P9-CND-777

TOURO COLLEGE LIBRARY
Kings Hwy

WITHDRAWN

ESSENTIAL CONCEPTS &
SCHOOL-BASED CASES IN
SPECIAL EDUCATION LAW

To Debbie and Debbie
With all of our love, now, always, and forever

ESSENTIAL CONCEPTS &
SCHOOL-BASED CASES IN
SPECIAL EDUCATION LAW

TOURO COLLEGE LIBRARY
Kings Hwy

CHARLES J.
RUSSO

ALLAN G.
OSBORNE, Jr.

CORWIN PRESS
A SAGE Company
Thousand Oaks, CA 91320

KH

Copyright © 2008 by Corwin Press

All rights reserved. When forms and sample documents are included, their use is authorized only by educators, local school sites, and/or noncommercial or nonprofit entities that have purchased the book. Except for that usage, no part of this book may be reproduced or utilized in any form or by any means, electronic or mechanical, including photocopying, recording, or by any information storage and retrieval system, without permission in writing from the publisher.

For information:

Corwin Press
A SAGE Company
2455 Teller Road
Thousand Oaks, California 91320
www.corwinpress.com

SAGE Ltd.
1 Oliver's Yard
55 City Road
London EC1Y 1SP
United Kingdom

SAGE India Pvt. Ltd.
B 1/I 1 Mohan Cooperative Industrial Area
Mathura Road, New Delhi 110 044
India

SAGE Asia-Pacific Pte. Ltd.
33 Pekin Street #02-01
Far East Square
Singapore 048763

Printed in the United States of America.

Library of Congress Cataloging-in-Publication Data

Russo, Charles J.
Essential concepts and school-based cases in special education law/by Charles J. Russo and Allan G. Osborne, Jr.
    p. cm.
Includes bibliographical references and index.
ISBN 978-1-4129-2703-1 (cloth)
ISBN 978-1-4129-2704-8 (pbk.)
    1. Special education—Law and legislation—United States .
2. Educators—United States—Handbooks, manuals, etc. I. Osborne, Allan G. II. Title.

KF4209.3.Z9R87 2008
344.73'0791—dc22   2007021925

This book is printed on acid-free paper.

07 08 09 10 11 10 9 8 7 6 5 4 3 2 1

Acquisitions Editor:	Elizabeth Brenkus
Managing Editor:	Arnis Burvikovs
Editorial Assistants:	Ena Rosen, Desirée Enayati
Production Editor:	Cassandra Margaret Seibel
Copy Editor:	Jamie Robinson
Typesetter:	C&M Digitals (P) Ltd.
Proofreader:	Caryne Brown
Indexer:	Jean Casalegno
Cover Designer:	Lisa Miller

2/15/08

Contents

Preface

Twenty-one years after the Supreme Court initiated the era of equal educational opportunity in striking down racial segregation in schools in *Brown v. Board of Education* (1954), Congress enacted sweeping legislation mandating that students with disabilities be provided with appropriate special education services tailored to their unique needs. Most recently reauthorized in 2004, this law, now known as the Individuals with Disabilities Education Act (IDEA), and its accompanying regulations, dramatically altered the continuum of programs that states, through local school boards, are required to provide for students with disabilities. Moreover, as an introductory note, it is worth pointing out that while some refer to the IDEA by the title it was assigned in the reauthorization process, the Individuals with Disabilities Education Improvement Act (IDEIA), we have not adopted this approach. Instead, we prefer to follow the very first section of the revised IDEA, according to which "This chapter may be cited as the 'Individuals with Disabilities Education Act'" (20 U.S.C. § 1400(a)).

The IDEA and its regulations are designed to be comprehensive in addressing the needs of students with disabilities. Even so, the IDEA and its regulations have generated more litigation than any other educational law in American legal history. These suits arose due to two interrelated reasons. First, no statute can anticipate all legal issues that can arise. Second, the IDEA affords parents a variety of rights, not the least of which are to request that fair and impartial third-party decision-makers resolve disagreements at due process hearings over whether school officials have provided their children with a free appropriate public education (FAPE) (20 U.S.C. § 1415(f)(1)(a)) and to bring civil actions in federal or state courts challenging the results of hearings once they have exhausted administrative remedies (20 U.S.C. § 1415(i)(2)(A)). Insofar as we live in a litigious society wherein parents are well aware of their rights and those of their children, and are willing to seek judicial recourse, it should not be surprising that these conflicts would lead to litigation, a small portion of which is excerpted in this case book.

As witnessed with *Brown v. Board of Education* and many other cases, one judicial opinion has the ability to change the very nature of American public schools. As such, each chapter in this book includes carefully selected, and edited, excerpts from leading cases that helped to shape the face of the law of special education. We include these cases because they help to illustrate the points that the text makes in the narrative. Further, by reviewing the actual words of the justices of the Supreme Court and judges in lower courts, readers can develop a deeper understanding of how well-thought-out their opinions are, even in cases with which they may disagree.

Aware of the complexity of the IDEA, its regulations, and the many cases that they have generated, this book is designed to provide educators, whether in preservice programs preparing to become teachers, administrators, counselors, or a variety of other positions in schools, or professionals already serving in these capacities, with wide-ranging information on the law of special education. This book combines a narrative approach with selected cases that illuminate how federal and state courts have interpreted the IDEA and its regulations, addressing the delivery of special education and related services to students with disabilities. As such, one of our goals is to offer a book that is comprehensive in its coverage of the law of special education. In this respect, we believe that this casebook can serve as a text in courses on legal issues in special education and as a supplementary text in general education law courses.

At the same time, this book is not intended to serve as a "how-to manual." Rather, this text is designed to help to make educators aware of the many requirements governing the law of special education, in the hope that this increased understanding will put them in a better position to implement the IDEA as they deal with parents and students. In light of the detail that the book provides, we believe that it can also serve as a current and concise desk reference for practicing educators ranging from building- or district-level administrators to classroom teachers of all kinds and resource specialists in special education and related fields such as counseling.

When referring to parents, for the sake of brevity, and consistency, even though the IDEA acknowledges that parental rights apply to parents, including natural, adoptive, or foster parents, guardians, and individuals acting in the place of natural or adoptive parents (including grandparents, stepparents, or other relatives) with whom children live, or individuals who are legally responsible for their welfare (20 U.S.C. §§ 1402 (23)), this book uses the term *parents* throughout to refer to all of these groups of adults unless otherwise noted by the circumstances.

This casebook is organized around the major issues in the law of special education. The book thus examines the substantive and procedural requirements that the IDEA, its regulations, and litigation place on educators. Among the major topics that this book addresses are the rights of students with disabilities to a free appropriate public education (FAPE), procedural due process, proper placement, the delivery of related services, discipline, and remedies if school officials fail to adhere to the IDEA. The book also traces the legal history of special education while briefly discussing other statutes that affect the delivery of special education services.

Insofar as there are many issues to cover in a book on special education law, it is a double challenge selecting both the issues to be grouped in each chapter and the order of the chapters themselves. To address this challenge, we have organized the chapters in this book around the major procedural and substantive issues in the law of special education.

Chapter 1 offers a brief historical perspective of the legal development of special education in the United States. It begins with an overview of the sources of law in order to place the rest of the book in its proper legal context before discussing the forces that led to the development of special education legislation in the United States. The remainder of the chapter reviews the federal statutes currently impacting the delivery of special education services for children with disabilities. Of particular interest should be a brief section that highlights some of the major changes to the IDEA.

The second chapter presents information pertaining to the rights of students to receive special education and related services. The chapter considers who is eligible to receive services, along with the legal requirements for providing a free appropriate public education in the least restrictive environment (LRE).

Among the IDEA's many unique features is its elaborate system of due process safeguards that are designed to ensure that students with disabilities receive a FAPE. Chapter 3 thus highlights the identification and assessment of students, the development of their individualized education programs (IEPs), parental rights, and changes in placements under the IDEA.

Chapter 4 discusses the components of FAPE and the factors that IEP teams must examine when making decisions that place children in the LRE. This chapter also includes material about when school boards are required to place children in private day schools or residential programs and when students are entitled to extended school-year programs

The IDEA requires states, through local school boards, to provide students with disabilities related, or supportive, services to the extent that they are necessary for them to benefit from their special education programs. Accordingly, Chapter 5 provides detailed information concerning the supportive services that qualify as related services and the circumstances under which they must be provided. In addition, the chapter examines issues surrounding assistive technology and transition services.

Chapter 6 reviews what may be the most complex, and contentious, of all issues dealing with students with disabilities: discipline. To this end, this chapter discusses the special procedures that school officials must adhere to when disciplining special education students, including those who may be suspended or expelled but have yet to be formally identified as having disabilities under the IDEA.

When Congress enacted the IDEA, it envisioned a system whereby school officials and parents would work together to plan appropriate placements for qualified students with disabilities. Yet, since Congress recognized that disputes would arise, it included procedures in the IDEA to help parents and school boards to resolve their differences. In order to keep educators up to date on these important issues, Chapter 7 examines the IDEA's dispute resolution provisions, focusing on resolution sessions, mediation, due process hearings, and judicial proceedings.

Chapter 8 focuses on the remedies available to parents when school boards fail to meet their duties to provide children with a FAPE. This chapter primarily addresses awards of tuition reimbursement, compensatory educational services, attorney and other fees, as well as a general discussion on punitive damages.

Insofar as a variety of emerging and recurring issues do not lend themselves to being included in other parts of this book, Chapter 9 reflects on selected topics that are not addressed elsewhere. More specifically, this chapter reviews state testing programs, state responsibility to ensure compliance with the IDEA, the responsibilities of insurance carriers, policy letters, supervision of students with disabilities, and Part C of the IDEA.

Chapter 10 deals with antidiscrimination laws and special education. After briefly comparing and contrasting the IDEA, Section 504 of the Rehabilitation Act of 1973 (Section 504), and the Americans with Disabilities Act (ADA), the remainder of the chapter primarily focuses on what school systems must do to comply with Section 504 and the ADA. The chapter examines the key issues of what it means to be otherwise qualified, reasonable accommodations, and the provision of comparable facilities.

The book includes a brief glossary of terms that are in bold but not defined or explained within the text. Instead, it is designed to define legal and technical terms with which readers may be unfamiliar. The book also offers a list of Internet resources, including Web sites of state departments of education, special education services, and education law.

Acknowledgments

We could not have written a book of this nature without the encouragement, support, and assistance of many friends, colleagues, and family members. Thus, while it may be almost impossible to acknowledge all who have influenced us in some way and so contributed to this book, we would at least like to extend our gratitude to those who have had the greatest impact in our lives. This group includes all who have contributed to our knowledge and understanding of the subject matter of this book, most notably our many friends and colleagues who are members of the Education Law Association. These professionals have not only consistently shared their knowledge with us but also, more importantly, provided constructive criticism and constantly challenged our thinking.

We are also most fortunate to work with a group of professionals who understand the importance of our work and provide us with the resources to continue our research. The contributions of many colleagues from the University of Dayton and Quincy Public Schools can never be adequately acknowledged.

At the University of Dayton, I (Charlie Russo) would like to express my thanks to the Rev. Joseph D. Massucci, Chair of the Department of Educational Leadership; Dean Thomas Lasley, Dean of the School of Education and Allied Professions at the University of Dayton; and Associate Dean Dr. Dan Raisch for their ongoing support and friendship. I also extend a special note of thanks to my assistant Ms. Elizabeth Pearn, for her valuable assistance in helping to process the manuscript and Ms. Colleen Wildenhaus for assistance in proofreading the final manuscript.

I would like to extend a special note of appreciation to two of my former professors and long-term friends from my student days at St. John's: Many thanks to Dr. David B. Evans who, even while I was an undergraduate, taught me a great deal about the skills necessary to succeed in an academic career. In addition, I would like to thank my doctoral mentor, Dr. Zarif Bacilous, for helping me to complete my studies and enter the academy.

I (Allan Osborne) especially thank Richard DeCristofaro and Carmen Mariano, Superintendent and former Assistant Superintendent, respectively, and the entire administrative team of the Quincy Public Schools for their continuing encouragement and support. I would also like to extend a very warm thank-you to the faculty, parents, and students of the Snug Harbor Community School in Quincy, Massachusetts, for over two decades of inspiration. Special thanks are extended to Bob Limoncelli, Chris Karaska, and Amy Carey-Shinney, who provide a wonderful network of support on a daily basis. A school administrator is no better than his or her secretarial staff. I am fortunate to have the best. Much appreciation and love are extended to Angie Priscella and Jeanne Furlong for still putting up with me. Finally, I wish to thank two good friends and colleagues: Dennis Carini, for providing me with encouragement, and a few laughs when they were most needed, and Carol Shiffer, who is a constant inspiration.

I also wish to thank my friend and former doctoral mentor, Dr. Phil DiMattia of Boston College, for first encouraging me to investigate many of the issues contained in this book and for continuing to challenge my thinking.

We would both like to thank our acquisitions editor at Corwin Press, Lizzie Brenkus, and her predecessor, Robb Clouse, for their support as we conceptualized and wrote this book, as well as our copy editor, Jamie Robinson. It is a pleasure working with such outstanding professionals and their colleagues at Corwin Press. They certainly helped to make our jobs easier.

On a more personal note, we both extend our appreciation to our parents, Helen J. Russo and the late James J. Russo and the late Allan G. Osborne and late Ruth L. Osborne. We can never adequately express our gratitude to our parents for the profound influences that they have had on our lives.

I (Charles Russo) also extend a special note of thanks and appreciation to my two wonderful children, David Peter and Emily Rebecca. The two bright and inquisitive children that my wife Debbie and I raised have grown to be wonderful young adults who provide me with a constant source of inspiration and love.

Our wonderful wives, the two Debbies, have been the major influence in our lives and professional careers. Our best friends, they encourage us to write, show great patience as we ramble on endlessly about litigation in special education, and understand when we must spend countless hours working on a manuscript. We would not be able to do all that we do if it were not for their constant love and support. Thus we dedicate this book to them with all of our love.

C. J. R.

A. G. O.

Corwin Press gratefully acknowledges the contributions of the following individuals:

Bob Algozzine, Professor
Corwin Press Author
University of North Carolina
Charlotte, NC

Dennis Dunklee, Professor
Corwin Press Author
George Mason University
Fairfax, VA

Laurie Emery, Principal
Old Vail Middle School
Vail, AZ

Daniel P. Gaffney, Principal
Howard R. Yocum Elementary School
Maple Shade, NJ

Peter Hilts, Principal
The Classical Academy
Colorado Springs, CO

Marian White Hood, Principal
Ernest Just Middle School
Mitchellville, MD

Michelle Kocar, Principal
Heritage South Elementary School
Avon, OH

Pamela Norris, 11th Grade Language Arts Teacher
Renaissance High School
Detroit, MI

Belinda J. Raines, Principal
Frank Cody High School
Detroit, MI

About the Authors

Charles J. Russo, JD, EdD, is the Joseph Panzer Chair in Education in the School of Education and Allied Professions and Adjunct Professor in the School of Law at the University of Dayton. The 1998–1999 President of the Education Law Association and 2002 winner of its McGhehey (Lifetime Achievement) Award, he is the author or coauthor of more than 170 articles in peer-reviewed journals and the author, coauthor, editor, or coeditor of 26 books. He has been the editor of the *Yearbook of Education Law* for the Education Law Association since 1995 and has written or coauthored in excess of 600 publications. In addition to serving on a variety of editorial boards, he speaks and teaches extensively on issues in education law in the United States and throughout the world, having spoken in more than 20 countries. In recognition of his work on School Law, Charles J. Russo received an honorary PhD from Potchefstroom University (now the Potchefstroom Campus of North-West University) in Potchefstroom, South Africa, in May of 2004.

Allan G. Osborne, Jr., EdD, is the Principal of the Snug Harbor Community School in Quincy, Massachusetts, and a former visiting Associate Professor at Bridgewater State College. He received his doctorate in educational leadership from Boston College. Allan Osborne has authored or coauthored numerous articles, monographs, textbooks, and textbook chapters on special education law, along with textbooks on other aspects of special education. A past President of the Education Law Association (ELA), he has been a frequent presenter at ELA conferences and writes the "Students with Disabilities" chapter of the *Yearbook of Education Law*, which is published by ELA. Allan Osborne is on the Editorial Advisory Committee of *West's Education Law Reporter* and is coeditor of the "Education Law Into Practice" section of that journal. He also serves as an editorial consultant for many other publications in education law and special education.

1

Introduction: The Law of Special Education

Key Concepts in This Chapter

- ❖ Sources of Law
- ❖ History of Special Education Law
- ❖ Individuals with Disabilities Education Act
- ❖ Section 504 of the Rehabilitation Act
- ❖ Americans with Disabilities Act

This chapter begins with a brief overview of the American legal system in order to assist readers who may be unfamiliar with general principles of educational law in better understanding the discussions in subsequent chapters. Next, the chapter reviews the history of the movement to obtain equal educational opportunities for students with disabilities; this section highlights important cases that led to federal and state legislation mandating a free appropriate public education for students with disabilities. After reviewing the legislation, the chapter explains the dispute resolution procedures established by federal law before examining the role courts play in enforcing statutory rights.

Readers who are not familiar with legal terminology should consult the glossary at the end of this work for definitions of the terms used in this chapter and throughout the book.

SOURCES OF LAW

There are four sources of law in the United States: constitutions, statutes, regulations, and judicial **opinions**. These sources of law exist at both the federal and state levels.

A constitution is the fundamental law of a nation or state (Garner, 2004). A statute is an act of the legislative body—basically, a law that the Congress or a state legislature has passed (Garner, 2004). Statutes must be consistent with their controlling constitutions. Most statutes are supplemented by implementing regulations or guidelines written by officials in the agencies that are charged with their implementation and enforcement. Regulations are typically more specific than the statutes that they are designed to implement or carry out because they "flesh out" legislative intent as to how laws should work in practice. Finally, the many decisions of the courts interpreting the constitutions, statutes, and regulations comprise a body of law known as case law or **common law,** relying heavily on the concept of binding **precedent**, that a ruling of the highest court in a jurisdiction is binding on all lower courts in that jurisdiction. Cases from other jurisdictions that are of no binding effect are referred to as persuasive precedent, meaning that courts are not bound to follow their **holdings**.

The federal judicial system, like most state systems, has three levels. At the lowest level, trial courts are known as federal district courts. Each state has at least one federal district court, while some, such as California and New York, have as many as four. Trial courts are the basic triers of fact in legal disputes. As triers of fact in **special education** suits, federal trial courts review the record of administrative hearings and additional evidence and hear the testimony of witnesses. Trial courts render **judgments** based on the evidence presented by the parties to the dispute. Parties not satisfied with the decisions of trial courts may **appeal** to federal circuit courts of appeals within which they are located. For example, the First Circuit Court of Appeals consists of Maine, New Hampshire, Massachusetts, Rhode Island, and Puerto Rico. There are thirteen federal judicial circuits in the United States. However, circuit courts are not required to hear all appeals. Parties not satisfied with the judgments of circuit courts may appeal to the Supreme Court, which also does not hear all cases brought before it on appeal. In fact, the Supreme Court accepts less than one percent of the cases in which parties seek further review. Cases typically reach the Court in requests for a writ of *certiorari*, literally "to be informed of" (Russo, 2006). The Supreme Court may decide, for whatever reason, that a case is not worthy of review. Generally, if the Supreme Court agrees to hear an appeal, the justices grant a writ of *certiorari*. At least four of the nine justices must vote to grant *certiorari* in order for a case to be heard (Russo, 2006). Denying a writ has the effect of leaving a lower court's decision unchanged (Garner, 2004).

Each of the fifty states and various territories has a similar arrangement, except that the names of the courts vary. Generally speaking, there are three levels of state courts: trial courts, intermediate **appellate courts**, and courts of last resort. One has to be careful with the names of state courts. For example, most people probably think of "supreme court" being the name of a state's highest court; however, in New York, the trial court is known as the Supreme Court, while the high court is called the Court of Appeals.

When a court hands down a decision, its judgment is binding only within its **jurisdiction**. Keeping in mind that the concept of jurisdiction can refer to either the types of cases that courts can hear or the geographic area over which they have authority, this instance refers to the latter situation. By way of illustration, a judgment of the federal district court for New Hampshire is binding only in New Hampshire. The federal district court in Massachusetts might find a decision of the New Hampshire court persuasive, but it is not bound by its order. However, a decision of the First Circuit Court of Appeals is binding on all states within its jurisdiction, and lower courts in those states must rule consistently. A decision by the Supreme Court of the United States is enforceable in all fifty states and American territories.

The written opinions of most cases are readily available in a variety of published formats. The official version of Supreme Court opinions are in the *United States Reports,* abbreviated U.S. The same opinions, with additional research aids, are published in the *Supreme Court Reporter* (S. Ct.) and the *Lawyer's Edition,* now in its second series (L. Ed.2d). Decisions of the federal circuit courts are found in the *Federal Reporter,* now in its third series (F.3d), while federal trial court opinions are in the *Federal Supplement,* now in its second series (F. Supp.2d). State cases are published in a variety of publications, most notably West's National Reporter System, which divides the country up into seven regions: Atlantic, North Eastern, North Western, Pacific, South Eastern, South Western, and Southern. Most education-related cases are also republished in West's *Education Law Reporter.* Prior to being published in bound volumes, most cases are available in what are known as slip opinions, a variety of loose-leaf services, and electronic sources. Special education cases, as well as due process hearing decisions, are reproduced in a loose-leaf format in the *Individuals with Disabilities Education Law Reporter* (IDELR) published by LRP Publications.

Statutes and regulations are also available in similar readily accessible formats. Federal statutes are in the United States Code (**U.S.C.**), the official version, or the United State Code Annotated (U.S.C.A.), published by West. Agency regulations are published in the Code of Federal Regulations (**C.F.R.**). Links for downloading copies of education statutes and regulations appear on the U.S. Department of Education's Web site. Legal materials are also available online from a variety of sources, most notably WestLaw. State laws and regulations are generally available online from the Web sites of their states.

Legal citations are easy to read. The first number indicates the volume number where the case, statute, or regulation is located; the abbreviation refers to the book or series in which the material may be found; the second number indicates the page on which a case begins or the section number of a statute or regulation; the last part of a citation includes the name of the court, for lower court cases, and the year in which the dispute was resolved. For instance, the citation for *Barnett v. Memphis City School System*, 294 F. Supp.2d 924 (W.D. Tenn. 2003) can be located in volume 294 of the *Federal Supplement, Second Series* beginning on page 924. The case was resolved in the federal trial court in the Western Division of Tennessee. Similarly, the citation for the No Child Left Behind Act, 20 U.S.C. § 6301 (2002) can be found in volume 20 of the United States Code beginning with section 6301.

THE DEVELOPMENT OF SPECIAL EDUCATION LAWS

The federal government did not require states to provide special education services to students with disabilities until 1975 but did offer financial incentives for states to provide some level of services. Prior to 1975 some states enacted legislation mandating special education services to students with disabilities, but those states were in the minority. Before states enacted their own laws safeguarding the educational rights of students with disabilities, many local school boards routinely excluded children who were difficult to educate. When challenged, the courts often upheld these exclusionary practices until the early 1970s. It was only through the long-term efforts of advocates of the disabled that the federal government intervened. Initially, the battle for the educational rights of the disabled was fought in the courts, much of it coming about as a result of the civil rights movement.

Exclusionary Practices

In the early years of public education, school programs were not usually available to students with disabilities. In fact, the exclusion of students with disabilities frequently was sanctioned by the courts. For example, in 1893 the Supreme Judicial Court of Massachusetts supported a school committee's exclusion of a student who was mentally retarded (*Watson v. City of Cambridge*, 1893). The student was excluded because he was too "weak minded" to profit from instruction. School records indicated that the student was "troublesome" and was unable to care for himself physically. The court wrote that by law the school committee (as school boards in Massachusetts are known) had general charge of the schools and refused to interfere with its judgment. The court explained that if acts of disorder interfered with the operation of the schools, whether committed voluntarily or because of imbecility, the school committee should have been able to exclude the offender without being overruled by a jury that lacked expertise in educational matters.

In another dispute, the Supreme Court of Wisconsin, in 1919, upheld the exclusion of a student with a form of paralysis (*State ex rel. Beattie v. Board of Education of Antigo*, 1919). The student had normal intelligence, but his condition caused him to drool and make facial contortions. The student attended public schools through grade five but was excluded since school officials claimed that his physical appearance nauseated teachers and other students, his disability required an undue amount of his teacher's time, and he had a negative impact on the discipline and progress of the school. School officials suggested that the student attend a day school for students with hearing impairments and defective speech, but the student refused and was supported by his parents. When the board refused to reinstate the student, the court **affirmed** its decision, maintaining that his right to attend the public schools was not absolute when his presence there was harmful to the best interests of others. The court went so far as to suggest that insofar as the student's presence was not in the best interests of the school, the board had an obligation to exclude the student.

An appellate court in Ohio, even in affirming the authority of the state to exclude certain students, recognized the dilemma that was created by exclusionary practices as they conflicted with compulsory education statutes (*Board of Education of Cleveland Heights v. State ex rel. Goldman*, 1934). At issue was the state's compulsory attendance law, which called for children between the ages of six and eighteen to attend school. Further, the court decided that the Department of Education had the authority to consider whether certain students were incapable of profiting from instruction. The controversy arose when the board in one community adopted a rule excluding any child with an IQ score below 50, subsequently excluding a student with IQ scores ranging from 45 to 61. In rendering its judgment, the court conceded that the Department of Education could exclude some students. Even so, the court ordered the student's reinstatement because it was a local board and not the state that had excluded the child. The court noted that education was so essential that it was compulsory between certain ages.

Civil Rights Movement

The greatest advancements in special education have come since World War II. These advancements have not come easily, but resulted from improved professional knowledge, social advancements, and legal mandates initiated by concerned parents, educators, and citizens. The civil rights movement in the United States provided the initial impetus for the efforts to secure educational rights for students with disabilities.

In *Brown v. Board of Education* (1954), the landmark school desegregation case, the Supreme Court unknowingly laid the foundation for future right to education cases on behalf of students with disabilities. Chief Justice Warren, writing for the majority, characterized education as the most important function of government. Warren, pointing out that education was necessary for citizens to exercise their most basic civic responsibilities, explained:

> In these days, it is doubtful that any child may reasonably be expected to succeed in life if he is denied the opportunity of an education. Such an opportunity, where the State has undertaken to provide it, is a right that must be made available to all on equal terms. (*Brown*, 1954, p. 493)

Other courts, dealing with later cases seeking equal educational opportunities for students with disabilities, either directly quoted or paraphrased Warren's comment. As a result, students with disabilities became known as the other minority as they, largely through their parents and advocacy groups, demanded that they be accorded the same rights to an equal educational opportunity that had been gained by racial and ethnic minorities (Osborne, 1988).

Equal Educational Opportunity Movement

The movement to procure equal educational opportunities for students with disabilities gained momentum in the late 1960s and early 1970s when parent activists filed suits seeking educational equality for the poor, language minorities, and racial minorities. Although not all of these cases were successful, as with *Brown,* much of the language that emerged from the judicial opinions had direct implications for the cause of students with disabilities.

Discriminatory Tracking

In a groundbreaking suit, the federal trial court in the nation's capital, as part of a much larger suit dealing with educational equity, declared that the tracking system used by the city's public schools was discriminatory (*Hobson v. Hansen,* 1969). As part of this system, students were placed in tracks, or curriculum levels, as early as elementary school based on an ability assessment that relied heavily on nationally normed standardized aptitude tests. Once they were placed, it was difficult for students to ever move out of their assigned tracks. The court ordered school board officials to abolish the tracking system after hearing testimony suggesting that the tests could have produced inaccurate and misleading results when used with populations other than white middle-class students. The court found that using these tests with poor minority students often resulted in their being placed according to environmental and psychological factors rather than innate ability.

The court saw that since the school board lacked the ability to render scores that accurately reflected the innate learning abilities of a majority of its students, the students' placements in lower tracks was not justified. The court was of the opinion that tracking denied the class of students who were in the lower tracks equal educational opportunities because they received a limited curriculum. The court concluded that school officials also denied students in the lower tracks equal educational opportunities by failing to provide them with compensatory educational services that would have helped to bring them back into the mainstream of public education.

Culturally Biased Testing

At least two courts forbade school systems from placing students in segregated programs on the basis of culturally biased assessments. In the first case, a student who was Spanish-speaking was placed in a class for the mentally retarded on the basis of an IQ test administered in English (*Diana v. State Board of Education,* 1970, 1973). The issue was similar in the second case, except that the student was African American (*Larry P. v. Riles,* 1972, 1974, 1979, 1984). In the latter case the court held that standardized IQ tests were inappropriate because they had not been validated for the class of students on whom they were used. This resulted in the students being placed disproportionately in special education classes. In both instances, the courts ordered the respective school boards to develop nondiscriminatory procedures for placing students in special education classes. However, in a separate case, another federal trial court commented that standardized IQ tests commonly used in schools were not culturally or racially biased (*Parents in Action on Special Education v. Hannon,* 1980).

Language Minorities

In 1974 the Supreme Court ruled that the failure to provide remedial English language instruction to non-English-speaking students violated Section 601 of the Civil Rights Act of 1974 (*Lau v. Nichols,* 1974). **Plaintiffs** filed a **class action** suit on behalf of Chinese students in the San Francisco school system who did not speak English and who had not been provided with English language instruction. The Court found that the board's denying the students the chance to receive remedial instruction denied them meaningful opportunities to participate in public education. The Court contended that, as a recipient of federal funds, the school board was bound by Title VI of the Civil Rights Act of 1964 and a Department of Health, Education, and Welfare regulation that required it to take affirmative steps to rectify language deficiencies.

Equal Expenditure of Funds

In a variety of suits plaintiffs claimed that the poor were discriminated against insofar as the quality of education that they received was based on school district wealth. By way of background, it is worth noting that in most of these disputes property taxes were used to finance education, resulting in great disparities in educational expenditures between and among a state's school districts. The differences in expenditure levels, the plaintiffs alleged, resulted in differences in the quality of education that the students received. However, in its only case ever addressing school finance directly, *San Antonio v. Rodriguez* (*Rodriguez*) (1973), the Supreme Court rejected the claim that these disparities violated the federal Constitution. Postulating that the poor were not a suspect class and that education was not a fundamental right, the Court commented that at least where wealth was concerned, the Constitution did not require absolute equality.

In *Rodriguez,* the Court delineated the criteria for what constitutes a suspect class: a group "saddled with such disabilities or subjected to such a history of purposeful unequal treatment, or relegated to such a position of political powerlessness as to command extraordinary protection from the majoritarian political process" (p. 28). Under equal protection analysis, categorization as a suspect class requires the courts to use what is known as the strict scrutiny test, a measure that imposes a higher standard on governmental units to justify unequal treatment. Conversely, subjecting a claim to the rational relations test, such as when dealing with issues of general welfare, requires states to meet a lower standard of duty. In practical terms, then, delineation as a suspect class makes it easier for a plaintiff class to show that disparate treatment was discriminatory. To drive home its point, the Supreme Court emphasized that "Education, of course, is not among the rights afforded explicit protection under our Federal Constitution. Nor do we find any basis for saying it is implicitly so protected" (p. 35).

In a bellwether state case involving school finance, the Supreme Court of California applied the strict scrutiny test in striking down the state's school finance system as violative of the equal protection clause of the state constitution because the inadequate system failed to serve a compelling state interest (*Serrano v. Priest*, 1971). Over the past thirty-five years, almost forty states have faced similar litigation. Overall, state courts are almost evenly split on the issue of whether their financing systems meet state constitutional requirements.

A New Era for Students with Disabilities

State and federal court cases addressing equal educational opportunities for the poor, language minorities, and racial minorities served as persuasive, rather than binding, precedent in later disputes over access to public school programs for students with disabilities. The legal principles remain the same regardless of why a particular group of students may be classified as a minority. Advocates for students with disabilities successfully used the cases dealing with equal educational opportunities discussed above to lobby for the passage of laws mandating equal treatment for these students.

The successes that advocates for students with disabilities enjoyed in mostly lower court cases are considered landmark opinions despite their limited precedential value since they provided the impetus for Congress to pass sweeping legislation mandating a free appropriate public education for students with disabilities, regardless of the severity or nature of their disabilities. These cases, which are listed by their conceptually related holdings rather than chronologically, occurred in less than a decade of each other and are important because they helped establish many of the legal principles that shaped the far-reaching federal legislation that is now known as the **Individuals with Disabilities Education Act (IDEA)** (2005).

Entitlement to an Appropriate Education Established

One of the first cases that shifted the tide in favor of students with disabilities, *Wolf v. State of Utah* (*Wolf*) (1969), was filed in a state court on behalf of two children with mental retardation who were denied admission to public schools. As a result, the parents of these children enrolled them in a private day-care center at their own expense. As background to the dispute, the parents, through their lawyer, pointed out that according to Utah's state constitution, the public school system should have been open to all children, a provision that the state supreme court interpreted broadly; other state statutes stipulated that all children between the ages of six and twenty-one who had not completed high school were entitled to public education at taxpayers' expense. In light of these provisions, the *Wolf* court, in language that was remarkably similar to portions of *Brown*, declared that children who were mentally retarded were entitled to a free appropriate public education under the state constitution.

Landmark Decisions

Two federal class action suits combined to have a profound impact on the education of students with disabilities. The first case, *Pennsylvania Association for Retarded Children (PARC) v. Commonwealth of Pennsylvania* (1971, 1972), was initiated on behalf of a class of all mentally retarded individuals between the ages of six and twenty-one who were excluded from public schools. Commonwealth officials justified the exclusions on the basis of four statutes that relieved them of any obligation to educate children who were certified, in the terminology used at that time, as uneducable and untrainable by school psychologists, allowed officials to postpone the admission to any children who had not attained the mental age of five years, excused children who were found unable to profit from education from compulsory attendance, and defined compulsory school age as eight to seventeen while excluding children who were mentally not between those ages. The plaintiff class sought a declaration that the statutes were unconstitutional while also seeking preliminary and permanent **injunctions** against their enforcement.

PARC was resolved by means of a consent agreement between the parties that was endorsed by a federal trial court. In language that presaged the IDEA, the stipulations maintained that no mentally retarded child, or child thought to be mentally retarded, could be assigned to a special education program or be excluded from the public schools without due process. The consent agreement added that school systems in Pennsylvania had the obligation to provide all mentally retarded children with a free appropriate public education and training programs appropriate to their capacities. Even though *PARC* was a **consent decree**, thereby arguably limiting its precedential value to the parties, there can be no doubt that it helped to usher in significant positive change with regard to protecting the educational rights of students. *PARC* helped to establish that students who were mentally retarded were entitled to receive a free appropriate public education.

The second case, *Mills v. Board of Education of the District of Columbia* (*Mills*) (1972), extended the same right to other classes of students with disabilities, establishing the principle that a lack of funds was an insufficient basis for denying these children services. Moreover, *Mills* provided much of the due process language that was later incorporated into the IDEA and other federal legislation.

Mills, like *PARC*, was a class action suit brought on behalf of children who were excluded from the public schools in the District of Columbia after they were classified as being behavior problems, mentally retarded, emotionally disturbed, and hyperactive. In fact, in an egregious oversight, the plaintiffs estimated that approximately 18,000 out of 22,000 students with disabilities in the district were not receiving special education services. The plaintiff class sought a declaration of rights and an order directing the school board to provide a publicly supported education to all students with disabilities either within its system of public schools or at alternative programs at public expense. School officials responded that while the board had the responsibility to provide a publicly supported education to meet the needs of all children within its boundaries and that it had failed to do so, it was impossible to afford the plaintiff class the relief it sought due to a lack of funds. Additionally, school personnel admitted that they had not provided the plaintiffs with due process procedures prior to their exclusion.

Entering a judgment on the merits in favor of the plaintiffs, meaning that it went beyond the consent decree in *PARC*, the federal trial court pointed out that the United States Constitution, the District of Columbia Code, and its own regulations required the board to provide a publicly supported education to all children, including those with disabilities. The court explained that the board had to expend its available funds equitably so that all students would have received a publicly funded education consistent with their needs and abilities. If sufficient funds were not available, the court asserted that existing funds would have to be distributed in such a manner that no child was entirely excluded and the inadequacies could not be allowed to bear more heavily on one class of students. In so ruling, the court directed the board to provide due process safeguards before any children were excluded from the public schools, reassigned, or had their special education services terminated. At the same time, as part of its opinion, the court outlined elaborate due process procedures that it expected the school board to follow. These procedures later formed the foundation for the due process safeguards that were mandated in the federal special education statute.

Other Significant Decisions

A number of subsequent cases were not as high profile as *PARC* and *Mills*, but nonetheless helped to establish many of the legal principles that were later incorporated into the federal special education law. In one such case, **In re G.H.** (1974), the Supreme Court of North Dakota maintained that a student with disabilities had a right to an education under the state's constitution. The child's parents moved out of state leaving her behind at the residential school she had been attending. The school board that had been paying the child's tuition and the welfare department disputed which party was responsible for her educational expenses. The court concluded that the board was liable after acknowledging that the child had the right to have her tuition paid because special education students were entitled to no less than other pupils under the state constitution. The court suggested that students with disabilities constituted a suspect class because their disabilities were characteristics that were established solely by the accident of birth. The court reasoned that the deprivation of an equal educational opportunity to a student with disabilities was a similar denial of equal protection as had been held to be unconstitutional in racial discrimination cases.

A year after the second judgment in *PARC* and *Mills,* an order of the Family Court of New York City helped establish the principle that special education programs had to be free of all costs to parents. *In re Downey* (1973) was filed on behalf of a student with disabilities who attended an out-of-state school because the city did not have an adequate public facility that could have met his instructional needs. As a result, the child's parents challenged their having to pay the difference between the actual tuition costs and the state aid that they received. The court found that requiring the parents to contribute to the costs of their child's education violated the equal protection clauses of both the federal and state constitutions. In ordering reimbursement for the parents' out-of-pocket expenses, the court was of the view that since children, not their parents, had the right to receive an education, their right should not have been limited by their parents' inability to pay for an education.

In *Fialkowski v. Shapp* (*Shapp*) (1975), another case from Pennsylvania, a federal trial court helped to define what constituted an adequate program for a student with disabilities. Here the parents of two students with severe disabilities claimed that their children were not getting an appropriate education because they were being taught academic subjects instead of self-help skills. School officials, relying on the Supreme Court's decision in *Rodriguez,* argued that the claim should have been dismissed because the children did not have a fundamental right to an education. The court responded that *Rodriguez* was not controlling and that the students had not received adequate educations because their programs were not giving them the tools they would need in life. At the same time, although agreeing with the parents that their children who were mentally retarded could have constituted a suspect class, the court did not find it necessary to consider this question because it was satisfied that the parents had presented a claim that warranted greater judicial scrutiny than was necessary by the claim of unequal financial expenditures among school systems. A year after *Shapp,* the same federal trial court in Pennsylvania heard a class action suit filed on behalf of students with specific learning disabilities who allegedly were deprived of an education appropriate to their specialized needs. The complaint in *Frederick L. v. Thomas* (1976, 1977) charged that students with specific learning disabilities who were not receiving instruction suited to their needs were being discriminated against while children who did not have disabilities were receiving a free public education appropriate to their needs, that mentally retarded children were being provided with a free public education suited to their needs, and that some children with specific learning disabilities were receiving special instruction. Therefore, the plaintiffs claimed, students with specific learning disabilities who were not receiving an education designed to overcome their conditions were being denied equal educational opportunities. In refusing to dismiss the claim, the court was convinced that the students did not receive appropriate educational services in violation of state special education statutes and regulations as well as Section 504 of the Rehabilitation Act of 1973. The Third Circuit agreed that while the trial court's remedial order requiring the local school board to submit a plan identifying all students who were learning disabled was an appealable injunctive order, the court neither abused its discretion in refusing to abstain nor erred in mandating the identification of all children in the district who had learning disabilities.

A federal trial court in West Virginia, in *Hairston v. Drosick* (1976), established that basic due process safeguards needed to be put in place before a student could be excluded from general education classes. The court held that a local school board violated federal law when officials excluded a minimally disabled student from its public schools without a legitimate educational reason. The student, who had spina bifida, was excluded from general classes even though she was mentally competent to attend school. Further, officials excluded the student even though they did not give her parents any prior written notice or other due process safeguards. The court concluded that the actions of school officials in excluding the student from general education and placing her in special education without prior written notice, the opportunity to be heard, and other basic procedural safeguards violated the due process clause of the Fourteenth Amendment.

The final groundbreaking lower court case arose in Wisconsin. In *Panitch v. State of Wisconsin* (1977), a federal trial court observed that not providing an appropriate education at public expense to mentally retarded students violated the equal protection clause of the Fourteenth Amendment to the United States Constitution. Although the state enacted legislation in 1973 that should have provided the relief the plaintiffs sought, by the time that the court issued its order four years later, public officials had yet to carry out the law's dictates. Believing that the delay was a sufficient indication of intentional discrimination in violation of the equal protection clause, the court ordered the state to provide an appropriate education at public expense to the students in question.

LEGISLATIVE INITIATIVES

With the prospect of additional litigation looming, Congress, along with selected state legislatures, passed new laws expanding the rights of students with disabilities to receive an appropriate education. In so doing, the legislatures incorporated many of the legal principles that emerged from the cases discussed above.

Special education in the United States is now governed primarily by three federal laws and numerous state laws. The federal laws are the Individuals with Disabilities Education Act, Section 504 of the Rehabilitation Act, and the Americans with Disabilities Act. Each is discussed in the following sections; these latter two statutes are discussed in more detail in Chapter 10.

Individuals with Disabilities Education Act

In 1975 Congress passed Public Law (**P.L.**) 94–142, which at that time was known as the Education for All Handicapped Children Act. In a 1990 amendment, this landmark statute was given its current title, the Individuals with Disabilities Education Act (IDEA). P.L. 94–142, signifying that it was the 142nd piece of legislation introduced during the Ninety-Fourth Congress, was not an independent act. Instead, the IDEA was an amendment to previous legislation that provided funds to the states for educating students with disabilities. The important aspect of the IDEA is that it is permanent legislation, while previous laws expired unless they were reauthorized.

The IDEA mandates a free appropriate public education (FAPE) in the least restrictive environment (LRE) for all students with disabilities between the ages of three and twenty-one based on the contents of their Individualized Education Programs (IEPs). Educators must develop IEPs in conferences with students' parents for any children who require special education and related services. The IDEA specifies how IEPs are to be developed and what they must contain. Additionally, the IDEA includes elaborate due process safeguards to protect the rights of students and ensure that its provisions are enforced. As part of the IDEA's funding formula that allows all school districts to qualify for funds, boards receiving funds are subject to fairly rigid auditing and management requirements.

The IDEA has been periodically amended, or reauthorized, since its original enactment in 1975. The Handicapped Children's Protection Act (1986), an important modification, added a clause that allows parents who prevail in litigation against their school boards to recover legal expenses. Another amendment, the Education of the Handicapped Amendments of 1986, provided grants to states that wish to provide services to children with disabilities from birth to age two. The 1990 amendments, mentioned above, changed the statute's name and abrogated the states' Eleventh Amendment **sovereign immunity** to litigation.

Another important reauthorization, the Individuals with Disabilities Education Act Amendments of 1997, which was passed after a great deal of debate, incorporated disciplinary provisions into the IDEA. The most recent amendments, the Individuals with Disabilities Education Improvement Act of 2004, now codified as the IDEA, modified the 1997 disciplinary provisions and brought the IDEA in line with other federal legislation.

Among the key changes in the 2004 version of the IDEA are the following; these changes appear in the order in which they appear in the statute (Russo, Osborne, & Borreca, 2005).

Students with learning disabilities: These provisions modify the evaluation of students with learning disabilities by not requiring educators to consider whether children have severe discrepancies between achievement and intellectual ability in oral expression, listening comprehension, written expression, basic reading skill, reading comprehension, mathematical calculation, or mathematical reasoning (20 U.S.C. §§ 1402, 1407(b), 1414(b)(6)). Instead, educators may use processes that determine whether children respond to scientific, research-based intervention as part of evaluation procedures.

Highly qualified teachers: The IDEA's definition of "highly qualified" teachers is almost identical to that in the No Child Left Behind Act (20 U.S.C. §§ 1402 (10), 1412 (a)(14)).

In meeting the IDEA's standard, which is to be set by state rather than federal law, subject-area teachers must be either certified fully in special education or pass state-designed special education licensure examinations, and they also need to have bachelor's degrees while demonstrating knowledge of all subjects for which they are primary instructors.

Parent: An expanded definition of *parent* now includes natural, adoptive, or foster parents, guardians, and individuals acting in the place of natural or adoptive parents (including grandparents, stepparents, or other relatives) with whom children live, or individuals who are legally responsible for the welfare of children (20 U.S.C. § 1402 (23)).

Risk pools for high-need children with disabilities: This addition permits states to use IDEA funds to establish and maintain "risk pools" to aid local educational agencies in providing high-cost IDEA services or for the unexpected enrollment of students with disabilities (20 U.S.C. § 1411(e)(3)). In addition, this change permits local boards to use unexpended funds in the next fiscal year.

Early intervention: This update allows states to extend Part C services for families and children with disabilities until a child reaches the age of five (20 U.S.C. §§ 1411 (e)(7), 1419, 1435 (c)).

Funding: The 2004 act set the goal of achieving the IDEA's initial 1975 promise of funding 40 percent of the national average of per-pupil spending by 2011; the authorized levels for funding the excess costs associated with educating students with disabilities has been increased by approximately $2.3 billion each year (20 U.S.C. § 1411(i)). However, since these levels are not mandatory, it remains to be seen whether they will be achieved.

Child Find: This far-reaching and potentially costly major change requires public school officials to identify and possibly serve children who attend private schools in the districts where they attend school rather than where they live (20 U.S.C. § 1412 (a)(10)(A)(i), (ii)). In addition to calling for child find activities for students in private schools that are comparable to those used in public schools, officials must record and report to state education agencies the number of children from private schools who are evaluated, determined to have disabilities, and served.

Minority students: This significant addition directs states to develop policies and procedures for preventing the overidentification or disproportionate representation by race and ethnicity of children with disabilities, to record the number of students from minority groups in special education classes, and to provide early intervening services for children in groups deemed to be over represented (20 U.S.C. §§ 1412 (a)(24), 1418 (d)(1)(A)(B)).

Early intervening services: This modification allows local school boards to spend up to 15 percent of their federal special education funds on early intervening services designed to help children before they are placed in special education. (20 U.S.C. § 1413 (f)).

Prohibition against mandatory medication of students: This change forbids state and local educational agencies from requiring parents to obtain prescriptions for their children for substances such as Ritalin that are covered by the Controlled Substances Act as a condition of attending school, being evaluated, or receiving special education services (20 U.S.C. § 1412(a)(25)).

Parental consent for services: This modification maintains that states and local education agencies can neither be liable for violating the IDEA's requirement of providing students with a FAPE nor be required to develop IEPs for children whose parents either refuse to consent to the receipt of special education services or fail to respond to requests to provide consent (20 U.S.C. § 1414 (a)(1)(D)(ii)(II)(III)).

IEPs: This change eliminates benchmarks and short-term objectives for children with disabilities other than those who take alternate assessments aligned to alternate achievement standards; this provision also adds that the statement of the special education and related services and supplementary aids and services "be based on peer-reviewed research to the extent practicable" (20 U.S.C. §§ 1414(d)(1)(A)(I)(cc), (d)(1)(A)(IV), (d)(1)(A)(I)(cc), (d)(1)(A)(IV), (d)(5), 1414(f)). In addition, these sections permit up to fifteen states to pilot comprehensive multiyear IEPs that do not exceed three years and that are designed to coincide with natural transition points in a child's education while also allowing minor changes to IEPs to be made by means of conference calls or letters.

Dispute resolution: This important addition imposes, in effect, a two-year **statute of limitations** on parental ability to file special education complaints while setting a ninety-day limit for appeals (20 U.S.C. §§ 1415(f)(3)(C), (i)(2)(B), (i)(3)(B)(i)(2)). These provisions also require hearing officers to focus on whether children were denied appropriate educations rather than emphasize procedural errors and make lawyers potentially liable for filing complaints that courts deem frivolous.

Student discipline: These changes grant school officials greater freedom to remove disruptive students with disabilities from classes if their behavior is unrelated to their disabilities (20 U.S.C. § 1415 (f)). Even though the law still requires IEP teams to conduct manifestation determinations, the process requires that misbehaviors be directly related to students' disabilities before relationships can be found. Moreover, students whose parents request due process hearings challenging manifestation determinations must remain in their disciplinary placements until hearing officers resolve complaints. Even so, special education students who are removed from classes are still entitled to the educational and medical services in alternative settings. These changes also expand the conditions under which students can be placed in alternative educational settings.

Further, students who carry or possess weapons to or at schools, on school premises, or to or at school functions, or knowingly possess or use illegal drugs, or sell or solicit the sale of controlled substances, while at school, on school premises, or at school functions, or who have inflicted serious bodily injury on other persons while at schools, on school premises, or at school functions can be placed in such settings.

Model forms: This section directs the Secretary of Education to provide copies of model forms for IEPs, individualized family service plans, the procedural safeguards described in Section 1415(d), and the prior written notice described in Sections 1415(b)(3) and (c)(1) no later than when the IDEA's final regulations are promulgated (20 U.S.C. § 1417 (e)).

Section 504, The Rehabilitation Act

According to Section 504 of the Rehabilitation Act of 1973:

No otherwise qualified individual with a disability in the United States . . . shall, solely by reason of her or his disability, be excluded from the participation in, be denied the benefits of, or be subjected to discrimination under any program or activity receiving Federal financial assistance or under any program or activity conducted by any Executive agency or by the United States Postal Service.

Section 504 was the first **civil rights** legislation that specifically guaranteed the rights of the disabled, even though it relies on the broader term *impairment* in offering its protections to qualified individuals. Section 504's provisions that prohibit discrimination against individuals with disabilities in programs receiving federal funds are similar to those in Titles VI (2005) and VII of the Civil Rights Act of 1964 (2005), which forbids employment discrimination in programs that receive federal financial assistance on the basis of race, color, religion, sex, or national origin. Section 504 effectively prohibits discrimination by any recipient of federal funds in the provision of services or employment.

Individuals are covered by Section 504 if they have physical or mental impairments that substantially limit one or more of life's major activities, have a record of such impairments, or are regarded as having impairments (29 U.S.C. § 706(7)(B)). Major life activities are "functions such as caring for oneself, performing manual tasks, walking, seeing, hearing, speaking, breathing, learning, and working" (28 C.F.R.f § 41.31).

Americans with Disabilities Act

The Americans with Disabilities Act (ADA), passed in 1990, prohibits discrimination against individuals with disabilities in the private sector. The ADA's preamble explains its purpose as acting "to provide a clear and comprehensive national mandate for the elimination of discrimination against individuals with disabilities" (42 U.S.C. § 12101). Basically, the intent of the ADA is to extend the protections afforded by Section 504 to programs and activities that are not covered by Section 504 because they do not receive federal funds.

While the ADA is aimed primarily at the private sector, public agencies are not immune to its provisions. Compliance with Section 504 does not automatically translate to compliance with the ADA. The legislative history of the ADA indicates that it also addresses what the judiciary had perceived as shortcomings or loopholes in Section 504 (Marczely, 1993).

No Child Left Behind Act

A more recent, controversial, federal education law is the No Child Left Behind Act (NCLB) that was signed into law in 2002. The NCLB, which is actually an extension of the original Elementary and Secondary Education Act of 1965, has the potential to impact the delivery of special education services (Raisch & Russo, 2006). The key elements in the NCLB are to improve the academic achievement of students who are economically disadvantaged; assist in preparing, training, and recruiting highly qualified personnel; provide improved language instruction for children of limited English proficiency; make school systems accountable for student achievement, particularly by imposing standards for annual yearly progress for students and districts; require school systems to rely on teaching methods that are research based and that have been proven effective; and afford parents better choices while creating innovative educational programs, especially if local school systems are unresponsive to their needs (Wenkart, 2003). As part of the process of complying with the revised IDEA and the NCLB, school officials must "take measurable steps to recruit, hire, train, and retain highly qualified school personnel to provide special education and related services" for students with disabilities (20 U.S.C. § 1412 (a)(14)(D)).

The IDEA and NCLB are, at the same time, similar and dissimilar. The laws are alike to the extent that each addresses the needs of students with disabilities through state agencies and local school systems, focusing on student achievement and outcomes, emphasizing parental participation, and requiring the regular evaluation or assessment of students and staffs. However, the laws have some important differences. The most significant difference between the two statutes is that the IDEA focuses on the performances of individual students in an array of areas, while the NCLB is more interested in systemwide outcomes.

One of the IDEA's most controversial additions from the 2004 amendments, which parallels the language of the NCLB, is its definition of "highly qualified" teachers (20 U.S.C. §§ 1402(10), 1412 (a)(14)). This provision also applies to related services personnel and paraprofessionals (20 U.S.C. § 1412 (a)(14)(B)). In order to be classified as "highly qualified," a standard that is based on state rather than federal criteria, subject-area teachers in public schools not only have to be certified fully in special education or pass state-designed special education licensure examinations, but they also have to possess bachelor's degrees and demonstrate knowledge of each subject for which they are the primary instructors (20 U.S.C. § 1402(10)). Under these provisions, which apply the same deadlines as the NCLB, currently employed teachers needed to meet the standards by the end of the 2005–2006 school year, even if they teach multiple subjects. New special education teachers have until up to two years after they are hired to become approved as "highly qualified" in different subjects as long as they are fully certificated in at least one. The IDEA adds that while teachers who satisfy its requirements as highly qualified also qualify for this title under the NCLB (20 U.S.C. § 1402 (10)(F)), the law does not create a private right of action that can be judicially enforced to ensure that children are taught by such teachers (20 U.S.C. § 1412(a) (14)(E)). In other words, parents cannot file a suit to ensure that their children are taught by teachers who meet the standards under the IDEA and the NCLB. The IDEA's regulations specify that the requirements concerning how to be categorized as highly qualified do not apply to teachers in private schools (300 C.F.R. § 300.18(g)).

State Statutes

Since education is a function of the states rather than the federal government, special education is governed by state laws in addition to the federal statutes discussed above. While state special education laws must be consistent with federal laws to the extent that they cannot do less than the federal statutes require, states can provide greater protection for children with disabilities should they wish to do so. To this end, while most states have laws that are similar in scope and language to the IDEA, several jurisdictions include provisions in their legislation that exceed the IDEA's requirements. For example, some states have higher standards of what constitutes an appropriate education for a student with disabilities. Other states have stricter procedural requirements. Most have established procedures for program implementation that are either not covered by federal law or have been left to the states to determine for themselves. If a conflict develops between provisions of the IDEA or other federal statutes and state laws, federal law is considered to be supreme under Article VI of the United States Constitution.

A comprehensive discussion of the laws of each of the fifty states, the District of Columbia, and various American possessions and territories is beyond the scope of this book. Each of these governmental entities has its own terminology, laws, regulations, funding schemes, and legal systems. Indeed, entire books could be written on the special education laws of each state. The purpose of this book is to provide comprehensive information on the federal mandate, the law that encompasses the entire nation. As such, readers are cautioned that they cannot have a complete understanding of special education law if they are not familiar with state law. Thus, readers are advised to seek out sources of information on the pertinent laws of their states to supplement this book.

❖

CASE NO. 1—RIGHTS OF STUDENTS WITH DISABILITIES TO AN EDUCATION

PENNSYLVANIA ASSOCIATION FOR RETARDED CHILDREN

v.

COMMONWEALTH OF PENNSYLVANIA

United States District Court, E. D. Pennsylvania, 1972

343 F. Supp. 279

OPINION, ORDER AND INJUNCTION

MASTERSON, District Judge.

This civil rights case, a class action, was brought by the Pennsylvania Association for Retarded Children and the parents of thirteen individual retarded children on behalf of all mentally retarded persons between the ages 6 and 21 whom the Commonwealth of Pennsylvania, through its local school districts and intermediate units, is presently excluding from a program of education and training in the public schools. Named as **defendants** are the Commonwealth of Pennsylvania, Secretary of Welfare, State Board of Education and thirteen individual school districts scattered throughout the Commonwealth. In addition, plaintiffs have joined all other school districts in the Commonwealth as class defendants of which the named districts are said to be representative.

The exclusions of retarded children complained of are based upon four State statutes: (1) . . . which relieves the State Board of Education from any obligation to educate a child whom a public school psychologist certifies as uneducable and untrainable. The burden of caring for such a child then shifts to the Department of Welfare which has no obligation to provide any educational services for the child; (2) . . . which allows an indefinite postponement of admission to public school of any child who has not attained a mental age of five years; (3) . . . which appears to *excuse* any child from compulsory school attendance whom a psychologist finds unable to profit therefrom and (4) . . . which defines compulsory school age as 8 to 17 years but has been used in practice to postpone admissions of retarded children until 8 or to eliminate them from public schools at age 17 . . .

. . . [T]he parties agreed upon a Stipulation which basically provides that no child who is mentally retarded or thought to be mentally retarded can be assigned initially (or re-assigned) to either a regular or special educational status, or excluded from a public education without a prior recorded hearing before a special hearing officer. At that hearing, parents have the right to representation by counsel, to examine their child's records, to compel the attendance of school officials who may have relevant evidence to offer, to cross-examine witnesses testifying on behalf of school officials and to introduce evidence of their own. . . .

AUTHORS' NOTE: In this case, as in others, the authors have left the language in the original opinions unchanged. Thus, while terms such as *handicapped* are no longer used today, they are preserved so as to reflect historical accuracy.

... [T]he parties submitted a Consent Agreement to this Court which, along with the ... Stipulation, would settle the entire case. Essentially, this Agreement deals with the four state statutes in an effort to eliminate the alleged equal protection problems. As a proposed cure, the defendants agreed, that since "the Commonwealth of Pennsylvania has undertaken to provide a free public education for all of its children between the ages of six and twenty-one years" ... therefore, "it is the Commonwealth's obligation to place each mentally retarded child in a *free, public program of education and training appropriate to the child's capacity...."*

The lengthy Consent Agreement concludes by stating that "[e]very retarded person between the ages of six and twenty-one shall be provided access to a free public program of education and training appropriate to his capacities as soon as possible but in no event later than *September 1, 1972...."* Finally, and perhaps most importantly, the Agreement states that:

"The defendants shall formulate and submit ... *a plan to be effectuated by September 1, 1972,* to commence or recommence a free public program of education and training for all mentally retarded persons ... aged between four and twenty-one years as of the date of this Order, and for all mentally retarded persons of such ages hereafter. The plan shall specify the range of programs of education and training, there [*sic*] kind and number, necessary to provide an appropriate program of education and training to all mentally retarded children, where they shall be conducted, arrangements for their financing, and, if additional teachers are found to be necessary, the plan shall specify recruitment, hiring, and training arrangements...."

Thus, if all goes according to plan, Pennsylvania should be providing a meaningful program of education and training to every retarded child in the Commonwealth by September, 1972....

Notes

1. Although *PARC* dealt only with the right to an education for students who suffered from mental retardation it is considered a landmark case. Why is this decision important for students with other types of disabilities?

2. The fact that this dispute was settled by a stipulation and consent agreement indicates that the Commonwealth of Pennsylvania accepted its obligation to provide appropriate educational opportunities for its students with disabilities. Compare this to the following case, in which the District of Columbia claimed that it did not have the resources to educate its students with disabilities properly.

CASE NO. 2—ESTABLISHMENT OF DUE PROCESS RIGHTS FOR STUDENTS WITH DISABILITIES

MILLS

v.

BOARD OF EDUCATION OF THE DISTRICT OF COLUMBIA

United States District Court, District of Columbia, 1972

348 F. Supp. 866

MEMORANDUM OPINION, JUDGMENT AND DECREE

WADDY, District Judge.

This is a **civil action** brought on behalf of seven children of school age by their next friends in which they seek a declaration of rights and to enjoin the defendants from excluding them from the District of Columbia Public Schools and/or denying them publicly supported education and to compel the defendants to provide them with immediate and adequate education and educational facilities in the public schools or alternative placement at public expense. They also seek additional and ancillary relief to effectuate the primary relief. They allege that although they can profit from an education either in regular classrooms with supportive services or in special classes adopted to their needs, they have been labeled as behavioral problems, mentally retarded, emotionally disturbed or hyperactive, and denied admission to the public schools or excluded therefrom after admission, with no provision for alternative educational placement or periodic review. . . .

The defendants are the Board of Education of the District of Columbia and its members, the Superintendent of Schools for the District of Columbia and subordinate school officials, the Commissioner of the District of Columbia and certain subordinate officials and the District of Columbia.

THE PROBLEM

The genesis of this case is found (1) in the failure of the District of Columbia to provide publicly supported education and training to plaintiffs and other "exceptional" children, members of their class, and (2) the excluding, suspending, expelling, reassigning and transferring of "exceptional" children from regular public school classes without affording them due process of law.

The problem of providing special education for "exceptional" children (mentally retarded, emotionally disturbed, physically handicapped, hyperactive and other children with behavioral problems) is one of major proportions in the District of Columbia. The precise number of such children cannot be stated because the District has continuously failed to comply with Section 31–208 of the District of Columbia Code which requires a census of all children aged 3 to 18 in the District to be taken. Plaintiffs estimate that there are " . . . 22,000 retarded, emotionally disturbed, blind, deaf, and speech or learning disabled children, and perhaps as many as 18,000 of these children are not being furnished with programs of specialized education." According to data prepared by the Board of Education, . . . the District of Columbia provides publicly supported special education programs of various descriptions to at least 3880 school age children. However, in a 1971 report to the Department of Health, Education and Welfare, the District of Columbia Public Schools admitted that an estimated 12,340 handicapped children were not to be served in the 1971–72 school year....

THERE IS NO GENUINE ISSUE OF MATERIAL FACT

... Defendants have admitted in these proceedings that they are under an affirmative duty to provide plaintiffs and their class with publicly supported education suited to each child's needs, including special education and tuition grants, and also, a constitutionally adequate prior hearing and periodic review. They have also admitted that they failed to supply plaintiffs with such publicly supported education and have failed to afford them adequate prior hearing and periodic review....

PLAINTIFFS ARE ENTITLED TO RELIEF

Plaintiffs' entitlement to relief in this case is clear. The applicable statutes and regulations and the Constitution of the United States require it....

Thus the Board of Education has an obligation to provide whatever specialized instruction that will benefit the child. By failing to provide plaintiffs and their class the publicly supported specialized education to which they are entitled, the Board of Education violates the ... statutes and its own regulations.

The Constitution—Equal Protection and Due Process

The Supreme Court in Brown v. Board of Education stated:

"Today, education is perhaps the most important function of state and local governments. Compulsory school attendance laws and the great expenditures for education both demonstrate our recognition of the importance of education to our democratic society. It is required in the performance of our most basic public responsibilities, even service in the armed forces. It is the very foundation of good citizenship. Today it is a principal instrument in awakening the child to cultural values, in preparing him for later professional training, and in helping him to adjust normally to his environment. In these days, it is doubtful that any child may reasonably be expected to succeed in life if he is denied the opportunity of an education. *Such an opportunity, where the state has undertaken to provide it, is a right which must be made available to all on equal terms.* (emphasis supplied)

... Not only are plaintiffs and their class denied the publicly supported education to which they are entitled many are suspended or expelled from regular schooling or specialized instruction or reassigned without any prior hearing and are given no periodic review thereafter. Due process of law requires a hearing prior to exclusion, termination of [sic] classification into a special program.

The Defense

The Answer of the defendants to the Complaint contains the following:

"These defendants say that it is impossible to afford plaintiffs the relief they request unless:

(a) The Congress of the United States appropriates millions of dollars to improve special education services in the District of Columbia; or

(b) These defendants divert millions of dollars from funds already specifically appropriated for other educational services in order to improve special educational services. These defendants suggest that to do so would violate an Act of Congress and would be inequitable to children outside the alleged plaintiff class."

This Court is not persuaded by that contention.

The defendants are required by the Constitution of the United States, the District of Columbia Code, and their own regulations to provide a publicly-supported education for these "exceptional" children. Their failure to fulfill this clear duty to include and retain these children in the public school system, or otherwise provide them with publicly-supported education, and their failure to afford them due process hearing and periodical review, cannot be excused by the claim that there are insufficient funds. . . . [T]he District of Columbia's interest in educating the excluded children clearly must outweigh its interest in preserving its financial resources. If sufficient funds are not available to finance all of the services and programs that are needed and desirable in the system then the available funds must be expended equitably in such a manner that no child is entirely excluded from a publicly supported education consistent with his needs and ability to benefit therefrom. The inadequacies of the District of Columbia Public School System whether occasioned by insufficient funding or administrative inefficiency, certainly cannot be permitted to bear more heavily on the "exceptional" or handicapped child than on the normal child.

IMPLEMENTATION OF JUDGMENT

This Court has pointed out that Section 31–201 of the District of Columbia Code requires that every person residing in the District of Columbia " . . . who has custody or control of a child between the ages of seven and sixteen years shall cause said child to be regularly instructed in a public school or in a private or parochial school or instructed privately. . . ." It is the responsibility of the Board of Education to provide the opportunities and facilities for such instruction.

The Court has determined that the Board likewise has the responsibility for implementation of the judgment and decree of this Court in this case. Section 31–103 of the District of Columbia Code clearly places this responsibility upon the Board. It provides:

"The Board shall determine all questions of general policy relating to the schools, shall appoint the executive officers hereinafter provided for, define their duties, and direct expenditures."

JUDGMENT AND DECREE

Plaintiffs having filed their verified complaint seeking an injunction and declaration of rights as set forth more fully in the verified complaint and the prayer for relief contained therein; and having moved this Court for summary judgment pursuant to [the rules of civil procedure], and this Court having reviewed the record of this cause . . . it is hereby ordered, adjudged and decreed that summary judgment in favor of plaintiffs and against defendants be, and hereby is, granted, and judgment is entered in this action as follows:

1. That no child eligible for a publicly supported education in the District of Columbia public schools shall be excluded from a regular public school assignment by a

Rule, policy, or practice of the Board of Education of the District of Columbia or its agents unless such child is provided (a) adequate alternative educational services suited to the child's needs, which may include special education or tuition grants, and (b) a constitutionally adequate prior hearing and periodic review of the child's status, progress, and the adequacy of any educational alternative.

2. The defendants, their officers, agents, servants, employees, and attorneys and all those in active concert or participation with them are hereby enjoined from maintaining, enforcing or otherwise continuing in effect any and all rules, policies and practices which exclude plaintiffs and the members of the class they represent from a regular public school assignment without providing them at public expense (a) adequate and immediate alternative education or tuition grants, consistent with their needs, and (b) a constitutionally adequate prior hearing and periodic review of their status, progress and the adequacy of any educational alternatives; and it is further ORDERED that:

3. The District of Columbia shall provide to each child of school age a free and suitable publicly-supported education regardless of the degree of the child's mental, physical or emotional disability or impairment. Furthermore, defendants shall not exclude any child resident in the District of Columbia from such publicly-supported education on the basis of a claim of insufficient resources.

4. Defendants shall not suspend a child from the public schools for disciplinary reasons for any period in excess of two days without affording him a hearing pursuant to the provisions of Paragraph 13.f., below, and without providing for his education during the period of any such suspension.

5. Defendants shall provide each identified member of plaintiff class with a publicly-supported education suited to his needs within thirty (30) days of the entry of this order. With regard to children who later come to the attention of any defendant, within twenty (20) days after he becomes known, the evaluation (case study approach) called for in paragraph 9 below shall be completed and within 30 days after completion of the evaluation, placement shall be made so as to provide the child with a publicly supported education suited to his needs.

In either case, if the education to be provided is not of a kind generally available during the summer vacation, the thirty-day limit may be extended for children evaluated during summer months to allow their educational programs to begin at the opening of school in September.

6. Defendants shall cause announcements and notices to be placed in the Washington Post, Washington Star-Daily News, and the Afro-American, in all issues published for a three week period commencing within five (5) days of the entry of this order, and thereafter at quarterly intervals, and shall cause spot announcements to be made on television and radio stations for twenty (20) consecutive days, commencing within five (5) days of the entry of this order, and thereafter at quarterly intervals, advising residents of the District of Columbia that all children, regardless of any handicap or other disability, have a right to a publicly-supported education suited to their needs, and informing the parents or guardians of such children of the procedures required to enroll their children in an appropriate educational program. Such announcements should include the listing of

a special answering service telephone number to be established by defendants in order to (a) compile the names, addresses, phone numbers of such children who are presently not attending school and (b) provide further information to their parents or guardians as to the procedures required to enroll their children in an appropriate educational program.

7. Within twenty-five (25) days of the entry of this order, defendants shall file with the Clerk of this Court, an up-to-date list showing, for every additional identified child, the name of the child's parent or guardian, the child's name, age, address and telephone number, the date of his suspension, expulsion, exclusion or denial of placement and, without attributing a particular characteristic to any specific child, a breakdown of such list, showing the alleged causal characteristics for such nonattendance (e. g., educable mentally retarded, trainable mentally retarded, emotionally disturbed, specific learning disability, crippled/other health impaired, hearing impaired, visually impaired, multiple handicapped) and the number of children possessing each such alleged characteristic.

8. Notice of this order shall be given by defendants to the parent or guardian of each child resident in the District of Columbia who is now, or was during the 1971–72 school year or the 1970–71 school year, excluded, suspended or expelled from publicly-supported educational programs or otherwise denied a full and suitable publicly-supported education for any period in excess of two days. Such notice shall include a statement that each such child has the right to receive a free educational assessment and to be placed in a publicly-supported educational program suited to his needs. Such notice shall be sent by registered mail within five (5) days of the entry of this order, or within five (5) days after such child first becomes known to any defendant. Provision of notification for non-reading parents or guardians will be made.

9. a. Defendants shall utilize public or private agencies to evaluate the educational needs of all identified "exceptional" children and, within twenty (20) days of the entry of this order, shall file with the Clerk of this Court their proposal for each individual placement in a suitable educational program, including the provision of compensatory educational services where required.

b. Defendants, within twenty (20) days of the entry of this order, shall, also submit such proposals to each parent or guardian of such child, respectively, along with a notification that if they object to such proposed placement within a period of time to be fixed by the parties or by the Court, they may have their objection heard by a Hearing Officer in accordance with procedures required in Paragraph 13.e., below.

10. a. Within forty-five (45) days of the entry of this order, defendants shall file with the Clerk of the Court, with copy to plaintiffs' counsel, a comprehensive plan which provides for the identification, notification, assessment, and placement of class members. Such plan shall state the nature and extent of efforts which defendants have undertaken or propose to undertake to

(1) describe the curriculum, educational objectives, teacher qualifications, and ancillary services for the publicly-supported educational programs to be provided to class members; and,

(2) formulate general plans of compensatory education suitable to class members in order to overcome the present effects of prior educational deprivations,

(3) institute any additional steps and proposed modifications designed to implement the matters decreed in paragraph 5 through 7 hereof and other requirements of this judgment.

11. The defendants shall make an interim report to this Court on their performance within forty-five (45) days of the entry of this order. Such report shall show:

(1) The adequacy of Defendants' implementation of plans to identify, locate, evaluate and give notice to all members of the class.

(2) The number of class members who have been placed, and the nature of their placements.

(3) The number of contested hearings before the Hearing Officers, if any, and the findings and determinations resulting therefrom.

12. Within forty-five (45) days of the entry of this order, defendants shall file with this Court a report showing the expunction from or correction of all official records of any plaintiff with regard to past expulsions, suspensions, or exclusions effected in violation of the procedural rights set forth in Paragraph 13 together with a plan for procedures pursuant to which parents, guardians, or their counsel may attach to such students' records any clarifying or explanatory information which the parent, guardian or counsel may deem appropriate.

13. Hearing Procedures.

a. Each member of the plaintiff class is to be provided with a publicly-supported educational program suited to his needs, within the context of a presumption that among the alternative programs of education, placement in a regular public school class with appropriate ancillary services is preferable to placement in a special school class.

b. Before placing a member of the class in such a program, defendants shall notify his parent or guardian of the proposed educational placement, the reasons therefor, and the right to a hearing before a Hearing Officer if there is an objection to the placement proposed. Any such hearing shall be held in accordance with the provisions of Paragraph 13.e., below.

c. Hereinafter, children who are residents of the District of Columbia and are thought by any of the defendants, or by officials, parents or guardians, to be in need of a program of special education, shall neither be placed in, transferred from or to, nor denied placement in such a program unless defendants shall have first notified their parents or guardians of such proposed placement, transfer or denial, the reasons therefor, and of the right to a hearing before a Hearing Officer if there is an objection to the placement, transfer or denial of placement. Any such hearings shall be held in accordance with the provisions of Paragraph 13.e., below.

d. Defendants shall not, on grounds of discipline, cause the exclusion, suspension, expulsion, postponement, interschool transfer, or any other denial of access to regular instruction in the public schools to any child for more than two days without first notifying the child's parent or guardian of such proposed action, the reasons therefor, and of the hearing before a Hearing Officer in accordance with the provisions of Paragraph 13.f., below.

e. Whenever defendants take action regarding a child's placement, denial of placement, or transfer, as described in Paragraphs 13.b. or 13.c., above, the following procedures shall be followed.

(1) Notice required hereinbefore shall be given in writing by registered mail to the parent or guardian of the child.

(2) Such notice shall:

(a) describe the proposed action in detail;

(b) clearly state the specific and complete reasons for the proposed action, including the specification of any tests or reports upon which such action is proposed;

(c) describe any alternative educational opportunities available on a permanent or temporary basis;

(d) inform the parent or guardian of the right to object to the proposed action at a hearing before the Hearing Officer;

(e) inform the parent or guardian that the child is eligible to receive, at no charge, the services of a federally or locally funded diagnostic center for an independent medical, psychological and educational evaluation and shall specify the name, address and telephone number of an appropriate local diagnostic center;

(f) inform the parent or guardian of the right to be represented at the hearing by legal counsel; to examine the child's school records before the hearing, including any tests or reports upon which the proposed action may be based, to present evidence, including expert medical, psychological and educational testimony; and, to confront and cross-examine any school official, employee, or agent of the school district or public department who may have evidence upon which the proposed action was based.

(3) The hearing shall be at a time and place reasonably convenient to such parent or guardian.

(4) The hearing shall be scheduled not sooner than twenty (20) days waivable by parent or child, nor later than forty-five (45) days after receipt of a request from the parent or guardian.

(5) The hearing shall be a closed hearing unless the parent or guardian requests an open hearing.

(6) The child shall have the right to a representative of his own choosing, including legal counsel. If a child is unable, through financial inability, to retain counsel, defendants shall advise child's parents or guardians of available voluntary legal assistance including the Neighborhood Legal Services Organization, the Legal Aid Society, the Young Lawyers Section of the D. C. Bar Association, or from some other organization.

(7) The decision of the Hearing Officer shall be based solely upon the evidence presented at the hearing.

(8) Defendants shall bear the burden of proof as to all facts and as to the appropriateness of any placement, denial of placement or transfer.

(9) A tape recording or other record of the hearing shall be made and transcribed and, upon request, made available to the parent or guardian or his representative.

(10) At a reasonable time prior to the hearing, the parent or guardian, or his counsel, shall be given access to all public school system and other public office records pertaining to the child, including any tests or reports upon which the proposed action may be based.

(11) The **independent Hearing Officer** shall be an employee of the District of Columbia, but shall not be an officer, employee or agent of the Public School System.

(12) The parent or guardian, or his representative, shall have the right to have the attendance of any official, employee or agent of the public school system or any public employee who may have evidence upon which the proposed action may be based and to confront, and to cross-examine any witness testifying for the public school system.

(13) The parent or guardian, or his representative, shall have the right to present evidence and testimony, including expert medical, psychological or educational testimony.

(14) Within thirty (30) days after the hearing, the Hearing Officer shall render a decision in writing. Such decision shall include findings of fact and conclusions of law and shall be filed with the Board of Education and the Department of Human Resources and sent by registered mail to the parent or guardian and his counsel.

(15) Pending a determination by the Hearing Officer, defendants shall take no action described in Paragraphs 13.b. or 13.c., above, if the child's parent or guardian objects to such action. Such objection must be in writing and postmarked within five (5) days of the date of receipt of notification hereinabove described.

f. Whenever defendants propose to take action described in Paragraph 13.d., above, the following procedures shall be followed.

(1) Notice required hereinabove shall be given in writing and shall be delivered in person or by registered mail to both the child and his parent or guardian.

(2) Such notice shall

   (a) describe the proposed disciplinary action in detail, including the duration thereof;

   (b) state specific, clear and full reasons for the proposed action, including the specification of the alleged act upon which the disciplinary action is to be based and the reference to the regulation subsection under which such action is proposed;

   (c) describe alternative educational opportunities to be available to the child during the proposed suspension period;

   (d) inform the child and the parent or guardian of the time and place at which the hearing shall take place;

   (e) inform the parent or guardian that if the child is thought by the parent or guardian to require special education services, that such child is eligible to receive, at no charge, the services of a public or private agency for a diagnostic medical, psychological or educational evaluation;

   (f) inform the child and his parent or guardian of the right to be represented at the hearing by legal counsel; to examine the child's school records before the hearing, including any tests or reports upon which the proposed action may be based; to present evidence of his own; and to confront and cross-examine any witnesses or any school officials, employees or agents who may have evidence upon which the proposed action may be based.

(3) The hearing shall be at a time and place reasonably convenient to such parent or guardian.

(4) The hearing shall take place within four (4) school days of the date upon which written notice is given, and may be postponed at the request of the child's parent or guardian for no more than five (5) additional school days where necessary for preparation.

(5) The hearing shall be a closed hearing unless the child, his parent or guardian requests an open hearing.

(6) The child is guaranteed the right to a representative of his own choosing, including legal counsel. If a child is unable, through financial inability, to retain counsel, defendants shall advise child's parents or guardians of available voluntary legal assistance including the Neighborhood Legal Services Organization, the Legal Aid Society, the Young Lawyers Section of the D. C. Bar Association, or from some other organization.

(7) The decision of the Hearing Officer shall be based solely upon the evidence presented at the hearing.

(8) Defendants shall bear the burden of proof as to all facts and as to the appropriateness of any disposition and of the alternative educational opportunity to be provided during any suspension.

(9)   A tape recording or other record of the hearing shall be made and tran-
      scribed and, upon request, made available to the parent or guardian or
      his representative.

(10) At a reasonable time prior to the hearing, the parent or guardian, or the
      child's counsel or representative, shall be given access to all records of
      the public school system and any other public office pertaining to the
      child, including any tests or reports upon which the proposed action
      may be based.

(11) The independent Hearing Officer shall be an employee of the District
      of Columbia, but shall not be an officer, employee or agent of the Public
      School System.

(12) The parent or guardian, or the child's counsel or representative, shall have
      the right to have the attendance of any public employee who may have
      evidence upon which the proposed action may be based and to confront
      and to cross-examine any witness testifying for the public school system.

(13) The parent or guardian, or the child's counsel or representative, shall
      have the right to present evidence and testimony.

(14) Pending the hearing and receipt of notification of the decision, there
      shall be no change in the child's educational placement unless the prin-
      cipal (responsible to the Superintendent) shall warrant that the contin-
      ued presence of the child in his current program would endanger the
      physical well-being of himself or others. In such exceptional cases, the
      principal shall be responsible for insuring that the child receives some
      form of educational assistance and/or diagnostic examination during the
      interim period prior to the hearing.

(15) No finding that disciplinary action is warranted shall be made unless the
      Hearing Officer first finds, by clear and convincing evidence, that the
      child committed a prohibited act upon which the proposed disciplinary
      action is based. After this finding has been made, the Hearing Officer
      shall take such disciplinary action as he shall deem appropriate. This
      action shall not be more severe than that recommended by the school
      official initiating the suspension proceedings.

(16) No suspension shall continue for longer than ten (10) school days after
      the date of the hearing, or until the end of the school year, whichever
      comes first. In such cases, the principal (responsible to the Superintendent)
      shall be responsible for insuring that the child receives some form of
      educational assistance and/or diagnostic examination during the suspen-
      sion period.

(17) If the Hearing Officer determines that disciplinary action is not war-
      ranted, all school records of the proposed disciplinary action, including
      those relating to the incidents upon which such proposed action was
      predicated, shall be destroyed.

(18) If the Hearing Officer determines that disciplinary action is warranted,
      he shall give written notification of his findings and of the child's right to

appeal his decision to the Board of Education, to the child, the parent or guardian, and the counsel or representative of the child, within three (3) days of such determination.

(19) An appeal from the decision of the Hearing Officer shall be heard by the Student Life and Community Involvement Committee of the Board of Education which shall provide the child and his parent or guardian with the opportunity for an oral hearing, at which the child may be represented by legal counsel, to review the findings of the Hearing Officer. At the conclusion of such hearing, the Committee shall determine the appropriateness of and may modify such decision. However, in no event may such Committee impose added or more severe restrictions on the child.

14. Whenever the foregoing provisions require notice to a parent or guardian, and the child in question has no parent or duly appointed guardian, notice is to be given to any adult with whom the child is actually living, as well as to the child himself, and every effort will be made to assure that no child's rights are denied for lack of a parent or duly appointed guardian. Again provision for such notice to non-readers will be made.

15. Jurisdiction of this matter is retained to allow for implementation, modification and enforcement of this Judgment and Decree as may be required.

Notes

1. The plaintiffs in *Mills* estimated that as many as 18,000 of the District of Columbia's 22,000 students with disabilities were not receiving specialized educational services. In today's world that would be unconscionable, but sadly, in 1972 it was not that unusual.

2. The Board of Education in *Mills* basically claimed that it could not afford to provide the required services to give the plaintiffs the relief they sought. The court responded that the available funds needed to be expended equitably so that students with disabilities would not be disproportionately deprived of an equal educational opportunity. How does this decision compare with other equal educational opportunity opinions?

3. Many legal commentators have expressed the view that *Mills* laid the groundwork for the elaborate due process provisions that were included in the IDEA. Compare the due process procedures outlined in this decision with those currently included in § 1415 of the IDEA. What are the similarities and differences?

REFERENCES

Americans with Disabilities Act, 42 U.S.C. §§ 12101–12213 (1990).

Board of Education of Cleveland Heights v. State ex rel. Goldman, 47 Ohio App. 417 (Ohio Ct. App. 1934).

Brown v. Board of Education, 347 U.S. 483 (1954).

Civil Rights Act of 1964, Title VI, 42 U.S.C. §§ 2000 *et seq.* (2005).

Civil Rights Act of 1964, Title VII, 42 U.S.C. §§ 2000 *et seq.* (2005).

Diana v. State Board of Education, Civ. No. C-70–37 RFP (N.D. Cal. 1970 & 1973).

Downey, In re, 72 Misc.2d 772 (N.Y. Fam. Ct. 1973).

Education for All Handicapped Children Act, 20 U.S.C. § 1400 *et seq.* (1975).

Education of the Handicapped Amendments of 1986, P.L. 99–457, 100 Stat. 1145 (1986).

Fialkowski v. Shapp, 405 F. Supp. 946 (E.D. Pa. 1975).

Frederick L. v. Thomas, 408 F. Supp. 832, 419 F. Supp. 960 (E.D. Pa. 1976), *affirmed*, 557 F.2d 373 (3d Cir. 1977), *appeal after remand*, 578 F.3d 513 (3d Cir. 1978).

Garner, B. A. (2004). *Black's Law Dictionary* (8th ed.). St. Paul, MN: West.

G.H., In re, 218 N.W.2d 441 (N.D. 1974).

Hairston v. Drosick, 423 F. Supp. 180 (S.D.W.V. 1976).

Handicapped Children's Protection Act, P.L. 99–372, 100 Stat. 796 (1986).

Hobson v. Hansen, 269 F. Supp. 401 (D.D.C. 1967), *affirmed* sub nom. *Smuck v. Hanson*, 408 F.2d 175 (D.C. Cir. 1969).

Individuals with Disabilities Education Act, 20 U.S.C. § 1400–1491 (2005).

Individuals with Disabilities Education Act Amendments of 1997, P.L. 105–17, 11 Stat. 37 (1997).

Individuals with Disabilities Education Improvement Act of 2004, P.L. 108–446, 118 Stat. 2647 (2004).

Larry P. v. Riles, 343 F. Supp. 1306 (N.D. Cal. 1972), *affirmed*, 502 F.2d 963 (9th Cir. 1974), *further action* 495 F. Supp. 926 (N.D. Cal. 1979), *affirmed*, 793 F.2d 969 (9th Cir. 1984).

Lau v. Nichols, 414 U.S. 563 (1974).

Marczely, B. (1993). The Americans with Disabilities Act: Confronting the shortcomings of Section 504 in public education. *Education Law Reporter, 78,* 199–207.

Mills v. Board of Education of the District of Columbia, 348 F. Supp. 866 (D.D.C. 1972).

No Child Left Behind Act, 20 U.S.C. §§ 6301–7941 (2002).

Osborne, A. G. (1988). *Complete legal guide to special education services: A handbook for administrators, counselors, and supervisors.* West Nyack, NY: Parker.

Panitch v. State of Wisconsin, 444 F. Supp. 320 (E.D. Wis. 1977).

Parents in Action on Special Education v. Hannon, 506 F. Supp. 831 (N.D. Ill. 1980).

Pennsylvania Association for Retarded Children v. Commonwealth of Pennsylvania, 334 Fu. Supp. 1257 (E.D. Pa. 1971), 343 F. Supp. 279 (E.D. Pa. 1972).

Raisch, C. D., & Russo, C. J. (2006). The No Child Left Behind Act: Federal over-reaching or necessary educational reform? *Education Law Journal, 7*(4), 255–265.

Rehabilitation Act, Section 504, 29 U.S.C. § 794 (1973).

Russo, C. J. (2006). *Reutter's The Law of Public Education* (6th ed.). New York: Foundation Press.

Russo, C. J., Osborne, A. G., & Borreca, E. (2005). Special education update: The 2004 revisions of the IDEA. *School Business Affairs, 71*(5), 41–44.

San Antonio v. Rodriguez, 411 U.S. 1 (1973).

Serrano v. Priest, 5 Cal.3d 584, 487 P.2d 1241 (Cal. 1971)

State ex rel. Beattie v. Board of Education of Antigo, 169 Wis. 231 (Wis. 1919).

Watson v. City of Cambridge, 157 Mass. 561 (Mass. 1893).

Wenkart, R. D. (2003). The No Child Left Behind Act and Congress' power to regulate under the Spending Clause. *Education Law Reporter, 174,* 589–597.

Wolf v. State of Utah, Civ. No. 182646 (Utah Dist. Ct. 1969).

Entitlement to Special Education and Related Services

❖

The Individuals with Disabilities Education Act (IDEA) requires school boards to provide students with disabilities with a free appropriate public education (FAPE), consisting of any needed special education and related services (20 U.S.C. § 1401(26)). Yet, the IDEA does not establish substantive standards by which to judge the adequacy of these services. In addition, the IDEA requires officials to provide students with disabilities with specially designed instruction (20 U.S.C. § 1401(29)) that conforms to their Individualized Education Programs (IEPs) (20 U.S.C. § 1401(9)(D)). IEPs are written statements, essentially agreements between parents and school boards, outlining current levels of student performance, detailing annual goals and short-term objectives, and detailing specific educational services to be provided (20 U.S.C. § 1401(14)).

In *Board of Education of the Hendrick Hudson Central School District v. Rowley* (*Rowley*) (1982), its first case ever dealing with special education, the United States Supreme Court ruled that students with disabilities are entitled to personalized instruction with support services sufficient to permit them to benefit from the instruction that they receive. At the same time, the Court cautioned lower courts not to impose their views of preferable educational methods on school districts. Nevertheless, lower courts frequently are asked to determine what level of services educators must provide to children with disabilities in order to meet the IDEA's minimum standards.

The IDEA provides students with disabilities with unprecedented access to American public schools. As the first chapter indicated, prior to the passage of the IDEA, students with disabilities routinely were denied access to public school programs. Children with disabilities who were not excluded from schools generally were relegated to second-class-citizen status insofar as they did not receive adequate services. Now well-established in American law, the IDEA defines a child with a disability as one:

(i) with mental retardation, hearing impairments (including deafness), speech or language impairments, visual impairments (including blindness), serious emotional disturbance . . . , orthopedic impairments, autism, traumatic brain injury, other health impairments, or specific learning disabilities; and

(ii) who, by reason thereof, need special education and related services. (20 U.S.C. § 1401(3)(A))

Under the IDEA's definition, a student is not considered to be a child with a disability unless that child requires special education services. The IDEA goes on to define special education as "specially designed instruction, at no cost to the parents or guardians, to meet the unique needs of a child with a disability" (20 U.S.C. § 1401(29)). Moreover, the IDEA directs educators to provide special education for all eligible students between the ages of three and twenty-one (20 U.S.C. § 1412(a)(1)(A)).

This chapter presents information on who is eligible to receive special education and related services. Questions of eligibility often arise, as students must fit into one of the IDEA's disability categories in order to be eligible for services in most states. This chapter also delineates specific rights of access to services and programs for students in public schools as well as for students who may not be enrolled in public schools.

ENTITLEMENT TO SERVICES

The IDEA unambiguously dictates that states, typically through local school boards or educational agencies, must ensure that all age-eligible children receive a FAPE (20 U.S.C. § 1412(a)(1)(A)). The courts have made it clear that educators cannot deny a FAPE to students regardless of the severity of their disability. For example, the First Circuit, in a case that now stands for the proposition of "zero reject," found that the unequivocal language of the IDEA neither includes an exception for those with severe disabilities nor requires children to demonstrate an ability to benefit from services to be eligible (*Timothy W. v. Rochester, N.H. School District*, 1989). In its **opinion**, the court referred to the original title of the law, the Education for All Handicapped Children Act, in support of its proposition that no child could be excluded. The court also defined education in a broad sense, encompassing training in basic life skills. The Supreme Court commented that even students with disabilities who are dangerous cannot be excluded from the benefits of the IDEA (*Honig v. Doe*, 1988). Yet, not all students with disabilities must be educated within public school settings, since the IDEA does allow for the placement of children, whose unique needs require it, in residential or institutional settings (20 U.S.C.§ 1412(a)(10)(B)).

Students with disabilities are entitled to access educational programs and activities that are available to the general student population as long as they qualify for participation. Denying such access would violate Section 504 of the Rehabilitation Act. Moreover, the IDEA's regulations require school officials to provide students with disabilities with nonacademic and extracurricular services and activities (34 C.F.R. § 300.107), while explaining that they should participate in these activities with children who do not have disabilities to the maximum extent appropriate (34 C.F.R. § 300.117). Section 504 requires all recipients of federal funds to provide reasonable accommodations to any child with a disability who would be otherwise qualified to participate in any of these programs (34 C.F.R. § 104.12(a)).

The IDEA requires states to provide special education services to students up to the age of twenty-one, unless doing so would be inconsistent with state law, practice, or court orders (20 U.S.C. § 1412(a)(1)(B)). The IDEA also grants an exemption for incarcerated youth between the ages of eighteen and twenty-one if they did not have IEPs prior to being incarcerated and state law does not require the provision of services (20 U.S.C. § 1412(a)(1)(B)(ii)). As a case from Indiana illustrates, a state may not discontinue services to students with disabilities over a certain age if it customarily provides services to students without disabilities over the same age (*Evans v. Tuttle*, 1993). The court struck down a state law that had the effect of automatically terminating services for some special education students at the age of nineteen while giving school boards the option of providing services to other students over the age of eighteen.

On the other hand, students may not continue to receive services until the age of twenty-one if they no longer require those services. To this end, a federal trial court in Michigan confirmed a school board's decision to graduate a student with disabilities and terminate special education services after the court determined that he received a FAPE and adequate transition services (*Chuhran v. Walled Lake Consolidated Schools*, 1993). The court noted that insofar as the student completed all of his graduation requirements and demonstrated exceptional performance in mainstream classes, he was no longer eligible for special education services. Similarly, a federal trial court in Tennessee pointed out that a student who graduated was not entitled to continued services under the IDEA (*Daugherty v. Hamilton County Schools*, 1998). Even so, a school board may not graduate a student who has not met the normal requirements to simply terminate special education services. In an early case, the Supreme Judicial Court of Massachusetts decided that a school board inappropriately graduated a student who had not met all of the usual graduation standards (*Stock v. Massachusetts Hospital School*, 1984). The court thus directed school officials to rescind the student's diploma and to conduct a hearing to consider what additional services he might have been entitled to receive, even if doing so meant that he had to continue to receive services beyond the time when his right to a FAPE might otherwise have expired.

Eligibility

As straightforward as the IDEA's requirements may seem, controversies have arisen over who is eligible for special education and related services. Much of the ensuing litigation evolved over the specified disability categories defined in the statute and its regulations and whether students were eligible for services under those definitions. Students who are classified under any of the categories of disabilities specifically defined in the IDEA's regulations (34 C.F.R. § 300.8) are eligible for services as long as they are necessary. Students are generally considered to require services if their educational performances are adversely affected by their disabilities. Individual states may specify disability categories in addition to those listed in the IDEA or may provide special education services on a noncategorical basis. The Supreme Court reasoned that only a level of services needed to permit eligible students to receive some educational benefit is required by the IDEA (*Board of Education of the Hendrick Hudson Central School District v. Rowley*, 1982). The Court further indicated that students who earn passing grades and advance from grade to grade are receiving educational benefits.

One disability category listed in the IDEA that has been controversial is that of seriously emotionally disturbed. The IDEA's regulations specify that in order to be classified as seriously emotionally disturbed, the educational performances of students must be adversely affected by their condition (34 C.F.R. § 300.8(c)(4)). The definition lists characteristics of emotional disturbance as an inability to learn that cannot be explained by other factors, an inability to build and maintain interpersonal relationships, inappropriate behavior or feelings under normal circumstances, a general pervasive mood of unhappiness or depression, or a tendency to develop physical symptoms or fears. That definition includes schizophrenia but excludes children who are socially maladjusted.

As noted above, the definition of "seriously emotionally disturbed" is controversial. This means that the outcome of cases may hinge on the extent to which the emotional difficulties of students affect their academic performance. In at least one such case, a court decided that a gifted student who was hospitalized due to emotional concerns but was not seriously emotionally disturbed, was ineligible to receive special education services because his emotional difficulties did not adversely affect his educational performance (*Doe v. Board of Education of the State of Connecticut,* 1990). Likewise, the Second Circuit agreed that a gifted student was not entitled to special education because his emotional and behavioral problems had not adversely affected his educational performance (*J.D. v. Pawlet School District,* 2000). In contrast, the Sixth Circuit held that a student who had average intelligence but had a long history of academic failure, difficulty making and maintaining friendships, and an inability to create normal social bonds was seriously emotionally disturbed and entitled to services under the IDEA (*Babb v. Knox County School System,* 1992). The court emphasized that school officials failed to make the proper determination that the student was disabled since they did not fully examine his academic, emotional, and psychological profile. Similarly, the Second Circuit (*Muller v. Committee on Special Education of the East Islip Union Free School District,* 1998) and Eighth Circuit (*Independent School District No. 284 v. A.C.,* 2001) agreed that students whose emotional disabilities adversely affected their educational development were entitled to special education

Students who have attention deficit hyperactivity disorder (ADHD) are not eligible for services under the IDEA unless they qualify under another category, such as learning disabled, seriously emotionally disturbed, or other health impaired (Hueffner, 2006). The federal trial court for the District of Columbia upheld a school board's finding that a student with ADHD was not eligible for special education services (*Lyons v. Smith,* 1993). The court agreed with the evidence that school personnel provided, namely that the student's educational performance had not been adversely affected by the ADHD since his academic achievement was superior.

Another controversial disability classification is that of "other health impaired." Students so classified must have "limited strength, vitality, or alertness" caused by chronic or acute health problems (34 C.F.R. § 300.8(c)(9)). Moreover, the health problems must adversely affect students' educational performance in order to entitle children to receive services. One question that has arisen is whether having HIV, AIDS, or hepatitis B qualifies students as being other health impaired. The answer depends on how far the diseases have progressed and the effect that they have had on students. In an early case, a state court in New York held that students were not disabled merely because they had AIDS but that they could qualify for IDEA services if their disease progressed (*District 27 Community School Board v. Board of Education of the City of New York,* 1986). According to the court, students' educational performance must be adversely affected as a result of limited strength, vitality, or alertness resulting from the AIDS in order for them to be eligible for IDEA services. At the same time, the court concluded that the automatic exclusion from school of all children with AIDS would have violated their rights under Section 504 of the Rehabilitation Act and to equal protection of the laws. Yet another court pointed out that the IDEA would apply to students with AIDS only if their physical condition adversely affected their ability to learn and complete the required classroom work (*Doe v. Belleville Public School District No. 118*, 1987). Using the language of the IDEA's regulations, the court established a three-part test for evaluating whether students could be classified as other health impaired. Under this tripartite test, students must have limited strength, vitality, or alertness due to chronic or acute health problems; their health problems must adversely affect their school performance; and the children must require special education and related services.

In another highly contentious area, the 2004 IDEA amendments made a significant change with regard to the criteria for diagnosing students with learning disabilities. These amendments modified existing evaluation procedures by no longer requiring educators to consider whether qualified students have severe discrepancies between achievement and intellectual ability in oral expression, listening comprehension, written expression, basic reading skills, reading comprehension, mathematical calculation, or mathematical reasoning (20 U.S.C. § 1401(30)). Instead, officials may use processes that consider whether children respond to scientific, research-based interventions as part of evaluation procedures (20 U.S.C. § 1401(c)(5)(F)). Children who fail to respond to such interventions may be considered eligible for special education services.

Medical Exclusion

It is well settled that students with disabilities cannot be excluded from public schools due to their health problems, even when they are afflicted with contagious diseases, if the risk of transmission of the diseases is low. Excluding students with health problems from the public schools violates Section 504 as well as the IDEA. The Second Circuit pointed out that students who were carriers of the hepatitis B virus could not be excluded from, or segregated in, their public schools because of their medical condition (*New York State Association for Retarded Children v. Carey*, 1979). Similarly, a state court in Illinois asserted that a student with hepatitis B was entitled to an education in a mainstream setting (*Community High School District 155 v. Denz*, 1984). Both courts agreed that the risk of transmission was low and could have been reduced further through the use of proper prophylactic procedures. The reasoning in the hepatitis B cases can also be applied to situations where students have AIDS or other contagious diseases.

As illustrated by a case from the Eleventh Circuit, school officials must consider whether reasonable accommodations can reduce the risk of transmission before excluding students who have contagious diseases (*Martinez v. School Board of Hillsborough County, Florida*, 1988, 1989). In this case, officials excluded a student who was mentally retarded and had AIDS from the public schools in part because she was incontinent and drooled. After **remand** from an appellate panel, a trial court found that because the risk of transmission from the student's bodily secretions was remote, officials had to admit her to a special education classroom.

Incarcerated Youth

Students with disabilities who previously were identified as such do not lose their eligibility due to incarceration (*Alexander v. Boyd*, 1995). While students' status as being incarcerated requires adjustments in the delivery of educational programming, it does not eliminate their entitlement to those services (*Donnell C. v. Illinois State Board of Education*, 1993; *Green v. Johnson*, 1981).

At the same time, youth who were not identified as students with disabilities prior to being incarcerated are ineligible for services if state law does not require that they continue to receive special education and related services while in custody (20 U.S.C. § 1412(a)(1)(B)(ii)). Even so, as recipients of federal funds, insofar as juvenile detention facilities would be subject to Section 504 and the Americans with Disabilities Act (ADA), they may have to provide some special education and related services for students who are incarcerated.

STUDENTS IN RELIGIOUS AND OTHER PRIVATE SCHOOLS

In spite of the many rights granted by the IDEA, students with disabilities whose parents place them in private schools, including religious schools, do not have individual entitlements to receive special education and related services (*Foley v. Special School District of St. Louis County*, 1998). However, as a group, students in religious schools are entitled to some IDEA benefits. More specifically, public school officials must locate, identify, and evaluate all parentally placed private school students with disabilities within their jurisdictions, including those who may live outside of district boundaries but attend school within those boundaries (34 C.F.R. § 300.131(a)). Additionally, school boards are required to develop plans to permit students in private schools to participate in programs that are delivered pursuant to the IDEA (34 C.F.R. § 300.132). The regulation defines students in private schools as those whose parents voluntarily enrolled them in such schools or facilities (34 C.F.R. § 300.130). Thus this definition does not include students whose school boards placed them in private facilities at public expense to provide each of them with a FAPE.

It almost goes without saying that many disputes over the delivery of special education services to children who attend religiously affiliated private schools often involve the Establishment Clause to the First Amendment of the United State Constitution, according to which "Congress shall make no law respecting an establishment of religion, or prohibiting the free exercise thereof." This section does not engage in a full discussion of the lengthy and complex history of litigation involving the limits of aid to religious schools under the Establishment Clause. Rather, it is sufficient to acknowledge that since the Supreme Court first enunciated the Child Benefit test, which permits a variety of forms of aid to children in nonpublic schools (*Everson v. Board of Education,* 1947) on the basis that the aid is directed at children (and their families), not their schools, it has had a checkered history. Put another way, depending on the composition of the Court, some justices have been more supportive of the Child Benefit Theory than others. Further, virtually all litigation involving the Establishment Clause has been examined in light of the tripartite test enunciated by the Supreme Court in *Lemon v. Kurtzman* (*Lemon*) (1971). Under this seemingly ubiquitous test,

> Every analysis in this area must begin with consideration of the cumulative criteria developed by the Court over many years. Three such tests may be gleaned from our cases. First, the statute must have a secular legislative purpose; second, its principal or primary effect must be one that neither advances nor inhibits religion; finally, the statute must not foster "an excessive government entanglement with religion. . . ." (*Lemon,* 1971, pp. 612–613; internal citations omitted)

In reviewing entanglement and state aid to religiously affiliated schools, the *Lemon* Court noted that three additional factors came into consideration: "[W]e must examine the character and purposes of the institutions that are benefitted, the nature of the aid that the State provides, and the resulting relationship between the government and religious authority" (p. 615).

The low point of the Child Benefit test occurred in 1985 when, in *Aguilar v. Felton,* the Supreme Court banned the on-site delivery of remedial Title I services in religiously affiliated nonpublic schools in New York City. The Court struck down the program, even in the absence of any allegation of misconduct or misappropriation of public funds, based on the fear that having public school educators provide services in religious schools might have created "excessive entanglement" between the government and religion. As a result, since school boards still had to provide services at public schools or neutral sites, many students who attended religiously affiliated nonpublic schools were denied equal educational opportunities under Title I.

The landscape with regard to state aid to K–12 education began to evolve in 1993 when the Supreme Court revitalized the Child Benefit test in *Zobrest v. Catalina Foothills School District* (*Zobrest*). In *Zobrest* the Court ruled that the Establishment Clause did not bar a public school board in Arizona from providing the on-site delivery of the services of a sign language interpreter for a student who attended a Roman Catholic high school. The Court reasoned that since the interpreter was essentially a conduit through whom information passed, the on-site delivery of such assistance did not violate the Establishment Clause. Four years later, in *Agostini v. Felton* (1997), following up on *Aguilar,* the Court essentially repudiated its earlier order in dissolving the injunction that banned the on-site delivery of services to students who attended religiously affiliated nonpublic schools in New York City since appropriate safeguards were in place (Osborne & Russo, 1997).

The Court evidenced increased support for the Child Benefit test in *Mitchell v. Helms* (2000). In a plurality, meaning that the Court lacked the necessary five-justice majority needed to make its opinion binding precedent, the constitutionality of Chapter 2, now Title VI, of Title I of the Elementary and Secondary Education Act was upheld. Chapter 2 is a far-reaching federal statute that permits the loan of state-owned instructional materials such as computers, slide projectors, television sets, tape recorders, maps, and globes to nonpublic schools. In the part of the case most relevant to special education but that was not appealed to the Supreme Court, the Fifth Circuit (*Helms v. Picard*, 1998) upheld state laws that permitted the on-site delivery of special education services to children who attended Catholic schools and that granted them free transportation to and from school.

A major statutory change occurred in 1997 when congressional reauthorization of the IDEA included provisions clarifying the obligations of public school systems to provide special education and related services to students in non-public schools. Unfortunately, neither Congress nor the courts conclusively answered questions about the delivery of special education for children in religiously affiliated nonpublic schools. Regulatory modifications that were adopted in 1999 and that changed little in the 2004 amendments, created a dilemma. The regulations and earlier **case law** made it clear that children in religious schools were entitled to receive some special education services, but the laws set funding restrictions in place that limited the amount of services that these children could receive on-site in their religious schools. The net result is that these students are likely to receive fewer services if public school officials follow the letter of the law and do not make additional services available to qualified students in religious schools.

The IDEA (20 U.S.C.A. § 1412(a)(10)) and its regulations (34 C.F.R. § 300.132) make it clear that children whose parents voluntarily enroll them in private schools are entitled to some level of special education services. Further, the IDEA permits the on-site delivery of special education for students with disabilities whose parents have placed them in "private," including religious, elementary and secondary schools (20 U.S.C.A. § 1412(a)(10)(A)(i)(III)), as long as safeguards are in place to avoid "excessive entanglement" between public school systems and religious institutions. Such an approach is consistent with settled law that public school personnel can conduct diagnostic tests on-site in religiously affiliated nonpublic schools to evaluate whether children are eligible for services in programs that are supported by public funds (*Meek v. Pittenger*, 1975; *Wolman v. Walter*, 1977).

The regulations incorporate statutory changes and provide guidance on meeting the IDEA's requirements while borrowing from preexisting Education Department General Administrative Regulations (EDGAR regulations) (34 C.F.R. § 76.1 *et seq.*). The EDGAR regulations require school boards to provide students in nonpublic schools with opportunities for equitable participation in federal programs (34 C.F.R. § 76.651(a)(1)). This means that students in nonpublic schools are entitled to opportunities to participate in federal programs that are comparable in quality to those available to children in public schools (34

C.F.R. § 76.654(a)). In developing programs, public school personnel must consult with representatives of the nonpublic schools to consider which students will be served, how their needs will be identified, what benefits they will receive, how the benefits will be delivered, and how the programs will be evaluated (34 C.F.R. §§ 76.652(a)(1)–(5)).

Fiscal Provisions

The IDEA limits the amount of money that school boards must spend to provide services to students who are enrolled in private schools (34 C.F.R. § 300.133). The total is limited to a proportionate share of the federal funds that boards receive based on the number of students in private schools in relation to the overall number of pupils in a district (20 U.S.C. §§ 1412(a)(10)(A)(i)(I), (II)). Nothing in the IDEA or its regulations prohibits school boards from using state or local funds to offer more than the IDEA calls for, because the regulations establish only a minimum amount that must be spent on qualified children (34 C.F.R. § 300.133(d)).

Under the regulations, consistent with long-standing case law, IDEA funds cannot be used to benefit private schools (34 C.F.R. § 300.141). Put another way, public funds cannot be used to offer impermissible aid to religious institutions by financing existing instructional programs. Under this limitation, school boards cannot provide private schools with direct financial benefits such as money, or organizing classes based on students' religions or the schools students attend (34 C.F.R. § 300.143). On the other hand, the regulations do allow boards to employ public school personnel in these private schools as long as they are not supplanting services that are normally provided by those facilities (34 C.F.R. § 300.142(a)). The regulations also permit boards to hire personnel from private schools to provide services outside of their regular hours of work as long as they are under the supervision and control of officials from public schools (34 C.F.R. § 300.142(b)). Finally, any property, equipment, and/or supplies purchased with IDEA funds can be used only on-site in private schools for the benefit of students with disabilities (34 C.F.R. § 300.144.).

Comparable Services

The regulations point out that students whose parents voluntarily place them in private schools do not have the individual right to receive some or all of the special education and related services that they might have been entitled to had they attended public schools (34 C.F.R. § 300.137(a)); *Fowler v. Unified School District*, 1997). Even so, this does not mean that children in private schools are denied all services under the IDEA. Instead, the regulations afford public school officials the authority to develop service plans and to decide which students from private schools are to be served (34 C.F.R. § 300.137(b)(2)). The regulations also require public school officials to ensure that representatives of private or religious schools have the opportunity to attend these meetings or participate by other means, such as individual or conference calls (34 C.F.R. § 300.137(c)).

Students in private schools are entitled to receive services from personnel who meet the same standards as educators in public schools (34 C.F.R. § 300.138(a)(1)), even if these children receive a different amount from their peers in public schools (34 C.F.R. § 300.138(a)(2)). To the extent that students with disabilities who attend private schools are not entitled to the same amount of services as their peers who attend a public school, the regulations do not require the development of an IEP. Instead, the regulations require school officials to develop service plans describing the aid that they will provide to students (34 C.F.R. § 300.138(b)(1)). Service plans must not only meet the same content requirements as IEPs but also must be developed, reviewed, and revised in a manner consistent with the IEP process (34 C.F.R. § 300.138(b)(2)).

Delivery of Services

It is well settled that the provision of special education services on the premises of religious schools is not unconstitutional (*Helms v. Picard*, 1998; *Zobrest v. Catalina Foothills School District*, 1993; 34 C.F.R. § 300.139(a)). Yet, this does not necessarily require school boards to provide services on-site (*Bristol Warren Regional School Committee v. Rhode Island Department of Education and Secondary Education*, 2003; *KDM ex rel. WJM v. Reedsport School District*, 1999; *Peter v. Wedl*, 1998).

In order to differentiate between schools, the regulations specifically use the term "including religious schools" to reflect the fact that these schools are included within the IDEA's framework (34 C.F.R. § 300.139(a)). However, the services offered on-site by school boards may not supplant those that would otherwise have been provided by religious schools. In this regard, the Sixth Circuit found no evidence that offering occupational or physical therapy services to students who attend religious schools constituted impermissible supplanting of services (*Peck v. Lansing School District*, 1998).

If it is necessary for children to benefit from services that are not offered on-site and students must be transported to alternate locations to receive them, school boards must provide transportation between their schools or homes to sites other than the private schools (34 C.F.R. § 300.139(b)(1)(i)(A)). As part of their duties, public school boards must transport students from their service sites to their private schools or homes, depending on the time of day (34 C.F.R. § 300.139(b)(1)(i)(B)), but not from their homes to their private schools (34 C.F.R. § 300.139(b)(i)(ii)). Moreover, it is important to recognize that the cost of transportation may be included in calculating the minimum amount of federal funds that school boards must spend on students in nonpublic schools (34 C.F.R. § 300.139(b)(2)).

Child Find in Private Schools

The 2004 modifications of the IDEA require officials in public schools to identify children whose parents enrolled them in private, including religious, elementary and secondary schools in their districts rather than simply those who live within school districts (20 U.S.C. § 1412(a)(10)(A)(I); 34 C.F.R. § 300.131(a)). Under these provisions, officials in public schools must provide accurate counts to state education agencies of the number of children from private schools who are evaluated, identified as having disabilities, and served (34 C.F.R. § 300.131(b)).

These changes also require school boards to employ child-find activities for students in private schools that are similar to those used to identify children who attend public schools (34 C.F.R. § 300.131(c)). Further, the cost of such activities does not count in evaluating whether school systems have exceeded the amount that they must spend serving students who attend private schools (34 C.F.R. § 300.131(e)).

Dispute Resolution

The IDEA's procedural safeguards generally do not apply to complaints that school boards failed to deliver services to students in private schools (34 C.F.R. § 300.140(a)(1)). The due process provisions do apply to complaints that boards failed to comply with the child find requirements that apply to students in private schools (34 C.F.R. § 300.140(a)(2)) and to those pursuant to allegations arising in connection with state administration of special education (34 C.F.R. § 300.140(b)). Insofar as there are no individually enforceable rights to receive special education and related services, students in private schools do not have individual rights to a due process hearing (*Gabel ex rel. L.G. v. Board of Education of the Hyde Park Central School District*, 2005; *Gary S. v. Manchester School District*, 2004).

HOMESCHOOLED STUDENTS

Whether students who are homeschooled by their parents, a practice that should not be confused with the delivery of homebound instruction under the IDEA, are entitled to special education and related services depends largely on state law. The Ninth Circuit ruled that the IDEA grants states discretion to decide whether home education that is exempted from a state's compulsory attendance requirements constitutes an IDEA-qualifying private school (*Hooks v. Clark County School District*, 2000). Accordingly, individual states may consider whether students with disabilities who are homeschooled are to be counted as part of a district's private school population. If state law treats children who are being homeschooled as private school students, then all of the IDEA's provisions regarding private school students with disabilities apply to eligible children.

❖

TIMOTHY W.

v.

ROCHESTER, NEW HAMPSHIRE, SCHOOL DISTRICT

United States Court of Appeals, First Circuit, 1989

875 F.2d 954

BOWNES, Circuit Judge.

Plaintiff-appellant Timothy W. appeals an order of the district court which held that under the Education for All Handicapped Children Act [now IDEA], a handicapped child is not eligible for special education if he cannot benefit from that education, and that Timothy W., a severely retarded and multiply handicapped child was not eligible under that standard. We reverse.

I. BACKGROUND

Timothy W. was born two months prematurely on December 8, 1975 with severe respiratory problems, and shortly thereafter experienced an intracranial hemorrhage, subdural effusions, seizures, hydrocephalus, and meningitis. As a result, Timothy is multiply handicapped and profoundly mentally retarded. He suffers from complex developmental disabilities, spastic quadriplegia, cerebral palsy, seizure disorder and cortical blindness. His mother attempted to obtain appropriate services for him, and while he did receive some services from the Rochester Child Development Center, he did not receive any educational program from the Rochester School District when he became of school age.

On February 19, 1980, the Rochester School District convened a meeting to decide if Timothy was considered educationally handicapped under the state and federal statutes, thereby entitling him to special education and related services. . . . The school district adjourned without making a finding. In a meeting on March 7, 1980, the school district decided that Timothy was not educationally handicapped—that since his handicap was so severe he was not "capable of benefitting" from an education, and therefore was not entitled to one. During 1981 and 1982, the school district did not provide Timothy with any educational program.

In May, 1982, the New Hampshire Department of Education reviewed the Rochester School District's special education programs and made a finding of non-compliance, stating that the school district was not allowed to use "capable of benefitting" as a criterion for eligibility. No action was taken in response to this finding until one year later, on June 20, 1983, when the school district met to discuss Timothy's case. . . . The school district, however, continued its refusal to provide Timothy with any educational program or services.

In response to a letter from Timothy's attorney, on January 17, 1984, the school district's placement team met. . . . The placement team recommended that Timothy be placed at the Child Development Center so that he could be provided with a special education program. The Rochester School Board, however, refused to authorize the placement team's recommendation to provide educational services for Timothy, contending that it still needed more information. The school district's request to have Timothy be given a neurological evaluation, including a CAT Scan, was refused by his mother.

On April 24, 1984, Timothy filed a complaint with the New Hampshire Department of Education requesting that he be placed in an educational program immediately. On October 9, 1984, the Department of Education issued an order requiring the school district to place him, within five days, in an educational program, until the appeals process on the issue of whether Timothy was educationally handicapped was completed. The school district, however, refused to make any such educational placement. On October 31, 1984, the school district filed an appeal of the order. There was also a meeting on November 8, 1984, in which the Rochester School Board reviewed Timothy's case and concluded he was not eligible for special education.

On November 17, 1984, Timothy filed a complaint in the United States District Court, . . . alleging that his rights under the Education for All Handicapped Children Act [now IDEA] . . . , the corresponding New Hampshire state law (RSA 186-C), § 504 of the Rehabilitation Act of 1973 . . . , and the equal protection and due process clauses of the United States and New Hampshire Constitutions, had been violated by the Rochester School District. The complaint sought preliminary and permanent injunctions directing the school district to provide him with special education, and $175,000 in damages.

A hearing was held in the district court on December 21, 1984. . . . On January 3, 1985, the district court denied Timothy's motion for a preliminary injunction, and on January 8, stated it would abstain on the damage claim pending exhaustion of the state administrative procedures.

In September, 1986, Timothy again requested a special education program. In October, 1986, the school district continued to refuse to provide him with such a program, claiming it still needed more information. Various evaluations were done at the behest of the school district. . . .

On May 20, 1987, the district court found that Timothy had not exhausted his state administrative remedies before the New Hampshire Department of Education, and precluded pretrial discovery until this had been done. On September 15, 1987, the hearing officer in the administrative hearings ruled that Timothy's capacity to benefit was not a legally permissible standard for determining his eligibility to receive a public education, and that the Rochester School District must provide him with an education. The Rochester School District, on November 12, 1987, appealed this decision to the United States District Court by filing a counterclaim, and on March 29, 1988, moved for summary judgment. Timothy filed a cross motion for summary judgment. . . .

On July 15, 1988, the district court rendered its opinion. . . . It first ruled that "under EAHCA [the Education for All Handicapped Children Act], an initial determination as to the child's ability to benefit from special education, must be made in order for a handicapped child to qualify for education under the Act." After noting that the New Hampshire statute (RSA 186-C) was intended to implement the EAHCA, the court held: "Under New Hampshire law, an initial decision must be made concerning the ability of a handicapped child to benefit from special education before an entitlement to the education can exist." The court then . . . found that "Timothy W. is not capable of benefitting from special education. . . . As a result, the defendant [school district] is not obligated to provide special education under either EAHCA [the federal statute] or RSA 186-C [the New Hampshire statute]." Timothy W. has appealed this order. . . .

The primary issue is whether the district court erred in its rulings of law. Since we find that it did, we do not review its findings of fact.

II. THE LANGUAGE OF THE ACT

A. The Plain Meaning of the Act Mandates a Public Education for All Handicapped Children

The Education for All Handicapped Children Act, [hereinafter the Act], . . . was enacted in 1975 to ensure that handicapped children receive an education which is appropriate to their unique needs. In assessing the plain meaning of the Act, we first look to its title: The Education for *All* Handicapped Children Act. (Emphasis added) . . . . Congress concluded that "State and local educational agencies have a responsibility to provide education for *all* handicapped children. . . ." (emphasis added). . . . The Act's stated purpose was "to assure that *all* handicapped children have available to them . . . a free appropriate public education which emphasizes special education and related services designed to meet their unique needs, . . . [and] to assist states and localities to provide for the education of *all* handicapped children . . ." (emphasis added).

The Act's mandatory provisions require that for a state to qualify for financial assistance, it must have "in effect a policy that assures *all* handicapped children the right to a free appropriate education." . . . The state must "set forth in detail the policies and procedures which the State will undertake . . . to assure that—there is established a goal of providing full educational opportunity to *all* handicapped children . . . , [and that] a free appropriate public education will be available for *all* handicapped children between the ages of three and eighteen . . . not later than September 1, 1978, and for *all* handicapped children between the ages of three and twenty-one . . . not later than September 1, 1980. . . ." (emphasis added). The state must also assure that "*all* children residing in the State who are handicapped, *regardless of the severity of their handicap,* and who are in need of special education and related services are identified, located, and evaluated . . ." (emphasis added). . . . The Act further requires a state to:

> establish[ ] *priorities* for providing a free appropriate public education to *all* handicapped children, . . . first with respect to handicapped children who are not receiving an education, and second *with respect to handicapped children, within each disability, with the most severe handicaps* who are receiving an inadequate education . . . (emphasis added). . . .

Thus, not only are severely handicapped children not excluded from the Act, but the most severely handicapped are actually given *priority* under the Act. . . .

The language of the Act could not be more unequivocal. The statute is permeated with the words "*all* handicapped children" whenever it refers to the target population. It never speaks of any exceptions for severely handicapped children. Indeed, as indicated *supra,* the Act gives priority to the most severely handicapped. Nor is there any language whatsoever which requires as a prerequisite to being covered by the Act, that a handicapped child must demonstrate that he or she will "benefit" from the educational program. Rather, the Act speaks of the *state's* responsibility to design a special education and related services program that will meet the unique "needs" of all handicapped children. The language of the Act in its entirety makes clear that a "zero-reject" policy is at the core of the Act, and that no child, regardless of the severity of his or her handicap, is to ever again be subjected to the deplorable state of affairs which existed at the time of the Act's passage, in which millions of handicapped children received inadequate education or none at all. In summary, the Act mandates an appropriate public education for all handicapped children, regardless of the level of achievement that such children might attain.

B. Timothy W.: A Handicapped Child Entitled to An Appropriate Education

Given that the Act's language mandates that all handicapped children are entitled to a free appropriate education, we must next inquire if Timothy W. is a handicapped child, and if he is, what constitutes an appropriate education to meet his unique needs.

(1) handicapped children:

The implementing regulations define handicapped children as "being mentally retarded, hard of hearing, deaf, speech impaired, visually handicapped, seriously emotionally disturbed, orthopedically impaired, other health impaired, deaf-blind, multi-handicapped, or as having specific learning disabilities, who because of those impairments need special education and related services." ... "Mentally retarded" is described as "significantly subaverage general intellectual functioning existing concurrently with deficits in adaptive behavior and manifested during the developmental period, which adversely affects a child's educational performance." ... "Multi-handicapped" is defined as "concomitant impairments (such as mentally retarded—blind, mentally retarded—orthopedically impaired, etc.), the combination of which causes such severe educational problems that they cannot be accommodated in special education programs solely for one of the impairments." ...

There is no question that Timothy W. fits within the Act's definition of a handicapped child: he is multiply handicapped and profoundly mentally retarded. He has been described as suffering from severe spasticity, cerebral palsy, brain damage, joint contractures, cortical blindness, is not ambulatory, and is quadriplegic.

(2) appropriate public education:

The Act and the implementing regulations define a "free appropriate public education" to mean "special education and related services which are provided at public expense ... [and] are provided in conformity with an individualized education program." ...

The record shows that Timothy W. is a severely handicapped and profoundly retarded child in need of special education and related services. Much of the expert testimony was to the effect that he is aware of his surrounding environment, makes or attempts to make purposeful movements, responds to tactile stimulation, responds to his mother's voice and touch, recognizes familiar voices, responds to noises, and parts his lips when spoon fed. The record contains testimony that Timothy W.'s needs include sensory stimulation, physical therapy, improved head control, socialization, consistency in responding to sound sources, and partial participation in eating. The educational consultants who drafted Timothy's individualized education program recommended that Timothy's special education program should include goals and objectives in the areas of motor control, communication, socialization, daily living skills, and recreation. The special education and related services that have been recommended to meet Timothy W.'s needs fit well within the statutory and regulatory definitions of the Act.

We conclude that the Act's language dictates the holding that Timothy W. is a handicapped child who is in need of special education and related services because of his handicaps. He must, therefore, according to the Act, be provided with such an educational program. There is nothing in the Act's language which even remotely supports the district court's conclusion that "under [the Act], an initial determination as to a child's ability to benefit from special education, must be made in order for a handicapped child to qualify for education under the Act." The language of the Act is directly to the contrary: a school district has a duty to provide an educational program for every handicapped child in the district, regardless of the severity of the handicap.

III. LEGISLATIVE HISTORY

An examination of the legislative history reveals that Congress intended the Act to provide a public education for all handicapped children, without exception; that the most severely handicapped were in fact to be given priority attention; and that an educational benefit was neither guaranteed nor required as a prerequisite for a child to receive such education. These factors were central, and were repeated over and over again, in the more than three years of congressional hearings and debates, which culminated in passage of the 1975 Act. . . .

Moreover, the legislative history is unambiguous that the primary purpose of the Act was to remedy the then current state of affairs, and provide a public education for *all* handicapped children. . . .

A. Priority For The Most Severely Handicapped

Not only did Congress intend that all handicapped children be educated, it expressly indicated its intent that the most severely handicapped be given priority. This resolve was reiterated over and over again in the floor debates and congressional reports, as well as in the final legislation. . . .

This priority reflected congressional acceptance of the thesis that early educational intervention was very important for severely handicapped children. . . .

If the order of the district court denying Timothy W. the benefits of the Act were to be implemented, he would be classified by the Act as in even greater need for receiving educational services than a severely multi-handicapped child receiving inadequate education. He would be in the *highest priority*—as a child who was not receiving any education at all.

B. Guarantees of Educational Benefit Are Not A Requirement For Child Eligibility

In mandating a public education for all handicapped children, Congress explicitly faced the issue of the possibility of the non-educability of the most severely handicapped. . . .

Thus, the district court's major holding, that proof of an educational benefit is a prerequisite before a handicapped child is entitled to a public education, is specifically belied, not only by the statutory language, but by the legislative history as well. We have not found in the Act's voluminous legislative history, nor has the school district directed our attention to, a single affirmative averment to support a benefit/eligibility requirement. But there is explicit evidence of a contrary congressional intent, that *no* guarantee of any particular educational outcome is required for a child to be eligible for public education.

We sum up. In the more than three years of legislative history leading to passage of the 1975 Act, covering House and Senate floor debates, hearings, and Congressional reports, the Congressional intention is unequivocal: Public education is to be provided to all handicapped children, unconditionally and without exception. It encompasses a universal right, and is not predicated upon any type of guarantees that the child will benefit from the special education and services before he or she is considered eligible to receive such education. Congress explicitly recognized the particular plight and special needs of the severely handicapped, and rather than excluding them from the Act's coverage, gave them priority status. The district court's holding is directly contradicted by the Act's legislative history, as well as the statutory language.

C. Subsequent Amendments to the Act

In the 14 years since passage of the Act, it has been amended four times. Congress thus has had ample opportunity to clarify any language originally used, or to make any modifications that it chose. Congress has not only repeatedly reaffirmed the original intent of the Act, to educate all handicapped children regardless of the severity of their handicap, and to give priority attention to the most severely handicapped, it has in fact *expanded* the provisions covering the most severely handicapped children. Most significantly, Congress has never intimated that a benefit/eligibility requirement was to be instituted. . . .

In summary, the Congressional reaffirmation of its intent to educate all handicapped children could not be any clearer. It was unequivocal at the time of passage of the Act in 1975, and it has been equally unequivocal during the intervening years. The school district's attempt in the instant case to "roll back" the entire thrust of this legislation completely ignores the overwhelming congressional consensus on this issue.

IV. CASE LAW

A. Cases Relied on in the Act

In its deliberations over the Act, Congress relied heavily on two landmark cases, Pennsylvania Association for Retarded Children v. Commonwealth of Pennsylvania (PARC) and Mills v. Board of Education of the District of Columbia which established the principle that exclusion from public education of any handicapped child is unconstitutional. . . .

B. All Handicapped Children are Entitled to a Public Education

Subsequent to the enactment of the Act, the courts have continued to embrace the principle that all handicapped children are entitled to a public education, and have consistently interpreted the Act as embodying this principle. . . .

C. Education is Broadly Defined

The courts have also made it clear that education for the severely handicapped under the Act is to be broadly defined. . . .

In the instant case, the district court's conclusion that education must be measured by the acquirement of traditional "cognitive skills" has no basis whatsoever in the 14 years of case law since the passage of the Act. All other courts have consistently held that education under the Act encompasses a wide spectrum of training, and that for the severely handicapped it may include the most elemental of life skills.

D. Proof of Benefit is Not Required

The district court relied heavily on *Rowley* in concluding that as a matter of law a child is not entitled to a public education unless he or she can benefit from it. The district court, however, has misconstrued *Rowley*. In that case, the Supreme Court held that a deaf child, who was an above average student and was advancing from grade to grade in a regular public school classroom, and who was already receiving substantial specialized instruction and related services, was not entitled, in addition, to a full time sign-language interpreter, because she was already benefitting from the special education and services she was receiving. The Court held that the school district was not required to *maximize* her educational achievement. It stated, "if personalized instruction is being provided with sufficient supportive services to permit the child to benefit from the instruction, . . . the child is receiving a 'free appropriate public education' as defined by the Act," . . . , and that "certainly the language of the statute contains no requirement . . . that States maximize the potential of handicapped children." . . .

Rowley focused on the *level* of services and the quality of programs that a *state* must provide, not the criteria for *access* to those programs. . . . The Court's use of "benefit" in *Rowley* was a substantive limitation placed on the state's choice of an educational program; it was not a license for the state to exclude certain handicapped children. In ruling that a state was not required to provide the maximum benefit possible, the Court was *not* saying that there must be proof that a child will benefit before the state is obligated to provide any education at all. Indeed, the Court in *Rowley* explicitly acknowledged Congress' intent to ensure public education to all handicapped children without regard to the level of achievement that they might attain. . . .

Rowley simply does not lend support to the district court's finding of a benefit/eligibility standard in the Act. As the Court explained, while the Act does not require a school to maximize a child's potential for learning, it does provide a "basic floor of opportunity" for the handicapped, consisting of "*access* to specialized instruction and related services" . . . (emphasis added). Nowhere does the Court imply that such a "floor" contains a trap door for the severely handicapped. Indeed, *Rowley* explicitly states: "[t]he Act requires special educational services for children 'regardless of the severity of their handicap,'" . . . , and "[t]he Act requires participating States to educate a wide spectrum of handicapped children, from the marginally hearing-impaired to the profoundly retarded and palsied." . . .

And most recently, the Supreme Court, in *Honig v. Doe* has made it quite clear that it will not rewrite the language of the Act to include exceptions which are not there. The Court, relying on the plain language and legislative history of the Act, ruled that dangerous and disruptive disabled children were not excluded from the requirement of [the IDEA], that a child "shall remain in the then current educational placement" pending any proceedings, unless the parents consent to a change. The Court rejected the argument that Congress could not possibly have meant to allow dangerous children to remain in the classroom. The analogous holding by the district court in the instant case—that Congress could not possibly have meant to "legislate futility," i.e. to educate children who could not benefit from it—falls for the reasons stated in *Honig*. The Court concluded that the language and legislative history of the Act was unequivocal in its mandate to educate all handicapped children, with no exceptions. The statute "means what it says," and the Court was "not at liberty to engraft onto the statute an exception Congress chose not to create." . . . . As Justice Brennan stated: "We think it clear . . . that Congress very much meant to strip schools of the *unilateral* authority they had traditionally employed to exclude disabled students . . . from school" . . . (emphasis in original). Such a stricture applies with equal force to the case of Timothy W., where the school is attempting to employ its unilateral authority to exclude a disabled student that it deems "uneducable."

The district court in the instant case, is, as far as we know, the only court in the 14 years subsequent to passage of the Act, to hold that a handicapped child was not entitled to a public education under the Act because he could not benefit from the education. This holding is contrary to the language of the Act, its legislative history, and the case law.

V. CONCLUSION

The statutory language of the Act, its legislative history, and the case law construing it, mandate that all handicapped children, regardless of the severity of their handicap, are entitled to a public education. The district court erred in requiring a benefit/eligibility test as a prerequisite to implicating the Act. School districts cannot avoid the provisions of the Act by returning to the practices that were widespread prior to the Act's passage, and which indeed were the impetus for the Act's passage, of unilaterally excluding certain handicapped children from a public education on the ground that they are uneducable.

The law explicitly recognizes that education for the severely handicapped is to be broadly defined, to include not only traditional academic skills, but also basic functional life skills, and that educational methodologies in these areas are not static, but are constantly evolving and improving. It is the school district's responsibility to avail itself of these new approaches in providing an education program geared to each child's individual needs. The only question for the school district to determine, in conjunction with the child's parents, is what constitutes an appropriate individualized education program (IEP) for the handicapped child. We emphasize that the phrase "appropriate individualized education program" cannot be interpreted, as the school district has done, to mean "no educational program." . . .

The judgment of the district court is reversed, judgment shall issue for Timothy W. The case is remanded to the district court which shall retain jurisdiction until a suitable individualized education program (IEP) for Timothy W. is effectuated by the school district. Timothy W. is entitled to an interim special educational placement until a final IEP is developed and agreed upon by the parties. The district court shall also determine the question of damages. . . .

Notes

1. The trial court in *Timothy W.* relied on *Rowley's* educational-benefit analysis to pronounce that a child who could not benefit from education was not entitled to services under the federal special education law. Why was the court's reliance on *Rowley* misplaced?

2. Many students with severe disabilities require expensive special education and related services. Should the cost of services be a factor in a school board's decision regarding what services it will provide to these students? Why? Should school boards be able to use cost-benefit analysis in evaluating whether to provide expensive services? Why?

CASE NO.4—ON-SITE SERVICES AT A RELIGIOUS SCHOOL

ZOBREST

v.

CATALINA FOOTHILLS SCHOOL DISTRICT

Supreme Court of the United States, 1993

509 U.S. 1

Chief Justice REHNQUIST delivered the opinion of the Court.

Petitioner James Zobrest, who has been deaf since birth, asked respondent school district to provide a sign-language interpreter to accompany him to classes at a Roman Catholic high school in Tucson, Arizona, pursuant to the Individuals with Disabilities Education Act (IDEA), . . . , and its Arizona counterpart, . . . The United States Court of Appeals for the Ninth Circuit decided, however, that provision of such a publicly employed interpreter would violate the Establishment Clause of the First Amendment. We hold that the Establishment Clause does not bar the school district from providing the requested interpreter.

James Zobrest attended grades one through five in a school for the deaf, and grades six through eight in a public school operated by respondent. While he attended public school, respondent furnished him with a sign-language interpreter. For religious reasons, James' parents . . . enrolled him for the ninth grade in Salpointe Catholic High School, a sectarian institution. When petitioners requested that respondent supply James with an interpreter at Salpointe, respondent referred the matter to the county attorney, who concluded that providing an interpreter on the school's premises would violate the United States Constitution. . . . Pursuant to [state law], the question next was referred to the Arizona attorney general, who concurred in the county attorney's opinion. . . . Respondent accordingly declined to provide the requested interpreter.

Petitioners then instituted this action in the United States District Court for the District of Arizona under [the IDEA], which grants the district courts jurisdiction over disputes regarding the services due disabled children under the IDEA. Petitioners asserted that the IDEA and the Free Exercise Clause of the First Amendment require respondent to provide James with an interpreter at Salpointe, and that the Establishment Clause does not bar such relief. The complaint sought a preliminary injunction and "such other and further relief as the Court deems just and proper." . . . The District Court denied petitioners' request for a preliminary injunction, finding that the provision of an interpreter at Salpointe would likely offend the Establishment Clause. . . . The court thereafter granted respondent summary judgment, on the ground that "[t]he interpreter would act as a conduit for the religious inculcation of James—thereby, promoting James' religious development at government expense." . . . "That kind of entanglement of church and state," the District Court concluded, "is not allowed."

The Court of Appeals affirmed by a divided vote, . . . applying the three-part test announced in *Lemon v. Kurtzman.* It first found that the IDEA has a clear secular purpose: "'to assist States and Localities to provide for the education of all handicapped children.'... "Turning to the second prong of the *Lemon* inquiry, though, the Court of

Appeals determined that the IDEA, if applied as petitioners proposed, would have the primary effect of advancing religion and thus would run afoul of the Establishment Clause. "By placing its employee in the sectarian school," the Court of Appeals reasoned, "the government would create the appearance that it was a 'joint sponsor' of the school's activities." . . . This, the court held, would create the "symbolic union of government and religion" found impermissible in *School Dist. of Grand Rapids v. Ball.* In contrast, the dissenting judge argued that "[g]eneral welfare programs neutrally available to all children," such as the IDEA, pass constitutional muster, "because their benefits diffuse over the entire population." . . . We granted certiorari . . . and now reverse.

Respondent has raised in its brief in opposition to certiorari and in isolated passages in its brief on the merits several issues unrelated to the Establishment Clause question. Respondent first argues that . . . a regulation promulgated under the IDEA, precludes it from using federal funds to provide an interpreter to James at Salpointe. . . . In the alternative, respondent claims that even if there is no affirmative bar to the relief, it is not *required* by statute or regulation to furnish interpreters to students at sectarian schools. . . . And respondent adds that providing such a service would offend Art. II, § 12, of the Arizona Constitution. . . .

We have never said that "religious institutions are disabled by the First Amendment from participating in publicly sponsored social welfare programs." . . . For if the Establishment Clause did bar religious groups from receiving general government benefits, then "a church could not be protected by the police and fire departments, or have its public sidewalk kept in repair." . . . Given that a contrary rule would lead to such absurd results, we have consistently held that government programs that neutrally provide benefits to a broad class of citizens defined without reference to religion are not readily subject to an Establishment Clause challenge just because sectarian institutions may also receive an attenuated financial benefit.

. . . The service at issue in this case is part of a general government program that distributes benefits neutrally to any child qualifying as "disabled" under the IDEA, without regard to the "sectarian-nonsectarian, or public-nonpublic nature" of the school the child attends. By according parents freedom to select a school of their choice, the statute ensures that a government-paid interpreter will be present in a sectarian school only as a result of the private decision of individual parents. In other words, because the IDEA creates no financial incentive for parents to choose a sectarian school, an interpreter's presence there cannot be attributed to state decisionmaking. . . . When the government offers a neutral service on the premises of a sectarian school as part of a general program that "is in no way skewed towards religion," . . . [I]t follows under our prior decisions that provision of that service does not offend the Establishment Clause. . . . [U]nder the IDEA, no funds traceable to the government ever find their way into sectarian schools' coffers. The only indirect economic benefit a sectarian school might receive by dint of the IDEA is the disabled child's tuition—and that is, of course, assuming that the school makes a profit on each student; that, without an IDEA interpreter, the child would have gone to school elsewhere; and that the school, then, would have been unable to fill that child's spot.

. . . [T]he task of a sign-language interpreter seems to us quite different from that of a teacher or guidance counselor. Notwithstanding the Court of Appeals' intimations to the contrary, . . . the Establishment Clause lays down no absolute bar to the placing of a public employee in a sectarian school. Such a flat rule, smacking of antiquated notions of "taint," would indeed exalt form over substance. Nothing in this record suggests that a sign-language interpreter would do more than accurately interpret whatever material is presented to the class as a whole. In fact, ethical guidelines require interpreters to "transmit everything that is said in exactly the same way it was intended." ... James' parents have chosen of their own free will to place him in a pervasively sectarian environment. The sign-language interpreter they have requested will neither add to nor subtract from that environment, and hence the provision of such assistance is not barred by the Establishment Clause.

The IDEA creates a neutral government program dispensing aid not to schools but to individual handicapped children. If a handicapped child chooses to enroll in a sectarian school, we hold that the Establishment Clause does not prevent the school district from furnishing him with a sign-language interpreter there in order to facilitate his education. The judgment of the Court of Appeals is therefore

Reversed.

Notes

1. School boards are often willing to provide special education and related services to private school students within public school settings under dual enrollment arrangements. However, the services of a sign-language interpreter can only be provided on-site. How does this affect a board's ability to provide services to a group of students with similar disabilities? Should this be a factor in a board's decision regarding what services it will provide to students who are enrolled in private schools?

2. *Zobrest* makes it clear that school boards may provide services on-site in religious schools. Are boards required to do so? What if boards provide on-site services to students attending non-sectarian private schools?

3. Although the sign-language interpreter in *Zobrest* could, and most likely would, have interpreted religious content along with the secular material in the student's instruction, the majority did not see this as a problem because the interpreter would not have originated the religious message but would only have conveyed it, much in the manner of a tape or video recorder. The majority saw this as a permissible action under the Establishment Clause. Would the result have been different if the student was visually impaired and requested the services of a public school employee to transcribe written materials, including materials that had a religious content?

REFERENCES

Agostini v. Felton, 521 U.S. 203 (1997).

Aguilar v. Felton, 473 U.S. 402 (1985).

Alexander v. Boyd, 876 F. Supp. 773 (D.S.C. 1995).

Americans with Disabilities Act, 42 U.S.C.A. §§ 12101–12213 (1990).

Babb v. Knox County School System, 965 F.2d 104 (6th Cir. 1992).

Board of Education of the Hendrick Hudson Central School District v. Rowley, 458 U.S. 176 (1982).

Bristol Warren Regional School Committee v. Rhode Island Department of Education and Secondary Education, 253 F. Supp.2d 236 (D.R.I. 2003).

Chuhran v. Walled Lake Consolidated Schools, 839 F. Supp. 465 (E.D. Mich. 1993).

Community High School District 155 v. Denz, 463 N.E.2d 998 (Ill. App. Ct. 1984).

Daugherty v. Hamilton County Schools, 21 F. Supp.2d 765 (E.D. Tenn. 1998).

District 27 Community School Board v. Board of Education of the City of New York, 502 N.Y.S.2d 325 (N.Y. Sup. Ct. 1986).

Doe v. Belleville Public School District No. 118, 672 F. Supp. 342 (S.D. Ill. 1987).

Doe v. Board of Education of the State of Connecticut, 753 F. Supp. 65 (D. Conn. 1990).

Donnell C. v. Illinois State Board of Education, 829 F. Supp. 1016 (N.D. Ill. 1993).

Evans v. Tuttle, 613 N.E.2d 854 (Ind. Ct. App. 1993).

Everson v. Board of Education, 330 U.S. 1 (1947).

Foley v. Special School District of St. Louis County, 153 F.3d 863 (8th Cir. 1998).

Fowler v. Unified School District, 107 F.3d 797, 129 F.3d 1431 (10th Cir. 1997).

Gabel ex rel. L.G. v. Board of Education of the Hyde Park Central School District, 368 F. Supp.2d 313 (S.D.N.Y. 2005).

Gary S. v. Manchester School District, 374 F.3d 15 (1st Cir. 2004).

Green v. Johnson, 513 F. Supp. 965 (D. Mass. 1981).

Helms v. Picard, 151 F.3d 347 (5th Cir. 1998).

Honig v. Doe, 484 U.S. 305 (1988).

Hooks v. Clark County School District, 228 F.3d 1036 (9th Cir. 2000).

Huefner, D. S. (2006). *Getting comfortable with special education law: A framework for working with children with disabilities*. (2nd ed.). Norwood, MA: Christopher-Gordon.

Independent School District No. 284 v. A.C., 258 F.3d 769 (8th Cir. 2001).

Individuals with Disabilities Education Act, 20 U.S.C. §§ 1400–1491 (2005).

J.D. v. Pawlet School District, 224 F.3d 60 (2d Cir. 2000).

KDM ex rel. WJM v. Reedsport School District, 196 F.3d 1046 (9th Cir. 1999).

Lemon v. Kurtzman, 403 U.S. 602 (1971).

Lyons v. Smith, 829 F. Supp. 414 (D.D.C. 1993).

Martinez v. School Board of Hillsborough County, Florida, 861 F.2d 1502 (11th Cir. 1988), *on remand* 711 F. Supp. 1066 (M.D. Fla. 1989).

Meek v. Pittenger, 421 U.S. 349 (1975).

Mitchell v. Helms, 530 U.S. 793 (2000), *on remand*, 229 F.3d 467 (5th Cir. 2000).

Muller v. Committee on Special Education of the East Islip Union Free School District, 145 F.3d 95, (2d Cir. 1998).

New York State Association for Retarded Children v. Carey, 612 F.2d 644 (2d Cir. 1979).

Osborne, A. G., & Russo, C. (1997). The ghoul is dead, long live the ghoul: *Agostini v. Felton* and the delivery of Title I services in nonpublic schools. *Education Law Reporter*, 119, 781–797.

Peck v. Lansing School District, 148 F.3d 619 (6th Cir. 1998).

Peter v. Wedl, 155 F.3d 992 (8th Cir. 1998).

Rehabilitation Act, Section 504, 29 U.S.C. § 794 (1973).

Stock v. Massachusetts Hospital School, 467 N.E.2d 448 (Mass. 1984).

Timothy W. v. Rochester, N.H. School District, 875 F.2d 954 (1st Cir. 1989).

Wolman v. Walter, 433 U.S. 229 (1977).

Zobrest v. Catalina Foothills School District, 509 U.S. 1 (1993).

3

Procedural Due Process

❖

Key Concepts in This Chapter
❖ Student Records
❖ Evaluation and Classification of Students With Disabilities
❖ Individualized Education Programs
❖ Rights of Parents and Guardians
❖ Status Quo Provision

Among the many unique elements of the Individuals with Disabilities Education Act (IDEA) is its complex system of due process safeguards to ensure that students with disabilities are properly identified, evaluated, and placed according to the procedures detailed in its provisions (20 U.S.C. § 1415). The primary function of the IDEA's safeguards is to make parents equal partners with school personnel in the education of their children.

The IDEA requires teams to develop Individualized Education Programs (IEPs) for every child found to need special education and related services (20 U.S.C. § 1414(d)(5)). As part of this process, the parents of children with disabilities must be provided with opportunities to participate in the development of the IEPs (20 U.S.C. § 1414(d)(1)(B)(i)).

Prior to the IDEA's initial implementation in 1977, school officials were allowed to make placement decisions concerning children with disabilities without regard for the wishes of their parents. This approach led to the exclusionary policies outlined in the first chapter. The IDEA's provisions ensure that school boards cannot act without parental knowledge by requiring school officials to obtain parental consent prior to evaluating students or making initial placements (20 U.S.C. § 1414(a)(D)) and by requiring proper notice before initiating changes in placements once students are in their original placements (20 U.S.C. § 1415(b)(3)).

The architects of the IDEA anticipated that parents and school officials would work together. Even so, Congress was pragmatic enough to realize that agreements regarding classification and placement would not always be reached easily. Thus, Congress created a dispute resolution process that allows parents to bring grievances to impartial third-party hearing officers and eventually to the courts, if necessary. Chapter 7 reviews the IDEA's dispute resolution process.

This chapter discusses the IDEA's due process scheme as it pertains to the identification, evaluation, and placement of a student with disabilities, emphasizing the procedural rights of students and their parents. To this end, the importance of procedural compliance cannot be overemphasized. In fact, the Supreme Court ruled that a special education placement is not appropriate if it is not developed according to the IDEA's procedures (*Board of Education of the Hendrick Hudson Central School District v. Rowley*, 1982). Due to the large amount of record keeping that is associated with the special education process, this chapter begins with an overview of regulations regarding student records. This chapter then examines information on the evaluation process, development of IEPs, and the procedures that teams must follow when attempting to change the placements of students.

STUDENT RECORDS

Congress passed the Family Educational Rights and Privacy Act (FERPA) (20 U.S.C. § 1232g) in 1974, a year before it enacted the original version of the IDEA. FERPA outlines the rights of students and their parents with regard to educational records. FERPA has two main goals: to grant parents and eligible students access to their educational records and to limit the access of outsiders to those records. FERPA and the IDEA and its regulations apply with equal force to parents (20 U.S.C. 1232(g); 34 C.F.R. § 99.4) and eligible students with disabilities. Insofar as parents, rather than students, typically exercise the right to access records, this section focuses more on parental rights. Due to the fact that numerous records are kept pertaining to students in special education placements, a large part of the IDEA's regulations (34 C.F.R. §§ 300.611–300.627) deal with this important topic. The IDEA's regulations prohibit school authorities from disclosing any personally identifiable information about students with disabilities (34 C.F.R. § 300.622) while requiring school boards to protect the confidentiality of this information (34 C.F.R. § 300.623).

Records Covered by FERPA

FERPA covers all "educational records" maintained by educational agencies or by persons acting on their behalf that contain personally identifiable information relating to students (20 U.S.C. § 1232g(a)(4)(A)). To the extent that "educational records" may include information about more than one student, parents (20 U.S.C. § 1232g(a)(1)(A)) who review the records of their children can examine only those portions of group data that are specific to their own children (20 U.S.C. § 1232g(a)(1)(A)).

Two cases highlight the importance of safeguarding student records in the context of special education. In the first, the federal trial court in Connecticut decided that school board officials violated parents' privacy rights when they released their names and that of their child to a local newspaper following a due process hearing (*Sean R. v. Board of Education of the Town of Woodbridge*, 1992). In the second case, the Eighth Circuit, noting that strong public policy favors protection of the privacy of minors where sensitive matters are concerned, affirmed that judicial proceedings under the IDEA can be closed to the public (*Webster Groves School District v. Pulitzer Publishing Co.*, 1990). The court also pointed out that the IDEA restricts the release of information concerning students with disabilities without parental permission. In an attempt to so safeguard that information and prevent stigmatization of the student, the court emphasized that access to the courtroom could be restricted and the files sealed.

Many school boards record directory information that may include each child's "name, address, telephone listing, date and place of birth, major field of study, participation in officially recognized activities and sports, weight and height of members of athletic teams, degrees and awards received, and the most recent previous educational agency or institution attended by the student" (20 U.S.C. § 1232g(a)(5)(A)). Before school officials can release directory information on current students, they must provide parents with public notice of the categories of records that are designated as directory and afford them a reasonable time to request that the material not be released without their consent (20 U.S.C. § 1232g(a)(5)(B); 34 C.F.R. § 99.37). Inasmuch as the disclosure provisions relating to directory information do not apply to former students, school officials can release such data without obtaining any prior approvals (34 C.F.R. § 99.37(b)).

FERPA requires school personnel to inform parents annually of their right to inspect and review, request amendment of, and consent to disclosure of educational records, along with the right to file a complaint with the federal Department of Education alleging failures to comply with the dictates of the statute (34 C.F.R. §§ 99.7, 300.612). Typically, parents receive a single notice by a means that is reasonably likely to inform them of their rights. This notice may be included in school newsletters, student handbooks, notes home, local access TV announcements, e-mail, or other methods or combination of means designed to ensure that they receive notice.

In spite of FERPA's comprehensiveness, the statute grants exceptions so that a variety of documents are not considered to be educational records subject to the statute's mandatory disclosure provisions (34 C.F.R. § 99.3(b)). Four exemptions, in particular, are relevant to special education. First, records generated by educational personnel that are in the sole possession of their makers and are not accessible by or revealed to any other persons except temporary substitutes are not subject to release (20 U.S.C. § 1232g (a)(4)(B)(1)). Second, records kept separately by the law enforcement units of educational agencies that are used only for their own purposes cannot be accessed by third parties (20 U.S.C. § 1232g(a)(4)(B)(2)). Third, records that are made in the ordinary course of events relating to individuals who work at but who do not attend educational institutions and that refer exclusively to individuals in their capacity as employees, and are not available for any other purpose, are not subject to disclosure (20 U.S.C. § 1232g(a)(4)(B)(3)). Fourth, records relating to students who are eighteen years of age or older or who attend postsecondary educational institutions, which are made by physicians, psychiatrists, psychologists, or other professionals or paraprofessionals for use in their treatment and are not available to others, except at the request of the students, cannot be released (20 U.S.C. § 1232g(a)(4)(B)(4)).

Rights to Inspect and Review Records

As indicated previously, parents have the right to inspect and review records containing personally identifiable information relating to the education of their children (20 U.S.C. § 1232g(a)(1)(A), 34 C.F.R. § 300.613). In this respect, FERPA grants noncustodial parents the same right of access to educational records as custodial parents, absent court orders or applicable state laws to the contrary (34 C.F.R. § 99.4). Along with access rights, FERPA requires school officials to provide parents with reasonable interpretations and explanations of information contained in the records of their children (34 C.F.R. § 99.10(c)).

Under FERPA, parental permission or consent is transferred to eligible students who reach their eighteenth birthday or who attend postsecondary institutions (20 U.S.C. § 1232g(d); 34 C.F.R. § 300.625(b)). In an important exception relating to special education, school officials can take the age and the type or severity of student disabilities into consideration when granting rights of access (34 C.F.R. §§ 300.574, 300.625(a)). Other restrictions of interest are that postsecondary institutions do not have to permit students to inspect financial records in their files that include information about the resources of their parents (20 U.S.C. § 1232g(a)(1)(B); 34 C.F.R. § 99.12(b)(1)) or letters of recommendation where they waived their rights of access (20 U.S.C. § 1232g(a)(1)(C); 34 C.F.R. § 99.37(b)(2)(3)). Further, school officials are not required to grant access to records pertaining to individuals who are not or never have been students at their institutions (20 U.S.C. § 1232g(a)(6)).

Exceptions

Parties generally can access school records other than directory information only if parents provide written consent (20 U.S.C. §§ 1232g(b)(1), 1232g(b)(2)(A)). However, FERPA contains nine major exceptions where parental permission is not required before officials can review educational records. The purpose of these exceptions is to assist in the smooth administration of schools, especially as personnel from different school systems interact with one another. First, school employees with legitimate educational interests can access student records (20 U.S.C. § 1232g(b)(1)(A)). Second, officials representing schools to which students apply for admission can access their records as long as parents receive proper notice that the information has been sent to the receiving institution (20 U.S.C. § 1232g(b)(1)(B)). Third, authorized representatives of the U.S. Comptroller General, the Secretary of the Department of Education, and state and local education officials who are authorized to do so by state law can view student records for law enforcement purposes (20 U.S.C. § 1232g(b)(1)(C)(E)). Fourth, persons who are responsible for evaluating eligibility for financial aid can review appropriate educational records of students (20 U.S.C. § 1232g(b)(1)(D)).

Fifth, members of organizations conducting studies on behalf of educational agencies or institutions developing predictive tests or administering aid programs and improving instruction can view records as long as doing so does not lead to the release of personal information about students (20 U.S.C. § 1232g(b)(1)(F)). Sixth, individuals acting in the course of their duties for accrediting organizations can review student records (20 U.S.C. § 1232g(b)(1)(G)). Seventh, parents of dependent children can access student records (20 U.S.C. § 1232g(b)(1)(H)). Eighth, persons who protect the health and safety of students or other persons can view records in emergency situations (20 U.S.C. § 1232g(b)(1)(I)). Ninth, written permission is unnecessary if student records are subpoenaed or otherwise obtained through judicial orders, except that the parents must be notified in advance of a school board's compliance (20 U.S.C. §§ 1232g(b)(1)(J), 1232g(b)(2)(B)). Prior to ordering the release of information, courts weigh the need for access against the privacy interests of students. FERPA adds that its provisions do not prohibit educational officials from disclosing information concerning registered sex offenders who are required to register by federal law. Of course, in any of these instances, school officials cannot release or quote any personally identifiable information relating to children without parental consent.

A third party seeking disclosure of student records must have written consent from parents specifying the record(s) to be released, the reason(s) for the proposed release, and to whom the information is being given (34 C.F.R. § 99.30). FERPA further stipulates that parents have the right to receive a copy of the materials to be released (20 U.S.C. § 1232g(b)(2)(A)). In addition, school officials must keep records of all individuals or groups, except exempted parties, who request or obtain access to student records (20 U.S.C. § 1232g(b)(4)(A)). These records not only must explain the legitimate interests of those who are granted access to educational records but must also be kept with records of individual students whose files were accessed (20 U.S.C. § 1232g(b)(4)(A); 34 C.F.R. § 300.614).

Educational agencies that maintain student records must comply with parental requests for review without unnecessary delay. Unless parents agree otherwise, they must be granted access no later than 45 days after making their requests (20 U.S.C. § 1232g(a)(1)(A); 34 C.F.R. § 99.10(b)). Of course, nothing prohibits school officials from granting parental requests for access to student records more quickly. Agencies that receive parental requests for access to records cannot charge fees to search for or to retrieve student records (34 C.F.R.

§§ 99.11(b), 300.614(b)). Once materials are located, school officials may charge parents for copies if doing so does not effectively prevent them from exercising their rights to inspect and review the educational records of their children (34 C.F.R. §§ 99.11(a), 300.614(a)).

Amending Records

Parents who disagree with the content of educational records can ask school officials to amend the information (34 C.F.R. § 99.20(a), 300.618(a)). If officials refuse to amend records within a reasonable time (34 C.F.R. §§ 99.20(b)(c), 300.618(c)), parents are entitled to hearings at which hearing officers evaluate whether challenged material is accurate and appropriately contained within the educational records of students (34 C.F.R. §§ 99.21, 300.619).

Hearing officers must both conduct hearings and render decisions over amending student records within a reasonable time (34 C.F.R. § 99.22). If hearing officers are convinced that contested material is inaccurate, misleading, or otherwise violates student rights to privacy, school officials must amend it accordingly and inform the parents in writing that this has been done (34 C.F.R. §§ 99.21(b)(1), 300.620(a)). Conversely, if hearing officers believe that materials in educational records are not inaccurate or misleading or do not otherwise violate student rights to privacy, the challenged information need not be removed or amended (34 C.F.R. §§ 99.21(b)(2), 300.620(b)). Parents who remain concerned over the content of educational records relating to their children, even after hearing officers decide that the records are acceptable, can add statements explaining their objections that must be kept with the contested information for as long as it is kept on file (34 C.F.R. §§ 99.21(c), 300.620(c)).

Destruction of Special Education Records

Insofar as the number of records in student files can multiply rapidly, it should not be surprising that the IDEA's regulations allow for the destruction of information that is no longer needed. While neither the IDEA nor its regulations define the term, the latter does stipulate that records can be destroyed when they are no longer needed to provide children with services (34 C.F.R. § 300.624(a)). The regulation adds not only that parents must be advised that records are going to be destroyed but also that school officials can keep a record of student names, addresses, phone numbers, grades, attendance records, classes attended, grade levels completed, and years completed, with a time limitation (34 C.F.R. § 300.624(b)).

Enforcement

FERPA includes enforcement provisions for situations when parents are denied the opportunity to review the records of their children, or records are released impermissibly. In *Gonzaga University v. Doe* (2002), the Supreme Court confirmed that the sole remedy for aggrieved parties is to file written complaints detailing the specifics of an alleged violation with the federal Department of Education's Family Policy Compliance Office (FPCO) (34 C.F.R. § 99.63).

Complaints must be filed within 180 days of either alleged violations or the dates when the aggrieved party knew or reasonably should have known about violations (34 C.F.R. § 99.64). When the FPCO receives complaints, its staff must notify officials at the educational institutions in writing, detailing the substance of the alleged violations and asking them to respond before considering whether to proceed with investigations (34 C.F.R. § 99.65). If, after investigations are completed (34 C.F.R. § 99.66), the FPCO staff agree that violations occurred, the Department of Education can withhold further payments under its programs, issue orders to compel compliance, or ultimately terminate institutional eligibility to receive federal funding if officials refuse to comply within a reasonable time (34 C.F.R. § 99.67).

In the only other Supreme Court case involving FERPA, *Owasso Independent School District v. Falvo* (2002), the Court found that peer grading, whereby teachers permit students to grade the papers of classmates, does not turn the materials in question into educational records covered by FERPA. The Court concluded that a school board did not violate the law by permitting teachers to use the practice over the objection of a mother whose children attended schools in the district (Russo & Mawdsley, 2002).

EVALUATION

The IDEA requires states to establish procedures to ensure that all children with disabilities are properly identified and evaluated (20 U.S.C. § 1412(a)(3)). All testing and evaluation materials and procedures must be selected and administered in a manner that is not racially or culturally biased (20 U.S.C. §§ 1412(a)(6)(B), 1414(b)(3)(A)(i)) and students whose language or other mode of communication is not English need to be evaluated in their native language or other mode of communication (20 U.S.C. §§ 1412(a)(6)(B), 1414(b)(3)(A)(ii)).

Evaluation procedures must be multidisciplinary; in other words, no single procedure can be the sole criterion for determining eligibility or placement (20 U.S.C. § 1414(b)(2)(B)). Even so, eligibility decisions are to be made by teams of qualified professionals in consort with the parents of children who were assessed (20 U.S.C. § 1414(b)(4)(A)). Evaluations must be individualized. All assessments must be valid and reliable and should be administered by trained personnel in conformance with the instructions provided by their producers (20 U.S.C. §§ 1414(b)(3)(A)(iii)-(v)). Moreover, at least one member of **evaluation teams** must have knowledge in the area of suspected disability (*Seattle School District No. 1 v. B.S.*, 1996).

The 2004 IDEA amendments include a new provision addressing the status of students based on race and ethnicity. The IDEA now requires states and local school boards to develop policies and procedures to prevent the overidentification or disproportionate representation by race and ethnicity of children with disabilities (20 U.S.C. §§ 1412(a)(24), 1418 (d)(1)(A)(B)). This provision also requires school officials to record the number of students from minority groups in special education classes and to provide early intervention services for children in groups deemed to be overrepresented. In a related provision, the IDEA directs school officials to examine data, including information that is disaggregated by race and ethnicity, to evaluate whether there are significant discrepancies in the rate of long-term **suspensions** and **expulsions** of students with disabilities (20 U.S.C. §§ 1412 (a)(22)(A), 1418(d)(1)(C)). The IDEA further requires school personnel to review and if appropriate revise policies, procedures, and practices related to the implementation of IEPs. Additionally, the IDEA directs school staff to use positive behavioral interventions and supports as well as procedural safeguards to ensure that they comply with the law (20 U.S.C. § 1412(a) (22)(B)) in avoiding this problem.

School officials must undertake complete **reevaluations** for all children with disabilities at least every three years (20 U.S.C. § 1414(a)(2)(B)(ii)). More frequent reevaluations may be conducted when school officials think that they are warranted or when parents or teachers make such requests (20 U.S.C. § 1414(a)(2)(A); *Cartwright v. District of Columbia*, 2003). Reevaluations are also required whenever school boards propose significant changes in placements (*Brimmer v. Traverse City Area Public Schools*, 1994).

IEPs can be invalidated if they are not based on proper evaluations. For example, the federal trial court in New Jersey was of the opinion that a proposed IEP for a student who was deaf was not appropriate because school personnel failed to follow proper evaluation procedures (*Bonadonna v. Cooperman*, 1985). The court observed that the school's evaluation team based its conclusions regarding placement on simple observations. The court added that school personnel did not use validated instruments to measure the child's aptitude, and the procedures used tended to be biased against students with hearing impairments. At the same time, the court acknowledged that the board did not include an expert on the education of hearing-impaired students on the evaluation team. Similarly, in an early case involving the education of students with emotional problems resulting in acting out and aggressive behavior, a federal trial court in New York discovered that their placements were based on vague criteria that tended to discriminate against minorities (*Lora v. Board of Education of the City of New York*, 1978, 1980, 1984). The record also reflected the fact that, once placed, the students were not reevaluated as mandated by state and federal law. In order to remedy the situation, the court directed the parties to develop nondiscriminatory assessment procedures.

School officials must complete all evaluations of students suspected of having disabilities within sixty days of receiving parental consent for the evaluations (20 U.S.C. § 1414(a)(1)(C)(i)(I)). However, if state law dictates different time frames for completing evaluations, these requirements are controlling. Depending on how state laws are worded, school officials may be required to conduct evaluations over summer vacation periods if necessary in order to complete them within prescribed time limitations. By way of illustration, the federal trial court in Maryland, where the law at the time required evaluations to be completed within forty-five calendar days of referrals, held that a school board violated a student's rights by not conducting the evaluation within that time limitation (*Gerstmyer v. Howard County Public Schools*, 1994). The court pointed out that the student's mother requested the evaluation in May, but officials informed her that they could not complete it over the summer months.

The IDEA's sixty-day rule does not apply if "the parent of a child repeatedly fails or refuses to produce the child for the evaluation" (20 U.S.C. § 1414(a)(1) (C)(ii)(II)). Yet, if parents refuse to respond to requests to provide consent for initial evaluations or to services, educational officials may still continue with evaluations as long as they follow the procedures outlined in section 1415 of the IDEA (20 U.S.C. §§ 1414(a)(1)(D)(ii)(I), (II)). Even so, the Eighth Circuit noted that the IDEA allows parents to decline services and waive all benefits under the IDEA (*Fitzgerald v. Camdenton R-III School District*, 2006).

Parents have the right to obtain independent evaluations of their children if they disagree with the evaluations completed by their school board (20 U.S.C. § 1415(b)(1); 34 C.F.R. § 300.502(b)). These independent evaluations are at public expense if it can be shown that evaluations conducted by school board personnel were inappropriate. Parents cannot obtain independent evaluations at public expense simply to get another opinion (*R.L. ex rel Mr. and Mrs. L. v. Plainville Board of Education*, 2005).

School officials must consider the results of independent evaluations in decisions that they make about the provision of services as long as they meet the criteria established by their boards (34 C.F.R. § 300.502(c)(1)). Yet, this does not mean that the recommendations of independent evaluators must be adopted. In fact, the First Circuit specifically declared that the requirement that school personnel consider the results of independent evaluations does not mean that they must engage in a substantive discussion of those findings (*G.D. v. Westmoreland School District*, 1991). In like manner, the federal trial court in Connecticut asserted that the IDEA does not require school boards to accept the recommendations of independent evaluations or even that evaluations be accorded any particular weight (*T.S. v. Ridgefield Board of Education*, 1992, 1993). The Second Circuit affirmed that the plain meaning of the word *consider* is to reflect or think about with care. These cases make it clear that school personnel satisfy the requirement to consider independent evaluations if they review their results at IEP conferences.

Educational officials are not required to leave their states to evaluate students whose parents unilaterally placed them in out-of-state facilities. In this regard, a federal trial court in Michigan expressed the view that a school board had the right to evaluate a student whose parents requested payment of tuition for an out-of-state residential school, but officials were not required to leave the state to do so (*Lenhoff v. Farmington Public Schools*, 1988). The parents had enrolled their child in the school without the knowledge or consent of school officials. Subsequently, a federal trial court in Illinois explained that the IDEA clearly did not require a school board to send its personnel to an out-of-state facility to evaluate a student (*Patricia P. v. Board of Education of Oak Park and River Forest High School District No. 200*, 1998).

School boards have the right to conduct their own evaluations even when parents present them with the results of outside assessments (*Andress v. Cleveland Independent School District*, 1995; *Johnson v. Duneland School Corporation*, 1996). On the other hand, school officials may rely on evaluations conducted by personnel from other school systems when developing IEPs for students who moved into new districts as long as the results are still relevant (*Poolaw v. Bishop*, 1995). School boards may, if they choose, rely on outside assessments when developing IEPs (*Pitchford ex rel. M. v. Salem-Keizer School District No. 24J*, 2001).

DEVELOPMENT OF INDIVIDUALIZED EDUCATION PROGRAMS

IEPs are written documents that include statements of students' current academic achievement and functional performance, annual goals, how teams will measure progress toward those goals, the specific educational services to be provided, the extent to which children can participate in the general education program, accommodations the pupils will need on state assessments, and the date of initiation and duration of services (20 U.S.C. § 1414(d)). School personnel, acting in conjunction with parents, must develop IEPs before providing students with disabilities with special education and related services. IEPs must be in effect at the beginning of each school year (34 C.F.R. § 300.323).

The 2004 IDEA amendments include two significant changes affecting the development of IEPs. First, the IDEA no longer specifies the need for benchmarks and short-term objectives for children with disabilities, other than for those who take alternate assessments aligned to alternate achievement standards (20 U.S.C. § 1414(d)(1)(A)(I)). Even so, educators should note that state laws may still require IEPs to include benchmarks and short-term objectives. Second, the IDEA allows up to fifteen states to pilot comprehensive multiyear IEPs that do not exceed three years and that are designed to coincide with natural transition points in a child's education (20 U.S.C. § 1414(d)(5)(A)). Nothing in this new provision prevents parents or school officials from requesting shorter-term IEPs or earlier reviews if they think that doing so is in a child's best interests.

Two related changes accompany the proposed three-year IEP provision. The first addition seeks to help school personnel reduce the significant amount of paperwork associated with the delivery of special education services (20 U.S.C. §§ 1400(c)(5)(G), 1400(c)(9)). This addition permits selected states to pilot paperwork-reduction plans to reduce the burden on teachers, administrators, and related service providers (20 U.S.C. § 1414(d)(5)(B)(i)). The second enhancement complements the paperwork-reduction provisions. This change directs the Secretary of Education to provide copies of model forms for IEPs, individualized family service plans, the IDEA's procedural safeguards, and its prior written notice provisions no later than when the IDEA's final regulations are promulgated (20 U.S.C. § 1417(e)).

An overriding theme of the IDEA is that IEPs and educational programs for students with disabilities must be individualized. This means that IEPs must be designed according to the unique characteristics of each individual child, taking into consideration the child's strengths and weaknesses. Programs must be developed to fit each individual child. To this end, the courts have invalidated IEPs that are not individualized. In one such case, a federal court emphasized that an IEP that did not contain academic objectives and methods of evaluation that addressed the student's unique needs and abilities was not appropriate (*Chris D. v. Montgomery County Board of Education*, 1990). Another court criticized an IEP that was not specific to the student but, rather, was assembled using portions of IEPs that had been developed for other students (*Gerstmyer v. Howard County Public Schools*, 1994).

IEPs do not have to be written perfectly to pass judicial review. Courts generally allow some flaws in IEPs as long as they do not compromise the appropriateness of student educational programming (Osborne, 2004). Courts are generally more forgiving if the missing information was available or provided in another form. For example, the Sixth Circuit noted that an IEP that did not include current levels of performance or the objective criteria for evaluating progress was still appropriate because the information was known to all concerned (*Doe v. Defendant I*, 1990). The court was unwilling to exalt form over substance, positing that the emphasis on procedural safeguards referred to the process by which an IEP was developed, not the myriad technical items that are to be included in the written document. On the other hand, a federal trial court in California invalidated an IEP that did not address all areas of the student's disabilities and that did not contain any statement of the specific services to be provided (*Russell v. Jefferson*, 1985). The court was of the view that an IEP with those defects would have compromised the integrity of the student's educational program.

Student placements must be based on IEPs, not the other way around. Placements should be developed to fit the unique, individual needs of children. Courts have frequently struck down the practice of writing IEPs to fit placements. In such a situation, the Fourth Circuit observed that school officials violated the IDEA when they placed a child in a county facility and developed an IEP to carry out their judgment (*Spielberg v. Henrico County Public Schools*, 1988). In another case, the federal trial court in Connecticut held that school officials violated the IDEA when they proposed a placement without first evaluating the child or writing an IEP (*P.J. v. State of Connecticut Board of Education*, 1992).

IEP Teams

According to the IDEA, IEPs must be developed by teams that include a student's parents, a regular education teacher (if the child is or will be participating in regular education), a special education teacher or provider, a school board representative, and an individual who can interpret evaluation results (20 U.S.C. § 1414(d)(1)(B)). The school board representative must be someone who is qualified to either provide or supervise special education, knows the general education curriculum, and knows the availability of school board resources. Failure to include a district representative can be fatal to a school board, as it can be taken as an indication that the parents were denied full opportunity to discuss all options (*Pitchford ex rel M. v. Salem-Keizer School District No. 24J*, 2001). At the same time, the requirement that the IEP team include persons knowledgeable about placement options does not mandate the presence of an expert in the parents' preferred methodology (*Dong v. Board of Education of the Rochester Community Schools*, 1999).

In light of the IDEA's emphasis on inclusion, the need for the participation of a regular education teacher on IEP teams cannot be overemphasized. Courts have invalidated IEPs when regular education teachers were not included on teams and students either were or would be participating in general education curricula (*Arlington Central School District v. D.K. and K.K.*, 2002; *Deal ex rel. Deal v. Hamilton County Department of Education*, 2004; *M.L. v. Federal Way School District*, 2005). When participation in general education is not an issue, it is unnecessary for regular education teachers to be part of IEP teams (*Cone ex rel. Cone v. Randolph County Schools*, 2004). Other persons may be present at the request of either the parents or school boards, and students may attend if appropriate. Individual members of IEP teams may be excused from attending meetings with the consent of the parents, but they must file written reports (20 U.S.C. § 1414(d)(1)(C)).

IEP Meetings

IEP meetings are designed to provide parents with the best opportunity to participate in the development of appropriate educational programs for their children. The purpose of IEP meetings is to share evaluation results, develop IEPs, and make placement decisions. While parents may have attended meetings where they provided school officials with information about and discussed the educational status of their children, most decisions regarding placements are made at IEP conferences. The IDEA's regulations specify that school personnel must take steps to ensure that at least one of a student's parents is present at IEP meetings (34 C.F.R. § 300.322). IEP meetings must occur within thirty calendar days of a determination that children need special education and related services (34 C.F.R. § 300.323(c)(1)). Failure to meet this time line may result in IEPs being invalidated (*Knable v. Bexley City School District*, 2001). For students who attend private schools, a representative of the private schools must be present at IEP meetings (34 C.F.R. § 300.325).

Parental input into the IEP process cannot be minimized. One of the IDEA's unique features is that it provides for parental participation. Parents cannot simply be given token opportunities for participation. As such, parental input into the IEP process must be genuine. In one instance, the Ninth Circuit affirmed that an IEP that was developed without input from a student's parents and his teacher in a religiously affiliated school was invalid (*W.G. and B.G. v. Board of Trustees of Target Range School District No. 23*, 1992). The court emphasized that procedural violations that infringe on parents' opportunity to participate in the formulation of their child's IEP resulted in a denial of a free appropriate public education (FAPE).

Similarly, the federal trial court in the District of Columbia wrote that the failure of public school officials to attend an IEP meeting that took place at a private school in which the student was enrolled rendered the proposed placement invalid (*Smith v. Henson*, 1992). Additionally, informal contacts between parents and school officials do not fully meet the IDEA's parental participation requirements. To this end, a state court in Pennsylvania proclaimed that impromptu meetings between a student's mother and school officials did not satisfy the IDEA's requirement of affording her the opportunity to participate in the development of an IEP (*Big Beaver Falls Area School District v. Jackson*, 1992).

Parental participation is meaningless if parents do not understand what is going on at IEP (or other) meetings. Accordingly, school officials must take necessary steps to ensure that parents do understand the proceedings. This may require officials to provide interpreters if the parents' primary mode of communication is not standard English (*Rothschild v. Grottenthaler*, 1990). Officials must take other steps to ensure that parents fully understand the proceedings. In two separate cases, the federal district court in Connecticut ruled that parents have the right to tape-record IEP meetings. In the first dispute, the student's mother had limited English proficiency and requested permission to tape-record the proceedings so that she could better understand and follow what was said at the meeting (*E.H. and H.H. v. Tirozzi*, 1990). In the second case, the mother could not take notes at the meeting due to a disabling hand injury (*V.W. and R.W. v. Favolise*, 1990). In each case, since the court interpreted the IDEA's intent of parental participation as meaning more than mere presence at the IEP conference, it decided that tape recordings would have allowed the parents to become active and meaningful participants in planning for the education of their children.

As the above cases illustrate, procedural errors can be fatal to school boards in that they may cause courts to rule in favor of parents in disputes involving IEPs. However, as a ruling of the Sixth Circuit demonstrated, parents may give up some of their rights by failing to participate in the process (*Cordrey v. Euckert*, 1990). The parents unsuccessfully challenged the adequacy of an IEP because all of the required participants were not present at the planned session, but they rejected the school board's offer to convene a properly constituted IEP meeting. The court found that the parents relinquished their right to a procedurally correct IEP conference when they rejected the board's offer to schedule another meeting.

Draft IEPs and Interim IEPs

School personnel may present draft IEPs at meetings for purposes of discussion. Such a practice is not improper as long as the drafts are nothing more than drafts. In fact, nothing in the IDEA or its regulations prohibits school personnel from coming to IEP meetings with tentative recommendations for IEPs (*Blackmon v. Springfield R-XII School District*, 1999). Along the same lines, school personnel are not prohibited from meeting informally, reviewing evaluations, or discussing placement options prior to convening formal IEP meetings (*Tracy v.*

Beaufort County Board of Education, 2004). In one case, the federal trial court in Rhode Island was of the opinion that presenting parents with a completed IEP at the meeting did not mean that the parents were denied a meaningful opportunity to participate in the development of the IEPs (*Scituate School Committee v. Robert B.,* 1985, 1986). Along the same lines, the First Circuit declared that it is acceptable for one person to draft an IEP as long as the parents and other members of the team have an opportunity to provide input into its contents (*Hampton School District v. Dobrowolski,* 1992). In a like situation, the Third Circuit affirmed that a draft IEP did not violate the IDEA's parental participation requirement where there was evidence that the parents made suggestions for changes, some of which were incorporated into the final IEP (*Fuhrmann v. East Hanover Board of Education,* 1993).

The courts certainly frown on attempts by school officials to develop IEPs beforehand and then force them on parents without any meaningful discussion of the educational needs of their children. In this regard, a federal trial court in Virginia ascertained that while school officials must come to IEP conferences with open minds, this does not mean they must come with blank minds (*Doyle v. Arlington County School Board,* 1992). The court emphasized that school board officials may not finalize placement decisions before IEP meetings but should have given prior thought to such issues. Of course, school board representatives must remain receptive to all parental concerns.

School board officials sometimes develop interim IEPs for students to cover short periods of time while preparing permanent IEPs. Some courts have frowned on this practice, while others have allowed it to be employed. Much depends on why interim IEPs are needed. For example, two courts agreed that school boards must have permanent IEPs in place by the beginning of school years, even if they had to conduct meetings over the summer (*Gerstmyer v. Howard County Public Schools,* 1994; *Myles S. v. Montgomery County Board of Education,* 1993).

Interim IEPs may be acceptable for short periods of time once special education students move into school districts. In these instances, school personnel can develop interim IEPs to cover short periods of time while they assess the needs of students and write long-range IEPs. The 2004 IDEA amendments specifically provide for students who move from one district to another but make a distinction between those who transfer within the state and those who transfer from another state. When students transfer within states, receiving boards must provide services that are comparable to those in the student's previous IEP until such time as they either adopt the previous IEPs or develop new ones (20 U.S.C. § 1414(d)(2)(C)(i)(I)). On the other hand, when students transfer to districts in new states, receiving school boards must provide services comparable to those in their previous IEPs until such time as officials conduct evaluations, if necessary, and develop new IEPs (20 U.S.C. § 1414(d)(2)(C)(i)(II)). Although the difference is slight, this provision recognizes the fact that students who were eligible for services in one state may not necessarily qualify for them in another due to differing state standards.

IEP Revisions

From time to time school officials may need to modify IEPs. These alterations may be necessary due to changing circumstances in either educational environments or the needs of students. Minor adjustments that do not result in changes in student placements are of little consequence. Changes that alter IEPs substantially or result in their not being implemented as written trigger the IDEA's procedural protections. Parents must be notified of changes in the educational placements of their children and must be given the opportunity to object (20 U.S.C. § 1415(b)(3); 34 C.F.R. § 300.504).

IEPs for students with disabilities must be reviewed and revised, if necessary, at least annually (20 U.S.C. § 1414(d)(4)), but may occur more frequently if needed. Procedures for reviewing and amending IEPs are generally similar to those for developing initial IEPs. All of the IDEA's procedural and notification rights apply to meetings to review and possibly revise IEPs. Naturally, parents must be given input into the process just as they are with initial IEPs.

IEPs should be reviewed if parents express any dissatisfaction with the educational programs of their children. In one case, the federal trial court in the District of Columbia ruled that a parent's request for a due process hearing put the school board on notice that she was dissatisfied with her daughter's placement status and that school personnel were obligated to review and possibly revise her IEP (*Edwards-White v. District of Columbia*, 1992). Conversely, where parents unilaterally withdrew their son from a public school and placed him in a private school, the First Circuit affirmed that the board was not obligated to review and revise the child's IEP (*Amann v. Stow School System*, 1992).

PARENTAL RIGHTS

When Congress passed the IDEA, it intended for parents to become partners in the development of appropriate educational programs for their children. In order to accomplish this goal, Congress provided parents with substantial procedural due process rights. The provision of these rights was unprecedented in federal education legislation. As noted, the IDEA affords parents the right to examine all records relative to the special education process, to obtain independent evaluations if they disagree with the findings of their school boards, and to receive written notification of plans by their board to initiate or change, or refuse to initiate or change, the educational placements of their children (20 U.S.C. § 1415). In addition, parents have the right to participate in all meetings in which the evaluations or educational placements of their children are discussed (34 C.F.R. § 300.322). The IDEA also grants parents avenues through which they can dispute recommendations or decisions that school officials make concerning the provision of a FAPE to their children (20 U.S.C. § 1415).

The 2004 IDEA amendments expanded the definition of parent. According to the IDEA, the term *parent* now means a natural, adoptive, or foster parent of a child (unless a foster parent is prohibited by state law from serving as a parent);

a guardian (but not the state if the child is a ward of the state); an individual acting in the place of a natural or adoptive parent (including a grandparent, stepparent, or other relative) with whom the child lives, or an individual who is legally responsible for the child's welfare; or an individual assigned to be a surrogate parent (20 U.S.C. § 1402(23)).

The courts recognize the importance Congress placed on parental participation. While the judiciary has not insisted on absolute compliance with the letter of the law regarding parental rights, the courts have been diligent in upholding the rights of parents in the special education process. The courts allow school board proposals to stand if procedural violations neither prejudice the process in any way nor result in detriments to the students. Of course, courts have not tolerated egregious violations of parental rights (*DiBuo v. Board of Education of Worcester County*, 2002; *Magyar v. Tucson Unified School District*, 1997).

Notification

Parents cannot exercise rights of which they are unaware. The IDEA requires school boards to inform parents fully of their rights in writing (20 U.S.C. §§ 1415(b)(3), 1415(d)(1)(A); 34 C.F.R. § 300.503)). If boards fail to inform parents of their rights, the courts agree, this limits their ability to participate in the education of their children. The purpose of notifying parents of their rights is to provide them with sufficient information to protect their rights relative to their children, to allow them to make informed decisions, and to afford them the chance to participate fully in due process hearings, if necessary (*Kroot v. District of Columbia*, 1992).

School officials must provide parents with notification of any actions or proposed actions that they refuse to initiate along with explanations of why one was proposed or refused (*Magyar v. Tucson Unified School District*, 1997; *Tennessee Department of Mental Health and Mental Retardation v. Paul B.*, 1996). Further, officials must provide parents with a description of options that were considered and rejected, as well as reasons for their rejection. At the same time, educators must give parents information relative to evaluation procedures that they used as part of their decision-making process. All notices must be written in a language that can be understood by the general public and, if necessary, must be translated into the parents' native language or primary mode of communication. Oral notification may be appropriate in situations where written notification is not feasible (34 C.F.R. § 300.503(c)(2)(i)).

Parents are entitled to notice at specific points, such as when their children are first referred for evaluations, when they request evaluations or reevaluations, when they file IDEA-related complaints, and/or when they make such requests (20 U.S.C. § 1415(d)(1)(A)). In a new provision, the 2004 IDEA permits school boards to place notice of the procedural safeguards on their Internet Web sites (20 U.S.C. § 1415(d)(B)).

In an early case, a federal trial court in Illinois posited that a school board's failure to notify a student's parents of their right to review psychological evaluations and obtain an independent evaluation, as well as its failure to notify them of meetings in which their son's educational placement was discussed, violated the IDEA (*Max M. v. Thompson*, 1983). The court noted that these procedural violations had the effect of denying the parents the opportunity to participate in the development of their son's IEP. In another case, the Fourth Circuit maintained that a school board's failure to notify parents of their rights resulted in a failure to provide a FAPE under the Supreme Court's decision in *Board of Education of the Hendrick Hudson Central School District v. Rowley* (1982). Earlier, a trial court found that board officials consistently failed to comply with federal and state statutes concerning parental notification. The court reasoned that this failure relegated parental participation to little more than acquiescence.

The purpose of the IDEA's notice requirements is to give the parents information that allows them to participate actively in the educational planning process. In a case from the District of Columbia, parents unsuccessfully challenged the notice provided by their school board where the trial court was convinced that materials they received were statutorily sufficient (*Smith v. Squillacote*, 1992). The court was of the view that the notices informed parents about where the board proposed to place their son and why they selected that option. The court asserted that the information that the board supplied was adequate to provide the parents with the opportunity to have a meaningful role in the decision-making process and to draw informed conclusions about whether the proposed placement would have offered an appropriate education for their son.

Naturally, misleading notice is problematic for school boards. For example, the trial court for the District of Columbia ordained that a misleading notice violated the procedural rights of parents under the IDEA (*Smith v. Henson*, 1992). In this instance, school officials notified the parents that they had fifteen days in which to request a due process hearing, but the IDEA did not contain such a limitation at that time.

As noted earlier, the IDEA requires school board officials to notify parents of meetings in which the IEPs of their children are to be developed or revised. However, this does not mean that school officials must notify parents every time they discuss a student's educational progress. For example, the Fifth Circuit contended that school officials are not required to notify parents every time a teacher discusses a student's progress with an administrator (*Buser v. Corpus Christi Independent School*, 1995). The Sixth Circuit subsequently decreed that school personnel are allowed to confer prior to IEP team meetings to coordinate assessment results and develop ideas about a proper course of action (*N.L. ex rel. Ms. C. v. Knox County Schools*, 2003).

Noncustodial Parents

In today's world many students do not live with both parents. The parental rights granted by the IDEA also apply to parents who do not have custody of their children due to divorce, unless a divorce decree restricts the rights of noncustodial parents. In such a case, the federal trial court in Massachusetts declared that a divorced parent's right to be involved in his son's education was basic unless a restraining order indicates otherwise (*Doe v. Anrig*, 1987). On the other hand, a federal trial court in Pennsylvania dismissed a suit filed by a noncustodial father because the divorce decree gave the mother sole custody of the child, thereby extinguishing his legal rights (*Carpenter v. Pennell School District Elementary Unit*, 2002). In a similar situation, a federal trial court in Texas dismissed an action filed by a noncustodial father whose divorce decree conferred educational decision-making authority on the child's mother (*Schares v. Katy Independent School District*, 2003). Generally speaking, the allocation of parental rights is left to state domestic relations law (*Taylor v. Vermont Department of Education*, 2002).

Rights of Adult Students

Many students continue to receive special education services after they reach their eighteenth birthday. Although these students assume rights of their own on reaching the age of majority, their parents do not lose their own rights under the IDEA just because their children reached this milestone. The Second Circuit decided that the procedural safeguards of the IDEA apply to students between the ages of eighteen and twenty-one even if they have not been adjudicated incompetent (*Mrs. C. v. Wheaton*, 1990). In this case, a school board terminated special education services for a twenty-year-old student, with his consent, but without notifying his mother about the contemplated change. The court held that the termination of services without parental notification violated the IDEA.

In another case, a sixteen-year-old special education student was tried as an adult and sentenced to two years of incarceration. Once incarcerated, the student's parents were neither notified nor involved in meetings concerning his IEP. The Florida Department of Corrections claimed that because the student was incarcerated as an adult, he had the transferred right of an adult. A federal trial court disagreed, positing that the student's rights of majority did not transfer until he reached the age of majority under state law (*Paul Y. by Kathy Y. v. Singletary*, 1997).

CHANGE IN PLACEMENT

Once students with disabilities are placed in special education programs, their placements may not be changed unless their parents are notified in writing of the planned actions and have been given the opportunity to contest the proposed change (20 U.S.C. § 1415(b)(3)). The IDEA further provides that while administrative hearings or judicial proceedings are pending, students are to remain in their "then current placements" unless their parents and school boards agree otherwise (20 U.S.C. § 1415(j)). This section of the law has become known as the status quo or stay put provision and has been the subject of much litigation. The purpose of the status quo provision is to provide educational stability and consistency (*Gabel ex rel. L.G. v. Board of Education of the Hyde Park Central School District*, 2005). One major exception to the status quo requirement exists in situations involving students who present a danger to themselves or others. As is discussed in greater detail in Chapter 6, these situations require a hearing officer or judicial order to alter the status quo.

Status Quo

Generally, the programs that students attended at the time that actions arose are considered to be their then current placements or, as one court defined the term, the operative placements actually functioning at the time disputes first arose (*Thomas v. Cincinnati Board of Education*, 1990). Here the Sixth Circuit made it clear that a proposed placement that was never implemented did not qualify as the status quo. Accordingly, the status quo placement is usually whatever placement was last agreed on by parents and school boards. Even if parents withdraw their consent for placements, they remain the then current placements (*Clyde K. v. Puyallup School District*, 1994). It is important to note that the status quo provision is inapplicable after students reach the ceiling age for eligibility under the IDEA (*Board of Education of Oak Park & River Forest High School District 200 v. Illinois State Board of Education*, 1996) or graduate (*Sammons v. Polk County School Board*, 2006).

Sometimes school officials may make placements that are meant to be temporary. In such situations, school personnel are obliged to make their intentions clear, or courts consider these placements to be the then current placements. A variety of cases involving the District of Columbia public schools illustrate this point. In an early case, officials at the private facility that a child attended called for his being transferred to a residential school. The school board agreed to the new placement but a year later notified the student's parents that since officials saw no need for continued residential placement, they would no longer assume financial responsibility for the placement. The trial court declared that the residential school was the student's then current placement because board officials assumed responsibility for it and gave no indication at the time that they intended to do so for one year only (*Jacobsen v. District of Columbia Board of Education*, 1983). In a separate action, the same court proclaimed that any limitation on a placement must be spelled out clearly and described in a **settlement agreement** (*Saleh v. District of Columbia*, 1987). In this case, the student was placed by mutual consent of the school board and parents in a private school pending resolution of a placement dispute. The board argued that the private school was an interim placement only, but the court was of the view that it was the then current placement because its interim status had not been articulated clearly. In contrast, the District of Columbia Circuit affirmed that a private school placement ceased to be the then current placement at the end of the school year where a hearing officer's order indicated clearly that it was to be for one year only (*Leonard v. McKenzie*, 1989). In like manner, the First Circuit noted that a settlement agreement between the parties calling for a temporary placement in a private school did not make it the child's status quo placement (*Verhoeven v. Brunswick School Committee*, 1999).

A unilateral placement made by parents can be the then current placement if a school board failed to propose an appropriate program in a timely fashion. The federal trial court for the District of Columbia observed that since the board had not proposed a program by the deadline established by the hearing officer, parents were justified in placing their son in a private school, which essentially became his then current educational placement (*Cochran v. District of Columbia*, 1987).

If parents unilaterally remove their child from programs, the programs do not cease to be the then current placements. The Eighth Circuit insisted that the placement of the student when his parents removed him from public school was the status quo (*Digre v. Roseville Schools Independent School District No. 623*, 1988). The parents enrolled their son in a neighboring school system, but one month later reenrolled him in his former system. The mother sought to reenroll the child as a regular education, rather than special education, student, but the court was convinced that a one-month term as a regular education student in another school system did not negate his special education history. Similarly, a federal trial court in Illinois held that the status quo provision is inapplicable to students who are unilaterally placed in private schools by their parents (*Joshua B. v. New Trier Township High School District 203*, 1991).

An exception to the status quo provision does exist when school officials believe that keeping students in their then current placements presents a danger to them or others or a substantial disruption to the educational process (*Honig v. Doe*, 1988; 20 U.S.C. § 1415(k)(3)(B)(ii)). In such cases, school officials may seek change in placement orders from courts or hearing officers. Under these circumstances, school officials bear the burden of demonstrating that a change is necessary. This is discussed in greater detail in Chapter 6.

Placement Pending Appeals

In a dispute over where students should go when their IEPs are being challenged, the First Circuit remarked that Congress did not intend to freeze arguably inappropriate placements for the length of time it takes for review proceedings to culminate (*Doe v. Brookline School Committee*, 1983). Consequently, the question then arises as to when parents or school boards are entitled to change placements based on orders from hearing officers or courts. Some courts maintain that changes in placements can occur once administrative hearing decisions are rendered, even if they are appealed. For example, the Ninth Circuit announced that once a state educational agency decided that a parentally chosen placement was correct, it became the then current placement under the IDEA, requiring a local school board to treat it as such (*Clovis Unified School District v. California Office of Administrative Hearings*, 1990). Similarly, the federal trial court in Massachusetts explained that where a state-level agency, such as the Bureau of Special Education Appeals, and a student's parent agreed on a placement, local officials did not have to approve in order to make a change in placement (*Grace B. v. Lexington School Committee*, 1991).

The IDEA calls for agreements by either states or local education agencies and parents to effectuate changes in placements during the pendency of review proceedings. On the one hand, the Supreme Court, in **dicta**, decreed that a state-level hearing decision in favor of a parentally chosen placement seems to constitute agreement by the state to a change in placement (*Burlington School Committee v. Department of Education of the Commonwealth of Massachusetts (Burlington)*, 1985). The Third Circuit, citing *Burlington*, declared that a placement ordered by a due process appeals panel became a student's pendant placement even though local officials sought judicial review (*Susquenita School District v. Raelee S.*, 1996). In like fashion, a federal trial court in Alabama was convinced that an administrative adjudication effectively constituted an agreement between the state and the student's parents that established a new status quo placement (*Escambia County Board of Education v. Benton*, 2005).

Conversely, the District of Columbia Circuit wrote that the IDEA's status quo provision requires a student's placement to remain the same until all administrative hearings and trial court actions are completed (*Anderson v. District of Columbia*, 1989). The court emphasized that the IDEA did not entitle students to remain in private schools at public expense pending reviews by appellate panels. Here the hearing officer and trial court agreed that the school board's proposed IEPs were appropriate.

Whether a student should remain in a placement may well depend on a student's individual circumstances. In such a case, the District of Columbia trial court pointed out that the school board was required to fund a private school placement during the pendency of an appeal of a hearing officer's order (*Holmes v. District of Columbia*, 1988). The court added that since it would have been inappropriate, insensitive, and indefensible for it to have ordered a change in placement one semester before the student, or any other child, completed his formal education, the board was required to fund the private school until he graduated, even though a hearing officer found that the board's proposed change in placement was appropriate. Similarly, a federal trial court in New York indicated that the status quo provision prohibited a school board from graduating a student during the pendency of **administrative appeals** (*Cronin v. Board of Education of East Ramapo Central School District*, 1988).

According to the IDEA's status quo provision, during the pendency of appeals regarding students who are applying for initial admissions to public schools, children are to be placed in public school programs until all appeals are completed (20 U.S.C. § 1415(j)). The law does not specify whether these placements should be in general education classrooms or special education programs. In New York, a federal trial court held that Congress' goal could be satisfied by the provision of a public school placement, regardless of whether it was in special education or general education (*Logsdon v. Board of Education of the Pavilion Central School District*, 1991). The parents of the student in this case preferred placement in a regular kindergarten class while school officials recommended a special class placement. The court ascertained that the school board's recommendation would have provided the student with a FAPE.

Students whose school boards have yet to place them are not protected by the status quo provision. For example, an Illinois federal trial court offered that the IDEA's status quo provision was inapplicable to a student whose parents unilaterally placed him before public school officials had the opportunity to educate the child (*Joshua B. v. New Trier Township High School District 203*, 1991). The court noted that the status quo provision was designed to prevent interruptions in students' programs but was not intended to protect children whose school boards had yet to offer them special education placements.

Change in Program Location

The courts generally agree that the term *change in placement* as employed in the IDEA refers to modifications that affect the form of the educational instruction provided, not the location where it takes place. For various reasons, such as school closings, boards must occasionally move special education programs from one building to another. Courts have reasoned that transfers of entire classes or programs do not constitute changes in placement triggering the IDEA's due process procedures (*Concerned Parents and Citizens for the Continuing Education at Malcolm X. v. New York City Board of Education*, 1980; *Middlebrook v. School District of the County of Knox*, 1991).

When boards move programs from one location to another, they must remain substantially the same. The elimination of major components of programs is sufficient cause to trigger the IDEA's due process mechanism. In such a case, a federal trial court in New York was of the opinion that the elimination of the summer component of what had been a year-round residential program was of such critical magnitude that it constituted a change in placement (*Gebhardt v. Ambach*, 1982). Moreover, a federal trial court in Pennsylvania nullified the proposed transfer of two students from one program to another that would have involved a change in instructional methodology (*Visco v. School District of Pittsburgh*, 1988). The court decided that once students are making progress in programs, any changes must be considered with caution.

When transfers involve moving a single student, they may not be considered changes in placements if the new programs are substantially identical to the former ones. In an illustrative case, the District of Columbia Circuit declared that at a minimum a student must show that a fundamental change in or an elimination of a basic element of an educational program took place for a change in placement to have occurred (*Lunceford v. District of Columbia Board of Education*, 1984). Likewise, the Fifth Circuit determined that a transfer from one school building to another did not constitute a change in placement where the student's IEP was fully implemented following the move (*Weil v. Board of Elementary and Secondary Education*, 1991). Other courts agreed that students are not subject to change in placement as long as their IEPs can be implemented in the new locations (*AW ex rel. Wilson v. Fairfax County School Board*, 2004; *Hill v. School Board for Pinellas County*, 1997; *J.S. ex rel. D.S. v. Lenape Regional High School District Board of Education*, 2000).

Graduation

As noted, major changes to student IEPs are considered changes in placement. Courts have acknowledged that graduation is a change in placement because it terminates all student rights to educational services. In one of the earlier cases, the Supreme Judicial Court of Massachusetts ruled that failing to provide parents with formal written notice of a decision to graduate a student violated both the IDEA and commonwealth law (*Stock v. Massachusetts Hospital School*, 1984). Applying a similar rationale, a federal trial court in New York posited that graduation was analogous to an expulsion since it resulted in the student's total exclusion from an educational placement (*Cronin v. Board of Education of East Ramapo Central School District*, 1988). In addition, the Eighth Circuit declared that graduating an eighteen-year-old student who had not completed a secondary education program violated the IDEA (*Birmingham by Birmingham v. Omaha School District*, 2000). Even so, permitting a student to graduate cannot be based solely on the pupil's accumulation of sufficient credits. In one case, a federal trial court in Illinois maintained that a student who had enough credits but had not completed his IEP goals and objectives was inappropriately graduated (*Kevin T. v. Elmhurst Community School District No. 205*, 2002). Further, the Tenth Circuit held that although school officials must notify parents of their intent to permit students to graduate and give them the opportunity to object, they are not required to evaluate the pupils or conduct IEP meetings prior to graduation (*T.S. v. Independent School District No. 54*, 2001).

Modifications to an IEP

The general rule is that alterations to IEPs constitute changes in placement. Even so, school officials can make minor adjustments to IEPs. In an early case, the Third Circuit affirmed that the important element in evaluating whether a change in placement occurred is whether the modification is likely to affect a student's learning in some significant way (*DeLeon v. Susquehanna Community School District*, 1984). In this case the court thought that a minor modification in the student's transportation arrangements was not a change in placement, but warned that under some circumstances transportation could have an effect on a child's learning. The federal trial court in Massachusetts echoed the Third Circuit's criteria that a student's learning experience must be affected in some significant way in acknowledging that an adjustment to an IEP that was more superficial than substantive was not a change in placement (*Brookline School Committee v. Golden*, 1986). For similar reasons, a federal trial court in Maryland was satisfied that minor modifications to a student's schedule did not change his placement (*Cavanagh v. Grasmick*, 1999).

The Fifth Circuit agreed with school officials that a child's being transferred from his neighborhood school to one that was several miles from his home, even though the shift required him to ride a school bus for students with disabilities and share a transliterator, was not a change of placement (*Veazey v. Ascension Parish School Board*, 2005). The court affirmed that these changes did not fundamentally alter either the student's IEP or the fact that the IEP was reasonably calculated to enable him to receive educational benefits.

Services Not in IEPs

School boards sometimes provide students with disabilities with services that are not specified in their IEPs. If boards provide services that are not called for in IEPs, then they can change these without providing the IDEA's due process safeguards. In such case, the Ninth Circuit ruled that insofar as a tutoring program that a board provided a child was not included in his IEP as a special education service, replacing his then current tutor was not a change in placement (*Gregory K. v. Longview School District*, 1987). Similarly, the Sixth Circuit affirmed that a school board did not violate the IDEA's stay put provision when it refused to keep a student in an extended school year program that had never been written into his IEP (*Cordrey v. Euckert*, 1990).

The IDEA's change in placement requirements apply only to placements that are made pursuant to its provisions and to services only called for in IEPs. Even so, if a state agency makes a residential placement for social purposes, officials may not invoke the IDEA's change in placement requirements if they later attempt to transfer a student to another facility or otherwise remove the child from a facility (*Corbett v. Regional Center for the East Bay*, 1988).

When Programs Are No Longer Appropriate or Available

A special problem regarding the IDEA's status quo provision exists when it is no longer appropriate for students to remain in their programs. A change of this nature can occur for a variety of reasons, such as if programs lose their state approval, are found to be lacking in quality, or may no longer be able to serve given students. Generally, in such cases, the courts approve placements in similar facilities. Once again, the key element is that the new facilities must be able to implement students' IEPs fully in order to pass muster under the status quo provision.

A pair of early cases that arose in New York reached different results. In the first, a federal trial court recognized that the transfer of students from a private school that was found to be lacking to alternate facilities was not a change in placement (*Dima v. Macchiarola*, 1981). The dispute arose when the local school board terminated its contract with the private school after an audit disclosed several problems, including mismanagement of funds and serious educational deficiencies. Conversely, the Second Circuit affirmed that a placement in a facility in New York that lost its state approval could not be changed until officials identified an appropriate alternative (*Vander Malle v. Ambach*, 1982).

The Sixth Circuit affirmed that the transfer of students from a treatment facility that closed, due to budgetary constraints, to dissimilar alternate facilities was a change in placement (*Tilton v. Jefferson County Board of Education*, 1983). While the court acknowledged that since the closing occurred for financial reasons, the IDEA's procedural safeguards did not apply, it did permit the students to contest their new placements through the IDEA's administrative hearing process. In another case where a student attended a private school that closed, the trial court for the District of Columbia upheld a hearing officer's order that the school board fund a placement at another private school (*Block v. District of Columbia*, 1990).

In two separate cases the District of Columbia Circuit ruled that when officials at private schools realized that they could no longer serve students, the public school board was obligated to locate and fund similar programs (*McKenzie v. Smith*, 1985; *Knight v. District of Columbia*, 1989). In the more recent of the two cases, where the private school placement was no longer available, the court allowed the board to make an interim placement in a public school program that was not inherently dissimilar until officials could make a final placement.

Difficulties can emerge when students transition from programs under Part C to one under Part B of the IDEA. Part C (20 U.S.C. §§ 1431–1444) encourages states to provide early intervention services for children under the age of three who are at risk of having a developmental delay (20 U.S.C. § 1431(b)(4)), while Part B (20 U.S.C. §§ 1411–1419) covers students from ages three to twenty-one. Under Part C, officials must develop individualized family service plans (IFSPs) for children. Difficulties emerge because agencies other than school systems generally provide the services outlined in IFSPs. In such a case, the Ninth Circuit affirmed a hearing officer's order requiring a school board to maintain services in an IFSP but did not require it to use the same vendors (*Johnson v. Special Education Hearing Office, State of California*, 2002). The Third Circuit, noting that an IFSP could serve as a child's IEP in preschool, required a school board to continue the services provided by the IFSP until a dispute over an evaluation was settled (*Pardini v. Allegheny Intermediate Unit*, 2005). On the other hand, a federal trial court in Florida contended that when a student applied for initial admission to a public school, the pendency placement was the public school program and that there was no exception for a child who received services under Part C (*D.P. and L.P. ex rel E.P. v. School Board of Broward County*, 2005).

Challenges can also arise when students move from one school system to another, insofar as the programs in the new systems may not mirror those in the former ones. If students move within a state, receiving school systems must provide services that are comparable to those in the children's previous IEPs until such time as school personnel either adopt the previous IEPs or develop new ones (20 U.S.C. § 1414(d)(2)(C)(i)(I)). The situation can be more complicated when students move from one state to another due to the fact that each state may have different requirements. When students transfer to districts in new states, the receiving boards must provide services comparable to those in the students' previous IEPs until such time as officials conduct evaluations, if necessary, and develop new IEPs (20 U.S.C. § 1414(d)(2)(C)(i)(II)). In one case where a student transferred to a new school system, the Ninth Circuit affirmed that the status quo no longer existed. The court reasoned that the school board could satisfy the IDEA by either implementing the student's previous IEP or devising a plan that approximated the earlier IEP as closely as possible (*Ms. S. ex rel. G. v. Vashon Island School District*, 2003).

❖

❖ **CASE NO. 5**—DRAFT IEP DOES NOT VIOLATE THE IDEA

BLACKMON

v.

SPRINGFIELD R-XII SCHOOL DISTRICT

United States Court of Appeals, Eighth Circuit, 1999

198 F.3d 648

TUNHEIM, J.

Grace Blackmon ("Grace") brought claims against the School District of Springfield, R-12 (the "School District") under the Individuals with Disabilities Education Act, ... (the "IDEA"), alleging that the individual education program ("IEP") offered to her by the School District was not reasonably calculated to provide her with a free, appropriate, public education. Grace's parents requested an impartial due process hearing for a determination of their claims pursuant to [the IDEA]. The administrative hearing panel determined that the IEP offered to Grace was appropriate, and further determined that the alternative IEP advocated by Grace's parents was inappropriate. The hearing panel also found that the School District committed no procedural violations in developing an IEP for Grace. Grace's parents appealed the hearing panel's decision to the United States District Court for the Western District of Missouri. The district court reversed the hearing panel's determinations on December 4, 1998 and ordered the School District to reimburse Grace's parents for their expenses in educating her. By Order dated January 6, 1999, the district court further awarded attorney's fees to Grace and her parents. The School District appeals from both of the district court's orders. We reverse.

I.

... Physicians have diagnosed Grace as suffering from a severe, diffuse, bilateral brain injury with hypotonic and autistic behaviors. The School District does not dispute that Grace is developmentally disabled and thus entitled to the protections and benefits of the IDEA.

When Grace was approximately fifteen months old, her parents enrolled her in a program designed to evaluate and treat her disabilities called the "First Steps" program. The "First Steps" program is operated by the Springfield Regional Center, a division of the Department of Mental Health, and is not in any way affiliated with the School District. Under this program Grace received speech and occupational therapy for four to five months, and received physical therapy for approximately ten months. Grace's parent's describe the program's approach as "traditional." Although Grace showed no significant improvement in fine motor skills based on the four to five months of occupational therapy she received, she made improvements in other areas, including significant progress in her gross motor skills.

Grace's parents were dissatisfied with her progress in the First Steps program and discontinued her enrollment on September 6, 1995. They thereafter enrolled her in an alternative program that they had been researching that is promoted by an organization called the Institutes for the Achievement of Human Potential (the "Institutes"). The Institutes advocates an intensive, home-based training program requiring individualized therapy taught by a child's parents for twelve hours per day. The Institutes's program centers around the theory that stimulation of the brain, by repetitious activity and increased supplies of oxygen and carbon dioxide, will facilitate its growth. The Institutes's methodology is controversial and has been criticized in a number of medical journals.

. . . The Institutes conducted an evaluation of Grace and provided her parents with a plan for her development. The program requires Grace's parents to keep detailed records of her daily activities, and to travel to Philadelphia for an assessment once every six months. Between visits, Grace's parents provide her with individualized therapy for twelve hours per day based on techniques they have learned through the Institutes's literature and through training provided to them during visits to Philadelphia. Grace's communication and gross motor skills have improved significantly during her treatment under the Institutes's program, and her parents are satisfied with her progress.

When Grace was three years old, and thus old enough to receive benefits under the IDEA, her parents contacted the School District and requested that it pay for the cost of training her under the Institutes's program. The School District informed them that it would need to evaluate Grace before making a determination regarding her education placement. The School District thereafter scheduled an evaluation for Grace and provided her parents with a copy of the procedural safeguards for parents and children set forth under the IDEA, as required by [the IDEA]. The School District put together a team of six employees who evaluated Grace and observed her on two separate occasions. . . . At the conclusion of the evaluation process, the School District produced a twenty-five page "diagnostic summary" of Grace's health, skills and abilities. Although Grace's parents disagreed with parts of the diagnostic summary, and although they were aware of their statutory right to request an independent evaluation of Grace, . . . they did not seek an independent evaluation or request that the School District otherwise reevaluate her.

After completing Grace's diagnostic summary, the School District held a conference with her parents to review the diagnostic summary and to develop an IEP for her. Grace's parents and five School District employees attended the conference, which was held on December 10, 1996. Prior to the meeting, the School District prepared a proposed IEP for Grace with sections pertaining to Grace's "present level of performance" and "goals and objectives" tentatively completed. At the meeting, the School District went through each of these sections item-by-item with Grace's parents and asked them whether they agreed with the proposed statements. Grace's parents in general indicated their agreement.

The School District then engaged in a discussion with Grace's parents about her appropriate placement. The School District indicated that it recommend Grace be placed in a "reverse mainstream" classroom and that she additionally receive individualized speech, occupational and physical therapies. In addition to this option, the School District also discussed with Grace's parents the possibility that the School District would provide Grace with in-home individualized training, as well as the proposal that Grace's parents advocated, namely, that the School District reimburse them for Grace's in-home training through the Institutes. The School District nevertheless rejected these options because they would not provide Grace with the ability to interact with other children.

When Grace's parents learned of the School District's recommendation they became upset and left the IEP meeting before a discussion of Grace's placement could be completed. In a letter to the School District dated December 25, 1996, Grace's parents revealed that they were upset because the School District did not recommend the Institutes's program, stating:

[W]e thought the evaluators were simply going through the formalities before announcing that they thought our work with the Institutes was the ideal educational plan for Grace and we had their total support. . . . So, when the evaluators recommended the same program (we're pretty confident of this) for Grace they would have recommended before ever meeting us, we were totally outraged (and still are).

The School District provided Grace's parents with a written statement on December 11, 1996 confirming its decision to offer Grace education in a reverse mainstream classroom along with individualized speech, occupational and physical therapies. The School District further provided Grace's parents with another notice of the procedural safeguards under the IDEA. Subsequent efforts to resolve the differences between the School District and Grace's parents were unsuccessful. On December 20, 1996, the School District held an informal resolution conference with Grace's parents at its administrative offices that did not result in an agreement between the parties.

On January 3, 1997, Grace's parents exercised their rights under the IDEA to request an impartial due process hearing. . . .

During the due process hearing, Grace's parents raised as issues for the hearing panel's consideration whether the School District's proposed IEP met the requirements of the IDEA, whether their alternative IEP met the requirements of the IDEA, the amount that the School District should be required to reimburse them for Grace's education, if any, and whether the School District should pay the attorney's fees that they had expended. Grace's parents did not challenge the School District's compliance with the IDEA's procedural requirements. Indeed, their attorney explicitly volunteered:

I want to say to you gentlemen that the parents through their counsel has [sic] told the School District that they do not want this panel to decide this matter in favor of their child because of the School District's procedural violations, rather they want the decision based upon the merits of the IEPs put before them.

Later, counsel for the School District directly asked counsel for Grace's parents, if he did not intend to raise procedural issues in the case, whether he intended on behalf of Grace's parents to waive any violations that he perceived to exist. Counsel for Grace's parents responded, "I will." Based on these statements, the hearing panel determined that Grace's parents had waived any procedural violations that might exist. The hearing panel further determined that Grace's parents had presented no evidence of procedural violations. The hearing panel issued its decision against Grace's parents and in favor of the School District on all issues on September 12, 1997. . . .

III. Procedural Claims

A. Waiver

Grace's parents argued to the district court that the School District deprived them of their procedural rights under the IDEA by failing to afford them an opportunity to participate equally in the development of Grace's IEP at the IEP meeting. The district court sustained their challenge and reversed the hearing panel's determination that the School

District committed no procedural violations in handling Grace's claims. In so doing, the court rejected the School District's argument that Grace waived any existing procedural claims at the administrative due process hearing. The court acknowledged that Grace's counsel "did profess to waive 'procedural violations' in his opening statement at the due process hearing." Nevertheless, the court noted that in a post-hearing brief Grace's counsel argued that he did not intend to waive all procedural issues, but only procedural "technicalities," such as forms of notice, dates, times and places of the due process proceedings. Upon reviewing the administrative record the court also found that Grace's parents offered testimony at the due process hearing regarding the conduct of school district personnel during the IEP meeting. The court determined that this testimony was inconsistent with the hearing panel's conclusion that Grace's parents waived procedural objections to the manner in which the School District conducted the meeting. We disagree.

It is difficult to imagine how Grace's counsel could have set forth her parents' intent to waive their procedural objections more clearly.... Thus, we conclude that Grace's parents did not properly raise at the administrative level the issue of whether the School District permitted them to participate sufficiently in the development of her IEP....

B. Procedural Compliance

Even assuming that Grace's parents had properly raised their procedural objection to the administrative hearing panel, the record does not support the district court's conclusion that the School District's IEP should be set aside on the ground that it deprived Grace's parents of their procedural rights. Procedural deficiencies in the development of a child's IEP warrant rejecting the IEP only if they "compromised the pupil's right to an appropriate education, seriously hampered the parent's opportunity to participate in the formulation process, or caused a deprivation of educational benefits."... Such circumstances are not present in this case.

Grace's parents concede that the School District provided them with proper notice of their procedural rights under the IDEA, that it gave them sufficient opportunities to review Grace's records, that it provided them with notice of the IEP meeting's date and purpose, that it invited them to attend that meeting, and that they signed the IEP, either before or after the meeting, to indicate their participation in developing it.

They nevertheless assert that the School District failed to provide them with a meaningful opportunity to participate in the development of Grace's IEP. They specifically contend that the School District inappropriately drafted Grace's IEP in their absence, that they did not subjectively understand the purpose of the IEP meeting, and that the School District imposed its proposal on them at the IEP meeting as passive listeners without soliciting their input.

The record does not support reversing the hearing panel's decision on these grounds. The fact that the School District developed an unfinished draft of Grace's IEP in advance of the meeting is not cause for concern, as nothing in the IDEA or its regulations prohibits a school district from coming to an IEP meeting with tentative recommendations for its development prepared in the parents' absence.... Moreover, the record shows that School District personnel reviewed the pre-drafted "present level of performance" and "goals and objectives" sections of the IEP with Grace's parents carefully and asked whether they agreed with the statements contained therein.

Grace's parents argue that they did not understand that in giving their agreement they were participating in the development of her IEP. This misunderstanding is unfortunate, however, Grace's parents have not shown that it was caused by any wrongdoing on the part of the School District. When, as in this case, a school district provides parents with proper notice explaining the purpose of the IEP meeting, the meeting is conducted in a language that the parents can understand, . . . the parents are of normal intelligence, and they do not ask questions or otherwise express their confusion about the proceedings, the school district's failure to apprehend and rectify that confusion does not constitute a violation of the IDEA's procedural requirements.

More importantly, the main point of contention between Grace's parents and the School District arises not from the development of the "present level of performance" and "goals and objectives" portions of her IEP, but from the School District's placement recommendation. Grace's parents admit that they did not attend the IEP meeting with the expectation that the parties would consider the available options and develop a plan for Grace together, but rather, with the expectation that the School District without discussion would agree to reimburse them for their costs in educating Grace at home through the Institutes's program. Their disillusionment upon learning that the School District recommended a different course of action angered them and they abruptly terminated the meeting before the parties could reach a resolution to their conflicting proposals. In so doing, Grace's parents truncated their own procedural right to contribute to the development of her IEP. The School District cannot be faulted for failing to engage in an open discussion with Grace's parents about alternative options for her placement, when the parents themselves refused to participate in a discussion with the School District at the first hint of disagreement with the plan they advocated.

A school district's obligation under the IDEA to permit parental participation in the development of a child's educational plan should not be trivialized. . . . Nevertheless, the IDEA does not require school districts simply to accede to parents' demands without considering any suitable alternatives. In this case, the record shows that the School District considered both the possibility of providing Grace with in-home instruction and the possibility of reimbursing her parents for the cost of educating her at home through the Institutes, but rejected these options on the ground that they would not provide her with sufficient interaction with other children. The School District's adherence to this decision does not constitute a procedural violation of the IDEA simply because it did not grant Grace's parents' request. For these reasons we agree with the hearing panel's determination that the School District did not deprive Grace's parents of their procedural rights. . . .

Notes

1. While school personnel may come to IEP meetings with draft IEPs, they must be exactly that, drafts. The courts frown on any attempts by school personnel to present finalized IEPs to parents, even if they are called drafts. What actions did school personnel take in this case that convinced the court that their IEP truly was a draft?

2. The parents here left the IEP meeting when it was apparent to them that school personnel were proposing a placement that was not what they wanted. In doing so, did the parents waive any right to further input into the process?

3. Did school personnel here adhere to all other procedural requirements in the development of the IEP?

CASE NO. 6—GRADUATION IS A CHANGE IN PLACEMENT

STOCK

v.

MASSACHUSETTS HOSPITAL SCHOOL

Supreme Judicial Court of Massachusetts, 1984

467 N.E.2d 448

NOLAN, Justice.

The plaintiff, Richard Stock, has appealed the entry of summary judgment in favor of the defendants in the Superior Court. We allowed Stock's motion for direct appellate review. We hold that allowance of the defendants' motion for summary judgment was error, and we remand the case to the Superior Court.

1. *Factual background and prior proceedings.* Richard Stock, age 21, suffers from multiple cognitive and motor disabilities which are the result of a brain tumor and chemotherapy-radiation treatments received for that tumor at the age of ten. He also manifests emotional and behavioral difficulties which are concomitant with his physical condition. For the most part, he is confined to a wheelchair. At times he has demonstrated academic abilities ranging from the fourth through the ninth grade level. At the time he was awarded a high school diploma, a psychologist's evaluation indicated that his abilities were consistently below the norm for his age group and were consonant with brain damage.

At the age of fourteen, Stock entered the Massachusetts Hospital School, where he received special education services at the Brayton High School. In the fall of 1980, Stock's teachers met to formulate his Individualized Educational Plan (IEP) for the 1980–81 school year. The teachers intended that Stock be graduated at the end of the academic year. Neither Stock nor his parents were invited to this meeting. In the early part of the winter of 1981, Stock signed the IEP. The IEP does not show a parental signature. The IEP does not mention graduation. At no time were his parents provided formal, written notice of their right to challenge the IEP or of the procedural avenues open to them to make that challenge. Neither were they told that graduation would terminate their son's eligibility for special education services. In June, 1981, Stock was presented with a high school diploma. His eligibility for special education services was thereby terminated.

In the months following graduation, Stock remained at the hospital school. Although the record is unclear as to whether additional special education services were offered to him, or offered and refused, in the time between graduation and the commencement of this action, there is no question that Stock has received no further special education services since his graduation. He has failed to adapt either to sheltered workshop or to independent living settings. At the time appellate briefs were filed, he was hospitalized in a chronic care unit.

In December, 1981, Stock's parents sought legal counsel. In the proceedings below, Stock challenged the award of his diploma on procedural and substantive grounds, alleging violations of both State and Federal law. The defendants asserted that Stock had failed to exhaust administrative remedies. On March 29, 1983, a judge of the Superior Court issued a memorandum and order on cross-motions for summary judgment. In his memorandum, the judge ruled that Stock could not acquire the academic skills necessary for a regular high school education before reaching age twenty-two, the age at which special education entitlements terminate. The judge then concluded that Stock had not met the primary jurisdiction requirement of exhaustion of administrative remedies, ordered the entry of summary judgment in favor of all defendants, and dismissed Stock's complaint.

After judgment, Stock's counsel wrote to the Bureau of Special Education Appeals urging consideration of his client's appeal. The assistant director of the Bureau of Special Education Appeals took the position that, because Stock had received a high school diploma, the bureau no longer had jurisdiction of his case.

On appeal, Stock raises the following issues: (1) whether the defendants' failure to provide notice and procedural protections before terminating special education services violated his rights under State and Federal law; (2) whether presentation of a high school diploma to Stock in the absence of his attaining sufficient skills to warrant such presentation violated his rights under State and Federal law; . . . Stock requests a determination from this court that he had not acquired sufficient skills to graduate from high school without his express consent. He requests relief in the form of an order rescinding his diploma and directing the department to arrange for and fund appropriate special education services for him. . . .

For the reasons set forth below, we agree that Stock's graduation was procedurally and substantively defective. . . .

2. *Procedural safeguards.* The focus of Stock's argument is that the decision to graduate a child with special education needs is a change in placement, . . . triggering the mandatory procedural safeguards of EAHCA [now IDEA], described in 20 U.S.C. § 1415. The plaintiff cites no judicial discussion of this issue, nor have we found any. It seems obvious, however, that graduation, because it will cause the termination of a student's participation in special education programs, can hardly be characterized as anything other than a change in placement. This view accords with Federal law, which requires that States qualifying for Federal assistance provide special needs children with a free appropriate public education. . . . It also accords with the law of this Commonwealth, which mandates that the department administer special education programs so as to assure the maximum possible development of a child with special needs. G.L. 71B, § 2, as amended by St.1978, c. 552, § 19. No change in placement seems quite so serious nor as worthy of parental involvement and procedural protections as the termination of placement in special education programs. Under the Federal scheme, a change in placement requires formal, written notice of the decision to graduate a child, as well as notice of a parent's right to protest that decision, a description of the administrative remedies and procedures to be followed, and a description of any alternative services which may be available. To ensure conformity with Federal policy, the State must adhere to these notice and procedural requirements. This change requires significant parental involvement in the decision making process, . . . It is not enough, contrary to the defendants' argument, that Stock's parents received actual notice of the graduation or that they participated to a limited extent in the transitional planning surrounding the graduation. From all appearances, the Stocks received actual notice of a fait accompli,

without any notice that they might challenge the decision. It is difficult to find justification for permitting a young man with Stock's handicaps to pass through and out of the special education system by virtue of his signature on an IEP—which did not even mention the graduation decision—without some evidence that he or his parents were aware of the consequences of doing so and the alternatives available to them. We note that the conduct of which Stock complains was in direct violation of the department's special education regulations.

Failure to provide to Stock's parents formal, written notice concerning the graduation decision, failure to provide such notice regarding their rights to involvement in that decision, and failure to notify them as to rights to a hearing and administrative review, violate State and Federal statutory law. . . .

3. *Relief to be granted.* In view of our determination . . . the trial judge's entry of summary judgment in favor of the defendants must be reversed. Further, because the award of a diploma was both procedurally and substantively deficient, the diploma must be rescinded. This case is remanded to the Superior Court with directions that it order the department to take jurisdiction and to hold a hearing on the matter of providing special education services to Stock. Should it determine that further services are appropriate, the department shall take into account the period of about three years which has elapsed since the initial graduation in June, 1981. This is to be added to Stock's period of eligibility for special education services. . . .

Notes

1. This case clearly established the principle that graduation is a change in placement under the IDEA because it effectively terminates all educational services. In what situations, other than graduation, would this legal principle apply?

2. School personnel committed a number of procedural errors in this situation. Most seriously, they did not provide proper notice and did not include the student's parents in the decision-making process. Why is this a problem?

3. The IDEA now requires that transition services be written into IEPs well before students graduate or leave educational systems. If this provision had been in effect in this situation, would school officials have been less likely to make the decision to graduate Richard Stock? Why?

REFERENCES

Amann v. Stow School System, 982 F.2d 644 (1st Cir. 1992).

Anderson v. District of Columbia, 877 F.2d 1018 (D.C. Cir. 1989).

Andress v. Cleveland Independent School District, 64 F.3d 176 (5th Cir. 1995).

Arlington Central School District v. D.K. and K.K., 2002 WL 31521158 (S.D.N.Y. 2002).

AW ex rel. Wilson v. Fairfax County School Board, 372 F.3d 674 (9th Cir. 2004).

Big Beaver Falls Area School District v. Jackson, 615 A.2d 910 (Pa. Commw. Ct. 1992).

Birmingham by Birmingham v. Omaha School District, 220 F.3d 850 (8th Cir. 2000).

Blackmon v. Springfield R-XII School District, 198 F.3d 648 (8th Cir. 1999).

Block v. District of Columbia, 748 F. Supp. 891, (D.D.C. 1990).

Board of Education of the Hendrick Hudson Central School District v. Rowley, 458 U.S. 176 (1982).

Board of Education of Oak Park & River Forest High School District 200 v. Illinois State Board of Education, 79 F.3d 654 (7th Cir. 1996).

Bonadonna v. Cooperman, 619 F. Supp. 401 (D.N.J. 1985).

Brimmer v. Traverse City Area Public Schools, 872 F. Supp. 447 (W.D. Mich. 1994).

Brookline School Committee v. Golden, 628 F. Supp. 113 (D. Mass. 1986).

Burlington School Committee v. Department of Education of the Commonwealth of Massachusetts, 471 U.S. 359 (1985).

Buser v. Corpus Christi Independent School, 51 F.3d 490 (5th Cir. 1995).

Carpenter v. Pennell School District Elementary Unit, 2002 WL 1832854 (E.D. Pa. 2002).

Cartwright v. District of Columbia, 267 F. Supp.2d 83 (D.D.C. 2003).

Cavanagh v. Grasmick, 75 F. Supp.2d 446 (D. Md. 1999).

Chris D. v. Montgomery County Board of Education, 753 F. Supp. 922 (M.D. Ala. 1990).

Clovis Unified School District v. California Office of Administrative Hearings, 903 F.2d 635 (9th Cir. 1990).

Clyde K. v. Puyallup School District, 35 F.3d 1396 (9th Cir. 1994).

Cochran v. District of Columbia, 660 F. Supp. 314 (D.D.C. 1987).

Concerned Parents and Citizens for the Continuing Education at Malcolm X. v. New York City Board of Education, 629 F.2d 751 (2d Cir. 1980).

Cone ex rel. Cone v. Randolph County Schools, 302 F. Supp.2d 500 (M.D.N.C. 2004).

Corbett v. Regional Center for the East Bay, 676 F. Supp. 964 (N.D. Cal. 1988).

Cordrey v. Euckert, 917 F.2d 1460 (6th Cir. 1990).

Cronin v. Board of Education of East Ramapo Central School District, 689 F. Supp. 197 (S.D.N.Y. 1988).

Deal ex rel. Deal v. Hamilton County Department of Education, 392 F.3d 840 (6th Cir. 2004).

DeLeon v. Susquehanna Community School District, 747 F.2d 149 (3d Cir. 1984).

DiBuo v. Board of Education of Worcester County, 309 F.3d 184 (4th Cir. 2002).

Digre v. Roseville Schools Independent School District No. 623, 841 F.2d 245 (8th Cir. 1988).

Dima v. Macchiarola, 513 F. Supp. 565 (E.D.N.Y. 1981).

Doe v. Anrig, 651 F. Supp. 424 (D. Mass. 1987).

Doe v. Brookline School Committee, 722 F.2d 910 (1st Cir. 1983).

Doe v. Defendant I, 898 F.2d 1186 (6th Cir. 1990).

Dong v. Board of Education of the Rochester Community Schools, 197 F.3d 703 (6th Cir. 1999).

Doyle v. Arlington County School Board, 806 F. Supp. 1253 (E.D. Va. 1992).

D.P. and L.P. ex rel E.P. v. School Board of Broward County, 360 F. Supp.2d 1294 (S.D. Fla. 2005).

Edwards-White v. District of Columbia, 785 F. Supp. 1022 (D.D.C. 1992).

E.H. and H.H. v. Tirozzi, 735 F. Supp. 53 (D. Conn. 1990).

Escambia County Board of Education v. Benton, 358 F. Supp.2d 1112 (S.D. Ala. 2005).

Family Educational Rights and Privacy Act (FERPA), 20 U.S.C. § 1232g (1974).

Fitzgerald v. Camdenton R-III School District, 439 F.3d 773 (8th Cir. 2006).

Fuhrmann v. East Hanover Board of Education, 993 F.2d 1031 (3d Cir. 1993).

Gabel ex rel. L.G. v. Board of Education of the Hyde Park Central School District, 368 F. Supp.2d 313 (S.D.N.Y. 2005).

G.D. v. Westmoreland School District, 930 F.2d 942 (1st Cir. 1991).

Gebhardt v. Ambach, EHLR 554:130 (W.D.N.Y. 1982).

Gerstmyer v. Howard County Public Schools, 850 F. Supp. 361 (D. Md. 1994).

Gonzaga University v. Doe, 536 U.S. 273 (2002).

Grace B. v. Lexington School Committee, 762 F. Supp. 416 (D. Mass. 1991).

Gregory K. v. Longview School District, 811 F.2d 1307 (9th Cir. 1987).

Hampton School District v. Dobrowolski, 976 F.2d 48 (1st Cir. 1992).

Hill v. School Board for Pinellas County, 954 F. Supp. 251 (M.D. Fla. 1997).

Holmes v. District of Columbia, 680 F. Supp. 40 (D.D.C. 1988).

Honig v. Doe, 484 U.S. 305 (1988).

Individuals with Disabilities Education Act, 20 U.S.C. §§ 1400–1482 (2005).

Jacobsen v. District of Columbia Board of Education, 564 F. Supp. 166 (D.D.C. 1983).

Johnson v. Duneland School Corporation, 92 F.3d 554 (7th Cir. 1996).

Johnson v. Special Education Hearing Office, State of California, 287 F.3d 1176 (9th Cir. 2002).

Joshua B. v. New Trier Township High School District 203, 770 F. Supp. 431, (N.D. Ill. 1991).

J.S. ex rel. D.S. v. Lenape Regional High School District Board of Education, 102 F. Supp.2d 540 (D.N.J. 2000).

Kevin T. v. Elmhurst Community School District No. 205, 2002 WL 433061 (N.D. Ill. 2002).

Knable v. Bexley City School District, 238 F.3d 755 (6th Cir. 2001).

Knight v. District of Columbia, 877 F.2d 1025 (D.D.C. 1989)

Kroot v. District of Columbia, 800 F. Supp. 977 (D.D.C. 1992).

Lenhoff v. Farmington Public Schools, 680 F. Supp. 921 (E.D. Mich. 1988).

Leonard v. McKenzie, 869 F.2d 1558 (D.C. Cir. 1989).

Logsdon v. Board of Education of the Pavilion Central School District, 765 F. Supp. 66, (W.D.N.Y. 1991).

Lora v. Board of Education of the City of New York, 456 F. Supp. 1211 (E.D.N.Y. 1978), *affirmed in part*, 623 F.2d 248 (2d Cir. 1980), *final order*, 587 F. Supp. 1572 (E.D.N.Y. 1984).

Lunceford v. District of Columbia Board of Education, 745 F.2d 1577 (D.C. Cir. 1984).

Magyar v. Tucson Unified School District, 958 F. Supp. 1423 (D. Ariz. 1997).

Max M. v. Thompson, 566 F. Supp. 1330 (N.D. Ill. 1983).

McKenzie v. Smith, 771 F.2d 1527 (D.C. Cir. 1985).

Middlebrook v. School District of the County of Knox, 805 F. Supp. 534 (E.D. Tenn. 1991).

M.L. v. Federal Way School District, 394 F.3d 634 (9th Cir. 2005).

Mrs. C. v. Wheaton, 916 F.2d 69 (2d Cir. 1990).

Ms. S. ex rel. G. v. Vashon Island School District, 337 F.3d 1115 (9th Cir. 2003).

Myles S. v. Montgomery County Board of Education, 824 F. Supp. 1549 (M.D. Ala. 1993).

N.L. ex rel. Ms. C. v. Knox County Schools, 315 F.3d 688 (6th Cir. 2003).

Osborne, A. G. (2004). To what extent can procedural violations of the IDEA render an IEP invalid? *Education Law Reporter, 185*, 15–29.

Owasso Independent School District v. Falvo, 534 U.S. 426 (2002).

Pardini v. Allegheny Intermediate Unit, 420 F.3d 181 (3d Cir. 2005).

Patricia P. v. Board of Education of Oak Park and River Forest High School District No. 200, 8 F. Supp.2d 801 (N.D. Ill. 1998).

Paul Y. by Kathy Y. v. Singletary, 979 F. Supp. 1422 (S.D. Fla. 1997).

Pitchford ex rel. M. v. Salem-Keizer School District No. 24J, 155 F. Supp.2d 1213 (D. Or. 2001).

P.J. v. State of Connecticut Board of Education, 788 F. Supp. 673 (D. Conn. 1992).

Poolaw v. Bishop, 67 F.3d 830 (9th Cir. 1995).

R.L. ex rel. Mr. and Mrs. L. v. Plainville Board of Education, 363 F. Supp.2d 222 (D. Conn. 2005)

Rothschild v. Grottenthaler, 907 F.2d 286 (2d Cir. 1990).

Russell v. Jefferson, 609 F. Supp. 605 (N.D. Cal. 1985).

Russo, C. J., & Mawdsley, R. D. (2002). *Owasso Independent School District v. Falvo:* The Supreme Court upholds peer grading. *School Business Affairs, 68*(5), 34–36.

Saleh v. District of Columbia, 660 F. Supp. 212 (D.D.C. 1987).

Sammons v. Polk County School Board, 165 Fed. Appx. 750 (11th Cir. 2006).

Schares v. Katy Independent School District, 252 F. Supp.2d 364 (S.D. Tex. 2003).

Scituate School Committee v. Robert B., 620 F. Supp. 1224 (D.R.I. 1985), *affirmed,* 795 F.2d 77 (1st Cir. 1986) (mem.).

Sean R. v. Board of Education of the Town of Woodbridge, 794 F. Supp. 467 (D. Conn. 1992).

Seattle School District No. 1 v. B.S., 82 F.3d 1493 (9th Cir. 1996).

Smith v. Henson, 786 F. Supp. 43 (D.D.C. 1992).

Smith v. Squillacote, 800 F. Supp. 993 (D.D.C. 1992).

Spielberg v. Henrico County Public Schools, 853 F.2d 256 (4th Cir. 1988).

Stock v. Massachusetts Hospital School, 467 N.E.2d 448 (Mass. 1984).

Susquenita School District v. Raelee S., 96 F.3d 78 (3d Cir. 1996).

Taylor v. Vermont Department of Education, 313 F.3d 768 (2d Cir. 2002).

Tennessee Department of Mental Health and Mental Retardation v. Paul B., 88 F.3d 1466 (6th Cir. 1996).

Thomas v. Cincinnati Board of Education, 918 F.2d 618 (6th Cir. 1990).

Tilton v. Jefferson County Board of Education, 705 F.2d 800 (6th Cir. 1983).

Tracy v. Beaufort County Board of Education, 335 F. Supp.2d 675 (D.S.C. 2004).

T.S. v. Independent School District No. 54, 265 F.3d 1090 (10th Cir 2001).

T.S. v. Ridgefield Board of Education, 808 F. Supp. 926 (D. Conn. 1992), *affirmed sub nom. T.S. v. Board of Education of the Town of Ridgefield*, 10 F.3d 87 (2d Cir. 1993).

Vander Malle v. Ambach, 673 F.2d 49 (2d Cir. 1982).

Veazey v. Ascension Parish School Board, 121 Fed. Appx. 552 (5th Cir. 2005).

Verhoeven v. Brunswick School Committee, 207 F.3d 1 (1st Cir. 1999).

Visco v. School District of Pittsburgh, 684 F. Supp. 1310 (W.D. Pa. 1988).

V.W. and R.W. v. Favolise, 131 F.R.D. 654 (D. Conn. 1990).

Webster Groves School District v. Pulitzer Publishing Co., 898 F.2d 1371 (8th Cir. 1990).

Weil v. Board of Elementary and Secondary Education, 931 F.2d 1069 (5th Cir. 1991).

W.G. and B.G. v. Board of Trustees of Target Range School District No. 23, 960 F.2d 1479 (9th Cir. 1992).

4

Free Appropriate
Public Education

❖

Key Concepts in This Chapter

- ❖ Appropriate Education Defined
- ❖ Least Restrictive Environment
- ❖ Placement in Private Facilities
- ❖ Extended School Year Programs

The Individuals with Disabilities Education Act (IDEA) requires school boards to maintain a "continuum of alternative placements" to provide students with disabilities with the free appropriate public education (FAPE) mandated in its provisions (34 C.F.R. § 300.115). The continuum must range from placements within general education classrooms to private residential facilities to homebound or hospital instruction to instruction in residential facilities. Further, all placements must be made in the least restrictive environment (LRE), and students with disabilities can be removed from general educational environments only to the extent necessary for them to be provided with special education services (20 U.S.C. § 1412(a)(5)). All placements are to be at public expense and need to meet state educational standards (20 U.S.C. § 1401(9)). While states are required to adopt policies and procedures that are consistent with federal law, they may provide greater benefits than those required by the IDEA. If states establish higher standards, parents and children can enforce those higher standards in federal courts (*David D. v. Dartmouth School Committee*, 1985).

This chapter begins with an examination of how the courts defined the term *appropriate* as used in the IDEA. Then the chapter traces the evolving law regarding the IDEA's LRE provision, particularly as it relates to the inclusion of students with disabilities in general educational settings. Next, the chapter outlines the situations in which school boards may be required to place students with disabilities in private day or residential school facilities. Finally, the chapter looks at the circumstances under which school boards must provide educational programs for students with disabilities beyond the usual 180-day school year.

DEFINITION OF APPROPRIATE

School administrators, special educators, and parents began to speculate about what constituted an appropriate education almost as soon as the IDEA went into effect. Yet, the IDEA's language and legislative history provided little guidance. The IDEA's implementing regulations, echoing the statute, stipulate that an appropriate education consists of special education and related services that are provided in conformance with an individualized education program (IEP) (34 C.F.R. § 300.17). Another regulation defines special education as "specially designed instruction, at no cost to the parents, to meet the unique needs of a child with a disability . . ." (34 C.F.R. § 300.38). Insofar as all of these terms and definitions were open to interpretation, it is not surprising that a great deal of the early litigation concerned the meaning of the term *appropriate* as used in the IDEA (Osborne, 1992).

Early judicial interpretations of the IDEA defined an appropriate education as one that provided more than simple access to educational programs but fell somewhat short of the best that could possibly be provided (O'Hara, 1985). The courts emphasized that although appropriate did not mean best, the educational programs provided needed to be individually tailored to meet the specific needs of students (*Norris v. Massachusetts Department of Education*, 1981; *Rettig v. Kent City School District*, 1981, 1983, 1986; *Springdale School District v. Grace*, 1981, 1982). Other courts went so far as to agree that the existence of better programs did not automatically render given programs inappropriate (*Age v. Bullitt County Public Schools*, 1982; *Buchholtz v. Iowa Department of Public Instruction*, 1982). These differences aside, the courts did support the principle that when school personnel proposed IEPs for students with disabilities, they had to be developed to meet the needs of the children rather than those of the school systems (*Anderson v. Thompson*, 1980; *Gladys J. v. Pearland Independent School District*, 1981; *Campbell v. Talladega County Board of Education*, 1981; *Laura M. v. Special School District*, 1980).

In 1982 in *Board of Education of the Hendrick Hudson Central School District v. Rowley (Rowley)*, the first case wherein the Supreme Court resolved a dispute under the IDEA, the Justices defined the term *appropriate* as used in the act. The suit, which originated in New York, was filed in a dispute over the special education and related services to be provided to a student who was hearing impaired. The student, who had minimal residual hearing but was an excellent lip reader, was placed in a regular kindergarten class on a trial basis when she entered the public schools. The school's staff took sign-language courses, and installed a teletype machine to communicate with her parents, who were also deaf. While the student was given a sign-language interpreter, at the end of the trial period the interpreter reported that these services were not needed.

The dispute between the school board and the parents began when officials proposed an IEP for the student's first-grade placement. That IEP called for regular class placement, an FM hearing aid to amplify the spoken words of her teacher and classmates, one hour per day of instruction from a tutor for the deaf, and three hours per week of speech therapy. The parents agreed to the IEP but asked the board to continue the assistance of a sign-language interpreter. When the board refused to provide an interpreter, the parents asked for a due process hearing.

The school board prevailed in administrative hearings, but a federal trial court and the Second Circuit ruled in favor of the parents. The courts basically agreed that the proposed IEP was inappropriate because it did not provide the student with an opportunity to achieve her full potential commensurate with the opportunity provided to students who were not disabled. Dissatisfied with this outcome, the school board sought further review.

At issue before the Supreme Court in *Rowley* was the question about the level of services that school officials were required to provide in an IEP and a student's educational placement in order to be appropriate under the IDEA. In a six-to-three decision, the Court **reversed** in favor of the board, reasoning that the lower courts erred in interpreting the IDEA as requiring the board to provide a level of services such that the potential of students with disabilities must be maximized to be commensurate with opportunities provided to their peers who were not disabled.

In its majority opinion, the Court explained that school officials satisfy the IDEA's requirement of providing a FAPE when they provide "personalized instruction with sufficient support services to permit the child to benefit educationally from that instruction" (p. 203). The Court further noted that IEPs must be formulated in accordance with the IDEA's requirements. While the student was performing better than average and was receiving personalized instruction that was reasonably calculated to meet her educational needs, the Court held that the requested sign-language interpreter was not required.

As part of its analysis, the Court maintained that other provisions of the IDEA are pertinent to evaluating whether proposed IEPs are appropriate. Specifically, the court was of the view that educational programs must be provided in the LRE (20 U.S.C. § 1412(a)(5)), while related, or supportive, services that may be required to assist children in benefiting from special education programs must also be included (20 U.S.C. § 1401(26)). The Court reiterated that all services must both be furnished at public expense (20 U.S.C. § 1401(9)(A)) and meet state educational standards (20 U.S.C. § 1401(9)(B)).

Trivial Educational Benefit Is Not Sufficient

Most courts responded to *Rowley* by deciding that IEPs and the educational programs that they called for were appropriate if they resulted in some educational benefit to students, even if the benefits were minimal (Osborne, 1992). In the years immediately following *Rowley*, lower federal courts agreed that Congress only intended for the IDEA to provide students with disabilities with access to educational programs.

Rowley clearly stands for the proposition that students with disabilities must be placed in educational programs that confer some educational benefit. Even so, the First Circuit decided that a student with severe disabilities need not demonstrate an ability to benefit from a special education program in order to be eligible for services (*Timothy W. v. Rochester, NH School District* (*Timothy W.*), 1989). In upholding the IDEA's zero reject principle, the court declared that education encompasses a wide spectrum of training, including instruction in even the most basic life skills. Pursuant to *Timothy W.*, school boards cannot refuse to provide services to students if they deem children too disabled to derive benefit from those services.

Approximately three years after *Rowley*, the lower courts began to expand their interpretation of the *some educational benefit* criteria. Even though the initial cases indicated that minimal benefits met this standard, later opinions interpreted the IDEA as requiring more. For example, the Fourth Circuit affirmed that *Rowley* allowed the courts to make case-by-case analyses of the substantive standards needed to meet the criteria that IEPs must reasonably have been calculated to enable students to receive educational benefits (*Hall v. Vance County Board of Education*, 1985). Here the court agreed that the minimal progress that the student made was insufficient in view of his intellectual potential. The court thought that Congress certainly did not intend for this, or any, school board to provide programs that produced only trivial academic advancements. In another case, that same court was convinced that since a goal of four months' progress during an academic year was unlikely to allow a student to advance from grade to grade with passing marks, the board's plan was insufficient to provide her with an appropriate education (*Carter v. Florence County School District Four*, 1991, 1993).

Other similar judgments helped to clarify the axiom that trivial educational benefit is insufficient under the IDEA. On more than one occasion, the Third Circuit commented that satisfying *Rowley*'s mandate required plans likely to produce progress, not trivial educational advancements (*Board of Education of East Windsor Regional School District v. Diamond*, 1986; *M.C. ex rel. J.C. v. Central Regional School District*, 1996). In another case, the court reiterated that the IDEA calls for more than trivial educational benefit, adding that Congress intended to provide all students with disabilities with educational placements that would have resulted in meaningful benefits (*Polk v. Central Susquehanna Intermediate Unit 16*, 1988). The Eleventh Circuit went so far as to observe that an appropriate education may be defined as one wherein a student makes measurable and adequate gains in the classroom (*J.S.K. v. Hendry County School Board*, 1991).

Best Available Option Is Not Required

Rowley made it clear that school boards are not required to develop IEPs designed to maximize the potential of students with disabilities. In *Rowley*, the Court rejected the notion that the IDEA requires programs to provide students with disabilities with opportunities to achieve their full potential commensurate with the chances afforded peers who are not disabled.

In accord with *Rowley*, lower courts unanimously agreed that school boards are not required to maximize the potential of children with disabilities insofar as they are only obligated to meet the some educational benefit standard (*J.S.K. v. Hendry County School Board*, 1991). Even when faced with a choice between two competing programs, courts have not ordered boards to provide programs that would have given students the best educational options or result in the greatest progress (*Angevine v. Smith*, 1992; *Daniel G. v. Delaware Valley School District*, 2002; *Hessler v. State Board of Education of Maryland*, 1983; *Karl v. Board of Education of Genesco Central School District*, 1984; *Timms v. Metropolitan School District*, 1983).

Once school boards can show that they have met their obligations under *Rowley*, the courts have required no more. For example, a federal trial court in California declined a parental invitation to pick between competing methodologies, instead responding that the fact that the student made more progress in a private school program did not affect the appropriateness of the public school's proposal (*Bertolucci v. San Carlos Elementary School District*, 1989). Along the same line, a federal trial court in Virginia insisted that since a school board's proposed IEP offered an adequate degree of educational benefit, it was statutorily appropriate even in the face of evidence that the private school placement favored by the parents would have provided even greater benefit (*Lewis v. School Board of Loudoun County*, 1992).

In *Rowley* the Supreme Court cautioned judges not to substitute their views of proper educational methodology for that of competent school officials. Most jurists, recognizing that they are not experts in the field of education, typically defer to school officials on matters of methodology. It is thus well settled that parents do not have the right to compel school boards to provide specific programs or employ specific methodologies (*Blackmon v. Springfield R-XII School District*, 1999; *Logue v. Shawnee Mission Public School Unified School District No. 512*, 1997, 1998; *Renner v. Board of Education of the Public Schools of the City of Ann Arbor*, 1999; *Tucker v. Calloway County Board of Education*, 1998). In this regard, the federal trial court in Kansas commented that the IDEA did not require a school board to use one proven method over another (*O'Toole v. Olathe District Schools Unified School*

District No. 233, 1997, 1998). The Second Circuit explained that the fact that experts privately hired by parents may have recommended a different methodology did not undermine the deference that the judiciary owed to school officials (*Watson ex rel. Watson v. Kingston City School District*, 2005). As such, courts ordinarily support proposals from school board officials as long as the programs they select meet the IDEA's standards of appropriateness and are based on legitimate educational methodologies (*Dong v. Board of Education of the Rochester Community Schools*, 1999; *E.S. v. Independent School District, No 196*, 1998).

Effect of State Standards

States may establish standards of appropriateness that are higher than the federal benchmark set in *Rowley*. In fact, the Court emphasized that programs also must meet state educational standards in order to be appropriate. The First Circuit noted that the IDEA incorporates state procedural and substantive standards that exceed the federal level by reference (*Town of Burlington v. Department of Education, Commonwealth of Massachusetts*, 1984). When state standards exceed their federal counterparts, the former are employed in evaluating whether proposed IEPs are appropriate. Even though the vast majority of jurisdictions have statutes and regulations that define an appropriate education in a manner not unlike the federal standard, at least five states have established higher standards.

Courts agree that North Carolina (*Burke County Board of Education v. Denton*, 1990), New Jersey (*Geis v. Board of Education of Parsippany-Troy Hills*, 1985), Michigan (*Barwacz v. Michigan Department of Education*, 1988), Missouri (*Lagares v. Camdenton R-III School District*, 2001), and California (*Pink v. Mt. Diablo Unified School District*, 1990) have higher standards of appropriateness. These courts treated the higher state standards as incorporated into federal law because one of the IDEA's requirements is that special education programs must meet "the standards of the state educational agency" (20 U.S.C. § 1401(9)(B)). To this end, state statutes may require school boards to provide programs to maximize the potential of students with disabilities commensurate with the educational opportunities provided to their peers who are not disabled (*Brimmer v. Traverse City Area Public Schools*, 1994). In these states, the *Rowley* standard simply does not apply because it has been superseded.

Indicators of Educational Benefit

Pursuant to the *Rowley* standard, special education students who are placed in general education classrooms should receive a level of services sufficient to enable them to achieve passing marks and advance from grade to grade. Even so, courts have found that promotion to the next grade by itself is not proof that a student has received a FAPE. In one such case, the Fourth Circuit affirmed that promotion alone, especially in conjunction with test scores showing minimal progress, did not satisfy the *Rowley* standard of educational benefit (*Hall v. Vance County Board of Education*, 1985). Later, that same court held that while

TOURO COLLEGE LIBRARY

passing marks and annual grade promotions were important considerations under the IDEA, achieving them did not automatically mean that a student received a FAPE (*In re Conklin*, 1991).

The fact that students graduated and received high school diplomas also does not automatically signify that they received a FAPE. The Supreme Judicial Court of Massachusetts rescinded an eighteen-year-old student's diploma in ascertaining that he was unable to adapt to a sheltered workshop or independent living after his graduation (*Stock v. Massachusetts Hospital School*, 1984). The court contended that it was substantively inappropriate to award a diploma where the evidence indicated that the student would have been unable to earn one under normal requirements even by the age of twenty-two. Another case from Massachusetts illustrates that even where a student legitimately earned a high school diploma, it was not necessarily an indicator of having received a FAPE. The federal trial court reflected that the fact that a student earned a high school diploma did not mean that she had not needed special education services. Instead, the court interpreted the student's having been given a diploma as a sign that she succeeded despite the school board's failure to provide her with assistance (*Puffer v. Raynolds*, 1988). Conversely, a federal trial court in Michigan posited that completion of general graduation requirements with exceptional performance in mainstream classes indicated that a student received a FAPE (*Chuhran v. Walled Lake Consolidated Schools*, 1993).

In considering whether proposed IEPs are appropriate, some courts look at students' past progress in the same or similar programs as well as evidence as to whether their progress should continue. In this regard, many courts treated evidence of past progress in programs as indicators that they were appropriate placements (*Bonnie Ann F. v. Calallen Independent School District*, 1993, 1994; *Cypress-Fairbanks Independent School District v. Michael F.*, 1995, 1997; *Gill v. Columbia 93 School District*, 2000; *Petersen v. Hastings Public Schools*, 1993, 1994; *Walczak v. Florida Union Free School District*, 1998). On the other hand, courts agreed that the continuation of programs that had not resulted in educational benefits was inappropriate (*Manchester School District v. Christopher B.*, 1992; *Ojai Unified School District v. Jackson*, 1993; *Straube v. Florida Union Free School District*, 1992). As such, courts viewed regression after services or programs were discontinued as an indicator that the education provided following the discontinuation of the services was not meaningful (*Johnson v. Lancaster-Lebanon Intermediate Unit 13, Lancaster City School District*, 1991).

In general terms, student progress should be comparable with that achieved by other similarly situated students. In one such case, a federal trial court in New York specified that progress should be measured in terms of a student's abilities as a child with disabilities (*Mavis v. Sobol*, 1994). Further, a federal trial court in Texas noted that progress for a student with disabilities cannot be judged by making a comparison to the progress of peers who do not have disabilities (*El Paso Independent School District v. Robert W.*, 1995). On the other hand, lack of progress does not necessarily mean that student programs are inappropriate. Courts recognize that some students are not motivated or that other factors, such as poor conduct, lack of motivation, failure to complete homework, absenteeism, or even their failure to access provided special education services contribute to the lack of success that some children experience (*Cerra v. Pawling Central School District*, 2005; *Hampton School District v. Dobrowolski*, 1992; *Hiller v. Board of Education of the Brunswick Central School District*, 1990; *McDowell v. Fort Bend Independent School District*, 1990).

Courts rely on objective data, such as test scores, report card grades, and the opinions of experts in the field, such as psychologists and educational diagnosticians, in evaluating whether children have made meaningful or significant progress. Courts have thus viewed improved standardized test scores and positive report card grades as evidence that students with learning disabilities received educational benefit from their IEPs (*B.L. ex rel. Mr. and Mrs. T.L. v. New Britain Board of Education*, 2005; *Board of Education of the Avon Lake City School District v. Patrick M.*, 1998; *Coale v. State Department of Education*, 2001; *W.C. ex rel. Sue C. v. Cobb County School District*, 2005). Moreover, the Seventh Circuit affirmed that a student who achieved well-earned yearly promotions received an appropriate education (*Todd v. Duneland School Corporation*, 2002). Conversely, a federal trial court in Illinois thought that a student who failed half her courses and received poor grades in most others received only minimal educational benefit (*Board of Education of Oak Park & River Forest High School District No. 200 v. Illinois State Board of Education*, 1998).

IEPs are **prospective**, but reviews of IEPs by hearing officers or courts can be retrospective. While due process appeals and court action generally occur after IEPs should have been implemented, those reviewing IEPs have the benefit of hindsight in evaluating their appropriateness. The Third Circuit considered the amount of weight that subsequent history should be given, affirming that a school board's action cannot be judged exclusively in hindsight. Rather, the court reasoned that any decision should be based on whether an IEP was appropriate at the time it was developed, not on whether the child actually received benefit as a result of the placement (*Fuhrmann v. East Hanover Board of Education*, 1993). The court observed that a student's gains can also be attributed to other factors besides the educational program. In like fashion, the Eighth Circuit agreed that the role of the judiciary is to evaluate whether an IEP was appropriate when it was written (*Independent School District No. 283 v. S.D. by J.D.*, 1996). Even so, while courts may look at evidence that arose after IEPs were proposed, the Third Circuit posited that such evidence may be used only with respect to a school board's proposal at the time it was made (*Susan N. v. Wilson School District*, 1995).

Effect of Procedural Errors

In *Rowley*, the Supreme Court held that in order to be appropriate, an IEP must be developed in accordance with the procedures outlined in the IDEA. The importance of following correct procedure in the development of IEPs simply cannot be overemphasized. Although all procedural errors are not fatal, those that interfere with or thwart parental participation in the IEP process may cause courts to invalidate otherwise appropriate IEPs (Osborne, 2004). One of the major errors school officials can make is to not notify parents of their procedural rights under the IDEA and state laws (*Hall v. Vance County Board of Education*, 1985). Further, the failure of school officials to adhere to the time lines set out in the IDEA or state laws can be fatal if their actions interfere with the provision of a FAPE (*Tice v. Botetourt County School Board*, 1990). Perhaps the most egregious error that school officials can make is to fail to involve parents in the IEP process (*Board of Education of the County of Cabell v. Dienelt*, 1988; *W.G. and B.G. v. Board of Trustees of Target Range School District No. 23*, 1992). The failure of officials to develop IEPs in a timely fashion or conduct the required **annual reviews** could result in judgments that school boards did not provide students with disabilities with a FAPE (*Delaware County Intermediate Unit #25 v. Martin K.*, 1993).

On the other hand, courts do not wish to exalt form over substance. The judiciary recognizes that the IDEA's provisions are often difficult to implement and realizes that school officials may sometimes proceed in a manner that is technically incorrect but does not prejudice the IEP process. In these situations, courts overlook minor procedural flaws. For example, courts have allowed IEPs to remain in place when there were minor inadequacies in the notice provided to parents (*Adam J. ex rel. Robert J. v. Keller Independent School District*, 2003; *Doe v. Alabama State Department of Education*, 1990) or when an IEP did not contain all of the required elements but the missing information was known to all concerned (*A.I. ex rel. Iapalucci v. District of Columbia*, 2005; *Doe v. Defendant I*, 1990).

Courts generally approve IEPs that are appropriate despite the presence of minor procedural errors if those flaws did not interfere with parental participation or prejudice students in any way (*Alexis v. Board of Education for Baltimore County Public Schools*, 2003; *Hiller v. Board of Education of the Brunswick Central School District*, 1990; *Livingston v. DeSoto County School District*, 1992; *Myles S. v. Montgomery County Board of Education*, 1993). The First Circuit summed it up well in stating that before an IEP can be set aside, there must be some rational basis for believing that procedural errors compromised a student's right to a FAPE, seriously interfered with the parents' right to participate in the IEP process, or caused a deprivation of educational benefits (*Roland M. v. Concord School Committee*, 1990).

LEAST RESTRICTIVE ENVIRONMENT

A major element in the IDEA is its requirement that students with disabilities be educated in the LRE. This means that states, through local school boards or educational agencies, must establish procedures to assure that, to the maximum extent appropriate, students with disabilities are placed with children who do not have disabilities. In addition, the IDEA permits educators to place children with disabilities in special classes and/or separate facilities or institute other removals from the general education environment only when the nature or severity of the students' disabilities is such that instruction in general education classes cannot be achieved satisfactorily, even with supplementary aids and services. These provisions apply to students in private schools, institutions, and/ or other care facilities as well as to students in public schools and facilities (20 U.S.C. § 1412(a)(5)(A)).

The terms *least restrictive environment, inclusion,* and *mainstreaming* are often confused but are distinct. The difference between inclusion and mainstreaming is one of degree. Mainstreaming refers to the practice of placing special education class students in general education classes for a portion of the school day. Inclusion, on the other hand, refers to a philosophy where students with disabilities are enrolled in general education classes and are removed only when necessary to receive special education services. Often, special education services are provided within the general education environment so that students are not removed at all. While there is a slight difference between the two terms, for the sake of consistency, this book uses the more current term *inclusion. LRE* is the legal term used in the IDEA. The IDEA does not require inclusion in every situation but does mandate that all children be educated in environments that are the least restrictive possible and that removal from general education occur only when absolutely necessary.

Segregated Placements Are Not Prohibited

The Supreme Court, in *Rowley,* emphasized that special education programs must be provided in the LRE in order to be appropriate. In the early days of the IDEA, courts weighed the benefits of placements in less restrictive settings against the advantages of providing greater or more specialized services in segregated settings (*Bonadonna v. Cooperman,* 1985). The courts typically agreed that the LRE mandate was secondary to the provision of an appropriate instructional program (*Johnston v. Ann Arbor Public Schools,* 1983).

Insofar as the IDEA is premised on the notion that students with disabilities may be removed from the general education environment only to the extent necessary to provide needed special education services, one task for the courts is to ascertain whether required services warrant removal from the general education environment or if they can be provided in less restrictive settings. Even so, many of the early courts agreed that the LRE requirement could not be used to preclude placements in segregated settings if they were necessary to afford children with a FAPE (*Board of Education of East Windsor Regional School District v. Diamond,* 1986; *St. Louis Developmental Disabilities Center v. Mallory,* 1984). The courts thus allowed placements in restrictive environments when school officials showed that they could not deliver satisfactory education for children with disabilities in less restrictive settings, even with supplementary aids and services (*Lachman v. Illinois State Board of Education,* 1988; *Wilson v. Marana Unified School District,* 1984). The next section demonstrates that even with the current emphasis on inclusion, these legal principles are still valid.

Inclusion

Prior to 1989 most courts reviewing LRE issues agreed that inclusion was not required for all students with disabilities but had to have been provided, where appropriate, to the maximum extent feasible. In acknowledging the social benefits of inclusion, courts nevertheless noted that students should not have been placed in general education solely for the sake of inclusion. In balancing the need for specialized services against the LRE provision of the IDEA, early courts tipped the scales in favor of specialized services. In one notable exception, the Sixth Circuit, pointing out that the IDEA does not require mainstreaming or inclusion in every case, observed that it only had to be provided to the maximum extent appropriate (*Roncker v. Walter*, 1983). In what has become known as the portability standard, the court wrote that if the services that make particular placements better could be provided in less segregated settings, then the more restrictive placement would be inappropriate.

Beginning in the 1990s, the LRE provision of the IDEA played a more prominent role in litigation over the proper placement for students with disabilities. At this time, courts departed from previous case law and began to tip the scales in favor of inclusive programming for students with severe disabilities. As a result of cases from the Third (*Oberti v. Board of Education of the Borough of Clementon School District*, 1992, 1993), Fifth (*Daniel R.R. v. State Board of Education*, 1989), Ninth (*Sacramento City Unified School District, Board of Education v. Rachel H.*, 1994), and Eleventh (*Greer v. Rome City School District*, 1991) Circuits, courts now view the LRE provision as a mandatory requirement rather than a general goal of the IDEA.

The Fifth Circuit provided considerable guidance on the LRE issue in *Daniel R.R. v. State Board of Education* (*Daniel R.R.*) (1989). While the court affirmed that a substantially separate class was appropriate for a child with Down syndrome, it provided a general test for evaluating when students could be removed from general education settings. The court specified that students with severe disabilities may be removed from the general education environment when they cannot be satisfactorily educated in such a setting. In order to assist lower courts with LRE decisions, the panel created a test for considering when school boards have met their obligations under the IDEA's LRE provision. Borrowing language from the IDEA, the panel instructed lower courts to first examine whether education in general classrooms with supplementary aids and services could have been achieved satisfactorily. If school officials were unable to achieve this result and needed to offer children placements in special education settings, the court directed them to consider whether they included students in general education to the maximum extent appropriate. In answering its two-part inquiry, the Fifth Circuit advised lower courts to consider the ability of students to grasp the general education curriculum, the nature and severity of their disabilities, the effect that their presence would have had on the functioning of the general education classroom, their overall experience in the general education setting, and the amount of exposure the special education students would have to children who are not disabled.

The Fifth Circuit's two-part test has become the benchmark for LRE cases in recent years. Other courts have expanded on the *Daniel R.R.* test to provide a comprehensive set of guidelines for reviewing whether school boards have met their LRE obligations.

Decisions Ordering Less Restrictive Placements

The Eleventh Circuit, citing *Daniel R.R.,* upheld an earlier order placing a student with Down syndrome in a general education classroom (*Greer v. Rome City School District*, 1991). According to the court, before a school board could decide that children should be educated outside the general education setting, officials must evaluate whether their education cannot be achieved satisfactorily with one or more supplemental aids or services. In making such a determination, the court explained, school boards may compare the educational benefits that children will receive in regular classes with the benefits that they might acquire in special education environments. Noting that academic achievement is not the only benefit of inclusion, the court added that boards can also consider the nonacademic benefits that children receive, the effect that students with disabilities will have on classrooms and the education of peers, and the cost of the supplemental aids and services. However, the court declared that inclusion may not be appropriate if children would make significantly more progress in special education settings rather than in general education classrooms.

The Third Circuit provided guidelines on the extent to which school boards must go before recommending more restrictive placements. In another case involving the placement of a student with Down syndrome, the federal trial court in New Jersey observed that school boards have an affirmative obligation to consider placing students with disabilities in general education classrooms with the use of supplementary aids and services before exploring other alternatives (*Oberti v. Board of Education of the Borough of Clementon School District*, 1992, 1993). Citing the Fifth Circuit's *Daniel R.R.* test, the court was convinced that in order to meet the IDEA's goals, school officials must maximize opportunities for inclusion. The trial court decided that the preference for placements in the LRE can be rebutted only if officials can show that students' disabilities are so severe that they will receive little or no benefit from inclusion in regular classrooms, that they are so disruptive that the education of peers is impaired, or that the cost of providing supplementary services will have a negative effect on the provision of services to other children.

The court added that the IDEA requires school boards to supplement and realign their resources to move beyond the systems, structures, and practices that tend to unnecessarily segregate students with disabilities. The court recognized that including the student in a general education classroom clearly would have required a modification of the curriculum, but commented that this alone was not a legitimate basis on which to justify his exclusion. Describing inclusion as a right, not a privilege for a select few, the court placed ultimate responsibility on the board to show that the student could not have been educated in a general education setting with supplementary aids and services. Insofar as school officials were unable to do as the court directed, it ordered them to develop an inclusive educational plan for the student.

On further review, the Third Circuit affirmed the original order but applied a slightly different rationale. In so doing, the court adopted the Fifth Circuit's *Daniel R.R.* two-part test but expanded it with the notation that the judiciary should also consider the benefits that students with disabilities would receive in regular classrooms as opposed to segregated settings, along with the possible negative effects that their inclusion could have on the education of other children. The court agreed that a fundamental value of the right of a student with disabilities to an education is to associate with peers who do not have disabilities. The court emphasized that a full range of supplementary aids and services must be available to modify regular classroom programs to accommodate students with disabilities and that the fact that these children may learn differently from their being placed in general educational settings did not justify their exclusion from these kinds of placements.

In another major LRE dispute, the Ninth Circuit combined elements of the three previous decisions in providing a general summary of a school board's obligations (*Sacramento City Unified School District, Board of Education v. Rachel H.*, 1994). In affirming an earlier order, the Ninth Circuit decided school officials must consider four factors when devising LREs for students: the educational benefits of placements in regular classrooms, the nonacademic benefits of such placements, the effect that students would have on their teachers and other children in classes, and the costs of inclusion.

Decisions Approving More Restrictive Placements

The above opinions notwithstanding, students may be placed in more restrictive settings when necessary. In fact, the Ninth Circuit applied its own test in affirming that officials had the authority to transfer a student with serious behavioral problems to an off-campus alternative program (*Clyde K. v. Puyallup School District*, 1994). After finding that the student's disruptive behavior prevented him from learning in a general education setting and that he was receiving minimal nonacademic benefits from inclusion, the court approved the transfer. The court was persuaded by evidence that the student's presence had a negative effect on the staff and other children in the general education setting. In subsequent cases approving segregated placements, the same court was satisfied that inclusion that results in total failure is inappropriate (*Capistrano Unified School District v. Wartenberg*, 1995) and that some students may not derive any benefit from inclusion until they develop other skills (*Poolaw v. Bishop*, 1995).

Students may be moved from general educational environments to more restrictive settings if they are not making sufficient progress. The Fourth Circuit allowed a school board to transfer a student with autism to a self-contained special education class in interpreting the evidence as clearly demonstrating that he failed to make academic progress in a regular classroom even with supplementary aids and services (*Hartman v. Loudoun County Board of Education*,

1997). Further, the Seventh Circuit approved the transfer of a student with severe disabilities to a more restrictive setting in affirming that her academic progress in inclusionary settings was practically nonexistent (*Beth B. v. Van Clay*, 2002). As in the other cases, the student received supplementary aids and services in the general education setting. The Tenth Circuit also approved a more restrictive placement when a child could not be educated in a regular classroom even with supplementary aids and services (*T.W. ex rel. McCullough v. Unified School District No. 259*, 2005).

The Seventh Circuit, noting that a student's history in a public school setting with special education and related services was disastrous, affirmed a homebound instruction program (*School District of Wisconsin Dells v. Z.S. ex rel. Littlegeorge*, 2001, 2002). Insofar as the student had a long record of assaulting peers and staff members, the court was of the view that school administrators were reasonable in thinking that he would not have functioned in a regular school environment (Hazelkorn, 2004).

Placement in Neighborhood Schools

The LRE mandate does not require school boards to place students in their neighborhood schools in all situations. For reasons of economy, many school systems centralize parts of their special education programs, a practice that the courts uphold consistently. For example, the federal trial court in Virginia approved, and the Fourth Circuit affirmed, a centralized program for a high school student who was hearing impaired (*Barnett v. Fairfax County School Board*, 1989, 1991). Insofar as the high school that the student was required to attend was located five miles farther from his home than the neighborhood school, his parents objected to this arrangement and requested that a similar program be developed in the latter. Noting that the student was earning satisfactory grades, was participating in extracurricular activities, and was successfully included in the general education program, the court approved the centralized placement. Aware of the limited resources available to school boards, the court reasoned that centralized programs better served the interests of all students. The court concluded that centralizing programs for children with low-incidence disabilities allows school boards to better provide for all of their students. Using this rationale, the Fifth Circuit approved the placement of a hearing-impaired student in a regional school program (*Flour Bluff Independent School District v. Katherine M.*, 1996).

The Eighth Circuit approved a centralized program for a student who was wheelchair-bound in acknowledging that the school board was not required to modify her neighborhood school to make it wheelchair accessible (*Schuldt v. Mankato Independent School District No. 77*, 1991). By the same token, the First Circuit approved the placement of a student who had medical concerns in a program some distance from his home because it had a full-time nurse (*Kevin G. by Jo-Ann G. v. Cranston School Committee*, 1997). Thus if the services that students need are available only at centralized locations, school boards are not required to duplicate them in neighborhood schools in order to satisfy the IDEA. In fact, school officials have significant authority to select school sites for providing special education and related services for students with disabilities (*White v. Ascension Parish School Board*, 2003).

Placement Should Be as Close to Home as Possible

When it is not feasible to have students with disabilities attend their neighborhood schools, their placements should be as close to their homes as possible (34 C.F.R. § 300.116(a)(3)). This is particularly important when placements must be made outside of school systems. An order of the federal trial court in New Jersey illustrates this point. The court approved a mother's request to have her daughter with autism transferred from the facility she attended to one closer to her home (*Remis v. New Jersey Department of Human Services*, 1993). The court was convinced that the requested placement would have provided the child with an education that was comparable to the one that she received but would have been located within her hometown. In addition, the Tenth Circuit, acknowledging that students with disabilities should attend the schools they would have gone to if they were not disabled unless their IEPs required other arrangements, noted that when students' IEPs call for other arrangements, placements should be as close to their homes as possible (*Murray v. Montrose County School District*, 1995). The court added that the preference for placing students in neighborhood schools did not amount to a mandate.

PLACEMENT IN PRIVATE FACILITIES

The IDEA requires school boards to offer a continuum of placement alternatives to meet the special education and related services needs of students with disabilities (34 C.F.R. § 300.115(a)). This continuum includes placements in private day schools or residential facilities, if necessary. Placements in private day or residential schools are often necessary when students' disabilities are severe or are of a type that cannot adequately be addressed by a school system's own programs. When private placements are necessary, even in residential facilities, they must be at public expense (34 C.F.R. § 300.104). States or local school boards must bear all expenses, including nonmedical care and room and board, unless local boards enter into cost-share agreements with other agencies.

When Public School Programs Are Not Available

School boards are not required to place students with disabilities in private facilities if public school programs are available to provide them with a FAPE. However, particularly in smaller districts, appropriate public school programs are not always available. In these situations boards may be required to contract with private facilities to provide a FAPE. Even in large school systems it is not always feasible to develop programs for all students, and placements in private facilities are sometimes required.

Private school placements are most often sought for students with severe or profound disabilities or those with multiple disabilities. In one such case, the federal trial court in Rhode Island ordered, and the First Circuit affirmed, a residential placement for two students with learning disabilities and emotional disturbance in agreeing that the severity of their disabilities required a highly individualized, highly structured, and closely monitored program that could not have been provided in the public schools (*Colin K. v. Schmidt*, 1982, 1983).

When Twenty-Four-Hour Care and Instruction Are Needed

Courts often order residential placements when they find that the unique educational needs of students require constant care and supervision or instruction on a full-time basis. For some students, total immersion in a mode of instruction is required. Sometimes, only residential settings can provide students with the consistency that they need between educational and home environments. Residential placements are occasionally required for students with behavioral disorders. Insofar as most school boards do not operate residential programs, private placements must be obtained when students' needs require such services.

Residential placements are usually required when students suffer from severe or multiple disabilities. For example, in an early case, a federal trial court in Texas ordered a residential placement for a student who was diagnosed as being mentally retarded and schizophrenic after agreeing that she needed a constant structured environment, a 24-hour-per-day behavior-modification program, and an intensive language program (*Gladys J. v. Pearland Independent School District*, 1981). Further, a federal trial court in Tennessee ordered a residential placement for a student with mental retardation and emotional disturbance in asserting that a 24-hour behavior-modification program was required for her to receive a FAPE (*Brown v. Wilson County School Board*, 1990). The federal trial court in Massachusetts also found that the training a student with multiple disabilities needed had to be given around the clock, necessitating a residential placement (*Mohawk Trail Regional School District v. Shaun D.*, 1999).

Courts may require residential placements for students who are classified as emotionally disturbed. In an illustrative case, the federal trial court for the District of Columbia agreed with testimony indicating that a student with learning disabilities and an emotional disturbance required a 24-hour structured program in a residential placement (*Diamond v. McKenzie*, 1985). In like manner, a federal trial court in Alabama directed a school board to provide a residential placement for a student with emotional problems who required consistent and systematic round-the-clock behavioral training (*Chris D. v. Montgomery County Board of Education*, 1990). More recently, the First Circuit affirmed that a student who needed constant supervision and an in-school psychologist required a placement in a private facility (*Zayas v. Commonwealth of Puerto Rico*, 2005).

Residential placements are frequently required when students need consistency between their school and home environments. To this end, the Third Circuit affirmed that a student's unique combination of disabilities necessitated a greater degree of consistency of programming than most students with disabilities (*Kruelle v. New Castle*, 1981). The court acknowledged the need for such a placement because the student had intellectual challenges and cerebral palsy; could not walk, dress himself, or eat unaided; was not toilet trained; did not speak; and had a history of emotional difficulties. In a separate situation, the same court decreed that a student with multiple disabilities who required a constant, consistent, professionally administered behavior modification program was entitled to a residential placement (*Board of Education of East Windsor Regional School District v. Diamond*, 1986).

For Students Who Are Dangerous

Courts order residential placements for students who are shown to be dangerous or who have exhibited violent behavior. Again, students who exhibit aggressive, disruptive, or dangerous behavior may require specialized treatment approaches that must be consistently applied in the home and school environments. These students often need support services in addition to educational services that are better provided in residential settings.

A federal trial court in North Carolina approved a residential placement for a student who was diagnosed as having a schizoid personality and who exhibited behavior and learning problems throughout his schooling (*Hines v. Pitt County Board of Education*, 1980). The court was partly persuaded by the fact that the student's behavior deteriorated in previous public and private day school programs. Likewise, the Sixth Circuit directed school officials to provide a placement in a private residential facility for an eighteen-year-old student who had a history of psychiatric hospitalizations, after discovering that he required a secure, locked facility that specialized in long-term treatment (*Clevenger v. Oak Ridge School Board*, 1984).

When Emotional Support Is Needed

Judicial opinions are mixed in cases where the home environments of students with disabilities are not supportive or conducive to their making educational progress. While the need for residential placements under these circumstances may be clear, it is not necessarily a school board's responsibility to provide and fund entire programs. Often, the costs of residential placements are shared by school boards and other state social service agencies.

School boards may be required to provide full funding for residential placements when they are needed for students to learn. In such instances, as reflected by a case from New Jersey, the room and board portions of placements may be considered related services. In this case, the federal trial court maintained that a residential placement was necessary for learning to take place for a student who exhibited behavioral problems and had difficulty learning (*B.G. v. Cranford Board of Education*, 1988). The court viewed the student's emotional problems as being unseverable from the learning process. Similarly, the Eleventh Circuit affirmed that a student who suffered from a number of physical and emotional disabilities required an integrated program of educational and supportive services that could have been provided only in a residential setting (*Jefferson County Board of Education v. Breen*, 1988). In yet another case, the Second Circuit agreed that if a student needs a residential placement because emotional problems prevent the child from making meaningful educational progress, a school board must pay for its cost (*Mrs. B. v. Milford Board of Education*, 1997).

Placement for Other Than Educational Reasons

As noted earlier, when residential placements may be required for social, emotional, medical, or other noneducational reasons, school boards may not necessarily be responsible for all associated costs. Whether boards are responsible for the full costs of residential placements that are made for noneducational reasons depends on the extent to which the other conditions affect attainment of the educational objectives of student IEPs.

An early case from the District of Columbia provides an excellent example of a court's ordering a school board to provide and fund a residential placement for a student with antecedent needs. In deciding that the student's educational, emotional, social, and medical needs were so intimately intertwined that it was impossible to treat them separately, the court ordered a residential placement at public expense (*North v. District of Columbia Board of Education*, 1979). The record reflected that the student, who was diagnosed as being epileptic, emotionally disturbed, and learning disabled, required a residential placement that provided special education, medical supervision, and psychological support. The court wrote that insofar as it was impossible to distinguish which of the student's needs was dominant and assign financial responsibility to the appropriate agencies, the school board was required to assume the full costs of the placement.

Even when residential placements are made to address disabilities that stem from medical or psychiatric disorders, if it is necessary to make sure that students benefit from the educational components, then school boards are not absolved from paying for their costs (*Seattle School District, No. 1 v. B.S.*, 1996). As long as the primary reason for residential placements is educational, boards may be required to pay for them entirely (*County of San Diego v. California Special Education Hearing Office*, 1996). In contrast, the federal trial court in Delaware ascertained that a student with multiple disabilities did not require a residential placement in spite of having emotional problems because her difficulties did not interfere with her achievement (*Ahern v. Keene*, 1984). Even though the student's parents placed her in a residential facility after she began to exhibit behavioral problems in reaction to a stressful home environment, the court was satisfied that she was achieving academically up to expectations for her capacity.

An order of a federal trial court in Louisiana reveals that school boards are not responsible for problems students may have in their homes as long as they do not spill over into their classrooms (*Swift v. Rapides Parish Public School System*, 1993). Although his parents requested a residential placement for their son after his behavior at home became severe, school personnel testified that he was not violent at school and was progressing academically. The court thought that the public school placement was appropriate and that the board was not required to remedy the problems the student had at home. Along the same lines, a federal trial court in Illinois reasoned that a student who exhibited out-of-school behavior problems did not require a residential placement (*Board of Education of Oak Park & River Forest High School District No. 200 v. Illinois State Board of Education*, 1998). The First Circuit affirmed that even though a student experienced significant problems at home, he was not entitled to a residential placement because those difficulties did not affect his ability to learn (*Gonzalez v. Puerto Rico Department of Education*, 2001).

EXTENDED SCHOOL YEAR PROGRAMS

The IDEA and its regulations do not directly mandate the provision of special education and related services that extend beyond the traditional school year. However, if students with disabilities need extended school year (ESY) programming to receive a FAPE, then school boards must supply such programs. While most students with disabilities do not require services during school vacations, some with severe disabilities do need programming of this sort. Even so, since the IDEA and its regulations are silent as to the circumstances in which school boards must provide ESY programming, the courts have offered some guidance.

Early courts in three federal jurisdictions established the principle that programming beyond the traditional school year must be an available option. A federal trial court in Georgia, affirmed by the Eleventh Circuit, wrote that state practices that effectively limited educational programming to 180 days per year violated the IDEA (*Georgia Association of Retarded Citizens v. McDaniel*, 1981, 1983, 1984). Insofar as the IDEA requires the full consideration of the unique needs of each child, the court decided that any policy that prohibited or inhibited such full consideration violated the IDEA. In addition, the Fifth Circuit decreed that the IDEA did not tolerate policies or practices that imposed a rigid pattern on the education of students with disabilities, but instead favored the development of IEPs based on an individual evaluation (*Crawford v. Pittman*, 1983). The court ruled that categorical limitations on the length of special education programs were not consistent with the IDEA. Subsequently, a federal trial court in Missouri, affirmed by the Eighth Circuit, held that any policy that refused to consider ESY programming violated the IDEA (*Yaris v. Special School District, St. Louis County*, 1983, 1984).

Later cases established the principle that ESY programming is required when it is needed to prevent substantial regression if the time required for students to recoup lost skills would substantially impede their progress toward meeting the objectives contained in their IEPs. This axiom first surfaced in a case from Pennsylvania where a federal trial court discovered that some students with severe disabilities suffered substantial regression during breaks in programming and that the time required to regain lost skills was substantial (*Armstrong v. Kline*, 1979, 1980, 1981). The court concluded that these students would not receive a FAPE if they were not provided with programs in excess of the traditional 180-day school year.

Later cases further refined the so-called regression/recoupment standard. The Fifth Circuit reasoned that an ESY program is required when the benefits that accrued during a school year would be significantly jeopardized in the absence of a summer program (*Alamo Heights Independent School District v. State Board of Education*, 1986). The Sixth Circuit added that regression in the past does not need to be shown to justify the need for ESY programs (*Cordrey v. Euckert*, 1990). The court explained that the need for ESY programming could be established by expert opinion based on a professional individual evaluation. Still, past regression certainly would substantiate the need for an ESY.

The fact that the regression/recoupment standard has received almost universal adoption in ESY cases aside, some courts examined other factors in judging whether students should receive this form of programming. In such a case, the Tenth Circuit pointed out that educators must consider a student's degree of impairment, amount of regression, recoupment time, rate of progress, availability of other resources, and skill level in making such a determination (*Johnson v. Independent School District No. 4*, 1990).

The regression/recoupment standard does not require school officials to provide ESY programs in every instance where students with disabilities experience regressions. Courts recognize that regression during summer vacations is normal for all students. Courts require school boards to provide ESY programs only when the rate of regression and/or the recoupment time is excessive. A federal trial court in Wisconsin declined to order a school board to provide a summer school program because the student's regression was no greater than that of a child without disabilities (*Anderson v. Thompson*, 1980, 1981). The court asserted that the student would not have suffered an irreparable loss of progress without summer school. At the same time, the Sixth Circuit affirmed that if a child benefits meaningfully from an IEP for a traditional school year, an ESY program is unnecessary unless the IEP's benefits would be significantly jeopardized without summer programming (*Cordrey v. Euckert*, 1990). Moreover, the Fourth Circuit reiterated that ESY services are necessary only when the benefits that students with disabilities gain during school years are significantly jeopardized if children are not provided with educational programming during summer months (*MM v. School District of Greenville County*, 2002).

As with all cases under the IDEA, judgments regarding the duration of ESY programs must be made on individualized bases and may not be made in light of the length of existing programs (*Reusch v. Fountain*, 1994). Rather, the ESY services that school boards provide must be sufficient to accomplish the objective of preventing regression so that students may continue to make progress during the next school year (*J.P. ex rel. Popson v. West Clark Community Schools*, 2002).

❖

CASE NO. 7—DEFINITION OF FREE APPROPRIATE PUBLIC EDUCATION

BOARD OF EDUCATION OF THE HENDRICK HUDSON CENTRAL SCHOOL DISTRICT

v.

ROWLEY

Supreme Court of the United States, 1982

458 U.S. 176

Justice REHNQUIST delivered the opinion of the Court.

This case presents a question of statutory interpretation. Petitioners contend that the Court of Appeals and the District Court misconstrued the requirements imposed by Congress upon States which receive federal funds under the Education of the Handicapped Act. We agree and reverse the judgment of the Court of Appeals.

I

The Education of the Handicapped Act (Act) [now IDEA] . . . provides federal money to assist state and local agencies in educating handicapped children, and conditions such funding upon a State's compliance with extensive goals and procedures. The Act represents an ambitious federal effort to promote the education of handicapped children, . . . The Act's evolution and major provisions shed light on the question of statutory interpretation which is at the heart of this case. . . .

In order to qualify for federal financial assistance under the Act, a State must demonstrate that it "has in effect a policy that assures all handicapped children the right to a free appropriate public education." . . .

The "free appropriate public education" required by the Act is tailored to the unique needs of the handicapped child by means of an "individualized educational program" (IEP). . . . The IEP, which is prepared at a meeting between a qualified representative of the local educational agency, the child's teacher, the child's parents or guardian, and, where appropriate, the child, consists of a written document. . . .

II

This case arose in connection with the education of Amy Rowley, a deaf student at the Furnace Woods School in the Hendrick Hudson Central School District, Peekskill, N.Y. Amy has minimal residual hearing and is an excellent lipreader. During the year before she began attending Furnace Woods, a meeting between her parents and school administrators resulted in a decision to place her in a regular kindergarten class in order to determine what supplemental services would be necessary to her education. Several members of the school administration prepared for Amy's arrival by attending a course in sign-language interpretation, and a teletype machine was installed in the principal's office to facilitate communication with her parents who are also deaf. At the end of the trial period it was determined that Amy should remain in the kindergarten class, but that she should be provided with an FM hearing aid which would amplify words spoken into a wireless receiver by the teacher or fellow students during certain classroom activities. Amy successfully completed her kindergarten year.

As required by the Act, an IEP was prepared for Amy during the fall of her first-grade year. The IEP provided that Amy should be educated in a regular classroom at Furnace Woods, should continue to use the FM hearing aid, and should receive instruction from a tutor for the deaf for one hour each day and from a speech therapist for three hours each week. The Rowleys agreed with parts of the IEP, but insisted that Amy also be provided a qualified sign-language interpreter in all her academic classes in lieu of the assistance proposed in other parts of the IEP. Such an interpreter had been placed in Amy's kindergarten class for a 2-week experimental period, but the interpreter had reported that Amy did not need his services at that time. The school administrators likewise concluded that Amy did not need such an interpreter in her first-grade classroom. They reached this conclusion after consulting the school district's Committee on the Handicapped, which had received expert evidence from Amy's parents on the importance of a sign-language interpreter, received testimony from Amy's teacher and other persons familiar with her academic and social progress, and visited a class for the deaf.

When their request for an interpreter was denied, the Rowleys demanded and received a hearing before an independent examiner. After receiving evidence from both sides, the examiner agreed with the administrators' determination that an interpreter was not necessary because "Amy was achieving educationally, academically, and socially" without such assistance. . . . The examiner's decision was affirmed on appeal by the New York Commissioner of Education on the basis of substantial evidence in the record. . . . Pursuant to the Act's provision for judicial review, the Rowleys then brought an action in the United States District Court for the Southern District of New York, claiming that the administrators' denial of the sign-language interpreter constituted a denial of the "free appropriate public education" guaranteed by the Act.

The District Court found that Amy "is a remarkably well-adjusted child" who interacts and communicates well with her classmates and has "developed an extraordinary rapport" with her teachers. . . . It also found that "she performs better than the average child in her class and is advancing easily from grade to grade," but "that she understands considerably less of what goes on in class than she could if she were not deaf" and thus "is not learning as much, or performing as well academically, as she would without her handicap." This disparity between Amy's achievement and her potential led the court to decide that she was not receiving a "free appropriate public education," which the court defined as "an opportunity to achieve [her] full potential commensurate with the opportunity provided to other children." . . . According to the District Court, such a standard "requires that the potential of the handicapped child be measured and compared to his or her performance, and that the resulting differential or 'shortfall' be compared to the shortfall experienced by nonhandicapped children." The District Court's definition arose from its assumption that the responsibility for "giv[ing] content to the requirement of an 'appropriate education' " had "been left entirely to the [federal] courts and the hearing officers." . . .

A divided panel of the United States Court of Appeals for the Second Circuit affirmed. The Court of Appeals "agree[d] with the [D]istrict [C]ourt's conclusions of law," and held that its "findings of fact [were] not clearly erroneous ." . . .

We granted certiorari to review the lower courts' interpretation of the Act. . . . Such review requires us to consider two questions: What is meant by the Act's requirement of a "free appropriate public education"? And what is the role of state and federal courts in exercising the review granted by [the Act]? We consider these questions separately.

III

A

This is the first case in which this Court has been called upon to interpret any provision of the Act. As noted previously, the District Court and the Court of Appeals concluded that "[t]he Act itself does not define 'appropriate education,'" . . . but leaves "to the courts and the hearing officers" the responsibility of "giv[ing] content to the requirement of an 'appropriate education. . . .'" Petitioners contend that the definition of the phrase "free appropriate public education" used by the courts below overlooks the definition of that phrase actually found in the Act. Respondents agree that the Act defines "free appropriate public education," but contend that the statutory definition is not "functional" and thus "offers judges no guidance in their consideration of controversies involving 'the identification, evaluation, or educational placement of the child or the provision of a free appropriate public education. . . .'" The United States, appearing as *amicus curiae* on behalf of respondents, states that "[a]lthough the Act includes definitions of a 'free appropriate public education' and other related terms, the statutory definitions do not adequately explain what is meant by 'appropriate.' . . ."

We are loath to conclude that Congress failed to offer any assistance in defining the meaning of the principal substantive phrase used in the Act. It is beyond dispute that, contrary to the conclusions of the courts below, the Act does expressly define "free appropriate public education":

> "The term 'free appropriate public education' means *special education* and *related services* which (A) have been provided at public expense, under public supervision and direction, and without charge, (B) meet the standards of the State educational agency, (C) include an appropriate preschool, elementary, or secondary school education in the State involved, and (D) are provided in conformity with the individualized education program required under [this Act]."

> "Special education," as referred to in this definition, means "specially designed instruction, at no cost to parents or guardians, to meet the unique needs of a handicapped child, including classroom instruction, instruction in physical education, home instruction, and instruction in hospitals and institutions." . . . "Related services" are defined as "transportation, and such developmental, corrective, and other supportive services . . . as may be required to assist a handicapped child to benefit from special education."

Like many statutory definitions, this one tends toward the cryptic rather than the comprehensive, but that is scarcely a reason for abandoning the quest for legislative intent.

According to the definitions contained in the Act, a "free appropriate public education" consists of educational instruction specially designed to meet the unique needs of the handicapped child, supported by such services as are necessary to permit the child "to benefit" from the instruction. Almost as a checklist for adequacy under the Act, the definition also requires that such instruction and services be provided at public expense and under public supervision, meet the State's educational standards, approximate the grade levels used in the State's regular education, and comport with the child's IEP. Thus, if personalized instruction is being provided with sufficient supportive services to permit the child to benefit from the instruction, and the other items on the definitional checklist are satisfied, the child is receiving a "free appropriate public education" as defined by the Act.

Other portions of the statute also shed light upon congressional intent. Congress found that of the roughly eight million handicapped children in the United States at the time of enactment, one million were "excluded entirely from the public school system" and more than half were receiving an inappropriate education. . . . When these express statutory findings and priorities are read together with the Act's extensive procedural requirements and its definition of "free appropriate public education," the face of the statute evinces a congressional intent to bring previously excluded handicapped children into the public education systems of the States and to require the States to adopt *procedures* which would result in individualized consideration of and instruction for each child.

Noticeably absent from the language of the statute is any substantive standard prescribing the level of education to be accorded handicapped children. Certainly the language of the statute contains no requirement like the one imposed by the lower courts—that States maximize the potential of handicapped children "commensurate with the opportunity provided to other children." . . . That standard was expounded by the District Court without reference to the statutory definitions or even to the legislative history of the Act. Although we find the statutory definition of "free appropriate public education" to be helpful in our interpretation of the Act, there remains the question of whether the legislative history indicates a congressional intent that such education meet some additional substantive standard. For an answer, we turn to that history.

B

(i)

. . . By passing the Act, Congress sought primarily to make public education available to handicapped children. But in seeking to provide such access to public education, Congress did not impose upon the States any greater substantive educational standard than would be necessary to make such access meaningful. Indeed, Congress expressly "recognize[d] that in many instances the process of providing special education and related services to handicapped children is not guaranteed to produce any particular outcome." . . . Thus, the intent of the Act was more to open the door of public education to handicapped children on appropriate terms than to guarantee any particular level of education once inside.

Both the House and the Senate Reports attribute the impetus for the Act and its predecessors to two federal-court judgments rendered in 1971 and 1972. As the Senate Report states, passage of the Act "followed a series of landmark court cases establishing in law the right to education for all handicapped children." . . . The first case, *Pennsylvania Assn. for Retarded Children v. Commonwealth* (PARC), was a suit on behalf of retarded children challenging the constitutionality of a Pennsylvania statute which acted to exclude them from public education and training. The case ended in a consent decree which enjoined the State from "deny[ing] to any mentally retarded child *access* to a free public program of education and training." . . .

PARC was followed by *Mills v. Board of Education of District of Columbia,* . . . a case in which the plaintiff handicapped children had been excluded from the District of Columbia public schools. The court's judgment . . . provided that

> "no [handicapped] child eligible for a publicly supported education in the District of Columbia public schools shall be *excluded* from a regular school assignment by a Rule, policy, or practice of the Board of Education of the District of Columbia or its agents unless such child is provided (a) *adequate* alternative educational services suited to the child's needs, which may include special education or tuition grants, and (b) a constitutionally adequate prior hearing and periodic review of the child's status, progress, and the *adequacy* of any educational alternative." . . .

Mills and *PARC* both held that handicapped children must be given *access* to an adequate, publicly supported education. Neither case purports to require any particular substantive level of education. Rather, like the language of the Act, the cases set forth extensive procedures to be followed in formulating personalized educational programs for handicapped children. . . . The fact that both *PARC* and *Mills* are discussed at length in the legislative Reports suggests that the principles which they established are the principles which, to a significant extent, guided the drafters of the Act. Indeed, immediately after discussing these cases the Senate Report describes the 1974 statute as having "incorporated the major principles of the right to education cases." . . . Those principles in turn became the basis of the Act, which itself was designed to effectuate the purposes of the 1974 statute. . . .

That the Act imposes no clear obligation upon recipient States beyond the requirement that handicapped children receive some form of specialized education is perhaps best demonstrated by the fact that Congress, in explaining the need for the Act, equated an "appropriate education" to the receipt of some specialized educational services. . . .

(ii)

Respondents contend that "the goal of the Act is to provide each handicapped child with an equal educational opportunity." . . . We think, however, that the requirement that a State provide specialized educational services to handicapped children generates no additional requirement that the services so provided be sufficient to maximize each child's potential "commensurate with the opportunity provided other children . . ." and the United States correctly note that Congress sought "to provide assistance to the States in carrying out their responsibilities under . . . the Constitution of the United States to provide equal protection of the laws." . . . But we do not think that such statements imply a congressional intent to achieve strict equality of opportunity or services.

The educational opportunities provided by our public school systems undoubtedly differ from student to student, depending upon a myriad of factors that might affect a particular student's ability to assimilate information presented in the classroom. The requirement that States provide "equal" educational opportunities would thus seem to present an entirely unworkable standard requiring impossible measurements and comparisons. Similarly, furnishing handicapped children with only such services as are available to non-handicapped children would in all probability fall short of the statutory requirement of "free appropriate public education"; to require, on the other hand, the furnishing of every special service necessary to maximize each handicapped child's potential is, we think, further than Congress intended to go. Thus to speak in terms of "equal" services in one instance gives less than what is required by the Act and in another instance more. The theme of the Act is "free appropriate public education," a phrase which is too complex to be captured by the word "equal" whether one is speaking of opportunities or services.

The legislative conception of the requirements of equal protection was undoubtedly informed by the two District Court decisions referred to above. But cases such as *Mills* and *PARC* held simply that handicapped children may not be excluded entirely from public education. In *Mills,* the District Court said:

> "If sufficient funds are not available to finance all of the services and programs that are needed and desirable in the system then the available funds must be expended equitably in such a manner that no child is entirely excluded from a publicly supported education consistent with his needs and ability to benefit therefrom." . . .

The *PARC* court used similar language, saying "[i]t is the commonwealth's obligation to place each mentally retarded child in a free, public program of education and training appropriate to the child's capacity." . . . The right of access to free public education enunciated by these cases is significantly different from any notion of absolute equality of opportunity regardless of capacity. To the extent that Congress might have looked further than these cases which are mentioned in the legislative history, at the time of enactment of the Act this Court had held at least twice that the Equal Protection Clause of the Fourteenth Amendment does not require States to expend equal financial resources on the education of each child. . . .

In explaining the need for federal legislation, the House Report noted that "no congressional legislation has required a precise guarantee for handicapped children, i.e. a basic floor of opportunity that would bring into compliance all school districts with the constitutional right of equal protection with respect to handicapped children." Assuming that the Act was designed to fill the need identified in the House Report—that is, to provide a "basic floor of opportunity" consistent with equal protection—neither the Act nor its history persuasively demonstrates that Congress thought that equal protection required anything more than equal access. Therefore, Congress' desire to provide specialized educational services, even in furtherance of "equality," cannot be read as imposing any particular substantive educational standard upon the States.

The District Court and the Court of Appeals thus erred when they held that the Act requires New York to maximize the potential of each handicapped child commensurate with the opportunity provided nonhandicapped children. Desirable though that goal might be, it is not the standard that Congress imposed upon States which receive funding under the Act. Rather, Congress sought primarily to identify and evaluate handicapped children, and to provide them with access to a free public education.

(iii)

Implicit in the congressional purpose of providing access to a "free appropriate public education" is the requirement that the education to which access is provided be sufficient to confer some educational benefit upon the handicapped child. It would do little good for Congress to spend millions of dollars in providing access to a public education only to have the handicapped child receive no benefit from that education. The statutory definition of "free appropriate public education," in addition to requiring that States provide each child with "specially designed instruction," expressly requires the provision of "such . . . supportive services . . . as may be required to assist a handicapped child *to benefit* from special education." . . . We therefore conclude that the "basic floor of opportunity" provided by the Act consists of access to specialized instruction and related services which are individually designed to provide educational benefit to the handicapped child. . . .

The determination of when handicapped children are receiving sufficient educational benefits to satisfy the requirements of the Act presents a more difficult problem. The Act requires participating States to educate a wide spectrum of handicapped children, from the marginally hearing-impaired to the profoundly retarded and palsied. It is clear that the benefits obtainable by children at one end of the spectrum will differ dramatically from those obtainable by children at the other end, with infinite variations in between. One child may have little difficulty competing successfully in an academic setting with nonhandicapped children while another child may encounter great difficulty in acquiring even the most basic of self-maintenance skills. We do not attempt today to establish any one test for determining the adequacy of educational benefits conferred upon all children covered by the Act. Because in this case we are presented with a handicapped child who is receiving substantial specialized instruction and related services, and who is performing above average in the regular classrooms of a public school system, we confine our analysis to that situation.

The Act requires participating States to educate handicapped children with nonhandicapped children whenever possible. When that "mainstreaming" preference of the Act has been met and a child is being educated in the regular classrooms of a public school system, the system itself monitors the educational progress of the child. Regular examinations are administered, grades are awarded, and yearly advancement to higher grade levels is permitted for those children who attain an adequate knowledge of the course material. The grading and advancement system thus constitutes an important factor in determining educational benefit. Children who graduate from our public school systems are considered by our society to have been "educated" at least to the grade level they have completed, and access to an "education" for handicapped children is precisely what Congress sought to provide in the Act.

C

When the language of the Act and its legislative history are considered together, the requirements imposed by Congress become tolerably clear. Insofar as a State is required to provide a handicapped child with a "free appropriate public education," we hold that it satisfies this requirement by providing personalized instruction with sufficient support services to permit the child to benefit educationally from that instruction. Such instruction and services must be provided at public expense, must meet the State's educational standards, must approximate the grade levels used in the State's regular education, and must comport with the child's IEP. In addition, the IEP, and therefore the personalized instruction, should be formulated in accordance with the requirements of the Act and, if the child is being educated in the regular classrooms of the public education system, should be reasonably calculated to enable the child to achieve passing marks and advance from grade to grade....

IV

A

As mentioned in Part I, the Act permits "[a]ny party aggrieved by the findings and decision" of the state administrative hearings "to bring a civil action" in "any State court of competent jurisdiction or in a district court of the United States without regard to the amount in controversy." The complaint, and therefore the civil action, may concern "any matter relating to the identification, evaluation, or educational placement of the child, or the provision of a free appropriate public education to such child." ... In reviewing the complaint, the Act provides that a court "shall receive the record of the [state] administrative proceedings, shall hear additional evidence at the request of a party, and, basing its decision on the preponderance of the evidence, shall grant such relief as the court determines is appropriate." ...

The parties disagree sharply over the meaning of these provisions, petitioners contending that courts are given only limited authority to review for state compliance with the Act's procedural requirements and no power to review the substance of the state program, and respondents contending that the Act requires courts to exercise *de novo* review over state educational decisions and policies. We find petitioners' contention unpersuasive, for Congress expressly rejected provisions that would have so severely restricted the role of reviewing courts. In substituting the current language of the statute for language that would have made state administrative findings conclusive if supported by substantial evidence, the Conference Committee explained that courts were to make "independent decision[s] based on a preponderance of the evidence." ...

But although we find that this grant of authority is broader than claimed by petitioners, we think the fact that it is found in § 1415, which is entitled "Procedural safeguards," is not without significance. When the elaborate and highly specific procedural safeguards embodied in § 1415 are contrasted with the general and somewhat imprecise substantive admonitions contained in the Act, we think that the importance Congress attached to these procedural safeguards cannot be gainsaid. It seems to us no exaggeration to say that Congress placed every bit as much emphasis upon compliance with procedures giving parents and guardians a large measure of participation at every stage of the administrative process, ... as it did upon the measurement of the resulting IEP against a substantive standard. We think that the congressional emphasis upon full participation of concerned parties throughout the development of the IEP, as well as the requirements that state and local plans be submitted to the Secretary for approval, demonstrates the legislative conviction that adequate compliance with the procedures prescribed would in most cases assure much if not all of what Congress wished in the way of substantive content in an IEP.

Thus the provision that a reviewing court base its decision on the "preponderance of the evidence" is by no means an invitation to the courts to substitute their own notions of sound educational policy for those of the school authorities which they review. The very importance which Congress has attached to compliance with certain procedures in the preparation of an IEP would be frustrated if a court were permitted simply to set state decisions at nought. The fact that § 1415(e) requires that the reviewing court "receive the records of the [state] administrative proceedings" carries with it the implied requirement that due weight shall be given to these proceedings. And we find nothing in the Act to suggest that merely because Congress was rather sketchy in establishing substantive requirements, as opposed to procedural requirements for the preparation of an IEP, it intended that reviewing courts should have a free hand to impose substantive standards of review which cannot be derived from the Act itself. In short, the statutory authorization to grant "such relief as the court determines is appropriate" cannot be read without reference to the obligations, largely procedural in nature, which are imposed upon recipient States by Congress.

Therefore, a court's inquiry in suits brought under [the Act] is twofold. First, has the State complied with the procedures set forth in the Act? And second, is the individualized educational program developed through the Act's procedures reasonably calculated to enable the child to receive educational benefits? If these requirements are met, the State has complied with the obligations imposed by Congress and the courts can require no more.

B

In assuring that the requirements of the Act have been met, courts must be careful to avoid imposing their view of preferable educational methods upon the States. The primary responsibility for formulating the education to be accorded a handicapped child, and for choosing the educational method most suitable to the child's needs, was left by the Act to state and local educational agencies in cooperation with the parents or guardian of the child. . . .

We previously have cautioned that courts lack the "specialized knowledge and experience" necessary to resolve "persistent and difficult questions of educational policy." . . . We think that Congress shared that view when it passed the Act. As already demonstrated, Congress' intention was not that the Act displace the primacy of States in the field of education, but that States receive funds to assist them in extending their educational systems to the handicapped. Therefore, once a court determines that the requirements of the Act have been met, questions of methodology are for resolution by the States.

V

Entrusting a child's education to state and local agencies does not leave the child without protection. Congress sought to protect individual children by providing for parental involvement in the development of state plans and policies . . . and in the formulation of the child's individual educational program. . . . As this very case demonstrates, parents and guardians will not lack ardor in seeking to ensure that handicapped children receive all of the benefits to which they are entitled by the Act.

VI

Applying these principles to the facts of this case, we conclude that the Court of Appeals erred in affirming the decision of the District Court. Neither the District Court nor the Court of Appeals found that petitioners had failed to comply with the procedures of the Act, and the findings of neither court would support a conclusion that Amy's educational program failed to comply with the substantive requirements of the Act. On the contrary, the District Court found that the "evidence firmly establishes that Amy is receiving an 'adequate' education, since she performs better than the average child in her class and is advancing easily from grade to grade." ... In light of this finding, and of the fact that Amy was receiving personalized instruction and related services calculated by the Furnace Woods school administrators to meet her educational needs, the lower courts should not have concluded that the Act requires the provision of a sign-language interpreter. Accordingly, the decision of the Court of Appeals is reversed, and the case is remanded for further proceedings consistent with this opinion.

So ordered.

Notes

1. In a dissenting opinion Justice White wrote:

Providing a teacher with a loud voice would not meet Amy's needs and would not satisfy the Act. The basic floor of opportunity is instead, as the courts below recognized, intended to eliminate the effects of the handicap, at least to the extent that the child will be given an equal opportunity to learn if that is reasonably possible. Amy Rowley, without a sign-language interpreter, comprehends less than half of what is said in the classroom—less than half of what normal children comprehend. This is hardly an equal opportunity to learn, even if Amy makes passing grades. (p. 215)

Did the Court do little more than provide Amy Rowley with a "teacher with a loud voice"?

2. In addition to providing a more concrete definition of what constitutes an appropriate education, *Rowley* provided instructions for lower courts on how to resolve cases involving an appropriate education. This is discussed in greater detail in Chapter 7.

3. As noted, states are free to establish higher standards of appropriateness. As such, states may adopt the "commensurate with the opportunities provided to other children" standard enunciated by the lower courts in *Rowley*. Check the standard in your state.

4. By way of update, Amy Rowley is currently a clinical instructor in the Department of Exceptional Children at the University of Wisconsin in Milwaukee, where she coordinates the American Sign Language program. She earned a bachelor's degree from Gallaudet University and a master's degree from Western Maryland College. At this writing she is pursuing a doctorate in Second Language Education at the University of Wisconsin.

CASE NO. 8—LEAST RESTRICTIVE ENVIRONMENT

SACRAMENTO CITY UNIFIED SCHOOL DISTRICT, BOARD OF EDUCATION

v.

RACHEL H.

United States Court of Appeals, Ninth Circuit, 1994.

14 F.3d 1398

SNEED, Circuit Judge:

The Sacramento Unified School District ("the District") timely appeals the district court's judgment in favor of Rachel Holland ("Rachel") and the California State Department of Education. The court found that the appropriate placement for Rachel under the Individuals with Disabilities Act ("IDEA") was full-time in a regular second grade classroom with some supplemental services. The District contends that the appropriate placement for Rachel is half-time in special education classes and half-time in a regular class. We affirm the judgment of the district court.

I.

FACTS AND PRIOR PROCEEDINGS

Rachel Holland is now 11 years old and is mentally retarded. She was tested with an I.Q. of 44. She attended a variety of special education programs in the District from 1985–89. Her parents sought to increase the time Rachel spent in a regular classroom, and in the fall of 1989, they requested that Rachel be placed full-time in a regular classroom for the 1989–90 school year. The District rejected their request and proposed a placement that would have divided Rachel's time between a special education class for academic subjects and a regular class for non-academic activities such as art, music, lunch, and recess. The district court found that this plan would have required moving Rachel at least six times each day between the two classrooms. The Hollands instead enrolled Rachel in a regular kindergarten class at the Shalom School, a private school. Rachel remained at the Shalom School in regular classes and at the time the district court rendered its opinion was in the second grade.

The Hollands and the District were able to agree on an Individualized Education Program ("IEP") for Rachel. Although the IEP is required to be reviewed annually, . . . because of the dispute between the parties, Rachel's IEP has not been reviewed since January 1990.

The Hollands appealed the District's placement decision to a state hearing officer pursuant to [the IDEA]. They maintained that Rachel best learned social and academic skills in a regular classroom and would not benefit from being in a special education class. The District contended Rachel was too severely disabled to benefit from full-time placement in a regular class. The hearing officer concluded that the District had failed to make an adequate effort to educate Rachel in a regular class pursuant to the IDEA. The officer found that (1) Rachel had benefited from her regular kindergarten class—that she was motivated to learn and learned by imitation and modeling; (2) Rachel was not disruptive in a regular classroom; and (3) the District had overstated the cost of putting Rachel in regular education—that the cost would not be so great that it weighed against placing her in a regular classroom. The hearing officer ordered the District to place Rachel in a regular classroom with support services, including a special education consultant and a part-time aide.

The District appealed this determination to the district court. Pursuant to [the IDEA], the parties presented additional evidence at an evidentiary hearing. The court affirmed the decision of the hearing officer that Rachel should be placed full-time in a regular classroom.

In considering whether the District proposed an appropriate placement for Rachel, the district court examined the following factors: (1) the educational benefits available to Rachel in a regular classroom, supplemented with appropriate aids and services, as compared with the educational benefits of a special education classroom; (2) the non-academic benefits of interaction with children who were not disabled; (3) the effect of Rachel's presence on the teacher and other children in the classroom; and (4) the cost of mainstreaming Rachel in a regular classroom.

1. Educational Benefits

The district court found the first factor, educational benefits to Rachel, weighed in favor of placing her in a regular classroom. . . . The court noted that the District's evidence focused on Rachel's limitations but did not establish that the educational opportunities available through special education were better or equal to those available in a regular classroom. Moreover, the court found that the testimony of the Hollands' experts was more credible because they had more background in evaluating children with disabilities placed in regular classrooms and that they had a greater opportunity to observe Rachel over an extended period of time in normal circumstances. The district court also gave great weight to the testimony of Rachel's current teacher, Nina Crone, whom the court found to be an experienced, skillful teacher. Ms. Crone stated that Rachel was a full member of the class and participated in all activities. Ms. Crone testified that Rachel was making progress on her IEP goals: She was learning one-to-one correspondence in counting, was able to recite the English and Hebrew alphabets, and was improving her communication abilities and sentence lengths.

The district court found that Rachel received substantial benefits in regular education and that all of her IEP goals could be implemented in a regular classroom with some modification to the curriculum and with the assistance of a part-time aide.

2. Non-academic Benefits

The district court next found that the second factor, non-academic benefits to Rachel, also weighed in favor of placing her in a regular classroom. The court noted that the Hollands' evidence indicated that Rachel had developed her social and communications skills as well as her self-confidence from placement in a regular class, while the District's evidence tended to show that Rachel was not learning from exposure to other children and that she was isolated from her classmates. The court concluded that the differing evaluations in large part reflected the predisposition of the evaluators. The court found the testimony of Rachel's mother and her current teacher to be the most credible.

These witnesses testified regarding Rachel's excitement about school, learning, and her new friendships and Rachel's improved self-confidence.

3. Effect on the Teacher and Children in the Regular Class

The district court next addressed the issue of whether Rachel had a detrimental effect on others in her regular classroom. The court looked at two aspects: (1) whether there was detriment because the child was disruptive, distracting or unruly, and (2) whether the child would take up so much of the teacher's time that the other students would suffer from lack of attention. The witnesses of both parties agreed that Rachel followed directions and was well-behaved and not a distraction in class. The court found the most germane evidence on the second aspect came from Rachel's second grade teacher, Nina Crone, who testified that Rachel did not interfere with her ability to teach the other children and in the future would require only a part-time aide. Accordingly, the district court determined that the third factor, the effect of Rachel's presence on the teacher and other children in the classroom weighed in favor of placing her in a regular classroom.

4. Cost

Finally, the district court found that the District had not offered any persuasive or credible evidence to support its claim that educating Rachel in a regular classroom with appropriate services would be significantly more expensive than educating her in the District's proposed setting.

The District contended that it would cost $109,000 to educate Rachel full-time in a regular classroom. This figure was based on the cost of providing a full-time aide for Rachel plus an estimated $80,000 for school-wide sensitivity training. The court found that the District did not establish that such training was necessary. Further, the court noted that even if such training were necessary, there was evidence from the California Department of Education that the training could be had at no cost. Moreover, the court found it would be inappropriate to assign the total cost of the training to Rachel when other children with disabilities would benefit. In addition, the court concluded that the evidence did not suggest that Rachel required a full-time aide.

In addition, the court found that the District should have compared the cost of placing Rachel in a special class of approximately 12 students with a full-time special education teacher and two full-time aides and the cost of placing her in a regular class with a part-time aide. The District provided no evidence of this cost comparison.

The court also was not persuaded by the District's argument that it would lose significant funding if Rachel did not spend at least 51% of her time in a special education class. The court noted that a witness from the California Department of Education testified that waivers were available if a school district sought to adopt a program that did not fit neatly within the funding guidelines. The District had not applied for a waiver.

By inflating the cost estimates and failing to address the true comparison, the District did not meet its burden of proving that regular placement would burden the District's funds or adversely affect services available to other children. Therefore, the court found that the cost factor did not weigh against mainstreaming Rachel.

The district court concluded that the appropriate placement for Rachel was full-time in a regular second grade classroom with some supplemental services and affirmed the decision of the hearing officer....

IV.

DISCUSSION...

B. Mainstreaming Requirements of the IDEA

1. The Statute

The IDEA provides that each state must establish:

[P]rocedures to assure that, to the maximum extent appropriate, children with disabilities ... are educated with children who are not disabled, and that special classes, separate schooling, or other removal of children with disabilities from the regular educational environment occurs only when the nature or severity of the disability is such that education in regular classes with the use of supplementary aids and services cannot be achieved satisfactorily....

This provision sets forth Congress's preference for educating children with disabilities in regular classrooms with their peers....

3. Test for Determining Compliance with the IDEA's Mainstreaming Requirement

We have not adopted or devised a standard for determining the presence of compliance with [the IDEA's least restrictive environment provision] ....
Although the district court relied principally on *Daniel R.R.* and *Greer,* it did not specifically adopt the *Daniel R.R.* test over the *Roncker* test. Rather, it employed factors found in both lines of cases in its analysis. The result was a four-factor balancing test in which the court considered (1) the educational benefits of placement full-time in a regular class; (2) the non-academic benefits of such placement; (3) the effect Rachel had on the teacher and children in the regular class; and (4) the costs of mainstreaming Rachel. This analysis directly addresses the issue of the appropriate placement for a child with disabilities under the requirements of [the IDEA]. Accordingly, we approve and adopt the test employed by the district court.

4. The District's Contentions on Appeal

The District strenuously disagrees with the district court's findings that Rachel was receiving academic and non-academic benefits in a regular class and did not have a detrimental effect on the teacher or other students. It argues that the court's findings were contrary to the evidence of the state Diagnostic Center and that the court should not have been persuaded by the testimony of Rachel's teacher, particularly her testimony that Rachel would need only a part-time aide in the future. The district court, however, conducted a full evidentiary hearing and made a thorough analysis. The court found the Hollands' evidence to be more persuasive. Moreover, the court asked Rachel's teacher extensive questions regarding Rachel's need for a part-time aide. We will not disturb the findings of the district court.

The District is also not persuasive on the issue of cost. The District now claims that it will lose up to $190,764 in state special education funding if Rachel is not enrolled in a special education class at least 51% of the day. However, the District has not sought a waiver pursuant to California Education Code § 56101. This section provides that (1) any school district may request a waiver of any provision of the Education Code if the waiver is necessary or beneficial to the student's IEP, and (2) the Board may grant the waiver when failure to do so would hinder compliance with federal mandates for a free appropriate education for children with disabilities. . . .

Finally, the District . . . argues that Rachel must receive her academic and functional curriculum in special education from a specially credentialed teacher. . . . [T]he District's proposition that Rachel must be taught by a special education teacher runs directly counter to the congressional preference that children with disabilities be educated in regular classes with children who are not disabled. . . .

We affirm the judgment of the district court. While we cannot determine what the appropriate placement is for Rachel at the present time, we hold that the determination of the present and future appropriate placement for Rachel should be based on the principles set forth in this opinion and the opinion of the district court.

Notes

1. The Ninth Circuit ruled that although the trial court referenced cases from other circuits, it did not specifically adopt one test over another. How does the Ninth Circuit's test incorporate elements of the tests established by other circuits?

2. The student in *Rachel H.* (like the plaintiffs in several other LRE disputes) attended an elementary school. Would the results have been different if the student had been older and the issue was inclusion in a high school environment?

3. During the two years following *Rachel H.,* the Ninth Circuit used its own LRE test with different results in *Clyde K. v. Puyallup School District* (1994), *Capistrano Unified School District v. Wartenberg* (1995), and *Poolaw v. Bishop* (1995). Compare and contrast these cases. How did the unique facts of each case dictate their respective outcomes?

REFERENCES

Adam J. ex rel. Robert J v. Keller Independent School District, 328 F.3d 804 (5th Cir. 2003).

Age v. Bullitt County Public Schools, 673 F.2d 141 (6th Cir. 1982).

Ahern v. Keene, 593 F. Supp. 902 (D. Del. 1984).

A.I. ex rel. Iapalucci v. District of Columbia, 402 F. Supp.2d 152 (D.D.C. 2005).

Alamo Heights Independent School District v. State Board of Education, 790 F.2d 1153 (5th Cir. 1986).

Alexis v. Board of Education for Baltimore County Public Schools, 286 F. Supp.2d 551 (D. Md. 2003).

Anderson v. Thompson, 495 F. Supp. 1256 (E.D. Wis. 1980), *affirmed*, 658 F.2d 1205 (7th Cir. 1981).

Angevine v. Smith, 959 F.2d 292 (D.C. Cir. 1992).

Armstrong v. Kline, 476 F. Supp. 583 (E.D. Pa. 1979), *remanded sub nom. Battle v. Commonwealth of Pennsylvania*, 629 F.2d 269 (3d Cir. 1980), *on remand* 513 F. Supp. 425 (E.D. Pa. 1981).

Barnett v. Fairfax County School Board, 721 F. Supp. 757 (E.D. Va. 1989), *affirmed*, 927 F.2d 146 (4th Cir. 1991).

Barwacz v. Michigan Department of Education, 681 F. Supp. 427 (W.D. Mich. 1988).

Bertolucci v. San Carlos Elementary School District, 721 F. Supp. 1150 (N.D. Cal. 1989).

Beth B. v. Van Clay, 282 F.3d 493 (7th Cir. 2002).

B.G. v. Cranford Board of Education, 702 F. Supp. 1140 (D.N.J. 1988).

B.L. ex rel. Mr. and Mrs. T.L. v. New Britain Board of Education, 394 F. Supp.2d 522 (D. Conn. 2005).

Blackmon v. Springfield R-XII School District, 198 F.3d 648 (8th Cir. 1999).

Board of Education of the Avon Lake City School District v. Patrick M., 9 F. Supp.2d 811 (N.D. Ohio 1998).

Board of Education of the County of Cabell v. Dienelt, 843 F.2d 813 (4th Cir. 1988).

Board of Education of East Windsor Regional School District v. Diamond, 808 F.2d 987 (3d Cir. 1986).

Board of Education of Hendrick Hudson Central School District v. Rowley, 458 U.S. 176 (1982).

Board of Education of Oak Park & River Forest High School District No. 200 v. Illinois State Board of Education, 21 F. Supp.2d 862 (N.D. Ill. 1998), *vacated and remanded on other grounds*, 207 F.3d 931 (7th Cir. 2000).

Bonadonna v. Cooperman, 619 F. Supp. 401 (D.N.J. 1985).

Bonnie Ann F. v. Calallen Independent School District, 835 F. Supp. 340 (S.D. Tex. 1993), *affirmed*, 40 F.3d 386 (5th Cir. 1994) (mem.).

Brimmer v. Traverse City Area Public Schools, 872 F. Supp. 447 (W.D. Mich. 1994).

Brown v. Wilson County School Board, 747 F. Supp. 436 (M.D. Tenn. 1990).

Buchholtz v. Iowa Department of Public Instruction, 315 N.W.2d 789 (Iowa 1982).

Burke County Board of Education v. Denton, 895 F.2d 973 (4th Cir. 1990).

Campbell v. Talladega County Board of Education, 518 F. Supp. 47 (N.D. Ala. 1981).

Capistrano Unified School District v. Wartenberg, 59 F.3d 884 (9th Cir. 1995).

Carter v. Florence County School District Four, 950 F.2d 156 (4th Cir. 1991), *affirmed on other grounds sub nom. Florence County School District Four v. Carter*, 510 U.S. 7 (1993).

Cerra v. Pawling Central School District, 427 F.3d 186 (2d Cir. 2005).

Chris D. v. Montgomery County Board of Education, 743 F. Supp. 1524 (M.D. Ala. 1990).

Chuhran v. Walled Lake Consolidated Schools, 839 F. Supp. 465 (E.D. Mich. 1993).

Clevenger v. Oak Ridge School Board, 744 F.2d 514 (6th Cir. 1984).

Clyde K. v. Puyallup School District, 35 F.3d 1396 (9th Cir. 1994).

Coale v. State Department of Education, 162 F. Supp.2d 316 (D. Del. 2001).

Colin K. v. Schmidt, 536 F. Supp. 1375 (D.R.I. 1982), *affirmed*, 715 F.2d 1 (1st Cir. 1983).

Conklin, In re, 946 F.2d 306 (4th Cir. 1991).

Cordrey v. Euckert, 917 F.2d 1460 (6th Cir. 1990).

County of San Diego v. California Special Education Hearing Office, 93 F.3d 1458 (9th Cir. 1996).

Crawford v. Pittman, 708 F.2d 1028 (5th Cir. 1983).

Cypress-Fairbanks Independent School District v. Michael F., 931 F. Supp. 471 (S.D. Tex. 1995), *affirmed*, 118 F.3d 245 (5th Cir. 1997).

Daniel G. v. Delaware Valley School District, 813 A.2d 36 (Pa. Commw. Ct. 2002).

Daniel R.R. v. State Board of Education, 874 F.2d 1036 (5th Cir. 1989).

David D. v. Dartmouth School Committee, 775 F.2d 411 (1st Cir. 1985).

Delaware County Intermediate Unit #25 v. Martin K., 831 F. Supp. 1206 (E.D. Pa. 1993).

Diamond v. McKenzie, 602 F. Supp. 632 (D.D.C. 1985).

Doe v. Alabama State Department of Education, 915 F.2d 651 (11th Cir. 1990).

Doe v. Defendant I, 898 F.2d 1186 (6th Cir. 1990).

Dong v. Board of Education of the Rochester Community Schools, 197 F.3d 793 (6th Cir. 1999).

El Paso Independent School District v. Robert W., 898 F. Supp. 442 (W.D. Tex. 1995).

E.S. v. Independent School District, No 196, 135 F.3d 566 (8th Cir. 1998).

Flour Bluff Independent School District v. Katherine M., 91 F.3d 689 (5th Cir. 1996).

Fuhrmann v. East Hanover Board of Education, 993 F.2d 1031 (3d Cir. 1993).

Geis v. Board of Education of Parsippany-Troy Hills, 774 F.2d 575 (3d Cir. 1985).

Georgia Association of Retarded Citizens v. McDaniel, 511 F. Supp. 1263 (N.D. Ga. 1981), *affirmed*, 716 F.2d 1565 (11th Cir. 1983), *vacated and remanded*, 468 U.S. 1213 (1984) (mem.), *modified*, 740 F.2d 902 (11th Cir. 1984).

Gill v. Columbia 93 School District, 217 F.3d 1027 (8th Cir. 2000).

Gladys J. v. Pearland Independent School District, 520 F. Supp. 869 (S.D. Tex. 1981).

Gonzalez v. Puerto Rico Department of Education, 254 F.3d 350 (1st Cir. 2001).

Greer v. Rome City School District, 950 F.2d 688, (11th Cir. 1991), *withdrawn* 956 F.2d 1025 (11th Cir. 1992), *reinstated* 967 F.2d 470 (11th Cir. 1992), *affirming* 762 F. Supp. 936 (N.D. Ga. 1990).

Hall v. Vance County Board of Education, 774 F.2d 629 (4th Cir. 1985).

Hampton School District v. Dobrowolski, 976 F.2d 48 (1st Cir. 1992).

Hartman v. Loudoun County Board of Education, 118 F.3d 996 (4th Cir. 1997).

Hazelkorn, M. (2004). Reasonable v. reasonableness: The *Littlegeorge* standard. *Education Law Reporter, 182*, 655–682.

Hessler v. State Board of Education of Maryland, 700 F.2d 134 (4th Cir. 1983).

Hiller v. Board of Education of the Brunswick Central School District, 743 F. Supp. 958 (N.D.N.Y. 1990).

Hines v. Pitt County Board of Education, 497 F. Supp. 403 (E.D.N.C. 1980).

Independent School District No. 283 v. S.D. by J.D., 88 F.3d 556 (8th Cir. 1996), *affirming* 948 F. Supp. 860 (D. Minn. 1995).

Individuals with Disabilities Education Act, 20 U.S.C. §§ 1400–1482 (2005).

Jefferson County Board of Education v. Breen, 853 F.2d 853 (11th Cir. 1988).

Johnson v. Independent School District No. 4 of Bixby, 921 F.2d 1022 (10th Cir. 1990).

Johnson v. Lancaster-Lebanon Intermediate Unit 13, Lancaster City School District, 757 F. Supp. 606 (E.D. Pa. 1991).

Johnston v. Ann Arbor Public Schools, 569 F. Supp. 1502 (E.D. Mich. 1983).

J.P. ex rel. Popson v. West Clark Community Schools, 230 F. Supp.2d 910 (S.D. Ind. 2002).

J.S.K. v. Hendry County School Board, 941 F.2d 1563 (11th Cir. 1991).

Karl v. Board of Education of Genesco Central School District, 736 F.2d (2d Cir. 1984).

Kevin G. by Jo-Ann G. v. Cranston School Committee, 130 F.3d 481 (1st Cir. 1997).

Kruelle v. New Castle, 642 F.2d 687 (3d Cir. 1981).

Lachman v. Illinois State Board of Education, 852 F.2d 290 (7th Cir. 1988).

Lagares v. Camdenton R-III School District, 68 S.W.3d 518 (Mo. Ct. App. 2001).

Laura M. v. Special School District, EHLR 552:152 (D. Minn. 1980).

Lewis v. School Board of Loudoun County, 808 F. Supp. 523 (E.D. Va. 1992).

Livingston v. DeSoto County School District, 782 F. Supp. 1173 (N.D. Miss. 1992).

Logue v. Shawnee Mission Public School Unified School District No. 512, 959 F. Supp. 1338
(D. Kan. 1997), *affirmed*, 153 F.3d 727 (10th Cir. 1998) (mem.).

Manchester School District v. Christopher B., 807 F. Supp. 860 (D.N.H. 1992).

Mavis v. Sobol, 839 F. Supp. 968 (N.D.N.Y. 1994).

M.C. ex rel. J.C. v. Central Regional School District, 81 F.3d 389 (3d Cir. 1996).

McDowell v. Fort Bend Independent School District, 737 F. Supp. 386 (S.D. Tex. 1990).

MM v. School District of Greenville County, 303 F.3d 523 (4th Cir. 2002).

Mohawk Trail Regional School District v. Shaun D., 35 F. Supp.2d 34 (D. Mass. 1999).

Mrs. B. v. Milford Board of Education, 103 F.3d 1114 (2d Cir. 1997).

Murray v. Montrose County School District, 51 F.3d 921 (10th Cir.1995).

Myles S. v. Montgomery County Board of Education, 824 F. Supp. 1549 (M.D. Ala. 1993).

Norris v. Massachusetts Department of Education, 529 F. Supp. 759 (D. Mass. 1981).

North v. District of Columbia Board of Education, 471 F. Supp. 136 (D.D.C. 1979).

Oberti v. Board of Education of the Borough of Clementon School District, 789 F. Supp. 1322,
(D.N.J. 1992), 801 F. Supp. 1393 (D.N.J. 1992), *affirmed*, 995 F.2d 1204 (3d Cir. 1993).

O'Hara, J. (1985). Determinants of an appropriate education under 94–142. *Education
Law Reporter, 27*, 1037–1045.

Ojai Unified School District v. Jackson, 4 F.3d 1467 (9th Cir. 1993).

Osborne, A. G. (1992). Legal standards for an appropriate education in the post-*Rowley*
era. *Exceptional Children, 58*, 488–494.

Osborne, A. G. (2004). To what extent can procedural violations of the IDEA render an
IEP invalid? *Education Law Reporter, 185*, 15–29.

O'Toole v. Olathe District Schools Unified School District No. 233, 963 F. Supp. 1000 (D. Kan.
1997), *affirmed*, 144 F.3d 692 (10th Cir. 1998).

Petersen v. Hastings Public Schools, 831 F. Supp. 742 (D. Neb. 1993), *affirmed*, 31 F.3d 705
(8th Cir. 1994).

Pink v. Mt. Diablo Unified School District, 738 F. Supp. 345 (N.D. Cal. 1990).

Polk v. Central Susquehanna Intermediate Unit 16, 853 F.2d 171 (3d Cir. 1988).

Poolaw v. Bishop, 67 F.3d 830 (9th Cir. 1995).

Puffer v. Raynolds, 761 F. Supp. 838 (D. Mass. 1988).

Remis v. New Jersey Department of Human Services, 815 F. Supp. 141 (D.N.J. 1993).

Renner v. Board of Education of the Public Schools of the City of Ann Arbor, 185 F.3d 635 (6th
Cir. 1999).

Rettig v. Kent City School District, 539 F. Supp. 768 (N.D. Ohio 1981), *affirmed in part,
vacated and remanded in part*, 720 F.2d 463 (6th Cir. 1983), *reversed*, 788 F.2d 328 (6th Cir.
1986).

Reusch v. Fountain, 872 F. Supp. 1421 (D. Md. 1994).

Roland M. v. Concord School Committee, 910 F.2d 983 (1st Cir. 1990).

Roncker v. Walter, 700 F.2d 1058 (6th Cir. 1983).

Sacramento City Unified School District, Board of Education v. Rachel H., 14 F.3d 1398 (9th Cir. 1994), *affirming sub nom. Board of Education, Sacramento City Unified School District v. Holland,* 786 F. Supp. 874 (E.D. Cal. 1992).

School District of Wisconsin Dells v. Z.S. ex rel. Littlegeorge, 184 F. Supp.2d 860 (W.D. Wis. 2001), 295 F.3d 671 (7th Cir. 2002).

Schuldt v. Mankato Independent School District No. 77, 937 F.2d 1357 (8th Cir. 1991).

Seattle School District, No. 1 v. B.S., 82 F.3d 1493 (9th Cir.1996).

Springdale School District v. Grace, 656 F.2d 300 (8th Cir. 1981), 693 F.2d 41 (8th Cir. 1982).

St. Louis Developmental Disabilities Center v. Mallory, 591 F. Supp. 1416 (W.D. Mo. 1984).

Stock v. Massachusetts Hospital School, 467 N.E.2d 448 (Mass. 1984).

Straube v. Florida Union Free School District, 801 F. Supp. 1164 (S.D.N.Y. 1992).

Susan N. v. Wilson School District, 70 F.3d 751 (3d Cir. 1995).

Swift v. Rapides Parish Public School System, 812 F. Supp. 666 (W.D. La. 1993), *affirmed,* 12 F.3d 209 (5th Cir. 1993) (mem.).

Tice v. Botetourt County School Board, 908 F.2d 1200 (4th Cir. 1990).

Timothy W. v. Rochester, NH School District, 875 F.2d 954 (1st Cir. 1989).

Timms v. Metropolitan School District, 718 F.2d 212 (7th Cir. 1983), *amended* 722 F.2d 1310 (7th Cir. 1983).

Todd v. Duneland School Corporation, 299 F.3d 899 (7th Cir. 2002).

Town of Burlington v. Department of Education, Commonwealth of Massachusetts, 736 F.2d 773 (1st Cir. 1984) *affirmed on other grounds sub nom. Burlington School Committee v. Department of Education of the Commonwealth of Massachusetts,* 471 U.S. 359 (1985).

Tucker v. Calloway County Board of Education, 136 F.3d 495 (6th Cir. 1998).

T.W. ex rel. McCullough v. Unified School District No. 259, 136 Fed. Appx. 122 (10th Cir. 2005).

Walczak v. Florida Union Free School District, 142 F.3d 119 (2d Cir. 1998).

Watson ex rel. Watson v. Kingston City School District, 142 Fed. Appx. 9 (2d Cir. 2005).

W.C. ex rel. Sue C. v. Cobb County School District, 407 F. Supp.2d 1351 (N.D. Ga. 2005).

W.G. and B.G. v. Board of Trustees of Target Range School District No. 23, 960 F.2d 1479 (9th Cir. 1992).

White v. Ascension Parish School Board, 343 F.3d 373 (5th Cir. 2003).

Wilson v. Marana Unified School District, 735 F.2d 1178 (9th Cir. 1984).

Yaris v. Special School District, St. Louis County, 558 F. Supp. 545 (E.D. Mo. 1983), *affirmed,* 728 F.2d 1055 (8th Cir. 1984).

Zayas v. Commonwealth of Puerto Rico, 378 F. Supp.2d 13 (D.P.R. 2005), *affirmed,* 163 Fed. Appx. 4 (1st Cir. 2005).

5

Related Services,
Assistive Technology,
and Transition Services

❖

Key Concepts in This Chapter

- ❖ Required Related Services
- ❖ When Related Services Must Be Provided
- ❖ Assistive Technology Services
- ❖ Transition Services

The Individuals with Disabilities Education Act (IDEA) requires states, through local school boards, to provide related, or supportive, services to students with disabilities to the extent that these children need these services to benefit from their special education programs (20 U.S.C. § 1401(26)). In its definition of related services, the IDEA specifically lists developmental, supportive, and corrective services such as transportation, speech-language pathology, audiology, interpreting services, psychological services, physical therapy, occupational therapy, recreation (including therapeutic recreation), social work services, school nurse services, counseling services (including rehabilitation counseling), orientation and mobility services, and medical services (for diagnostic or evaluative purposes only). Insofar as this list is not exhaustive, other unlisted services may be considered to be related services if they help students with disabilities to benefit from special education. As such, services such as artistic and cultural programs or art, music, and dance therapy could be related services under the appropriate circumstances. Related services may be provided by persons of varying professional backgrounds with a variety of occupational titles.

The only limit placed on what school officials must provide as related services is that medical services are exempted unless they are for diagnostic or evaluative purposes. The 2004 IDEA amendments clarified that the term does not include a medical device that is surgically implanted or the replacement of such a device (20 U.S.C. § 1401(20)(B)).

Related services must be provided only to students who are receiving special education services. By definition, children are disabled under the IDEA only if they require special education and related services. In other words, there is no requirement to provide related services to students who are not receiving special education. However, since many special education services could qualify as accommodations under Section 504 of the Rehabilitation Act, it is not uncommon for school boards to provide related services to students who are qualified to receive assistance under Section 504 but do not qualify for help under the IDEA.

When Congress amended the IDEA in 1990 it added definitions of assistive technology devices and services. The most recent version of the IDEA clarified and expanded these definitions. An *assistive technology device* is defined as any item, piece of equipment, or product system that is used to increase, maintain, or improve the functional capabilities of individuals with disabilities. These devices may include commercially available, modified, or customized equipment (20 U.S.C. § 1401(1)(A)) but, as with related services, do not include surgically implanted medical devices (20 U.S.C. § 1401(1)(B)). The objective of assistive technology services is to assist students in the selection, acquisition, or use of assistive technology devices. In addition, assistive technology services include evaluations of the needs of children, provision of assistive technology devices, training in the use of these devices, coordination of other services with assistive technology, and maintenance and repair of devices (20 U.S.C. § 1401(2)).

Curiously, assistive technology is not explicitly included in either the definition of special education or related services, yet it does fit within the definition of special education, as specially designed instruction, and within the definition of related services, as a developmental, corrective, or supportive service. Rather than include assistive technology within either of these two definitions, Congress instead chose to create assistive technology as a category separate from both special education and related services. Assistive technology can thus be a special education service, a related service, or simply a supplementary aid or service (34 C.F.R. § 300.105(a)(1)). School boards are required to provide supplementary aids and services to students with disabilities to allow them to be educated in the least restrictive environment (LRE) (20 U.S.C. §§ 1401(33), 1412(a)(5)).

The IDEA requires school boards to provide transition services to students with disabilities to promote their movement from school to postschool activities such as employment, vocational training, and/or independent living. Transition services include related services, instruction, community experiences, and the acquisition of daily living skills (20 U.S.C. § 1401(34)). School personnel must include a statement of needed transition services in students' individualized education plans (IEPs) beginning no later than the age of sixteen (20 U.S.C. § 1414(d)(1)(A)(i)(VIII)).

As with special education, the provision of related services, assistive technology, and transition services must be done on an individual basis according to each student's unique needs. Not surprisingly, there have been many disputes between parents and school boards over whether some of the programs and devices that students with disabilities need qualified as required related services under the IDEA. Although each of the categories of related services listed in the IDEA is defined in the regulations, the precise parameters of some categories are subject to dispute. Moreover, where the list is not exhaustive, parents have filed suit seeking services that are not expressly mentioned in the IDEA. Similarly, there has been a small but significant amount of litigation over the IDEA's assistive technology and transition services mandates. The first part of this chapter reviews pertinent litigation under the IDEA's related services provision. The next two sections address assistive technology and transition services directives.

REQUIRED RELATED SERVICES

As indicated above, the list of required related services in the IDEA is not exhaustive. Thus, any developmental, supportive, or corrective service could be a required related service. In spite of the IDEA's fairly clear definition of related services, questions have often arisen as to what services are required and which students are entitled to related services. The following sections detail the most frequently litigated issues.

Counseling, Psychological, and Social Work Services

The IDEA's regulations define counseling as a service that is provided by a qualified social worker, psychologist, guidance counselor, or other qualified person (34 C.F.R. § 300.34(c)(2)). The definition of psychological services includes psychological counseling (34 C.F.R. § 300.34(c)(10)), while the definition of social work services includes group and individual counseling (34 C.F.R. § 300.34(c)(14)).

One of the controversies that developed over the medical exclusion clause of the related services mandate concerns the provision of psychotherapy. Insofar as counseling, psychological, and social work services are defined in the IDEA's regulations, they clearly are required related services when students with disabilities need them to benefit from their special education placements. On the other hand, psychotherapy is not defined. While psychotherapy can be classified as a psychological service, in some instances it may fit within the medical exclusion depending on individual state laws governing psychotherapy. Put another way, some states permit only psychiatrists to provide psychotherapy while other jurisdictions allow clinical psychologists to provide psychotherapy. To the extent that psychiatrists are licensed physicians, psychotherapy would be an exempted medical service in states that restrict its provision to psychiatrists.

The distinguishing criterion regarding whether psychotherapy is a related service or an exempted medical service is how it is defined by state law, not by who actually provides services. For example, a federal trial court in Illinois, a state that allows nonpsychiatrists to provide psychotherapy, ruled that a school board was responsible for the costs of psychotherapy even though it was actually provided by a psychiatrist (*Max M. v. Thompson*, 1983, 1984, 1986). The court explained that the fact that health services that must be provided by a physician are exempted from the related services mandate did not mean that services that may be performed by a nonphysician but in actuality were provided by a physcian were excluded. Even so, in such instances, boards are required to pay for the services only to the extent of the costs of their being performed by nonphysicians.

In many situations students with emotional difficulties may not be able to benefit from their special education programs until professionals address their emotional problems. Under these circumstances, counseling, psychotherapy, or social work services may be required as related services. In an early case, a federal trial court in Illinois concluded that psychotherapy is a required related service because it can be necessary for some children if they are to benefit from their educational programs (*Gary B. v. Cronin*, 1980). The court found that although psychotherapy is related to mental health, it may be required before a child can derive any benefit from education. In like manner, the federal trial court in New Jersey held that psychotherapy was an essential service that allowed a student who was emotionally disturbed to benefit from his educational program (*T.G. and P.G. v. Board of Education of Piscataway*, 1983).

Insofar as counseling is not considered to be a medical service, it may be a required related service. In another early case, the federal trial court in Connecticut pointed out that psychological and counseling services that a student with disabilities needed in order to benefit from his special education program were not embraced within the exempted medical services clause (*Papacoda v. State of Connecticut*, 1981). The court maintained that the therapy services offered as part of a residential placement were essential to rendering the student educable and thus were required related services.

An important element in the requirement to provide related services is that they must be necessary for the student if he or she is to benefit from special education services. In such a case, the Fourth Circuit reasoned that counseling services were unnecessary for a student who made great improvement under an

IEP that did not include counseling (*Tice v. Botetourt County School Board*, 1990). On the other hand, as reflected by a judgment of a federal trial court in Illinois, when therapeutic services are classified as psychiatric services, courts will declare that they fall within the medical exception. Here, since the court was convinced that psychiatric services are medical because psychiatrists are licensed physicians, it declared that they were not related services (*Darlene L. v. Illinois Board of Education*, 1983).

Whether placements in facilities that provide psychiatric services are primarily for medical or educational reasons may determine the costs that school boards must pay. Two cases that were resolved months apart by the Ninth Circuit are illustrative. The student in the first case was admitted to an acute-care psychiatric hospital when the residential school she attended could no longer control her behavior. The court compared the placement to one for a student suffering from a physical illness and declared that it had been made for medical reasons. The court decided that room and board costs were medically related, not educationally related, because the hospital did not provide educational services (*Clovis Unified School District v. California Office of Administrative Hearings*, 1990). In the second case, the student was placed in a residential school and psychiatric hospital after he assaulted a family member. In this instance the court affirmed that the residential facility was a boarding school that had the capacity to offer necessary medical services. The court observed that since the placement was made primarily for educational reasons, it was appropriate under the IDEA (*Taylor v. Honig*, 1990).

School Health, School Nurse, and Medical Services

The IDEA's regulations define school health and school nurse services as those designed to enable students with disabilities to receive a free appropriate public education (FAPE) (34 C.F.R. § 300.34(c)(13)). The two services are distinguished by virtue of the fact that school nurse services are performed by qualified school nurses, while school health services can be performed by other qualified persons. A great deal of controversy has developed over the provision of health-related services in the schools because of the medical exclusion clause. To the extent that a number of medical procedures can be performed by registered nurses, questions have arisen as to whether certain nursing services fall within the definition of school health services or are exempted medical services.

In one of its first special education cases, the United States Supreme Court, in *Irving Independent School District v. Tatro* (1984), ruled that catheterization was a required related service. In this case, since the student could not voluntarily empty her bladder due to spina bifida, she had to be catheterized every three to four hours. According to the Court, services that allow a student to remain in class during the school day, such as catheterization, are no less related to the effort to educate than services that allow the student to reach, enter, or exit the school. Considering that the catheterization procedure could be performed by a school nurse or trained health aide, the Court was of the opinion that Congress did not intend to exclude these services as medical services.

The Ninth Circuit affirmed that school boards are required to attend to such matters as a student's tracheotomy tube (*Department of Education, State of Hawaii v. Katherine D.*, 1982, 1983). Insofar as procedures such as reinserting the tube or suctioning students' lungs can be performed by school nurses or trained laypersons, the court treated them as required related services. In addition, services of this type can be required while students are being transported (*Skelly v. Brookfield LaGrange Park School District*, 1997). In one case, a federal trial court in Michigan specifically commented that the provision of an aide or other health professional on a school bus to attend to a medically fragile student did not constitute an exempted medical service (*Macomb County Intermediate School District v. Joshua S.*, 1989).

These cases reveal that services that may be provided by school nurses, health aides, or even trained laypersons fall within the IDEA's mandated related services provision. However, the fragile medical condition of some students requires the presence of full-time nurses. In its second case dealing with the IDEA's related services provision, the Supreme Court, in *Cedar Rapids Community School District v. Garret F.* (1999), affirmed that a school board was required to provide full-time nursing services for a student who was quadriplegic. The Court ruled that even though continuous services may have been more costly and may have required additional school personnel, this did not render them more medical. Emphasizing that cost was not a factor in the definition of related services, the Court asserted that even costly related services must be provided to help guarantee that students with significant medical needs are integrated into the public schools.

Diagnostic and Evaluative Services

The IDEA makes clear that medical services can be related services when used for diagnostic and evaluative purposes (34 C.F.R. § 300.34(a)). To this end, medical evaluations are often part of the proper diagnosis and evaluation of students suspected of having disabilities since this is an important component of the special education process.

An interesting case out of Tennessee illustrates many facets of a school board's responsibility in this regard. A federal trial court directed a school board to pay for neurological and psychological evaluations ordered by a student's pediatrician (*Seals v. Loftis*, 1985). School personnel had requested an evaluation by a pediatrician for a student who had a seizure disorder, visual difficulties, and learning disabilities, and whose behavior and school performance had deteriorated. The pediatrician referred the student to a neurologist, who subsequently referred him to a psychologist. A dispute arose over who was responsible for paying for the neurological and psychological evaluations. The court pointed out that since the student's needs were intertwined, the evaluations were necessary for him to benefit from his special education. The court added that the student's parents could have been required to use their health insurance to pay for the evaluations if doing so did not incur a cost to them.

However, since the parents' policy placed a lifetime cap on psychological services that would have been reduced by the amount of the evaluation bill, the court concluded that the board was responsible for payment. Where no such cap existed for neurological services, the court suggested that parents would have to use their insurance to pay for an evaluation.

School boards may even be responsible for hospitalization costs when they are an integral part of a child's overall evaluation for special needs. In such a case, the federal trial court in Hawaii ordered the Department of Education to reimburse parents for the cost of a hospital stay that it considered to be a significant part of the student's diagnosis and evaluation. The student was identified as having an emotional impairment and oppositional defiant disorder as a result of her hospitalization (*Department of Education, State of Hawaii v. Cari Rae S.*, 2001).

The phrase *diagnostic and evaluative services* does not refer only to assessments that may be conducted as part of an initial evaluation. An order of a federal trial court in Tennessee illustrates that ongoing monitoring of a student's condition could fall within the realm of diagnostic and evaluative services (*Brown v. Wilson County School Board*, 1990). The court wrote that since medical services that are provided to monitor and adjust a student's medication are medical services for diagnostic and evaluation purposes, they are the responsibility of the school board.

Physical, Occupational, and Speech Therapy

The IDEA's regulations define physical therapy simply as the services provided by a qualified physical therapist (34 C.F.R. § 300.34(c)(9)). Occupational therapy refers to services that improve, develop, or restore functions impaired or lost through illness, injury, or deprivation; improve a student's ability to perform tasks for independent functioning; and prevent initial or further loss of function (34 C.F.R. § 300.34(c)(6)). Speech pathology includes the identification, diagnosis, and appraisal of speech or language impairments and the provision of appropriate services for the habilitation or prevention of communication impairments (34 C.F.R. § 300.34(c)(15)). Students with disabilities often need these services in order to benefit from special education, since they facilitate the remediation of impediments to learning.

Improving the physical abilities of students frequently expedites their ability to benefit from their special education placements. The Third Circuit explained that for some children physical therapy is an important facilitator of classroom learning (*Polk v. Central Susquehanna Intermediate Unit 16*, 1988). Emphasizing that the IDEA requires boards to provide children with education services that provide meaningful benefit, the court was of the view that physical therapy is an essential prerequisite for learning for some children with severe disabilities.

A federal trial court in New York ordered a school board to provide occupational therapy to a student with disabilities over the summer months, recognizing that his regression in the areas of upper-body strength and ambulation skills would have adversely affected his classroom performance in the fall (*Holmes v. Sobol*, 1988). In like manner, the federal trial court for the District of Columbia posited that a proposed placement for a student with multiple disabilities was inappropriate since it did not provide for an integrated occupational therapy program as called for in her IEP (*Kattan v. District of Columbia*, 1988). The court contended that the student would not have benefited from her special education program without this service. Accordingly, it is important to keep in mind that the term *education* for many students with severe disabilities encompasses instruction in daily living skills. For this reason, occupational therapy can be a necessary part of overall student programs because it may address deficits in skills related to dressing and eating (*Glendale Unified School District v. Almasi*, 2000).

Insofar as an inability to communicate effectively may interfere with a student's learning, speech and language therapy, when needed, generally is considered to be a related service. Although there has been no major litigation involving the need for speech or language therapy, it is safe to say that courts would require its provision. Most school boards provide extensive speech and language therapy services, and in some states it is considered to be a special education service rather than a related service.

In providing various therapeutic services, school systems often employ qualified assistants who work under the direction of the therapist. In light of a judgment from a federal trial court in Tennessee, such a practice is acceptable. The court approved an IEP that called for occupational therapy assistants to provide services to a student with autism (*Metropolitan Nashville and Davidson County School System v. Guest*, 1995). The court was convinced that since the assistants were well trained and the student made progress working with them, the board could continue to use them to assist the child.

Alterations to the Physical Plant

School boards may be required to make alterations to their physical plants in order to allow students with disabilities to participate fully in and benefit from their educational programs. Most of these alterations, such as construction of wheelchair ramps, allow access to buildings. An early dispute from Texas illustrates the fact that modifications may be required to allow students to remain physically in classrooms. A federal trial court ordered a board to provide an air-conditioned classroom for a student who, due to brain injuries suffered in an accident, could not regulate his body temperature and consequently required a temperature-controlled environment (*Espino v. Besteiro*, 1981). Previously, the board had provided the student with an air-conditioned plexiglass cubicle, and, although he was achieving satisfactorily, he was restricted in his ability to socialize and participate in group activities. The court commented that since the use of the cubicle caused the student to miss out on class participation and group interactions that were important to his education, its continued use violated the IDEA's least restrictive environment mandate.

School boards are not required to make alterations to every building within districts in order to make them accessible to students with disabilities. A judgment of the Eighth Circuit demonstrates that boards comply with the IDEA's provisions as long as they offer students placements in accessible facilities that are reasonably close to their homes (*Schuldt v. Mankato Independent School District No. 77*, 1991). This case, which was filed on behalf of a student who used a wheelchair, sought to require the board to modify her neighborhood school to make it accessible. Based on the board's ability to demonstrate that three other schools in the district were accessible, and officials offered the student a placement in one of those schools, the court affirmed that this was an acceptable arrangement.

Transportation

It almost goes without saying that students cannot benefit from educational programs if they cannot get to school. As such, school boards must provide special transportation arrangements for students who are unable to access standard transportation provisions. As used in the IDEA's regulations, the term *transportation* encompasses travel to and from school, between schools, and around school buildings. Moreover, boards must provide students with disabilities with specialized equipment, such as adapted buses, lifts, and ramps, if needed, to provide the transportation (34 C.F.R. § 300.34(c)(16)).

The First Circuit, in a dispute from Rhode Island, affirmed that transportation may encompass transport from a student's house to a vehicle (*Hurry v. Jones*, 1983, 1984). The student challenged the denial of his request for assistance in getting from his house to a school bus. Insofar as the child could not get to the vehicle without assistance, his father transported him to school for a time. When the father was unable to transport his son to school, the student was unable to attend classes. The situation was finally resolved, but the court awarded the parents compensation for their efforts in transporting him to school after insisting that transportation clearly was the responsibility of the school board. In a similar situation, the federal trial court for the District of Columbia ordered the school board to provide an aide to convey a student from his apartment to the school bus (*District of Columbia v. Ramirez*, 2005). Even so, door-to-door transportation is required only when a student cannot get to school without such assistance (*Malehorn v. Hill City School District*, 1997).

Students whose IEP teams place them in private schools are entitled to transportation (*Union School District v. Smith*, 1994). However, if parents unilaterally place their children in the private schools, public school boards are not required to provide transportation (*A.A. v. Cooperman*, 1987; *McNair v. Cardimone*, 1987, 1989; *Work v. McKenzie*, 1987).

If students attend residential schools, they are entitled to transportation between their homes and schools for usual vacation periods. On the other hand, a state court in Florida ruled that a student was not entitled to additional trips home for therapeutic purposes even though improved family relations was a goal of his IEP (*Cohen v. School Board of Dade County*, 1984).

Transportation arrangements must be reasonable. Still, courts recognize that alterations to transportation plans for students may need to be made from time to time. The Third Circuit affirmed that a minor change in a student's transportation plan did not constitute a change in placement under the IDEA (*DeLeon v. Susquehanna Community School District*, 1984). The court realized that transportation could have an effect on the child's learning but found that a change that added ten minutes to his return trip home would not have had much of an impact. On the other hand, a federal trial court in Virginia ordered a school board to develop better arrangements for a student whose transportation took more than thirty minutes even though she lived only six miles from school (*Pinkerton v. Moye*, 1981).

In this day and age many students do not return home after school but go to caretakers. While courts have reached mixed results as to whether school boards are required to provide transportation to the homes or locations of caretakers, they generally agree that boards are not required to accommodate parents' personal or domestic circumstance. Yet, the Fifth Circuit affirmed that students with disabilities are entitled to transportation to caretakers even if the caretakers reside outside a school's attendance boundaries (*Alamo Heights Independent School District v. State Board of Education*, 1986). The court noted that the parents' request for transportation to a caretaker was reasonable and would not place any burden on the board. Conversely, the Eighth Circuit was of the opinion that a special education student was not entitled to be dropped off at a day-care center that was outside a school's attendance area. In this instance, the board's policy for all students dictated that children could be dropped off only within their school's attendance boundary. As such, the court was satisfied that the board did not violate the IDEA by refusing to transport the child to his day-care center because the policy was facially neutral and the parent's request was based on her personal convenience, not her daughter's educational needs (*Fick ex rel. Fick v. Sioux Falls School District*, 2003). The federal trial court in Maine reached the same outcome, denying the request of a mother that the bus driver ensure that an adult was present at the bus stop to meet her son, and if one was not, to then drop the student off at an alternative location (*Ms. S. ex rel. L.S. v. Scarborough School Committee*, 2005). In its analysis, the court specified that the mother was not entitled to have her request granted because it was motivated by her child-care arrangements with her ex-husband, with whom she shared joint custody, rather than her son's educational needs. Similarly, a state court in Pennsylvania refused to require a board to provide transportation on weeks a student stayed with his father, who had joint custody but lived out of the district's boundaries (*North Allegheny School District v. Gregory P.*, 1996). The court acknowledged that the request did not address any of the student's educational needs but served only to accommodate the parents' domestic situation.

School boards may not be required to provide transportation when parents send their children to schools other than the ones recommended by school personnel. A state court in Florida determined that a school board was not required to transport a student to a geographically distant facility after she was enrolled there at her parents' request. The court found that transportation was unnecessary since the student could have received an appropriate education at a closer facility (*School Board of Pinellas County v. Smith*, 1989).

In addition to providing specialized equipment, if needed, to transport students safely, school boards may be required to provide aides on the transportation vehicle. A federal trial court in Michigan ordered a school board to provide a trained aide to attend to a medically fragile student during transport (*Macomb County Intermediate School District v. Joshua S.*, 1989). The court asserted that under the IDEA students with disabilities were entitled to transportation and incidents thereto.

Extracurricular Activities

The IDEA specifically includes recreation and therapeutic recreation as related services (20 U.S.C. § 1402(22)). The definition of *recreation* indicates that it includes assessment of leisure function, recreation programs in schools and community agencies, and leisure education, along with therapeutic recreation (34 C.F.R. § 300.34(c)(11)). In addition, the IDEA's regulations require school boards to provide nonacademic and extracurricular services and activities to the extent necessary to afford students with disabilities equal opportunities for participation (34 C.F.R. § 300.107). Nonacademic and extracurricular services and activities may include athletics, recreational activities, special-interest groups or clubs, employment, and many of the services listed as related services. School officials must offer these activities in inclusive settings to the maximum extent appropriate (34 C.F.R. § 300.117).

If students with disabilities are unable to participate in general extracurricular programs, the regulations dictate that school boards may be required to develop special extracurricular programs for these children. Students who meet the eligibility requirements for participation in general extracurricular programs cannot be denied access to them under Section 504 of the Rehabilitation Act. School officials may have to provide reasonable accommodations to allow students with disabilities to participate in general extracurricular programs (Osborne & Battaglino, 1996; Rose & Huefner, 2005). For example, eligibility rules, particularly those dealing with age restrictions, that would prevent students with disabilities from participating due to their conditions, may have to be waived (*Crocker v. Tennessee Secondary School Athletic Association*, 1990; *Texas Education Agency v. Stamos*, 1991; *University Interscholastic League v. Buchanan*, 1993).

A state court in Michigan ordered a school board to provide a summer enrichment program to a student who was autistic (*Birmingham and Lamphere School Districts v. Superintendent of Public Instruction*, 1982). Where the testimony at trial revealed that the student needed a program that included outdoor activities, the court thought that the requested program fell within the parameters of special education and related services because physical education was included in the definition of special education and recreation was a related service. Further, a federal trial court in Ohio issued a preliminary injunction requiring a school board to include participation in interscholastic athletics in a student's IEP. The court was persuaded by evidence that the student's participation in sports resulted in academic, physical, and personal progress (*Kling v. Mentor Public School District*, 2001). Conversely, a state court in New York declared that a board was not required to provide an afterschool program when such participation was unnecessary for a student to receive a FAPE (*Roslyn Union Free School District v. University of the State of New York, State Education Department*, 2000).

ASSISTIVE TECHNOLOGY

Assistive technology may be provided as a special education service, a related service, or a supplementary aid and service. Assistive technology must be included in student IEPs when it is needed for children to receive a FAPE under the standard established by the United States Supreme Court in *Board of Education of the Hendrick Hudson School District v. Rowley* (1982). Additionally, since assistive technology may permit many students with disabilities to benefit from education in less restrictive settings, it may be required under the IDEA's least restrictive environment provision.

IEP teams must consider whether children require assistive technology devices and services in order to receive an appropriate education (34 C.F.R. § 300.324(a)(2)(v)). If teams determine that assistive technology is required, it must be written into IEPs. Unfortunately, though, there are no requirements that teams must document that they considered assistive technology devices and services if they agree that none were needed.

The IDEA's regulations specifically mandate that school boards ensure that assistive technology devices and services are made available to students if either or both are required as part of their special education, related services, or supplementary aids and services (34 C.F.R. § 300.105(a)). At the same time, boards must provide students with the use of school-provided assistive technology devices in their homes if IEP teams believe that children need access to these devices in order to receive a FAPE (34 C.F.R. § 300.105(a)(2)).

In explanatory material accompanying the 1999 IDEA regulations, the Department of Education made it clear that school boards are not required to provide personal devices that students would require regardless of whether they attended school (*Federal Register*, March 12, 1999, p. 12540). This directive included items such as eyeglasses, hearing aids, or braces. Of course, nothing prohibits school systems from providing students with these items. The current regulations do require boards to ensure that hearing aids worn in school are functioning properly (34 C.F.R. § 300.105(b)). At the same time, the Department of Education spelled out that students with disabilities are entitled to have access to any general technology that is available to peers who are not disabled. When students with disabilities require accommodations in order to use general technology, educators must make sure that these modifications are provided (*Federal Register*, March 12, 1999, p. 12540). Such accommodations are also required under Section 504.

In one of the first cases involving assistive technology, a federal trial court in Pennsylvania reasoned that a school board's provision of assistive technology to a student with multiple disabilities was inadequate (*East Penn School District v. Scott B.*, 1999). The court observed that the student required a laptop computer with appropriate software but that school personnel failed to obtain and set up the device for nearly a year. The court found fault with the school's chosen software program and keyboarding instruction. In like manner, the federal trial court in Maryland supported a hearing officer's order for a school board to provide a student with appropriate software to use at home and school while providing instruction in how to use the software (*Board of Education of Harford County v. Bauer*, 2000).

An order of the Second Circuit, in a case originating in New York, exemplifies the point that an assistive technology device should assist students in receiving a FAPE by mitigating the effects of their disability but should not compromise the learning process. The dispute involved a student who was allowed to use a calculator because he had learning disabilities that affected his ability in mathematics. School personnel denied the student's request to use a more advanced calculator on the basis that it would have circumvented the learning process. After a hearing officer ascertained that school officials provided the student with appropriate assistive technology and that the more advanced calculator was not needed, a trial court ruled in his favor. The Second Circuit, in vacating the earlier order in favor of the student, agreed with the hearing officer that the denial of his request to use an advanced calculator did not deprive him of a FAPE where the evidence demonstrated that he was capable of passing the class with the assistance of a less advanced calculator in a manner consistent with the education goals of the class's curriculum and that his own lack of effort contributed to his failing grade (*Sherman v. Mamaroneck Union Free School District*, 2003).

TRANSITION SERVICES

The IDEA requires school boards to provide transition services to students with disabilities in order to facilitate their passage from school to postschool activities. Transition services not only involve instruction and training but may also encompass related services. A major goal of transition services is to help students with disabilities make meaningful transitions from school to whatever they may face in the future (Ray, 2002).

Not surprisingly, courts disagree on whether school boards have provided appropriate transition services for students with disabilities. On the one hand, the federal trial court in Connecticut maintained that a twenty-year-old student was entitled to instruction in community and daily living skills as these skills fell within the scope of transition services (*J.B. v. Killingly Board of Education*, 1997). Similarly, a federal trial court in Pennsylvania, commenting that transition services should be designed to prepare a student for life outside the school system, insisted that providing him with only vocational evaluations and training was insufficient (*East Penn School District v. Scott B.*, 1999).

On the other hand, the federal trial court in Hawaii approved a coordinated set of activities that were clearly designed to promote a student's movement from school to postschool activities. The court ruled that these activities, which were included as part of the student's IEP, were aimed at assisting him in completing high school, becoming part of his community, exploring careers and colleges, and meeting with vocational counselors (*Browell v. LeMahieu*, 2000). Subsequently, a federal trial court in Louisiana, affirmed by the Fifth Circuit, agreed that transition plans that detailed desired adult outcomes and included school action steps and family action steps were appropriate (*Pace v. Bogulusa City School Board*, 2001, 2003).

❖

CASE NO. 9—PROVISION OF NURSING SERVICES FOR A MEDICALLY FRAGILE STUDENT

CEDAR RAPIDS COMMUNITY SCHOOL DISTRICT

v.

GARRET F.

Supreme Court of the United States, 1999

526 U.S. 66

Justice STEVENS delivered the opinion of the Court.

The Individuals with Disabilities Education Act (IDEA) . . . as amended, was enacted, in part, "to assure that all children with disabilities have available to them . . . a free appropriate public education which emphasizes special education and related services designed to meet their unique needs." . . . Consistent with this purpose, the IDEA authorizes federal financial assistance to States that agree to provide disabled children with special education and "related services." . . . The question presented in this case is whether the definition of "related services" in [the IDEA] requires a public school district in a participating State to provide a ventilator-dependent student with certain nursing services during school hours.

I

Respondent Garret F. is a friendly, creative, and intelligent young man. When Garret was four years old, his spinal column was severed in a motorcycle accident. Though paralyzed from the neck down, his mental capacities were unaffected. He is able to speak, to control his motorized wheelchair through use of a puff and suck straw, and to operate a computer with a device that responds to head movements. Garret is currently a student in the Cedar Rapids Community School District (District), he attends regular classes in a typical school program, and his academic performance has been a success. Garret is, however, ventilator dependent, and therefore requires a responsible individual nearby to attend to certain physical needs while he is in school.

During Garret's early years at school his family provided for his physical care during the school day. When he was in kindergarten, his 18-year-old aunt attended him; in the next four years, his family used settlement proceeds they received after the accident, their insurance, and other resources to employ a licensed practical nurse. In 1993, Garret's mother requested the District to accept financial responsibility for the health care services that Garret requires during the school day. The District denied the request, believing that it was not legally obligated to provide continuous one-on-one nursing services.

Relying on both the IDEA and Iowa law, Garret's mother requested a hearing before the Iowa Department of Education. An **administrative law judge** (ALJ) received extensive evidence concerning Garret's special needs, the District's treatment of other disabled students, and the assistance provided to other ventilator-dependent children in other parts of the country. In his 47-page report, the ALJ found that the District has about 17,500 students, of whom approximately 2,200 need some form of special education or special services. Although Garret is the only ventilator-dependent student in the District, most of the health care services that he needs are already provided for some other students. "The primary difference between Garret's situation and that of other students is his dependency on his ventilator for life support." . . . The ALJ noted that the parties disagreed over the training or licensure required for the care and supervision of such students, and that those providing such care in other parts of the country ranged from nonlicensed personnel to registered nurses. However, the District did not contend that only a licensed physician could provide the services in question.

The ALJ explained that federal law requires that children with a variety of health impairments be provided with "special education and related services" when their disabilities adversely affect their academic performance, and that such children should be educated to the maximum extent appropriate with children who are not disabled. In addition, the ALJ explained that applicable federal regulations distinguish between "school health services," which are provided by a "qualified school nurse or other qualified person," and "medical services," which are provided by a licensed physician. . . . The District must provide the former, but need not provide the latter (except, of course, those "medical services" that are for diagnostic or evaluation purposes. . . . According to the ALJ, the distinction in the regulations does not just depend on "the title of the person providing the service"; instead, the "medical services" exclusion is limited to services that are "in the special training, knowledge, and judgment of a physician to carry out." . . . The ALJ thus concluded that the IDEA required the District to bear financial responsibility for all of the services in dispute, including continuous nursing services.

The District challenged the ALJ's decision in Federal District Court, but that court approved the ALJ's IDEA ruling and granted summary judgment against the District. . . . The Court of Appeals affirmed. . . . It noted that, as a recipient of federal funds under the IDEA, Iowa has a statutory duty to provide all disabled children a "free appropriate public education," which includes "related services." . . . The Court of Appeals read our opinion in *Irving Independent School Dist. v. Tatro* to provide a two-step analysis of the "related services" definition in [the IDEA]—asking first, whether the requested services are included within the phrase "supportive services"; and second, whether the services are excluded as "medical services." . . . The Court of Appeals succinctly answered both questions in Garret's favor. The Court found the first step plainly satisfied, since Garret cannot attend school unless the requested services are available during the schoolday. . . . As to the second step, the court reasoned that *Tatro* "established a bright-line test: the services of a physician (other than for diagnostic and evaluation purposes) are subject to the medical services exclusion, but services that can be provided in the school setting by a nurse or qualified layperson are not." . . .

In its petition for certiorari, the District challenged only the second step of the Court of Appeals' analysis. The District pointed out that some federal courts have not asked whether the requested health services must be delivered by a physician, but instead have applied a multifactor test that considers, generally speaking, the nature and extent of the services at issue. We granted the District's petition to resolve this conflict. . . .

II

The District contends that [the IDEA] does not require it to provide Garret with "continuous one-on-one nursing services" during the schoolday, even though Garret cannot remain in school without such care. . . . However, the IDEA's definition of "related services," our decision in *Irving Independent School Dist. v. Tatro*, . . . and the overall statutory scheme all support the decision of the Court of Appeals.

The text of the "related services" definition . . . broadly encompasses those supportive services that "may be required to assist a child with a disability to benefit from special education." As we have already noted, the District does not challenge the Court of Appeals' conclusion that the in-school services at issue are within the covered category of "supportive services." As a general matter, services that enable a disabled child to remain in school during the day provide the student with "the meaningful access to education that Congress envisioned." *Tatro*, . . . ("'Congress sought primarily to make public education available to handicapped children' and 'to make such access meaningful'" (quoting *Board of Ed. of Hendrick Hudson Central School Dist., Westchester Cty. v. Rowley* . . .).

This general definition of "related services" is illuminated by a parenthetical phrase listing examples of particular services that are included within the statute's coverage. . . . "[M]edical services" are enumerated in this list, but such services are limited to those that are "for diagnostic and evaluation purposes." . . . The statute does not contain a more specific definition of the "medical services" that are excepted from the coverage of [the IDEA].

The scope of the "medical services" exclusion is not a matter of first impression in this Court. In *Tatro* we concluded that the Secretary of Education had reasonably determined that the term "medical services" referred only to services that must be performed by a physician, and not to school health services. . . . Accordingly, we held that a specific form of health care (clean intermittent catheterization) that is often, though not always, performed by a nurse is not an excluded medical service. We referenced the likely cost of the services and the competence of school staff as justifications for drawing a line between physician and other services, . . . but our endorsement of that line was unmistakable. It is thus settled that the phrase "medical services" in [the IDEA] does not embrace all forms of care that might loosely be described as "medical" in other contexts, such as a claim for an income tax deduction.

The District does not ask us to define the term so broadly. Indeed, the District does not argue that any of the items of care that Garret needs, considered individually, could be excluded from the scope of [the IDEA]. It could not make such an argument, considering that one of the services Garret needs (catheterization) was at issue in *Tatro,* and the others may be provided competently by a school nurse or other trained personnel. . . . As the ALJ concluded, most of the requested services are already provided by the District to other students, and the in-school care necessitated by Garret's ventilator dependency does not demand the training, knowledge, and judgment of a licensed physician. . . . While more extensive, the in-school services Garret needs are no more "medical" than was the care sought in *Tatro.*

Instead, the District points to the combined and continuous character of the required care, and proposes a test under which the outcome in any particular case would "depend upon a series of factors, such as [1] whether the care is continuous or intermittent, [2] whether existing school health personnel can provide the service, [3] the cost of the service, and [4] the potential consequences if the service is not properly performed." . . .

The District's multifactor test is not supported by any recognized source of legal authority. The proposed factors can be found in neither the text of the statute nor the regulations that we upheld in *Tatro.* Moreover, the District offers no explanation why these characteristics make one service any more "medical" than another. The continuous character of certain services associated with Garret's ventilator dependency has no apparent relationship to "medical" services, much less a relationship of equivalence. Continuous services may be more costly and may require additional school personnel, but they are not thereby more "medical." Whatever its imperfections, a rule that limits the medical services exemption to physician services is unquestionably a reasonable and generally workable interpretation of the statute. Absent an elaboration of the statutory terms plainly more convincing than that which we reviewed in *Tatro,* there is no good reason to depart from settled law.

Finally, the District raises broader concerns about the financial burden that it must bear to provide the services that Garret needs to stay in school. The problem for the District in providing these services is not that its staff cannot be trained to deliver them; the problem, the District contends, is that the existing school health staff cannot meet all of their responsibilities and provide for Garret at the same time. Through its multifactor test, the District seeks to establish a kind of undue-burden exemption primarily based on the cost of the requested services. The first two factors can be seen as examples of cost-based distinctions: Intermittent care is often less expensive than continuous care, and the use of existing personnel is cheaper than hiring additional employees. The third factor—the cost of the service—would then encompass the first two. The relevance of the fourth factor is likewise related to cost because extra care may be necessary if potential consequences are especially serious.

The District may have legitimate financial concerns, but our role in this dispute is to interpret existing law. Defining "related services" in a manner that *accommodates* the cost concerns Congress may have had, . . . is altogether different from using cost *itself* as the definition. Given that [the IDEA] does not employ cost in its definition of "related services" or excluded "medical services," accepting the District's cost-based standard as the sole test for determining the scope of the provision would require us to engage in judicial lawmaking without any guidance from Congress. It would also create some tension with the purposes of the IDEA. The statute may not require public schools to maximize the potential of disabled students commensurate with the opportunities provided to other children, . . . and the potential financial burdens imposed on participating States may be relevant to arriving at a sensible construction of the IDEA. . . . But Congress intended "to open the door of public education" to all qualified children and "require[d] participating States to educate handicapped children with nonhandicapped children whenever possible." . . .

This case is about whether meaningful access to the public schools will be assured, not the level of education that a school must finance once access is attained. It is undisputed that the services at issue must be provided if Garret is to remain in school. Under the statute, our precedent, and the purposes of the IDEA, the District must fund such "related services" in order to help guarantee that students like Garret are integrated into the public schools.

The judgment of the Court of Appeals is accordingly

Affirmed.

Notes

1. In a dissenting opinion, Justice Thomas noted that Congress had not included nursing services within the list of required related services. School nursing services have since been added to that list.

2. Justice Thomas in his dissent also stated that spending clause legislation must be interpreted narrowly. The Supreme Court has interpreted the IDEA very narrowly in more recent cases. Compare the results in the Court's decision in *Arlington Central School District Board of Education v. Murphy* 126 S. Ct. 2455 (2006) with *Cedar Rapids.*

❖ CASE NO. 10—LIMITATION ON REQUIREMENT TO PROVIDE TRANSPORTATION

FICK ex rel. FICK

v.

SIOUX FALLS SCHOOL DISTRICT

United States Court of Appeals, Eighth Circuit, 2003

337 F.3d 968

BYE, Circuit Judge.

This is a dispute over whether the Sioux Falls School District (the District) must transport Sarah Fick to a day care center after school, rather than to her home, in order to provide a free appropriate public education under the Individuals with Disabilities Education Act (IDEA). . . . Both a state hearing examiner and the district court held the District did not violate the IDEA, because transportation to the day care center was not necessary for Sarah to benefit educationally from her individualized education plan (IEP). We affirm.

I

Sarah Fick suffers from epileptic seizures. When a seizure occurs, Sarah must receive a shot of Valium from a qualified nurse within a short period of time. This condition requires the District to provide Sarah transportation to and from school as a "related service" under the IDEA. The District satisfies this requirement by providing Sarah with a nurse-accompanied taxi ride to school in the morning, and back to her home in the afternoon.

The District has created geographical "cluster sites" within its boundaries to provide better and more efficient education services to its students. For example, the cluster sites allow children to be with the same neighborhood peer groups as they move through elementary school, middle school, and high school. During the 2000–2001 school year, the District had three cluster sites for its elementary school children located at John Harris, John F. Kennedy, and Hawthorne Elementary Schools. Sarah Fick lived in the John Harris cluster site.

The District uses the cluster boundaries to establish transportation policies for all children, both regular and special education, who are eligible for transportation to and from school. Students are allowed one designated pick-up address before school and one drop-off address after school. The addresses do not have to be the same, but both must be located within the child's cluster boundaries. The District will, however, transport a disabled child outside her designated cluster site when the transportation is necessary for the child to benefit from her IEP.

In October 2000, Sarah's mother, Darlene, asked the District to change Sarah's designated drop-off address from her home to an after-school day care center called Liberty Center. The District refused to change Sarah's drop-off point because Liberty Center was outside the boundaries of Sarah's cluster site. Darlene renewed her request at an IEP meeting held in February 2001. When that request was denied as well, Darlene filed a complaint with the state Office of Special Education (OSE). After an informal investigation, the OSE determined the District violated the IDEA by failing to accommodate the transportation request, and ordered the District to pay for Sarah's transportation to Liberty Center.

The District requested a due process hearing to contest the OSE's decision. After a formal hearing, a state hearing examiner issued written findings of fact and conclusions of law determining the District had not violated the IDEA. The state hearing examiner concluded the transportation request was made for personal reasons unrelated to Sarah's educational needs, and therefore the District was not required to pay for the transportation.

Darlene Fick challenged the hearing examiner's decision by filing suit in the district court. Noting that Darlene made her request for personal reasons unrelated to Sarah's educational needs, the district court also concluded the District had not violated the IDEA by refusing to transport Sarah to a drop-off address outside her designated cluster site. Ms. Fick timely appealed the district court's decision.

II

In IDEA cases we review the district court's decision de novo . . . but, like the district court we must give "due weight" to the state administrative proceedings. . . .

We believe our decision in *Timothy H. v. Cedar Rapids Cmty. Sch. Dist.,* is dispositive. That case, like this one, involved a parental request to transport a disabled child to a school outside a neighborhood school boundary. The Cedar Rapids School District had an intra-district transfer policy which allowed parents to send their child to a school other than the neighborhood school as long as the parents paid for transportation. We held the school district did not violate Section 504 of the Rehabilitation Act of 1973 . . . , by refusing to pay to transport a disabled child to a school outside the neighborhood boundaries. Specifically, we said the child's parents failed to prove the child was denied the benefits of participating in the intra-district transfer program, because all parents in the district had to pay for transportation costs in order to participate in the program. . . . We concluded all of the disabled child's educational needs were being met by the school within the neighborhood boundaries, and the request for transportation to a school outside the boundaries was "for reasons of parental preference" only. . . .

In short, *Timothy H.* indicates a school district may apply a facially neutral transportation policy to a disabled child without violating the law when the request for a deviation from the policy is not based on the child's educational needs, but on the parents' convenience or preference . . . We conclude *Timothy H.* controls our decision here because the pertinent obligation of the District under Section 504 is the same as its obligation under the IDEA: "To provide disabled students with a free appropriate public education." . . . We therefore affirm the decision of the district court.

Notes

1. As noted in the text of this chapter, school boards have been upheld in their refusal to make transportation arrangements to suit parents' domestic situations when the parents are divorced and live separately. In *Fick* the requested alternate transportation arrangements had little to do with the student's disability but much to do with the parents' personal needs.

2. Consider the circumstances of the parent of a wheelchair-bound student who must get the student down several stairs to get to the school bus. Should a school board be required to provide a transportation aide to help get the student down the stairs? Would such a request be due to the student's disability or the parents' personal circumstances (i.e., their living arrangements)? How is this situation different from the situation in *Fick?*

REFERENCES

A.A. v. Cooperman, 526 A.2d 1103 (N.J. Super. Ct. App. Div. 1987).

Alamo Heights Independent School District v. State Board of Education, 790 F.2d 1153 (5th Cir. 1986).

Arlington Central School District Board of Education v. Murphy, 126 S. Ct. 2455 (2006).

Birmingham and Lamphere School Districts v. Superintendent of Public Instruction, 328 N.W.2d 59 (Mich. Ct. App. 1982).

Board of Education of Harford County v. Bauer, 2000 WL 1481464 (D. Md. 2000).

Board of Education of Hendrick Hudson Central School District v. Rowley, 458 U.S. 176 (1982).

Browell v. LeMahieu, 2000 WL 1117 (D. Haw. 2000).

Brown v. Wilson County School Board, 747 F. Supp. 436 (M.D. Tenn. 1990).

Cedar Rapids Community School District v. Garret F., 526 U.S. 66 (1999).

Clovis Unified School District v. California Office of Administrative Hearings, 903 F.2d 635 (9th Cir. 1990).

Cohen v. School Board of Dade County, 450 So. 2d 1238 (Fla. Dist. Ct. App. 1984).

Crocker v. Tennessee Secondary School Athletic Association, 735 F. Supp. 753 (M.D. Tenn. 1990), *affirmed sub nom. Metropolitan Government of Nashville and Davidson County v. Crocker*, 908 F.2d 973 (6th Cir. 1990).

Darlene L. v. Illinois Board of Education, 568 F. Supp. 1340 (N.D. Ill. 1983).

DeLeon v. Susquehanna Community School District, 747 F.2d 149 (3d Cir. 1984).

Department of Education, State of Hawaii v. Cari Rae S., 158 F. Supp.2d 1190 (D. Haw. 2001).

Department of Education, State of Hawaii v. Katherine D., 531 F. Supp. 517 (D. Haw. 1982), *affirmed*, 727 F.2d 809 (9th Cir. 1983).

District of Columbia v. Ramirez, 377 F. Supp.2d 63 (D.D.C. 2005).

East Penn School District v. Scott B., 1999 WL 178363 E.D. Pa. 1999).

Espino v. Besteiro, 520 F. Supp. 905 (S.D. Tex. 1981).

Federal Register, March 12, 1999, p. 12540.

Fick ex rel. Fick v. Sioux Falls School District, 337 F.3d 968 (8th Cir. 2003).

Gary B. v. Cronin, 542 F. Supp. 102 (N.D. Ill. 1980).

Glendale Unified School District v. Almasi, 122 F. Supp.2d 1093 (C.D. Cal. 2000).

Holmes v. Sobol, 690 F. Supp. 154 (W.D.N.Y. 1988).

Hurry v. Jones, 560 F. Supp. 500 (D.R.I. 1983), *affirmed in part, reversed in part*, 734 F.2d 879 (1st Cir. 1984).

Individuals with Disabilities Education Act, 20 U.S.C. §§ 1400–1482 (2005).

Irving Independent School District v. Tatro, 468 U.S. 883 (1984).

J.B. v. Killingly Board of Education, 900 F. Supp.2d 57 (D. Conn. 1997).

Kattan v. District of Columbia, 691 F. Supp. 1539 (D.D.C. 1988).

Kling v. Mentor Public School District, 136 F. Supp.2d 744 (N.D. Ohio 2001).

Macomb County Intermediate School District v. Joshua S., 715 F. Supp. 824 (E.D. Mich. 1989).

Malehorn v. Hill City School District, 987 F. Supp.2d 772 (D.S.D. 1997).

Max M. v. Thompson, 566 F. Supp. 1330 (N.D. Ill. 1983), 585 F. Supp. 317 (N.D. Ill. 1984), 592 F. Supp. 1437 (N.D. Ill. 1984), 592 F. Supp. 1450, (N.D. Ill. 1984), 629 F. Supp. 1504, (N.D. Ill. 1986).

McNair v. Cardimone, 676 F. Supp. 1361 (S.D. Ohio 1987), *affirmed sub nom. McNair v. Oak Hills Local School District*, 872 F.2d 153 (6th Cir. 1989).

Metropolitan Nashville and Davidson County School System v. Guest, 900 F. Supp.2d 905 (M.D. Tenn. 1995).

Ms. S. ex rel. L.S. v. Scarborough School Committee, 366 F. Supp.2d 98 (D. Me. 2005).

North Allegheny School District v. Gregory P., 687 A.2d 37 (Pa. Commw. Ct. 1996).

Osborne, A. G., & Battaglino, L. (1996). Eligibility of students with disabilities for sports: Implications for policy. *Education Law Reporter, 105,* 379–388.

Pace v. Bogulusa City School Board, 137 F. Supp.2d 711 (E.D. La. 2001), *affirmed,* 325 F.3d 609 (5th Cir. 2003).

Papacoda v. State of Connecticut, 528 F. Supp. 68 (D. Conn. 1981).

Pinkerton v. Moye, 509 F. Supp. 107 (W.D. Va. 1981).

Polk v. Central Susquehanna Intermediate Unit 16, 853 F.2d 171 (3d Cir. 1988).

Ray, J. M. (2002). Components of legally sound, high quality transition services planning under the IDEA. *Education Law Reporter, 170,* 1–13.

Rehabilitation Act, Section 504, 29 U.S.C. § 794 (2005).

Rose, T. E., & Huefner, D. S. (2005). High school athletic age-restriction rules continue to discriminate against students with disabilities. *Education Law Reporter, 196,* 385–401.

Roslyn Union Free School District v. University of the State of New York, State Education Department (711 N.Y.S.2d 582 (N.Y. App. Div. 2000).

School Board of Pinellas County v. Smith, 537 So. 2d 168 (Fla. Dist. Ct. App. 1989).

Schuldt v. Mankato Independent School District No. 77, 937 F.3d 1357 (8th Cir. 1991), *rehearing denied, cert. denied,* 502 U.S. (1992).

Seals v. Loftis, 614 F. Supp. 302 (E.D. Tenn. 1985).

Sherman v. Mamaroneck Union Free School District, 340 F.3d 87 (2d Cir. 2003).

Skelly v. Brookfield LaGrange Park School District, 968 F. Supp. 385 (N.D. Ill. 1997).

Taylor v. Honig, 910 F.2d 627 (9th Cir. 1990).

Texas Education Agency v. Stamos, 817 S.W.2d 378 (Tex. Ct. App. 1991).

T.G. and P.G. v. Board of Education of Piscataway, 576 F. Supp. 420 (D.N.J. 1983).

Tice v. Botetourt County School Board, 908 F.2d 1200 (4th Cir. 1990).

Union School District v. Smith, 15 F.3d 1519 (9th Cir. 1994).

University Interscholastic League v. Buchanan, 848 S.W.2d 298 (Tex. Ct. App. 1993).

Work v. McKenzie, 661 F. Supp. 225 (D.D.C. 1987).

6

Student Discipline

❖

Until the enactment of its most comprehensive amendment of the Individuals with Disabilities Act (IDEA) in 1997, neither the statute nor its regulations explicitly addressed the contentious topic of disciplining students with disabilities. Even so, many of the IDEA's provisions had implications that could be applied to instances when students with disabilities misbehaved. Early court cases agreed that students with disabilities had additional due process rights when faced with disciplinary action because sanctions such as expulsions or long-term suspensions deprived them of educational opportunities, thereby depriving them of their IDEA rights. Congress, in the IDEA (20 U.S.C. § 1415(k)), and the Department of Education, in promulgating regulations (34 C.F.R. §§ 300.530–537), have, in their most recent versions, refined the provisions governing the disciplinary process as applied to students with disabilities. As complex as the IDEA's discipline requirements are, educators can still extract guiding principles from the laws, regulations, and numerous court cases on this topic (Dayton, 2002).

This chapter details specific requirements for administering disciplinary penalties to students with disabilities. In order to provide perspective in understanding how and why many of the IDEA's current disciplinary provisions came into being, the chapter begins with a historical overview of the case law that developed before the enactment of the 1997 amendments. Insofar as much of the pre-1997 litigation is now incorporated into the IDEA, this examination should provide insight into how the law ought to be interpreted. The next sections review the specific requirements of the 2004 version of the IDEA and its accompanying regulations and recent litigation involving the disciplining of students with disabilities. Interestingly, as complicated and contentious as this topic is, there are as yet apparently no reported cases involving disputes over the discipline provisions in the 2004 IDEA and its regulations.

JUDICIAL HISTORY

The original version of the IDEA, initially known as the Education for All Handicapped Children's Act, did not directly address disciplining of students with disabilities. However, since courts were often asked to resolve disputes involving discipline, a large body of case law emerged. Even though the IDEA now contains disciplinary provisions, a brief review of the early case law is instructive because it provides the necessary background to understand the current version of the law.

Early Decisions

In apparently the first case involving discipline under the IDEA, *Stuart v. Nappi* (1978), school officials in Connecticut unsuccessfully tried to expel a student with disabilities who had been involved in several schoolwide disturbances. The student's attorney requested a due process hearing under the IDEA while obtaining an order from the federal trial court that prevented the school board from conducting an expulsion hearing. In addressing the issues, the court proclaimed that an expulsion was a change in placement that was inconsistent with the IDEA procedures that existed at that time, which required written prior notice before any proposed change in a student's educational placement occurred (20 U.S.C. § 1415(b)(3)). At the same time, the court added that school officials could temporarily suspend a disruptive special education student or change his or her placement to a more restrictive setting as long as they followed the statutory procedures.

A year later, a federal trial court in Indiana, in *Doe v. Koger* (1979), over-turned the expulsion of a student who was mildly mentally disabled. The court declared that school officials could not expel students whose disruptive con-duct was caused by their disabilities. The court implied that students with dis-abilities could be expelled when there was no relationship between their misconduct and their disabilities, a standard subsequently referred to as the manifestation of the disability doctrine. Additionally, the court reasoned that a disruptive student in a special education setting could be transferred to a more restrictive placement as long as school officials followed the proper change in placement procedures.

The Fifth Circuit expanded the manifestation of the disability doctrine in *S-1 v. Turlington* (1981) after one of at least seven students who were expelled from high school for a variety of acts of misconduct unsuccessfully requested a hearing. In rejecting the student's requests, the superintendent concluded that because the plaintiff was not classified as emotionally disturbed, the miscon-duct was not a manifestation of his disability. In overturning the expulsion, the court decided that a manifestation determination must be made by a special-ized and knowledgeable group of persons. Moreover, the court explained that officials could not completely cease the delivery of services, even where there was no relationship between the student's misconduct and disability and he was properly expelled in accord with the IDEA's procedures.

A case from the Fourth Circuit, affirming an earlier order from Virginia, illustrates that it is not always difficult to make the connection between a child's disability and misconduct. *School Board of the County of Prince William v. Malone* (1985) involved a student with a learning disability who participated in drug transactions. After a committee of special educators was satisfied that there was no causal relationship between the student's disability and his involvement in the drug transactions, he was expelled. Yet, on judicial review, a federal trial court found that a relationship did in fact exist because the student's learning disability caused him to have a poor self-image, which in turn led him to seek peer approval by becoming involved in the drug transactions. The court main-tained that since the student's learning disability prevented him from under-standing the long-term consequences of his actions, officials acted improperly in expelling him from school.

In a topic of great importance, the courts generally agreed that educators can exclude students who pose a danger to others as long as they follow proper procedures. In *Jackson v. Franklin County School Board* (1985), the Fifth Circuit supported a school board's exclusion of a student who was diagnosed as having a psychosexual disorder. After the court committed the student to a state hospital for treatment, educational officials refused to admit him when he tried to return to school following his release from the hospital. The court agreed with the recommendation of officials that the student had to be placed in a private facility on the basis that his presence might have endan-gered him and/or others while threatening to disrupt the otherwise safe school environment.

Honig v. Doe: The Supreme Court Enters the Fray

In 1988 the United States Supreme Court resolved its only dispute involving discipline of students with disabilities under the IDEA in *Honig v. Doe* (*Honig*). *Honig* concerned two special education students who were identified in court papers as John Doe and Jack Smith. Doe, an emotionally disturbed student with aggressive tendencies, attended a developmental center for children with disabilities. Soon after Doe was placed at the school, he assaulted a peer and broke a school window. Initially Doe was suspended for five days, but he was later placed on an indefinite suspension pending an expulsion hearing. Doe's counsel unsuccessfully requested that school officials cancel his expulsion hearing and that his individualized education program (IEP) team be reconvened to assess his situation. Judicial review began after school board representatives ignored the attorney's request. A federal trial court eventually cancelled the expulsion hearing, ordered Doe readmitted to school, and prevented officials from excluding him while they sought an alternative placement where he could attend classes.

Smith was also emotionally disturbed and displayed aggressive tendencies. Educators placed Smith in a special education program within a regular school on a trial basis. After he committed acts of misconduct, school authorities reduced Smith's program to a half-day schedule. Although his grandparents agreed to this reduction, they were not advised of their rights or options regarding Smith's IEP. Following an incident wherein he made sexual comments to female students, Smith was suspended for five days and recommended for expulsion. School officials continued Smith's suspension pending resolution of expulsion proceedings. When Smith's attorney objected to the expulsion hearing, the school board canceled it and offered to either restore the half-day program or provide home tutoring. Smith's grandparents chose the home tutoring option.

A federal trial court in California, the Ninth Circuit, and the Supreme Court all agreed that students with disabilities could not be expelled for behavior that was a manifestation of, or related to, their disabilities. The Supreme Court acknowledged that in passing the IDEA, Congress intended to limit the authority of school officials to exclude students with disabilities, even for disciplinary purposes:

> We think it clear, however, that Congress very much meant to strip schools of the *unilateral* authority they had traditionally employed to exclude disabled students, particularly emotionally disturbed students, from school. In so doing, Congress did not leave school administrators powerless to deal with dangerous students; it did, however, deny school officials their former right to "self help," and directed that in the future the removal of disabled students could be accomplished only with the permission of the parents or, as a last resort, the courts. (*Honig v. Doe,* 1988, pp. 323–324)

The Court did not leave school officials without recourse because it added that they could suspend students with disabilities for up to ten days if they posed immediate threats to the safety of others. During the ten-day "cooling-off" period, the Court suggested that educators could seek to reach agreements with parents for alternate placements. In the event that parents adamantly refused to consent to changes in the placement of their children, the Court explained, school officials could seek judicial assistance. Under such circumstances, the Court specified that school officials would not be required to exhaust administrative remedies prior to filing court action if they could show that administrative review would be futile or inadequate. The Court indicated that in appropriate cases the judiciary could temporarily prevent dangerous children from attending school. The Court concluded by pointing out that the IDEA created a presumption in favor of students' then current, or pendant, educational placements that school officials could overcome only by showing that preserving the status quo was substantially likely to result in injury to those children and/or others in school communities.

Post-*Honig* Lower Court Decisions

Honig cleared up many but not all issues regarding the discipline of special education students in acknowledging that they could not be expelled for misbehavior that was related to their disabilities. At the same time, *Honig* suggested that educators could employ other normal disciplinary sanctions that did not cause changes in placement, such as short-term suspensions. Not surprisingly, litigation continued.

The Tenth Circuit affirmed that short-term disciplinary measures were not changes in placement under the IDEA (*Hayes v. Unified School District No. 377*, 1989). The dispute began when the parents of two students with histories of academic and behavior problems objected to the use of in-school suspensions and time-outs. The court found that while these short-term measures did not amount to changes in placement, since they related to the education of the students, they were subject to the IDEA's due process procedures.

In sanctioning suspensions of up to ten school days, *Honig* envisioned that cooling-off periods would give school officials and parents time to work together to devise other placements for students if they were needed. Unfortunately, since educators and parents do not always agree, sometimes other options cannot be worked out during the ten-day suspension periods. When parents and school officials cannot agree, their disputes are subject to the often lengthy and contentious administrative and judicial processes.

Honig granted school officials the ability to seek injunctions to remove students with disabilities who are dangerous or create serious disruptions in schools while administrative and judicial proceedings continue. In these situations, the burden is on school officials to demonstrate that students are truly dangerous and that removing them from their current educational placement is the only feasible option.

In the face of disruptive behavior by children with disabilities, school boards began, with mixed results, seeking *Honig* injunctions to remove students who were dangerous. A court in Virginia granted a board's request to enjoin a twelve-year-old student who was involved in fights, struck and yelled obscenities at school officials, and had to be restrained by the police on several occasions from attending classes (*School Board of the County of Prince William v. Wills*, 1989). A year later another court in Virginia granted the request of school officials for an injunction to exclude a student who set a fire in a school locker, among other infractions (*School Board of the County of Stafford v. Farley*, 1990). Similarly, a federal trial court in Illinois enjoined a student from attending class after he had violently struck other children and threatened to kill students and staff (*Board of Education of Township High School District v. Kurtz-Imig*, 1989). Finally, a state court in New York asserted that educators met their burden of showing that a student who ran out of the school waving an iron bar while threatening to kill someone was likely to endanger other students if he returned to class (*East Islip Union Free School District v. Andersen*, 1994).

Courts have ordered alternative placements when granting *Honig* injunctions. A federal trial court in Texas prohibited a student who assaulted classmates and teachers, destroyed school property, used profanity, and threatened to kill himself and others from attending general education classes (*Texas City Independent School District v. Jorstad*, 1990). In addition, the court decreed that pending the completion of the administrative review process, the student could either attend a behavioral class recommended by school officials or receive home tutoring. In a dispute from New York, a federal trial court ordered school officials to place a student in a special education class pending completion of a due process hearing (*Binghampton City School District v. Borgna*, 1991). The student frequently exhibited such aggressive behavior as punching other children, sticking a pencil in another student's ear, throwing his shoes at staff, hitting faculty, tipping over desks, and throwing chairs. In like manner, a federal trial court in Florida allowed a school board to transfer a student who was involved in forty-three instances of aggressive behavior to a special education center (*School Board of Pinellas County v. J.M. by L.M.*, 1997).

As important as it is to place dangerous students in appropriate placements, not all courts have agreed that school boards were entitled to *Honig* injunctions. A federal trial court in Missouri refused to allow officials to remove a middle school student who made numerous threats to students and school officials, repeatedly exploded in anger, and threw furniture (*Clinton County R-III School District v. C.J.K.*, 1995). Although another child was injured during one of these incidents and teachers testified that they were afraid of him, the court did not think that this was enough to establish that serious personal injury was likely to occur if he remained in his current placement. In another case, a federal trial court in Pennsylvania refused to issue an injunction in declaring that school officials failed to show that they took every reasonable measure to mitigate the dangers that the student posed (*School District of Philadelphia v. Stephan M. and Theresa M.*, 1997).

The Eighth Circuit provided school administrators with practical guidance on the removal of students with disabilities from their current educational settings in *Light v. Parkway C-2 School District* (1994). The court allowed officials to remove a student with mental disabilities who exhibited a steady stream of aggressive and disruptive behaviors from her then current special education placement. In doing so, the court was of the opinion that even a child whose behaviors flowed directly from her disability was subject to removal if she posed a substantial risk of injury to herself or others. In addition to showing that the student presented such a danger, the court declared that school officials must also demonstrate that they had made a reasonable effort to accommodate the student's disabilities so as to minimize the likelihood that she would injure herself or others. The court emphasized that only a showing of the likelihood of injury was required and that serious harm need not be inflicted before a child could be considered likely to cause injury. The court added that injury is not defined solely as an infliction that draws blood or sends a victim to an emergency room but also includes bruises, bites, and poked eyes.

Another post-*Honig* issue that emerged was whether students who were not yet identified as disabled were entitled to the IDEA's protections if they claimed to be disabled. The Ninth Circuit, in *Hacienda La Puente Unified School District of Los Angeles v. Honig* (1992), interpreted *Honig v. Doe* as suggesting that all students with disabilities, regardless of whether they were previously identified, are entitled to the procedural protections of the IDEA. Similarly, in *M.P. by D.P. v. Governing Board of the Grossmont Union High School District* (1994) a federal trial court in California held that the IDEA's procedural safeguards must be applied regardless of whether a student was previously diagnosed as having a disability. The court recognized that a student who is not disabled could attempt to be labeled as disabled solely to gain the benefits of the IDEA, but it responded that the IDEA did not address this possibility. On the other hand, a federal trial court in Virginia decided that a student who was suspended on a weapons violation was not entitled to the protections of the IDEA because the question of her disability was raised well after she committed her infraction (*Doe v. Manning*, 1994).

A related issue is whether former special education students who were not receiving services at the time of their disciplinary infractions were entitled to the IDEA's protections. A federal trial court in Wisconsin answered this question in the affirmative where a student was removed from special education at the request of his mother. In *Steldt v. School Board of the Riverdale School District* (1995), the student was expelled for a series of acts, including assaults on peers and school personnel. Previously, officials removed the student from a special education class for emotionally disturbed children at his mother's request, but contrary to his teacher's recommendation. The court, noting that the mother's request for her son to be removed from special education did not change his status as a student in need of special education, insisted that he was entitled to the protections of the IDEA.

Another similar issue was how school officials should treat students who were evaluated but not classified as disabled. As with most issues, the answer was based on the unique facts of each case. In one instance, a school's IEP team was convinced that a student did not require special education, but his mother contested its action. The Seventh Circuit maintained that the student was not entitled to an injunction barring his expulsion while administrative proceedings were pending

(*Rodiriecus L. v. Waukegan School District No. 60,* 1996). In a circumstance such as this, the court stated, educators needed to employ a flexible approach when applying the IDEA's stay-put provision and should not have applied it automatically to every student who was referred for a placement in special education.

The *Honig* Court reasoned that students in special education placements could be suspended for up to ten days. Insofar as the Court failed to specify whether the ten-day limit was consecutive or cumulative, litigation ensued. The Ninth Circuit, in *Parents of Student W. v. Puyallup School District* (1994), interpreted *Honig* as not supporting the proposition that the ten-day limit referred to ten total days. The court affirmed that the school board's suspension guidelines, wherein each suspension triggered an evaluation to consider whether a student was receiving an appropriate education, were lawful. On the other hand, in *Manchester School District v. Charles M.F.* (1994), the federal trial court in New Hampshire held that cumulative suspensions that totaled more than ten days constituted a pattern of exclusion that resulted in a change of placement.

In *S-1 v. Turlington (Turlington)* (1981), discussed earlier, the Fifth Circuit asserted that even when a special education student was properly expelled by following all of the IDEA's due process procedures, a complete cessation of services was not authorized. According to *Turlington,* a school board would still have to provide special education and related services to an expelled student with disabilities.

This issue arose again in Virginia in 1992 when the commonwealth officials submitted their three-year plan for special education to the U. S. Department of Education. A regulation declaring that students with disabilities could be disciplined in the same manner as students who were not disabled, if there was no causal relationship between the misconduct and the disability, was included in that plan. The Department of Education responded by informing officials in Virginia that they could not discontinue educational services to expelled special education students, even if the discipline resulted from behavior unrelated to the students' disabilities. The officials in Virginia failed to change the regulation, and the dispute eventually ended up in the courts. Following years of litigation, the Fourth Circuit, in *Commonwealth of Virginia Department of Education v. Riley (Riley)* (1997), pointed out that the IDEA did not require local school boards to discipline disabled students differently from peers who were not disabled when their misconduct was unrelated to their disabilities. The court found that the IDEA required states to provide disabled students only with access to a free appropriate public education, which, as with any right, could be forfeited by conduct antithetical to the right itself. The court concluded that school boards were not required to provide educational services to students with disabilities who forfeited their right to a FAPE by willfully engaging in conduct so serious as to warrant the ultimate penalty of expulsion.

Later in the same year that the Fourth Circuit resolved *Riley,* the Seventh Circuit reached a similar outcome in *Doe v. Board of Education of Oak Park & River Forest High School District 200 (Oak Park)* (1997). When school officials expelled a student for possession of a pipe and a small amount of marijuana, the board's evaluation team did not think that there was a causal relationship between his disability and misconduct. Under the circumstances, a federal trial court was of the opinion that the school board was not required to provide alternative educational services during the expulsion period. The appeals court agreed that the IDEA was not intended to shield special education students from the usual consequences of their misconduct when it is unrelated to their disabilities.

Riley and *Oak Park* can be compared to the order of the federal trial court in Arizona. In *Magyar v. Tucson Unified School District* (1997), school officials expelled a student with a learning disability after he gave an assault-style knife to another child. In reinstating the student, the court decided that the IDEA requires school boards to provide an appropriate education for all students with disabilities. The court thought that since the use of the word *all* in the IDEA was clear and unequivocal, it did not include an exception for misbehaving students.

THE 1997 AND 2004 IDEA AMENDMENTS

Against this backdrop of litigation and amid pressure from advocates for both school administrators and students with disabilities, Congress added disciplinary provisions to the IDEA in 1997. The 1997 amendments implemented the most far-reaching changes to the IDEA since its original enactment in 1975. Some of these provisions simply codified existing case law, others clarified gray areas, and some settled judicial disagreements. However, since these amendments did not settle all issues, litigation continued (Daniel, 2001). When Congress amended the IDEA again in 2004, it further refined the disciplinary provisions. The cumulative result of these two amendments is that the statute now includes comprehensive guidelines dealing with discipline. Consequently, litigation in this area has decreased.

Authority of School Personnel

The IDEA now details the authority and obligations of school personnel regarding the discipline of students with disabilities. The current disciplinary language provides school officials with more guidance than at any time in the past. Still, questions do arise that need to be resolved by the courts.

Case-by-Case Determinations for Short-Term Suspensions

Recognizing that disciplinary infractions may present school administrators with some unique situations, Congress inserted a clause into the 2004 version of the IDEA that allows school officials some flexibility. The IDEA and its regulations permit educators to consider unique circumstances on case-by-case bases when evaluating whether changes in placement are necessary for students with disabilities who violate school rules (20 U.S.C. § 1415(k)(1)(A); 34 C.F.R. § 300.530(a)).

Officials may remove children with disabilities from their current settings to alternative interim placements, or other locations, or suspend them for no more than ten consecutive school days for violating school disciplinary rules. Further, such students can be removed for up to ten additional consecutive school days in the same academic year for separate disciplinary infractions as long as these moves do not constitute changes in placement. If children with disabilities are removed from their current placements for ten school days in an academic year, then educators must provide them with services pursuant to 34 C.F.R. § 300.530(b). At the same time, if misbehaviors that are not a manifestation of a student's disabilities lead to a change in placements that exceeds ten days, then the IDEA and its regulations afford officials the authority to make such a change as long as the same procedures would apply to students who are not disabled (20 U.S.C. § 1415(k)(1)(C); 300 C.F.R. § 300.53(c)). This means that students with disabilities who are removed from school must continue to receive services that enable them to continue to participate in the general education curriculum, even in other settings, and to progress toward meeting the goals established in their IEPs (34 C.F.R. § 300.530(d)(1)).

The regulation also requires educators to perform functional behavioral assessments, discussed later in this chapter, along with implementing behavioral intervention services and modifications that are designed to address the misbehavior of students so that they do not recur (34 C.F.R. § 300.530(d)(2)). However, the regulation requires educators to provide services to students who are removed for less than ten days only if they do so for students who do not have disabilities and are removed from school for misconduct (34 C.F.R. § 300.530(d)(3)). Further, the regulation neither indicates that school systems may deny services to students who are removed for more than ten days in an academic year nor requires that they receive assistance when they are out of class for shorter periods of time (34 C.F.R. § 300.530(d)(4)). Of course, nothing prevents school systems from providing services under these circumstances. If removals constitute changes in placement, then the IEP teams of these children must determine what appropriate services they are entitled to receive (34 C.F.R. § 300.530(d)(5)).

Suspensions and Placements in Interim Alternative Educational Settings

The IDEA clearly stipulates that school officials may remove students with disabilities who violate school rules to appropriate interim alternative settings, or other settings, or can suspend them for not more than ten school days (20 U.S.C. § 1415(k)(1)(B); 34 C.F.R. § 300.530(b)). Even so, educators can implement such measures only to the extent that they use similar punishments when disciplining students who are not disabled. In addition, students may be removed to interim alternative educational settings for up to forty-five days under specified circumstances, discussed below, without regard for whether their misbehavior is a manifestation of their disabilities (20 U.S.C. § 1415(k)(1)(G); 34 C.F.R. § 300.530(g)).

Short-Term Suspensions

The IDEA affords school personnel the explicit authority to suspend special education students for not more than ten school days as long as similar sanctions would apply to children who are not disabled (20 U.S.C. § 1415(k)(1)(B); 34 C.F.R. § 300.530(b)(1)). Under these circumstances, officials not only must conduct functional behavioral assessments for students if they have not already been completed but must also take steps to address the misconduct (20 U.S.C. § 1415(k)(1)(D)(ii); 34 C.F.R. § 300.530(d)(1)(ii)).

At the same time, the IDEA's regulations maintain that a series of removals resulting in a pattern of exclusion that cumulates to more than ten school days constitutes a change in placement (34 C.F.R. § 300.356(a)(2)(i)). The regulation on changes of placements due to disciplinary removals includes the significant modification that if students are suspended for misbehavior that was "substantially similar" to past infractions that were viewed as manifestations of their disabilities, then a change in placement also would have occurred (34 C.F.R. § 300.536(a)(2)(ii)). Moreover, where students have been subject to a series of removals that constitute a pattern, hearing officers and courts will consider the length of each removal, the total amount of time that students are removed, and the proximity of the exclusions to one another in evaluating whether changes in placement occurred (34 C.F.R. § 300.536(a)(2)(iii)).

Educators have the authority to remove children with disabilities who violate school codes of conduct in their current placements to appropriate interim alternative educational settings, other settings, or suspend them for not more than ten consecutive school days to the extent those alternatives are applied to children without disabilities (34 C.F.R. § 300.530(b)(1)). Under this provision, school officials can impose additional removals of not more than ten consecutive school days in the same academic year for separate incidents of misconduct as long as these removals do not constitute a change of placement. If subsequent suspensions exceed ten cumulative school days in one year, services must begin after the tenth day (34 C.F.R. § 300.356(b)(2)).

Transfers to Other Settings for Disciplinary Reasons

Beginning with its 1997 amendments, the IDEA allows for the placement of students with disabilities to interim alternative educational settings for up to forty-five days for weapons and drug violations. In an important clarification, the regulations permit students to be removed for up to forty-five school, as opposed to calendar, days, a time frame that grants educators more latitude (34 C.F.R. § 300.530(g)(1)).

The IDEA and its regulations now authorize school officials to transfer students to alternative settings if they carry or possess weapons at school, on school premises, or at school functions (20 U.S.C. § 1415(k)(1)(G)(i); 34 C.F.R. § 300.530(g)(1)). Similarly, educators can transfer students who knowingly possess, use, sell, or solicit drugs under those same circumstances (20 U.S.C. § 1415(k)(1)(G)(ii); 34 C.F.R. § 300.530(g)(2)). When it comes to drugs, their mere possession is not enough for exclusion. Instead, students must "knowingly" possess drugs before they can be excluded. Perhaps this difference can be explained by anecdotal reports that drug-dealing and drug-using students often ask children with disabilities, with whom they would not otherwise associate, to unknowingly transport their caches of drugs as a sign of friendship or as favors. Finally, officials can transfer students if they have inflicted bodily injury on other persons (20 U.S.C. § 1415(k)(1)(G)(iii); 34 C.F.R. § 300.530(g)(3)). The regulation eliminated any specific requirements that IEP teams must consider in selecting interim alternative placements, thereby affording them greater authority and discretion.

When students are placed in interim settings for possession of drugs, weapons, or having caused bodily harm, the duties of school officials are relaxed to the extent that they are no longer required to conduct functional behavioral assessments and implement behavioral intervention plans in doing so. Rather, on the date on which educators make removals that constitute changes in placement of children with disabilities due to violations of student codes of conduct, they must inform the parents of their doing so and provide them with notice of their procedural safeguards (34 C.F.R. § 300.530(h)).

If parents disagree with the placement of their children in interim alternative settings and request hearings, students must remain in these locations pending the outcomes of hearings, until the expiration of the forty-five-day period, or the parties agree otherwise (20 U.S.C. § 1415(k)(4)(A); 34 C.F.R. § 300.533). The new regulation on placements during appeals introduced an important new change, replacing a lengthier, more detailed rule, with its streamlined provisions. Under this regulation, children must remain in their alternative settings for all disciplinary appeals, not just those relating to challenges of forty-five-day placements or where school officials sought hearings under the IDEA's "dangerousness" provisions (34 C.F.R. § 300.533). Additionally, school officials are required to arrange for expedited hearings within twenty school days of when they receive a request for one and must render decisions within ten school days after hearings are completed (20 U.S.C. § 1415(k)(4)(B); 34 C.F.R. § 300.532 (c)(2)). At the expiration of the forty-five-day period, students are entitled to return to their former settings even if hearings about school board proposals to change their placement are pending (20 U.S.C. § 1415(k)(4)(A)).

Weapons, Alcohol, and Drugs. School officials have the explicit authority to transfer students with disabilities to appropriate interim alternative placements for up to forty-five days for weapon, drug, and alcohol violations (20 U.S.C. §§ 1415(k)(1)(G)(i)-(ii); 34 C.F.R. §§ 300.530(g)(1), (2), (4)). This clause expands the authority that the Gun-Free Schools Act of 1994 granted school officials to exclude students from schools for drug violations.

The IDEA defines weapons and illegal drugs by referencing other federal legislation (20 U.S.C. §§ 1415(k)(7)(A), (B); 34 C.F.R. § 300.530(i)(1), (2)). In this regard, the definition of a dangerous weapon is expanded beyond the previous definition enunciated in the Gun-Free Schools Act. Under the new definition, what can be considered a dangerous weapon includes other instruments, devices, materials, and substances capable of inflicting harm in addition to firearms, but it does not include small pocket knives (18 U.S.C. § 930(g)(2)). The IDEA defines illegal drugs as controlled substances, but it excludes controlled substances that may be legally prescribed by physicians (20 U.S.C. § 1415(k)(7)(B); 34 C.F.R. § 300.530(i)(1)). The Controlled Substances Act (21 U.S.C. § 812 (c)), which is too lengthy to repeat here, specifies the full list of controlled substances.

Infliction of Serious Bodily Injury. The IDEA also now allows school personnel to remove students to interim alternative settings for inflicting serious bodily injuries (20 U.S.C. § 1415(k)(1)(G)(iii); 34 C.F.R. § 300.530(g)(3)). The IDEA's definition of serious bodily injury, which refers to another section of the United States Code (20 U.S.C. § 1415(k)(7)(C); 34 C.F.R. § 300.530(I)(3)), is that which may involve a substantial risk of death; extreme physical pain; protracted and obvious disfigurement; or protracted loss or impairment of the function of a bodily member, organ, or mental faculty (18 U.S.C. § 1365(h)(3)). Serious bodily injury may be contrasted with bodily injury, which generally involves only cuts, abrasions, bruises, burns, or other temporary injuries (18 U.S.C. § 1365(h)(4)).

Other Infractions. The IDEA's disciplinary provisions permit school officials to remove students from fully inclusive settings and place them in interim alternative placements for infractions other than those specifically listed in its text as long as they are doing so under "unique circumstances" (20 U.S.C. § 1415(k)(1)(A); 34 C.F.R. § 300.530(a)). When exercising this case-by-case authority, it is likely that school officials will be faced with parental challenges. Even so, prior case law suggests that officials will be upheld as long as they can reasonably justify their actions.

As illustrated by a case from Texas that was resolved prior to the IDEA's reauthorization, a circumstance justifying a student's exclusion may be an act of sexual harassment. In *Randy M. v. Texas City ISD* (2000) educators recommended that a special education student be transferred to an alternative education program for the remainder of a school year after he, in consort with another child, ripped the pants off of a female student. Prior to making this recommendation, the IEP team agreed that the student's misconduct was not a manifestation of his disability. When the student's parents sought to prevent the transfer, a federal trial court refused their request to do so. The court expressed its view that the disciplinary actions of the school officials were entirely appropriate under the facts of the case. The court explained that school officials were justified in taking stern and aggressive remedial action when faced with such conduct.

Another circumstance that can lead to a student's removal is behavior that may not necessarily have caused serious bodily injury but that, if repeated, has the potential to do so. In such a case, an appellate court in New York approved the removal of a student who hit other children and teachers, conceding that educators demonstrated that allowing him to return to school would have been likely to result in injuries to the child and/or others (*Roslyn Union Free School District v. Geffrey W.*, 2002).

Functional Behavioral Assessments and Behavioral Intervention Plans

The IDEA requires school personnel to conduct functional behavioral assessments (FBAs) and implement behavioral intervention plans (BIPs), if they are not already in place, or review such assessments and plans if they have been implemented under certain circumstances. Specifically, officials must perform FBAs and implement BIPs whenever students with disabilities are removed from their current placements for disciplinary reasons for more than ten school days (20 U.S.C. § 1415(k)(1)(D)(ii); 34 C.F.R. § 300.530(d)(ii)). Further, educators must complete FBAs and BIPs if they determine that misbehavior is a manifestation of students' disabilities (20 U.S.C. § 1415(k)(1)(F)(i); 34 C.F.R. § 300.530(f)(1)). Surprisingly, since the IDEA is generally prescriptive about such concerns, the statute and its regulations are silent about the form that BIPs must take. Even though the Eighth Circuit, relying on the IDEA's facial language, ruled that there was no requirement that a BIP be in writing (*School Board of Independent School District No. 11 v. Renollett*, 2006), educators would be wise to reduce their agreements to writing both to avoid potential problems down the line and to be consistent with the statute's overall stance with regard to record keeping.

Neither the IDEA nor its regulations provide much guidance as to what should be included in FBAs or BIPs. As of this writing, there have been few reported judicial decisions or due process hearings dealing with the contents of either FBAs or BIPs. In one dispute over a school's BIP, the Seventh Circuit affirmed that since there are no substantive requirements for a BIP, the challenged BIP could not have fallen short of criteria that did not exist (*Alex R. v. Forrestville Valley Community Unit School District*, 2004). Yet, the fact that substantive criteria for FBAs and BIPs do not exist does not mean that developing them is unimportant. To this end, a federal trial court in New York overturned a school's manifestation determination, in part because school personnel had not conducted an FBA prior to acting (*Coleman v. Newburgh Enlarged City School District*, 2004).

Expulsions

The IDEA permits educators to expel students with disabilities as long as the behaviors that gave rise to the violations of school rules are not manifestations of their disabilities. Again, though, under these circumstances expulsions must be treated in the same manner and for the same duration as they would be for students who are not disabled (20 U.S.C. § 1415(k)(1)(C); 300 C.F.R. § 300.530(c)).

Provision of Special Education Services During Expulsions

The IDEA makes it clear that special education services must continue during expulsions (20 U.S.C. §§ 1412(a)(1)(A), 1415(k)(1)(D)(i); 34 C.F.R. § 530(d)(i)). This provision essentially codifies the position of the United States Department of Education and effectively reverses judicial orders to the contrary (*Commonwealth of Virginia Department of Education v. Riley*, 1997; *Doe v. Board of Education of Oak Park & River Forest High School District 200*, 1997). The addition of this section to the IDEA ended a controversy that existed among the federal circuits prior to the enactment of the 1997 amendments.

Manifestation Doctrine

As noted earlier, the courts have long recognized that expulsions of students in special education settings constitute changes in placements. Expelling students for misconduct that was a manifestation of their disabilities, the courts reasoned, would have been the equivalent of punishing children for behavior over which they had no control. Additionally, the courts agreed that expulsions would result in the denial of the FAPEs the students are entitled to under federal law.

When school officials contemplate the expulsion of special education students, the IDEA requires educators to first ascertain whether their misbehaviors are manifestations of their disabilities. If officials agree that there is no connection between disabilities and misconduct, they may expel students (20 U.S.C. § 1415(k)(1)(C); 34 C.F.R. § 300.530(c)). However, even if students with disabilities are expelled, they must continue to receive educational services that will permit them to make progress toward meeting the goals set out in their IEPs (34 C.F.R. § 300.530d(1)(I)). Insofar as it is highly likely that expulsions will be challenged, it is imperative for school officials to follow proper procedures when making manifestation determinations.

Personnel Making the Manifestation Determination

Whether student misconduct is a manifestation of a disability is a judgment for IEP teams (20 U.S.C. § 1415(k)(1)(E); 34 C.F.R. § 300.531), including parents. Members of IEP teams should have personal knowledge of the student involved and of special education, especially an understanding of the characteristics of the child's disability. The regulations require IEP teams to include a child's parents (34 C.F.R. § 300.321(1)); not less than one regular education teacher (34 C.F.R. § 300.321(2)); not less than one special education teacher (34 C.F.R. § 300.321(3)); a school board representative who is qualified to provide or supervise special education (34 C.F.R. § 300.321(4)); a person who is qualified to interpret evaluation data (34 C.F.R. § 300.321(5)); other persons, at the discretion of parents and school board officials, who have knowledge or special expertise about the child (34 C.F.R. § 300.321(6)); and the student when appropriate (34 C.F.R. § 300.321(7)).

Time line

Manifestation determinations must be made within ten school days of any decision to change the placements of children with disabilities who violated school codes of conduct (20 U.S.C. § 1415(k)(1)(E)(i); 34 C.F.R. § 300.530(e)(1)). As explicit as this language is, the federal trial court in Maine pointed out that a delay in conducting a manifestation hearing was of no consequence because the parents had the opportunity to participate and the delay did not affect its outcome (*Farrin v. Maine School Administrative District No. 59*, 2001). The court observed that the delay in convening the meeting was understandable because the school board's special education director made several unsuccessful attempts to contact the parents in trying to schedule the hearing within the ten-day time period.

Manifestation as Defined in the IDEA

Prior to 2004 the IDEA did not provide a precise definition of the term *manifestation*. Yet, as indicated, the IDEA now specifies the criteria that IEP teams should consider in evaluating whether misconduct is a manifestation of a disability. More specifically, IEP teams must review all relevant information in student files, including IEPs, teacher observations, and other relevant information from parents that can be used to evaluate whether students' conduct was caused by or had a direct and substantial relationship to their disabilities or was a direct result of a school board's failure to implement an IEP (20 U.S.C. § (k)(1)(E); 34 C.F.R. § 300.530(e)(1)). Earlier case law can provide some guidance on how this new language can be interpreted.

The IDEA's definition of manifestation is identical to the wording that the Ninth Circuit used in *Doe v. Maher* (1986), the case that became known as *Honig v. Doe* (1988) once it reached the Supreme Court. The court held that manifestation of a disability refers to "conduct that is caused by, or has a direct and substantial relationship" to the student's disability (pp. 1480–1481, n. 8). The court further clarified this by explaining that disabilities must significantly impair the ability of students' behavioral controls and that the term does not embrace conduct that "bears only an attenuated relationship" to the disabilities (pp. 1480–1481, n. 8).

In a judgment that was handed down before the current definition of manifestation took effect, a federal trial court in New York overturned a school panel's finding that a student's misconduct was not a manifestation of his disability. Although it is a pre-2004 amendment opinion, this case illustrates one way that a disability may be deemed to have a direct relationship to a student's misconduct. After the student was disciplined following an altercation with another child, he claimed that he was merely responding to taunting about his status as being in special education. Under the circumstances, the court was satisfied that the student's disability was directly involved in the altercation (*Coleman v. Newburgh Enlarged City School District*, 2004).

On the other hand, in another pre-2004 amendment case, the Fourth Circuit upheld a school board's manifestation determination where a student coerced another child into putting a threatening note in the computer file of a third child. The court decided that the student was aware of the consequences of sending the threatening note and even anticipated them by enlisting the services of another student. Uncovering nothing in the student's records indicating that he could not manage his emotional problems, the court agreed that his misconduct was not a manifestation of his disability (*AW ex rel. Wilson v. Fairfax County School Board*, 2004).

Decisions the Manifestation Team Must Make

Along with evaluating whether misconduct was caused by or had a direct and substantial relationship to a student's disability, an IEP team must consider whether it was due to an IEP that was not properly implemented (20 U.S.C. § 1415(k)(1)(E)(i)(II); 34 C.F.R. § 300.530(e)(1)(ii)). In reviewing whether a placement was inappropriate, an IEP team should use the same standards that apply when prospectively determining whether a proposed placement is appropriate. Unless state law dictates otherwise, the basic criterion of an appropriate placement is whether it resulted in educational benefit to the student (*Board of Education of the Hendrick Hudson Central School District v. Rowley*, 1982).

If IEP teams decide that misconduct either is a manifestation of student disabilities or results from inappropriate placements or IEPs, the children may neither be expelled nor suspended for more than ten days, and school officials must reconsider their current placements. Nonpunitive changes in placement may be appropriate and should be implemented subject to the applicable procedural safeguards and the IDEA's least restrictive environment provision. Students may be suspended for more than ten days, or expelled, if the misconduct was not caused by their disabilities or did not result from inappropriate IEPs or placements.

Consideration of the Student's Disability Classification

As with the formulations of IEPs, manifestation determinations must be individualized. Insofar as blanket judgments based on the characteristics generally exhibited by other students with the same disability are not allowed, IEP teams must consider whether disabilities, as they impact students, are related to specific misconduct. An important consideration in this regard is the severity of a student's disability (*Elk Grove Unified School District*, 1989). IEP teams should also evaluate whether students have any previously unidentified disabilities that could have caused their wrongdoing (*Modesto City Schools*, 1994). Further, manifestation determinations must refer to a specific incident since generalizations cannot be the deciding factor. As such, IEP teams must consider whether disabilities, as exhibited by students, could have caused the misconduct that gave rise to proposed expulsions.

Consideration of Causes Other Than Disability

IEP teams must consider other factors that could have caused misbehavior by students (*Elk Grove Unified School District*, 1989). When several factors contribute to misbehavior, and student disabilities are among them, as long as officials can uncover a connection between disabilities and misconduct, children may not be expelled.

Reevaluation Requirement

If evaluation data are not up to date, school officials should conduct reevaluations (*In re Child with Disabilities*, 1989). Even though the IDEA requires school officials to complete reevaluations every three years, unless parents and officials agree that it is not necessary (20 U.S.C. § 1414(a)(2)(B)(ii)), evaluations are warranted earlier if circumstances change or if parents or teachers request reevaluations (20 U.S.C. § 1414(a)(2)(A)(ii)).

As reflected by a case from Michigan, one circumstance that requires an earlier evaluation is whenever an IEP team is considering a significant change in placement (*Brimmer v. Traverse City Area Public Schools*, 1994). A reevaluation should include a psychological assessment designed specifically to elicit data relative to the behavior that led to the disciplinary action. If those who conducted the most recent assessments are not part of the group making the manifestation determination, they should be consulted regarding the specific incident in question. If available evaluation data are more than one year old, a reevaluation should be completed before the manifestation decision is undertaken.

Making a Manifestation Determination

In making a manifestation determination, IEP teams must consider all relevant information, including all evaluation and diagnostic results and observations of children (20 U.S.C. § 1415(k)(1)(E)(i); 34 C.F.R. § 300.530(e)(1)). After IEP teams consider all relevant information, they should proceed as they would in making any other identification, classification, or placement decisions. IEP teams must thus exercise sound professional judgment. Members of IEP teams must rely on their professional knowledge, knowledge of the students, and understanding of the circumstances that led to the misconduct in making this critical decision.

Appeals

Like any matters related to special education programs, manifestation determinations are subject to the IDEA's administrative appeals process. In the case of manifestation determinations, hearings must be expedited (20 U.S.C. § 1415(k)(4)(B); 34 C.F.R. § 300.532 (c)), meaning that they must take place within twenty school days of the date on which they were requested and decisions must be issued within ten days of hearings. If parents contest manifestation determinations, school officials must postpone any long-term suspensions or expulsions until hearings are completed, even though students must remain in their interim alternative educational settings (20 U.S.C. § 1415(k)(4)(A); 34 C.F.R. § 300.533).

Authority of Hearing Officers

The IDEA affords hearing officers the authority to issue change in placement orders (20 U.S.C. § 1415(k)(3)(B); 34 C.F.R. § 300.532(b)(2)(ii)). Essentially, when hearing appeals, officers have two options: They may either return students to the placements from which they were removed or order that they be placed in interim alternative settings. If hearing officers choose the latter option, placements may not be for any more than forty-five school days.

Placement Pending Appeals

Whenever parents challenge placements made by their school boards, the IDEA requires children to remain in their then current placements pending the outcome of hearings (20 U.S.C. § 1415(j)). An exception exists when parents challenge a school board's wish to place a child in an interim alternative setting for disciplinary reasons. The IDEA declares that while such appeals are pending, students are to remain in interim alternative settings until hearing officers render judgments or the forty-five-day limit has expired (20 U.S.C. § 1415(k)(3)(4)(A); 34 C.F.R. § 300.533). In these circumstances, hearings must take place within twenty days, and orders must be rendered within another ten days (20 U.S.C. § 1415(k)(3)(4)(B); 34 C.F.R. § 300.532(c)).

Injunctions to Allow School Boards to Exclude Dangerous Students

In *Honig* the Supreme Court gave school officials the authority to seek injunctions to exclude dangerous students with disabilities from the regular education environment. Although hearing officers have the authority to order changes in placement to appropriate interim alternative educational settings for periods of up to forty-five days, when school officials can demonstrate that maintaining students in their then current placement is substantially likely to result in injury to them or other children (20 U.S.C. § 1415(k)(3)(B)(ii); 34 C.F.R. § 300.532(b)(2)(ii)), they may still seek injunctive relief to bar students from attending school.

According to a federal trial court in Alabama, the IDEA allows school boards to seek orders from hearing officers but does not require them to do so before requesting injunctions (*Gadsden City Board of Education v. B.P.*, 1998). The court ruled that the expedited-hearing provision in the amended IDEA is permissive and that exhaustion of administrative remedies is not required if a board chooses to seek a *Honig* injunction.

An appellate court in New York affirmed an injunction that allowed a school board to exclude and place a student who committed acts of misconduct, including hitting other students and teachers, in homebound instruction (*Roslyn Union Free School District v. Geffrey W.*, 2002). The court observed that the evidence presented by school officials clearly demonstrated that allowing the student to return to school was substantially likely to result in his injuring himself or others.

Rights of Students Not Yet Identified as Disabled

The IDEA and its regulations require school boards to provide its protections to students who were not yet determined to be eligible for special education, if school officials knew that they were disabled before the misbehavior occurred (20 U.S.C. § 1415(k)(5); 34 C.F.R. § 300.534). The law and regulations outline the circumstances under which school board personnel are considered to have such knowledge (20 U.S.C. § 1415(k)(5)(B); 34 C.F.R. § 300.534(b)).

School officials are deemed to have knowledge that students are disabled before misbehavior that precipitated the disciplinary action occurred if their parents expressed written concern to school officials or one of their teachers voiced a similar concern that they needed special education and related services (34 C.F.R. § 300.534(b)(1)); if the parent requested IDEA evaluations (34 C.F.R. § 300.534(b)(2)); or one of a student's teachers or other staff expressed specific concerns to the district's director of special education or other supervisory personnel about a pattern of behavior demonstrated by the child (34 C.F.R. § 300.534(b)(3)). However, if parents refused permission for evaluation or declined offered special education services (20 U.S.C. § 1415(k)(5)(C); 34 C.F.R. § 300.534 (c)(1)) or school personnel conducted evaluations and decided that students did not have disabilities (20 U.S.C. § 1415(k)(5)(C); 34 C.F.R. § 300.534(c)(2)), then the board would not be considered to have knowledge of their disabilities under this section.

If school board officials lack prior knowledge that students are disabled, they may be disciplined in the same manner as peers who are not disabled (20 U.S.C. § 1415(k)(5)(D)(i); 34 C.F.R. § 300.534(d)(1)). At the same time, requests for evaluations during a time period in which disciplinary sanctions have been imposed must be conducted in an expedited manner (20 U.S.C. § 1415(k)(5)(D)(ii); 34 C.F.R. § 300.534(d)(2)). Moreover, until evaluations are completed, children remain in the educational placement determined by school officials, which can include suspension or expulsion without educational services (20 U.S.C. § 1415(k)(5)(D)(ii); 34 C.F.R. § 300.534(d)(2)(ii)). Further, if officials decide that students have disabilities, then they must provide the children with special education and related services (20 U.S.C. § 1415(k)(5)(D)(ii); 34 C.F.R. § 300.534(d)(2)(iii)).

In an interesting case, *Colvin v. Lowndes County, Mississippi, School District* (1999), a federal trial court held that parents had not shown that their son had a disability even though they made requests for an evaluation. The court did rule that the school board violated the IDEA by failing to provide some assessment procedure to consider whether the student had a disability.

Conversely, the federal trial court in Connecticut, in *J.C. v. Regional School District No. 10* (2000), found that a student whose parents expressed concern over his poor performance and requested evaluations was entitled to the protections of the IDEA when he was faced with expulsion. Here, the student was evaluated, but officials decided that he was not entitled to an IEP because he was not disabled. When he faced expulsion consistent with the IDEA's provisions, the child was again evaluated at his parents' request, and this time the school board agreed that he was eligible for special education. Similarly, the federal trial court in Massachusetts overturned the expulsion of a student who failed all of her courses. Prior to conducting the student's expulsion hearing, school personnel evaluated her and agreed that she was not disabled. Yet, her attorney requested a due process hearing to contest the board's determination. Noting that the evaluation team's finding that the student was not disabled was not final but was subject to the pending hearing, the court reasoned that the student sufficiently presented a claim that officials had knowledge that she was disabled and should have afforded her the protections of the IDEA (*S.W. and Joanne W. v. Holbrook Public Schools*, 2002).

Effect of the IDEA on the Juvenile
Court and Law Enforcement Authorities

The IDEA and its regulations continue to specify that nothing in their provisions may be interpreted as prohibiting school officials from reporting crimes committed by special education students to the proper authorities or to impede law enforcement and judicial authorities from carrying out their responsibilities (20 U.S.C. § 1415(k)(6); 34 C.F.R. § 300.535). If school officials do report crimes, the IDEA requires them to furnish the special education and disciplinary records of students to the appropriate authorities.

In a case from Massachusetts, an appellate court emphasized that a juvenile court proceeding did not constitute a change in placement under the IDEA even when it took place due to a student's misconduct at school (*Commonwealth v. Nathaniel N.*, 2002). The court, in upholding the student's adjudication as delinquent for possession of marijuana in school, concluded that the IDEA clearly authorized educators to report criminal activity to the proper authorities.

As reflected by a case from New York, some judicial proceedings may trigger the IDEA's change in placement procedures. School officials unsuccessfully initiated proceedings to have an eight-year-old student declared a person in need of supervision due to his tardiness, absenteeism, and misconduct. Before permitting officials to initiate such an action, which would have resulted in a material change in the student's placement because it was unlikely that he would have been able to be educated with peers who were not disabled to the same extent or to have the same opportunities to participate in nonacademic extracurricular services, the court explained that they should have reviewed his IEP to consider whether additional interventions may have been warranted (*In re Doe*, 2002).

❖

❖   CASE NO. 11—SUSPENSION AND EXPULSION OF STUDENTS WITH DISABILITIES

HONIG

v.

DOE

Supreme Court of the United States, 1988

484 U.S. 305

Justice BRENNAN delivered the opinion of the Court.

As a condition of federal financial assistance, the Education of the Handicapped Act requires States to ensure a "free appropriate public education" for all disabled children within their jurisdictions. In aid of this goal, the Act establishes a comprehensive system of procedural safeguards. . . . Among these safeguards is the so-called "stay-put" provision, which directs that a disabled child "shall remain in [his or her] then current educational placement" pending completion of any review proceedings, unless the parents and state or local educational agencies otherwise agree. Today we must decide whether, in the face of this statutory proscription, state or local school authorities may nevertheless unilaterally exclude disabled children from the classroom for dangerous or disruptive conduct growing out of their disabilities. . . .

I

. . . The present dispute grows out of the efforts of certain officials of the San Francisco Unified School District (SFUSD) to expel two emotionally disturbed children from school indefinitely for violent and disruptive conduct related to their disabilities. In November 1980, respondent John Doe assaulted another student at the Louise Lombard School, a developmental center for disabled children. Doe's April 1980 IEP identified him as a socially and physically awkward 17–year-old who experienced considerable difficulty controlling his impulses and anger. Among the goals set out in his IEP was "[i]mprovement in [his] ability to relate to [his] peers [and to] cope with frustrating situations without resorting to aggressive acts." Frustrating situations, however, were an unfortunately prominent feature of Doe's school career: physical abnormalities, speech difficulties, and poor grooming habits had made him the target of teasing and ridicule as early as the first grade; his 1980 IEP reflected his continuing difficulties with peers, noting that his social skills had deteriorated and that he could tolerate only minor frustration before exploding.

On November 6, 1980, Doe responded to the taunts of a fellow student in precisely the explosive manner anticipated by his IEP: he choked the student with sufficient force to leave abrasions on the child's neck, and kicked out a school window while being escorted to the principal's office afterwards. Doe admitted his misconduct and the school subsequently suspended him for five days. Thereafter, his principal referred the matter to the SFUSD Student Placement Committee (SPC or Committee) with the recommendation that Doe be expelled. On the day the suspension was to end, the SPC notified Doe's mother that it was proposing to exclude her child permanently from SFUSD and was therefore extending his suspension until such time as the expulsion proceedings were completed. The Committee further advised her that she was entitled to attend the November 25 hearing at which it planned to discuss the proposed expulsion.

After unsuccessfully protesting these actions by letter, Doe brought this suit.... [a]lleging that the suspension and proposed expulsion violated the EHA, he sought a temporary restraining order canceling the SPC hearing and requiring school officials to convene an IEP meeting. The District Judge granted the requested injunctive relief and further ordered defendants to provide home tutoring for Doe on an interim basis; shortly thereafter, she issued a preliminary injunction directing defendants to return Doe to his then current educational placement at Louise Lombard School pending completion of the IEP review process. Doe reentered school on December 15, 5 1/2 weeks, and 24 school-days, after his initial suspension.

Respondent Jack Smith was identified as an emotionally disturbed child by the time he entered the second grade in 1976. School records prepared that year indicated that he was unable "to control verbal or physical outburst[s]" and exhibited a "[s]evere disturbance in relationships with peers and adults." Further evaluations subsequently revealed that he had been physically and emotionally abused as an infant and young child and that, despite above average intelligence, he experienced academic and social difficulties as a result of extreme hyperactivity and low self-esteem. Of particular concern was Smith's propensity for verbal hostility; one evaluator noted that the child reacted to stress by "attempt[ing] to cover his feelings of low self worth through aggressive behavior ... primarily verbal provocations."

Based on these evaluations, SFUSD placed Smith in a learning center for emotionally disturbed children. His grandparents, however, believed that his needs would be better served in the public school setting and, in September 1979, the school district acceded to their requests and enrolled him at A.P. Giannini Middle School. His February 1980 IEP recommended placement in a Learning Disability Group, stressing the need for close supervision and a highly structured environment. Like earlier evaluations, the February 1980 IEP noted that Smith was easily distracted, impulsive, and anxious; it therefore proposed a half-day schedule and suggested that the placement be undertaken on a trial basis.

At the beginning of the next school year, Smith was assigned to a full-day program; almost immediately thereafter he began misbehaving. School officials met twice with his grandparents in October 1980 to discuss returning him to a half-day program; although the grandparents agreed to the reduction, they apparently were never apprised of their right to challenge the decision through EHA procedures. The school officials also warned them that if the child continued his disruptive behavior—which included stealing, extorting money from fellow students, and making sexual comments to female classmates—they would seek to expel him. On November 14, they made good on this threat, suspending Smith for five days after he made further lewd comments. His principal referred the matter to the SPC, which recommended exclusion from SFUSD. As it did in John Doe's case, the Committee scheduled a hearing and extended the suspension indefinitely pending a final disposition in the matter. On November 28, Smith's counsel protested these actions on grounds essentially identical to those raised by Doe, and the SPC agreed to cancel the hearing and to return Smith to a half-day program at A.P. Giannini or to provide home tutoring. Smith's grandparents chose the latter option and the school began home instruction on December 10; on January 6, 1981, an IEP team convened to discuss alternative placements.

After learning of Doe's action, Smith sought and obtained leave to intervene in the suit. The District Court subsequently entered summary judgment in favor of respondents on their EHA claims and issued a permanent injunction. In a series of decisions, the District Judge found that the proposed expulsions and indefinite suspensions of respondents for conduct attributable to their disabilities deprived them of their congressionally mandated right to a free appropriate public education, as well as their right to have that education provided in accordance with the procedures set out in the EHA. The District

Judge therefore permanently enjoined ... any disciplinary action other than a 2- or 5-day suspension against any disabled child for disability-related misconduct, or from effecting any other change in the educational placement of any such child without parental consent pending completion of any EHA proceedings. In addition, the judge barred the State from authorizing unilateral placement changes and directed it to establish an EHA compliance-monitoring system or, alternatively, to enact guidelines governing local school responses to disability-related misconduct. Finally, the judge ordered the State to provide services directly to disabled children when, in any individual case, the State determined that the local educational agency was unable or unwilling to do so.

... the Ninth Circuit affirmed the orders with slight modifications. Agreeing with the District Court that an indefinite suspension in aid of expulsion constitutes a prohibited "change in placement" under [the EHA], the Court of Appeals held that the stay-put provision admitted of no "dangerousness" exception and that the statute therefore rendered invalid those provisions of the California Education Code permitting the indefinite suspension or expulsion of disabled children for misconduct arising out of their disabilities. The court concluded, however, that fixed suspensions of up to 30 schooldays did not fall within the reach of [the EHA], and therefore upheld recent amendments to the state Education Code authorizing such suspensions. ...

Petitioner Bill Honig, California Superintendent of Public Instruction, sought review in this Court, claiming that the Court of Appeals' construction of the stay-put provision conflicted with that of several other Courts of Appeals which had recognized a dangerousness exception. ... We granted certiorari to resolve these questions and now affirm.

II

...

III

The language of [the EHA] is unequivocal. It states plainly that during the pendency of any proceedings initiated under the Act, unless the state or local educational agency and the parents or guardian of a disabled child otherwise agree, "the child *shall* remain in the then current educational placement." (emphasis added). Faced with this clear directive, petitioner asks us to read a "dangerousness" exception into the stay-put provision on the basis of either of two essentially inconsistent assumptions: first, that Congress thought the residual authority of school officials to exclude dangerous students from the classroom too obvious for comment; or second, that Congress inadvertently failed to provide such authority and this Court must therefore remedy the oversight. Because we cannot accept either premise, we decline petitioner's invitation to rewrite the statute.

Petitioner's arguments proceed, he suggests, from a simple, commonsense proposition: Congress could not have intended the stay-put provision to be read literally, for such a construction leads to the clearly unintended, and untenable, result that school districts must return violent or dangerous students to school while the often lengthy EHA proceedings run their course. We think it clear, however, that Congress very much meant to strip schools of the unilateral authority they had traditionally employed to exclude disabled students, particularly emotionally disturbed students, from school. In so doing, Congress did not leave school administrators powerless to deal with dangerous students; it did, however, deny school officials their former right to "self-help," and directed that in the future the removal of disabled students could be accomplished only with the permission of the parents or, as a last resort, the courts.

As noted above, Congress passed the EHA after finding that school systems across the country had excluded one out of every eight disabled children from classes. In drafting the law, Congress was largely guided by the recent decisions in Mills v. Board of Education of District of Columbia and PARC, both of which involved the exclusion of hard-to-handle disabled students. Mills in particular demonstrated the extent to which schools used disciplinary measures to bar children from the classroom. . . .

Congress attacked such exclusionary practices in a variety of ways. It required participating States to educate all disabled children, regardless of the severity of their disabilities, and included within the definition of "handicapped" those children with serious emotional disturbances. It further provided for meaningful parental participation in all aspects of a child's educational placement, and barred schools, through the stay-put provision, from changing that placement over the parent's objection until all review proceedings were completed. Recognizing that those proceedings might prove long and tedious, the Act's drafters did not intend to operate inflexibly and they therefore allowed for interim placements where parents and school officials are able to agree on one. Conspicuously absent from [the EHA], however, is any emergency exception for dangerous students. This absence is all the more telling in light of the injunctive decree issued in PARC, which permitted school officials unilaterally to remove students in "'extraordinary circumstances.'" Given the lack of any similar exception in Mills, and the close attention Congress devoted to these "landmark" decisions, we can only conclude that the omission was intentional; we are therefore not at liberty to engraft onto the statute an exception Congress chose not to create.

Our conclusion that [the EHA] means what it says does not leave educators hamstrung. The Department of Education has observed that, "[w]hile the [child's] placement may not be changed [during any complaint proceeding], this does not preclude the agency from using its normal procedures for dealing with children who are endangering themselves or others." Such procedures may include the use of study carrels, timeouts, detention, or the restriction of privileges. More drastically, where a student poses an immediate threat to the safety of others, officials may temporarily suspend him or her for up to 10 schooldays. This authority, which respondent in no way disputes, not only ensures that school administrators can protect the safety of others by promptly removing the most dangerous of students, it also provides a "cooling down" period during which officials can initiate IEP review and seek to persuade the child's parents to agree to an interim placement. And in those cases in which the parents of a truly dangerous child adamantly refuse to permit any change in placement, the 10-day respite gives school officials an opportunity to invoke the aid of the courts under, which empowers courts to grant any appropriate relief.

Petitioner contends, however, that the availability of judicial relief is more illusory than real, because a party seeking review under [the EHA] must exhaust time-consuming administrative remedies, and because under the Court of Appeals' construction of [the EHA's due process procedures], courts are as bound by the stay-put provision's "automatic injunction," as are schools. It is true that judicial review is normally not available under [the EHA] until all administrative proceedings are completed, but as we have previously noted, parents may bypass the administrative process where exhaustion would be futile or inadequate. While many of the EHA's procedural safeguards protect the rights of parents and children, schools can and do seek redress through the administrative review process, and we have no reason to believe that Congress meant to require schools alone to exhaust in all cases, no matter how exigent the circumstances. The burden in such cases, of course, rests with the school to demonstrate the futility or inadequacy of administrative review, but nothing in [the EHA] suggests that schools are completely barred from attempting to make such a showing. Nor do we think that [the EHA] operates to limit the equitable powers of district courts such that they cannot, in appropriate cases, temporarily enjoin a dangerous disabled child from attending school. As the EHA's legislative history makes clear, one of the evils Congress sought to remedy was the unilateral exclusion of disabled children by schools, not courts, and one of the purposes of [the EHA's procedural protections], therefore, was "to prevent school officials from removing a child from the regular public school classroom over the parents' objection pending completion of the review proceedings." The stay-put provision in no way purports to limit or pre-empt the authority conferred on courts by [the EHA]; indeed, it says nothing whatever about judicial power.

In short, then, we believe that school officials are entitled to seek injunctive relief under [the EHA] in appropriate cases. In any such action, [the EHA's procedural protections] effectively creates a presumption in favor of the child's current educational placement which school officials can overcome only by showing that maintaining the child in his or her current placement is substantially likely to result in injury either to himself or herself, or to others. In the present case, we are satisfied that the District Court, in enjoining the state and local defendants from indefinitely suspending respondent or otherwise unilaterally altering his then current placement, properly balanced respondent's interest in receiving a free appropriate public education in accordance with the procedures and requirements of the EHA against the interests of the state and local school officials in maintaining a safe learning environment for all their students.

IV

We believe the courts below properly construed and applied [the EHA], except insofar as the Court of Appeals held that a suspension in excess of 10 schooldays does not constitute a "change in placement." We therefore affirm the Court of Appeals' judgment on this issue as modified herein. . . .

Affirmed.

Notes

1. In *Honig* the Court did not mention or address whether school officials must determine whether a student's misbehavior is a manifestation of a disability. Perhaps because the students in this case were identified as having behavior problems, it was automatically assumed that their misbehavior was a manifestation of their disabilities. Recent amendments to the IDEA make it clear that the manifestation doctrine is alive and well. Is it appropriate to assume that behavior is a manifestation of a student's disability based on a disability classification?

2. As *Honig* indicated, suspensions of up to ten school days can be handed out in the same manner for students with disabilities as they are for those who are not disabled. However, serial suspensions that, when taken together, exceed ten days can be problematic if they create a pattern of exclusion. What factors need to be considered when a student's total suspension days in a year exceed ten?

3. School officials can sometimes be heard to lament that the IDEA creates a different standard of discipline for students with disabilities. Yet, commentators insist that the IDEA only creates different procedures. Does the IDEA's process for disciplining students with disabilities result in different codes of conduct? How would you explain this to the parents of a student who was not disabled but was disciplined for hitting back after being struck by a student with disabilities?

❖   **CASE NO. 12**—MANIFESTATION DETERMINATION

AW ex rel. WILSON

v.

FAIRFAX COUNTY SCHOOL BOARD

United States Court of Appeals, Fourth Circuit, 2004

372 F.3d 674

DUNCAN, Circuit Judge:

AW, a disabled student in Fairfax County, Virginia, appeals the district court's judgment in favor of the Fairfax County School Board ("FCSB") in his suit under the Individuals with Disabilities Education Act, . . . ("the IDEA"). In his complaint, AW asserted that the FCSB improperly refused to allow him to enroll at his preferred junior high school after a pattern of misbehavior in the preceding school year resulted in his mid-year transfer to an elementary school that sent its students on to a different junior high school. Specifically, AW alleged that the FCSB's transfer decision violated the procedural and substantive protections afforded him under the IDEA, including its "stay-put" provision requiring that the student's "educational placement" not change while disciplinary proceedings are pending. Because we conclude that the term "educational placement" as used in the stay-put provision refers to the overall educational environment rather than the precise location in which the disabled student is educated, we affirm.

I.

In March 2002, AW was a sixth-grade student assigned to the "gifted and talented" program (the "GT program") at his elementary school. During the prior school year, a committee at AW's school concluded that AW was eligible to receive special education assistance under the IDEA as a student with an emotional disability. That determination resulted in the formulation of an Individualized Educational Program ("IEP") for AW that devoted one hour of each school week to specialized education intended to alleviate AW's "difficulty maintaining focus and completing academic tasks as required" and avoidance of "many tasks, especially when they involve writing." . . . AW successfully completed the remainder of his fifth-grade year, and his IEP was revised the following year in accordance with IDEA procedure.

As a sixth-grader, AW began exhibiting behavior problems he had not displayed during the first year of his IDEA program. These disciplinary issues culminated in a March 2002 incident in which AW persuaded another student to place a threatening note in the computer file of a student that AW disliked. In the ensuing inquiry, AW admitted that his intent was to scare the targeted student away from school. Based on his admission and past behavioral problems, school administrators suspended AW from school for two school weeks and initiated proceedings to expel AW.

As required by the IDEA, school officials convened a Manifestation Determination Review ("MDR") committee in order to determine the extent to which AW could be disciplined. Under the IDEA, a disabled student may not be disciplined by his school unless an MDR committee concludes that the student's IEP was appropriate relative to his qualifying disability and that the student's disability did not inhibit his capacity either to appreciate that his behavior was inappropriate or to conform his behavior to expectations. . . .

On the ninth day of AW's suspension, the MDR committee concluded that AW's IEP appropriately compensated for his emotional disability and that AW's disability did not prevent him from either understanding that his actions violated school rules or behaving appropriately. This finding opened the door for the FCSB to discipline AW as it would any other student.... The following day, however, a FCSB administrator rejected the expulsion recommendation from the administrators of AW's school and directed instead that AW be transferred to the GT program at another FCSB elementary school for the remainder of the school year. It is undisputed that AW would continue to receive the one hour per week of special education at this new location.

Despite the transfer determination, AW returned to his original school at the conclusion of his suspension to complete the final week of school before spring break. During this week, AW continued to receive GT program course work but was separated from his class and assigned instead to an empty classroom. As the week drew to a close, AW's parents invoked their right under the due process procedures of the IDEA to a review of the MDR determination. The appointed due process review officer ("DPR Officer") issued a pre-hearing decision staying the FCSB administrator's transfer decision, and AW returned to his original school following spring break.

At the April 17, 2002 hearing regarding the MDR committee's findings, AW's psychologist testified that AW had Attention Deficit Hyperactivity Disorder ("ADHD") and Oppositional Defiance Disorder ("ODD"). AW's psychologist opined that AW's IEP failed to adequately compensate for ODD and that AW's combination of conditions figured prominently in the behavior for which he was disciplined. Nevertheless, the DPR Officer concluded that the MDR committee's conclusion was sound and that the FCSB could transfer AW to a nearby school with a comparable GT program, based in part on his conclusion that the evidence did not support the findings of AW's psychologist. The DPR Officer's order released the FCSB to transfer AW to another elementary school located approximately five miles away from AW's original school, and AW completed his sixth-grade year at that school.

Following their unsuccessful attempts to enroll AW at the junior high he would likely have attended but for his transfer, AW's parents filed the complaint in this case on AW's behalf on August 16, 2002. The complaint alleged that the FCSB violated the IDEA's "stay-put" provision by transferring AW despite the ongoing challenge to the MDR committee's determination under the IDEA's review procedures, and that the MDR committee erred in concluding that AW could be disciplined as any other student. The district court granted judgment in favor of the FCSB, and AW timely appealed.

II.

... AW challenges the substantive determination by the MDR committee that allowed the FCSB to discipline AW in the same manner as any non-disabled student....

III.

. . .

IV.

AW's substantive challenge to the FCSB's transfer decision addresses the adequacy of the MDR committee's determination that his disability did not factor into the conduct for which he was suspended. As noted above, the IDEA requires that before any school can discipline a student, the school must determine whether the student's misconduct is related to the student's disability. If it is, the school officials are confined to the limited disciplinary measures described in [the IDEA]. However, if the MDR committee concludes that the child's disability did not factor into the student's conduct, then the school may discipline that student as it would any other. . . .

The issues the MDR committee must consider are clearly defined by the IDEA. The MDR committee must gather "all relevant information," including any "evaluation or diagnostic results," any "observations of the child," and "the child's IEP and placement." The MDR committee must then decide whether: (1) "the child's IEP and placement were appropriate and the special education services . . . were provided consistent with the child's IEP and placement"; (2) the child's disability impaired his ability to understand "the impact and consequences of the behavior subject to disciplinary action"; and (3) the child's disability impaired his ability "to control the behavior subject to disciplinary action." . . . The parties disagree as to the nature of AW's disability. Although it is undisputed that AW suffers from ADHD and ODD, the hearing officer and district court concluded that these disorders did not figure in the "emotional disability," . . . that rendered AW eligible for special education under the IDEA. The hearing officer and district court concluded instead that these conditions constituted "social maladjustment," . . . which was not a basis for coverage under the IDEA, and therefore the MDR committee need not have inquired whether these conditions impacted the adequacy of AW's IEP or his conduct.

Based on our review of the record, we conclude the MDR committee's conclusion was sound, although for slightly different reasons than relied on by the district court. AW's IDEA eligibility form is only marginally instructive, as it states that AW is eligible based on his "difficulties maintaining focus and completing academic tasks as required" and avoiding "many tasks, especially when they involve writing." . . . Additionally, the form notes that "Social Maladjustment has been ruled out as the PRIMARY cause of identified characteristics," . . . but does not exclude the possibility that it plays a secondary role in his qualifying disability.

A psychological and educational evaluation conducted in December 2000, however, indicates that while ADHD was a central feature of the emotional disability that qualified AW for special education services under the IDEA, ODD was not. In that evaluation, a psychologist at AW's elementary school concluded that AW's primary difficulty was his inability to concentrate and hyperactivity, two undisputed symptoms of ADHD. Although the evaluation also noted AW's tendency towards "frequent confrontations with authority figures," and that "*[t]his behavioral pattern may also lead to difficulties relating to peers at times, . . .*" (emphasis added), the evaluation nevertheless makes clear that AW's primary difficulty was behavior associated with ADHD that hampered his ability to thrive educationally. The psychologist concluded that "structure, consistency, predictability, and immediate feedback are critical in the development of any plan to address difficulties related to attention, impulsivity and concentration," and recommended that due to AW's hyperactivity, "*teachers [should] consider a variety of modifications in his school program,*" which would apparently include the very special education services subsequently implemented through AW's IEP . . . (emphasis added). By contrast, with respect to AW's "interpersonal and emotional difficulties," the evaluation concluded that outside counseling should be encouraged. . . . This evaluation strongly suggests that ADHD figured prominently in AW's qualifying disability, but ODD did not.

We therefore find no error in the MDR committee's conclusion that AW's IEP and placement in a general curriculum GT program was appropriate, and that his ADHD did not figure into the behavior for which he was to be disciplined. With respect to the adequacy of AW's IEP, we note that the IEPs of February 2001 and February 2002 focused on the complications occasioned in AW's schoolwork by his ADHD and identified his "social/emotional" difficulties as a matter for out-of-school counseling with a private counselor. This approach conforms to the recommendations made by the school psychologist in his evaluation of AW just prior to AW's IDEA eligibility determination. Moreover, nothing in the IEPs or the school psychologist's evaluation suggests that AW's interpersonal difficulties were so substantial that they could not be managed by outside counseling or that they would be exacerbated by being placed in the general GT curriculum with other students.

We likewise find no basis in the administrative record to conclude that ADHD figured into the conduct for which AW was disciplined. It is undisputed that AW is an intelligent student, and that AW was not only aware of the consequences of sending the threatening message to the targeted student, but anticipated them by enlisting another student to actually place the note. To the extent that students with ADHD may be described as impulsive, the circumstances of the conduct for which AW was disciplined indicated forethought and investigation, as he had to figure out a way to gain access to his target's personal folder. Given these circumstances, we find no error in the MDR committee's conclusion that AW's IEP and placement were appropriate to his ADHD, and that his ADHD did not figure into the conduct for which he was disciplined by the FCSB.

V.

Because we find that the specific location where the student is being educated is not controlling in a determination of educational placement in this context, and that the MDR committee's evaluation was appropriate given the nature of AW's disability, we find no error in the reasoning of the DPR Officer or the district court. Accordingly, the district court's order is

AFFIRMED.

Notes

1. This case was decided under the 1997 version of the IDEA. When Congress passed the 2004 amendments, the inquiry into whether misconduct was a manifestation of the student's disability was simplified. IEP teams now must consider "(I) if the conduct in question was caused by, or had a direct and substantial relationship to, the child's disability; or (II) if the conduct in question was the direct result of the local education agency's failure to implement the IEP" (20 U.S.C. § 1415(k)(1)(E)(i)). If the answer to either subclause (I) or (II) is yes, then the team must evaluate whether students' misconduct is a manifestation of their disabilities.

2. Here the court also decided that school personnel had not changed the student's placement while an appeal of the manifestation determination was pending in violation of the IDEA. That portion of the opinion was not included in the edited version of this case because it was not pertinent to the material presented in this chapter. Please refer to Chapter 3 for a discussion of the IDEA's change in placement procedures.

3. Insofar as the student involved in this case was gifted, the court was of the opinion that he was well aware that his conduct was not appropriate and understood the consequences of his actions. Would the decision have been different if the student had cognitive limitations or was learning disabled?

REFERENCES

Alex R. v. Forrestville Valley Community Unit School District, 375 F.3d 603 (7th Cir. 2004), cert. denied, 543 U.S. 1009 (2004).

AW ex rel. Wilson v. Fairfax County School Board, 372 F.3d 674 (4th Cir. 2004).

Binghampton City School District v. Borgna, 17 EHLR 677 (N.D.N.Y. 1991).

Board of Education of the Hendrick Hudson Central School District v. Rowley, 458 U.S. 176 (1982).

Board of Education of Township High School District v. Kurtz-Imig, 16 EHLR 17 (N.D. Ill. 1989).

Brimmer v. Traverse City Area Public Schools, 872 F. Supp. 447 (W.D. Mich. 1994).

Child with Disabilities, In re, 16 EHLR 207 (SEA Cal. 1989).

Clinton County R-III School District v. C.J.K., 896 F. Supp. 948 (W.D. Mo. 1995).

Coleman v. Newburgh Enlarged City School District, 319 F. Supp.2d 446 (S.D.N.Y. 2004).

Colvin v. Lowndes County, Mississippi, School District, 114 F. Supp. 504 (N.D. Miss. 1999).

Commonwealth of Virginia Department of Education v. Riley, 106 F.3d 559 (4th Cir. 1997).

Commonwealth v. Nathaniel N., 764 N.E.2d 883 (Mass. Ct. App. 2002).

Controlled Substances Act, 21 U.S.C. § 812 (2006).

Daniel, P. T. K. (2001). Discipline and the IDEA reauthorization: The need to resolve inconsistencies. *Education Law Reporter, 142,* 591–607.

Dayton, J. (2002). Special education discipline law. *Education Law Reporter, 163,* 17–35.

Doe, In re, 753 N.Y.S.2d 656 (N.Y. Fam. Ct. 2002).

Doe v. Board of Education of Oak Park & River Forest High School District 200, 115 F.3d 1273 (7th Cir. 1997).

Doe v. Koger, 480 F. Supp. 225 (N.D. Ind. 1979).

Doe v. Maher, 793 F.2d 1470 (9th Cir. 1986), *affirmed, Honig v. Doe*, 484 U.S. 305 (1988).

Doe v. Manning, 1994 WL 99052, 21 IDELR 357 (W.D. Va. 1994).

East Islip Union Free School District v. Andersen, 615 N.Y.S.2d 852 (N.Y. Sup. Ct. 1994).

Elk Grove Unified School District, 16 EHLR 622 (SEA Cal. 1989).

Farrin v. Maine School Administrative District No. 59, 165 F. Supp.2d 37 (D. Me. 2001).

Gadsden City Board of Education v. B.P., 3 F. Supp.2d 1299 (N.D. Ala. 1998).

Gun-Free Schools Act of 1994, 20 U.S.C. § 8921 (1994).

Hacienda La Puente Unified School District of Los Angeles v. Honig, 976 F.2d 487 (9th Cir. 1992).

Hayes v. Unified School District No. 377, 877 F.2d 809 (10th Cir. 1989).

Honig v. Doe, 484 U.S. 305 (1988).

Individuals with Disabilities Education Act, 20 U.S.C. §§ 1400–1482 (2005).

Jackson v. Franklin County School Board, 765 F.2d 535 (5th Cir. 1985).

J.C. v. Regional School District No. 10, 115 F. Supp. 297 (D. Conn. 2000), *reversed on other grounds*, 278 F.3d 119 (2d Cir. 2002).

Light v. Parkway C-2 School District, 41 F.3d 1223 (8th Cir. 1994).

Magyar v. Tucson Unified School District, 958 F. Supp. 1423 (D. Ariz. 1997).

Manchester School District v. Charles M.F., 1994 WL 485754, 21 IDELR 732 (D.N.H. 1994).

Modesto City Schools, 21 IDELR 685 (SEA Cal. 1994).

M.P. by D.P. v. Governing Board of the Grossmont Union High School District, 858 F. Supp. 1044 (S.D. Cal. 1994).

Parents of Student W. v. Puyallup School District, 31 F.3d 1489 (9th Cir. 1994).

Randy M. v. Texas City ISD, 93 F. Supp.2d 1310 (S.D. Tex. 2000).

Rodiriecus L. v. Waukegan School District No. 60, 90 F.3d 249 (7th Cir. 1996).

Roslyn Union Free School District v. Geffrey W., 740 N.Y.S.2d 451 (N.Y. App. Div. 2002).

S-1 v. Turlington, 635 F.2d 342 (5th Cir. 1981).

School Board of Independent School District No. 11 v. Renollett, 440 F.3d 1007 (8th Cir. 2006).

School Board of Pinellas County v. J.M. by L.M., 957 F. Supp. 1252 (M.D. Fla. 1997).

School Board of the County of Prince William v. Malone, 762 F.2d 1210 (4th Cir. 1985).

School Board of the County of Prince William v. Wills, 16 EHLR 1109 (Va. Cir. Ct. 1989).

School Board of the County of Stafford v. Farley, 16 EHLR 1119 (Va. Cir. Ct. 1990).

School District of Philadelphia v. Stephan M. and Theresa M., 1997 WL 89113 (E.D. Pa. 1997).

Steldt v. School Board of the Riverdale School District, 885 F. Supp. 1192 (W.D. Wis. 1995).

Stuart v. Nappi, 443 F. Supp. 1235 (D. Conn. 1978).

S.W. and Joanne W. v. Holbrook Public Schools, 221 F. Supp.2d 222 (D. Mass. 2002).

Texas City Independent School District v. Jorstad, 752 F. Supp. 231 (S.D. Tex. 1990).

7

Dispute Resolution

❖

Key Concepts in This Chapter

❖ Resolution Sessions

❖ Mediation

❖ Administrative Due Process Hearings

❖ Court Proceedings

As discussed throughout this book, the Individuals with Disabilities Education Act (IDEA) was enacted, in part, to grant parents and school officials opportunities to work together to develop individualized educational programs (IEPs) for students with disabilities. Yet, in recognizing that parents and educators may not agree in all situations, Congress included dispute resolution provisions in the IDEA (20 U.S.C. § 1415).

Parents of students with disabilities may request mediation (20 U.S.C. § 1415(e)) or due process hearings (20 U.S.C. § 1415(f)) if they disagree with any actions of school boards regarding proposed IEPs or of the provision of a free appropriate public education (FAPE) for their children. Once they exhaust administrative remedies, parents may seek judicial review in federal or state courts (20 U.S.C. § 1415(i)(2)(A)). Courts can waive the exhaustion requirement only when it clearly is futile to pursue additional administrative remedies (*Honig v. Doe* (*Honig*) 1988). Students must remain in their then current placements while administrative or judicial actions are pending unless school officials and parents agree to the contrary (20 U.S.C. § 1415(j)), hearing officers order changes (20 U.S.C. § 1415(k)(3)(B)), or judicial decrees call for new placements (*Honig v. Doe*, 1988).

The IDEA empowers the judiciary to review the records of administrative proceedings, to hear additional evidence, and to "grant such relief as the court determines is appropriate" (20 U.S.C. § 1415(i)(2)(C)(iii)) based on a **preponderance of the evidence** (20 U.S.C. § 1415(i)(2)(C)(iii)). Even so, the Supreme Court cautioned judges not "to substitute their own notions of sound educational policy for those of the authorities which they review" (*Board of Education of Hendrick Hudson Central School District v. Rowley* (*Rowley*), 1982, p. 206).

MEDIATION

In providing parents with alternative remedies in disputes over the placements of their children, the IDEA (20 U.S.C. § 1415(e)(1)) and its accompanying regulations (34 C.F.R. § 300.506(a)) direct states and school boards to offer mediation at public expense (20 U.S.C. § 1415(e)(2)(D)) as an option when due process hearings may be possible. To date, these provisions have been subject to little litigation.

The IDEA specifies that mediation must be voluntary on the part of the parties; cannot be used to deny or delay parental rights to due process hearings or to deny any other rights under the IDEA; and must be conducted by trained, qualified, impartial mediators (20 U.S.C. § 1415(e)(2)(A)(iii); 34 C.F.R. § 300.506(b)(1)) whose names are on state-maintained lists of qualified mediators in special education (20 U.S.C. § 1415(e)(2)(C)).

Mediators cannot be employees of states, school boards, or other agencies that provide direct services to students who are subject to the mediation process, nor can they have personal or professional conflicts of interest (34 C.F.R. § 300.506(c)(1)). Individuals who otherwise qualify as mediators are not considered employees of states or boards solely by virtue of being paid to serve as mediators (34 C.F.R. § 300.506(c)(2)).

Mediation sessions must be scheduled in a timely manner in locations convenient to the parties (20 U.S.C. § 1415(e)(2)(E)). Agreements that the parties reach as a result of mediation must be formalized in writing (20 U.S.C. § 1415(e)(2)(F)). Discussions that occur during mediation must be kept confidential and cannot be used as evidence in subsequent due process hearings or civil proceedings; the parties may also be required to sign confidentiality pledges prior to initiating mediation (20 U.S.C. § 1415(e)(2)(G)). A new subsection in one of the regulations makes clear that the results of mediation agreements can be enforced in federal or state courts (34 C.F.R. § 300.506(b)(7)).

To the extent that mediation is voluntary, parents may choose to bypass the process. If parents choose not to participate in mediation, then states may establish procedures allowing the parties to meet at convenient times and locations with disinterested third parties who are under contract with parent training and information centers, community parent-resource centers, or appropriate alternative dispute resolution entities to encourage the use of, and explain the benefits of, the process (20 U.S.C. § 1415(e)(2)(B)).

RESOLUTION SESSIONS

As part of the dispute resolution process, school officials must convene meetings between parents and relevant members of the IEP teams of their children (34 C.F.R. § 300.510(a)(4)) within fifteen days of parental requests for due process hearings in attempt to resolve placement disputes (20 U.S.C. § 1415(f)(1)(B)(i); 34 C.F.R. § 300.510(a)). If educators do not convene requested resolution sessions within this fifteen-day time frame, parents can seek the intervention of hearing officers to begin this process (34 C.F.R. § 300.510(b)(5)).

Each resolution session must include a school board representative with decision-making authority on its behalf (34 C.F.R. § 300.510(a)(i)) but may not involve a board attorney unless parents are also accompanied by counsel (34 C.F.R. § 300.510(a)(ii)). However, if school officials are unable to get parents to participate in resolution sessions and can document their reasonable efforts to do so within thirty days, hearing officers can dismiss complaints (34 C.F.R. § 300.510 (b)(4)). The parties need not attend resolution sessions if they agree, in writing, to waive their meetings or instead agree to mediation (34 C.F.R. § 300.510(a)(3)).

If parties do not resolve their disputes within thirty days, they should schedule due process hearings (20 U.S.C. § 1415(f)(1)(B)(ii); 34 C.F.R. § 300.510(b)). If the parties do resolve their differences at resolution sessions, they must execute and sign legally binding settlement agreements (20 U.S.C. § 1415(f)(1)(B)(iii); 34 C.F.R. § 300.510(c)). Settlement agreements are enforceable in state or federal courts, but either party may void such agreements within three business days (20 U.S.C. § 1415(f)(1)(B)(iv); 34 C.F.R. § 300.510(d)).

The federal trial court in the District of Columbia has maintained that the school board was not required to schedule a due process hearing without first trying to convene a preliminary resolution session. According to the court, there was no legal authority supporting the parent's proposition that the school board was required to bypass the statutorily required resolution session at the mother's request (*Spencer v. District of Columbia*, 2006). As such, this is an indication that resolution sessions may be waived only by consent of both parties.

DUE PROCESS HEARINGS

Parents have the right to request due process hearings on any matters concerning the delivery of any aspect of the special education that their children receive, including identification, evaluation, and placement (20 U.S.C. § 1415(f)). School officials may request hearings if parents refuse to consent to evaluations (34 C.F.R. § 300.300(a)(3)) and must provide parents with proper notice of their rights when they make requests for the evaluation of their children (34 C.F.R. § 300.503(a)). While administrative or judicial actions are pending, students must remain in their then current placements unless parents and school officials agree to other settings (20 U.S.C. § 1415(j)), hearing officers order changes (20 U.S.C. § 1415(k)(3)(B)), or judicial decrees mandate changes in placement (*Honig v. Doe*, 1988).

The IDEA's regulations grant parents the right to choose whether to have their children present at hearings (34 C.F.R. § 300.512(c)(1)) and whether they should be open to the public (34 C.F.R. § 300.512(c)(2)). If parents cannot be identified, their whereabouts cannot be discovered, or children are wards of the state, surrogate parents who are appointed to safeguard the educational interests of children can request hearings (34 C.F.R. § 300.30(a)(5)). The IDEA's regulations specify that surrogate parents are not employees of school boards or state educational agencies, cannot have personal or professional conflicts of interest with regard to the interests of the children involved, and have the knowledge and skill to act in this capacity (34 C.F.R. § 300.519(d)(2)). Otherwise, state laws and regulations govern other qualifications for surrogate parents, such as necessary educational preparation and background.

Parties who file due process complaints must forward copies of the materials to their state education agencies (34 C.F.R. § 300.508(a)(2)). Complaints must include the names and addresses of the children, their schools, and, if they are homeless, available contact information. In addition, complaints must include descriptions of the nature of the problems relating to the proposed or refused initiations or changes in the placement of the children, including facts relating to the problems and proposed resolutions to the extent known and available to the parties (34 C.F.R. § 300.508(b)).

An IDEA regulation explains that due process hearings cannot take place until one of the parties or its attorney files a sufficient complaint (34 C.F.R. § 300.508(c)). Complaints must be deemed sufficient unless the parties receiving them notify the hearing officers and the other party in writing within fifteen days of their receipt that they are insufficient (34 C.F.R. § 300.508(d)(1)). Within five days of receipt of this response, hearing officers must evaluate whether complaints are sufficient on their face and must immediately notify the parties of their decisions (34 C.F.R. § 300.508(d)(2)).

Parties may amend due process complaints only if the opposing parties consent in writing, are given the opportunity to resolve the underlying disputes through resolution sessions, or hearing officers grant permission no later than five days before hearings begin (34 C.F.R. § 300.508(d)(3)). If parties file amended complaints, the time lines for the resolution sessions to resolve the dispute begin anew (34 C.F.R. § 300.508(d)(4)).

Assuming, as is almost always the case, that parents requested due process hearings, school officials must, within ten days of receiving complaints, respond. Responses must include explanations of why school officials proposed or refused to take the actions raised in the complaints; descriptions of other options that IEP teams considered and the reasons why they were rejected;

descriptions of each evaluation procedure, assessment, record, or report they relied on as the basis for the proposed or refused actions; and descriptions of the other factors that were relevant to their proposed or refused actions. A regulation adds that responses cannot be interpreted as precluding school officials from asserting, if appropriate, that parental due process complaints are insufficient (34 C.F.R. § 300.508(e)).

Depending on the law in a given jurisdiction, either states or local school boards may conduct due process hearings (20 U.S.C. § 1415(f)(1)(A)). States are free to establish either one- or two-tiered administrative due process mechanisms. If local boards conduct initial hearings, either party may initiate state-level appeals (20 U.S.C. § 1415(g)). While procedures vary from one state to another, most jurisdictions created two-tiered systems that begin with hearings before individual hearing officers with appeals to review panels. In two-tiered systems, both procedures cannot be at the state level (*Burr v. Ambach*, 1988, 1989a, 1989b, 1990).

In states with two-tiered administrative hearing systems, some courts agreed that appeals heard by the heads of state educational agencies failed to meet the IDEA's impartiality requirements. For example, the Third Circuit ruled that Pennsylvania's Secretary of Education was not an impartial third-party decision-maker (*Muth v. Central Bucks School District*, 1988; *Johnson v. Lancaster-Lebanon Intermediate Unit No. 13, Lancaster City School District*, 1991). In an earlier case, the same court maintained that employees of the Delaware Department of Public Instruction were forbidden from serving as **state-level review officers** (*Grymes v. Madden*, 1982). Similarly, courts in New York held that the State Commissioner of Education was not impartial (*Antkowiak v. Ambach*, 1988; *Burr v. Ambach*, 1988, 1989a, 1989b, 1990; *Holmes v. Sobol*, 1988; *Louis M. v. Ambach*, 1989). Yet, another court in New York found that review officers who were appointed to oversee adjudications of local hearing officers were impartial even though they were subordinate to the Commissioner (*Board of Education of the Baldwin Union Free School District v. Commissioner of Education*, 1994).

In the past, the IDEA did not contain a statute of limitations for requesting administrative due process hearings. Thus, time limitations needed to be either mandated by state law or borrowed from analogous state statutes. Congress remedied this situation with the passage of the 2004 IDEA amendments by instituting a two-year limitations period for requesting hearings (20 U.S.C. § 1415(f)(3)(C)). If state laws create other limitations periods, they prevail (34 C.F.R. § 300.507(a)(2)). Moreover, if parents can show that school officials misrepresented that they resolved the problems or if they withheld pertinent information from parents, the federal time line is to be stayed (20 U.S.C. § 1415(f)(3)(D)).

Subject Matter of Hearings

Parents can request due process hearings on any matters relating to the education of their children with disabilities (20 U.S.C. § 1415(f)(1)(A)). For instance, parents can request hearings if school officials refuse to assess whether their children have disabilities (*Hacienda La Puente Unified School District of Los Angeles v. Honig,* 1992), if they disagree with findings or recommendations offered by school officials (*Dong v. Board of Education of the Rochester Community Schools,* 1999), or if they are dissatisfied with the content or implementation of the IEPs of their children (*Kuszewski v. Chippewa Valley Schools,* 2000). State laws and regulations may provide parents with additional rights over the content and structure of due process hearings.

If parents whose children are either enrolled in public schools or seeking to enroll them fail, or refuse, to respond to requests to provide consent for initial evaluations, school officials may, but are not required to, request due process hearings to pursue initial evaluations, if appropriate, except to the extent that doing so would be inconsistent with state laws relating to parental consent (34 C.F.R. § 300.300(a)(3)(i)). If school officials choose not to pursue evaluations under the circumstances, parents may not accuse them of violating their duties under the IDEA (34 C.F.R. § 300.300(a)(3)(ii)). School officials can request hearings if parents refuse to consent to evaluations (34 C.F.R. § 300.300(a)(3)), but not if parents refuse to consent to the provision of services for their children (34 C.F.R. § 300.300(b)(2)).

Parents can also request due process hearings after the eligibility of their children to receive special education ends because students may be entitled to compensatory educational services if courts agree that they were denied a FAPE. In such a case, the Supreme Court of Ohio decided that a student was entitled to a hearing even though the request for it was submitted one day before the student's eligibility for special education services ended under state law (*Board of Education of Strongville City School District v. Theado,* 1991). The record reflected that school board officials objected to the hearing since the student was no longer eligible for services. Reversing in favor of the student, the court disagreed, reasoning that insofar as it was possible to award compensatory services to children who were denied an appropriate education, he was entitled to the hearing.

Pursuant to an important new limitation, parties requesting due process hearings pursuant to the IDEA are precluded from raising issues that were not included in the complaints that they filed to initiate the proceedings unless the other party agrees otherwise (20 U.S.C. § 1415(f)(3)(B); 34 C.F.R. § 300.511(d)).

Impartiality of Hearing Officers

Hearing officers, typically selected pursuant to provisions in state law (*Cothern v. Mallory,* 1983), must be impartial, meaning that they cannot be employees of the states or districts involved in the education of the children whose cases appear before them or have personal or professional interests in these students (20 U.S.C. § 1415(f)(3)(A); 34 C.F.R. § 300.511(c)). Individuals who otherwise qualify as hearing officers are not considered employees of states or local school boards solely by virtue of being paid to serve in this capacity (34 C.F.R. § 300.511(c)(2)). State education agencies are required to keep lists of qualified hearing officers along with explanations of their qualifications (34 C.F.R. § 300.511(c)(3)).

Just because hearing officers may be employed by other school boards does not automatically disqualify them from serving due to bias. In a representative case challenging the impartiality of a hearing officer, the Tenth Circuit reiterated the rule that an officer's being employed by another school board did not violate the IDEA prohibition against working for the district involved in a hearing (*L.B. and J.B. ex rel. K.B. v. Nebo School District*, 2004). The court confirmed that hearing officers must not have any personal or professional interest that would conflict with their objectivity.

Authority of Hearing Officers

In due process hearings, hearing officers must sort out what took place and apply the law to the facts in a manner similar to that of trial court judges. Like judges, hearing officers are empowered to issue orders and grant **equitable relief** regarding the provision of a FAPE for students with disabilities.

The importance of their duties aside, the authority of hearing officers is limited. Hearing officers generally do not have the authority to provide remedies when parties challenge broad policies or procedures that affect a large number of students or to address matters of law since they lack the ability to consider a statute's constitutionality. Rather, the power of hearing officers is limited to the facts of the disputes at hand. In such a case, the Ninth Circuit ruled that a hearing officer lacked the power to address the legislature's failure to appropriate sufficient funds for special education programs (*Kerr Center Parents Association v. Charles*, 1990). Along the same lines, a federal trial court in Indiana concluded that a hearing officer did not have the authority to rule on the legality of a state-required application review process for students who needed residential placements or to provide a remedy (*Bray v. Hobart City School Corporation*, 1993). In addition, the IDEA limits the awarding of attorneys fees to prevailing parents in special education disputes to the discretion of federal courts (20 U.S.C. §1415(i)(3)(B)).

An unresolved question remains over whether hearing officers can grant awards of compensatory services to students who were denied a FAPE. While the Third Circuit affirmed that hearing officers were powerless to address the question of compensatory education (*Lester H. v. Gilhool*, 1990), the Second Circuit reached the opposite result (*Burr v. Ambach*, 1988, 1989a, 1989b, 1990). Moreover, the federal trial court in New Hampshire asserted that a hearing officer erred in writing that he lacked the authority to award compensatory services. The court thought that in light of the importance Congress placed on the process, such power was coextensive with that of the judiciary (*Cocores v. Portsmouth, New Hampshire School District*, 1991). To the extent that hearing officers can grant awards of tuition reimbursement, it seems logical that they should have the authority to award compensatory educational services as well.

Preparation of Hearing Officers

Hearing officers must be impartial and have no personal or professional interest in the outcome of the disputes they resolve (34 C.F.R. § 300.511(c)). Insofar as the IDEA does not contain specific language regarding the qualifications of hearing officers, these criteria are left up to the states to establish. In one of the few cases on point, the federal trial court in Connecticut noted that the state's failure to train hearing officers was not a violation of the IDEA (*Canton Board of Education v. N.B. and R.B.,* 2004).

Burden of Proof

Until recently, the IDEA and its regulations were silent as to which party bore the burden of proof in due process hearings. As such, this important question was resolved based on state laws or judicial discretion, leading to a great deal of disagreement and inconsistency. Not surprisingly, two distinct perspectives emerged. On the one hand, the Fourth (*Weast v. Schaffer,* 2004), Fifth (*Alamo Heights Independent School District v. State Board of Education,* 1986), Sixth (*Doe v. Board of Education of Tullahoma City Schools,* 1993), and Tenth (*Johnson v. Independent School District No. 4,* 1990) Circuits agreed that the parties challenging IEPs bore the burden of proof. These courts assigned presumptions in favor of IEPs as long as they were developed according to the procedures outlined in the IDEA.

Conversely, the Second (*Grim v. Rhinebeck Central School District,* 2003), Third (*Carlisle Area School v. Scott P.,* 1995), Seventh (*Beth B. v. Van Clay,* 2002), Eighth (*Blackmon v. Springfield R-XII School District,* 1999), Ninth (*Seattle School District No. 1 v. B.S.,* 1996), and District of Columbia (*McKenzie v. Smith,* 1985) Circuits placed the burden of proof on school boards, regardless of whether they or parents wished to alter IEPs. These courts noted that since boards had the duty to provide a FAPE for students with disabilities, school officials should have been better able to meet the burden of proof due to their access to relevant information, coupled with parental lack of expertise in formulating an appropriate IEP.

The Supreme Court stepped into the fray and resolved the controversy over who bore the burden of proof in *Schaffer ex rel. Schaffer v. Weast* (*Schaffer*) (2005). In conceding that arguments could be made on both sides of the issue, the Court saw no reason to depart from the usual rule that the party seeking relief bears the burden of persuasion. In IDEA cases, this is generally the parents (Osborne & Russo, 2005). The issue was important since the assignment of the burden of proof can well impact the final outcome in close cases (Wenkart, 2004). Under *Schaffer,* parents who challenge proposed IEPs must now demonstrate that the IEPs are deficient unless state laws provide otherwise (Russo & Osborne, 2006). In the wake of *Schaffer,* at least two circuits placed the burden of proof on the party challenging the IEPs (*L.E. ex rel. E.S. v. Ramsey Board of Education,* 2006; *West Platte R-II School District v. Wilson ex rel. L.W.,* 2006).

Exhaustion of Administrative Remedies

As reflected by a case from New Mexico, "[t]he IDEA favors prompt resolution of disputes" (*Sanders v. Santa Fe Public Schools,* 2004, p. 1311) over the education of students with disabilities because Congress acknowledged the need to help children who may be at formative stages in their development. In this respect, the IDEA requires parties to exhaust administrative remedies before filing suits unless it clearly is futile to do so (*Honig v. Doe*, 1988). Courts can also excuse parental failure to exhaust administrative remedies if school officials deny their requests for due process hearings or frustrate their attempts to dispute the results of hearings (*Abney ex rel. Kantor v. District of Columbia*, 1988; *Independent School District No. 623 v. Digre*, 1990), or if it is impossible for parents to obtain adequate relief through hearings (*Padilla v. School District No. 1*, 2000). Exhaustion is not required to enforce final administrative orders, except that these cases must be filed under the Civil Rights Act of 1871, Section 1983 (42 U.S.C. § 1983), a statute that is discussed later in this chapter (*Robinson v. Pinderhughes*, 1987). Put another way, as reviewed in the next section, since parties may not file suit until administrative appeals are pursued, courts refuse to address issues that have not been subjected to complete exhaustion (*T.S. v. Ridgefield Board of Education*, 1993).

Exhaustion Required

The judiciary has long refused to hear cases in which parties bringing suits have not exhausted administrative remedies (*Riley v. Ambach*, 1981; *Christopher W. v. Portsmouth School Committee*, 1989; *Cox v. Jenkins*, 1989; *Doe v. Smith*, 1989; *Gardener v. School Board of Caddo Parish*, 1992; *T.S. v. Ridgefield Board of Education*, 1993; *N.B. v. Alachua County School Board*, 1996; *Doe v. Arizona Department of Education*, 1997; *D.C. ex rel. S.K. v. Hamamoto*, 2004). Exhaustion is required for a variety of reasons. By way of illustration, since judges consider themselves generalists when reviewing the educational needs of students with disabilities and hearing officers are more experienced in these matters (*Crocker v. Tennessee Secondary School Athletic Association*, 1989), courts want to be able to review complete records that have been developed by professionals with competence in this complex area of the law. In one case, where a student sought **damages** over a board's alleged failure to provide IDEA services, the Second Circuit decided that this did not entitle her to sidestep the exhaustion requirement because the real problem was the lack of specificity in her IEP rather than the board's failure to comply with its content (*Polera v. Board of Education of the Newburgh Enlarged City School District*, 2002).

The majority of courts treat class action suits, wherein one person or a small group of individuals files a case on behalf of a larger group of similarly aggrieved individuals with widespread application, as being subject to the exhaustion requirements (*Hoeft v. Tucson Unified School District*, 1992). One court went so far as to declare that all members of a class had to exhaust administrative remedies prior to bringing suit (*Jackson v. Fort Stanton Hospital and Training School*, 1990). Other courts have pointed out that filing representative claims served the purposes of exhaustion (*Association for Retarded Citizens of Alabama v. Teague*, 1987; *Association for Community Living in Colorado v. Romer*, 1993).

The Tenth Circuit stated that the issue of whether a state's policies denied students with disabilities a FAPE entailed a factually intensive inquiry into the circumstances of their cases and was the type of issue the administrative process was designed to address (*Association for Community Living in Colorado v. Romer,* 1993). A federal trial court in Indiana reached a different result in positing that plaintiffs representing a class need not exhaust administrative remedies because class action administrative hearings are not permitted (*Evans v. Evans,* 1993).

Insofar as parties must exhaust administrative remedies, they cannot initiate litigation on issues that have not already been addressed at due process hearings. In this regard, the Second Circuit affirmed that a student's attorney could not claim that a school board committed procedural violations since the issue had not been raised at a due process hearing on his request for compensatory education (*Garro v. State of Connecticut,* 1994). A federal court in New York also explained that parents could not raise the issue of the appropriateness of an evaluation facility since they failed to challenge the hearing officer's recommendation on the issue in the presence of a state-level review officer (*Stellato v. Board of Education of the Ellenville Central School District,* 1994).

Parties must exhaust administrative remedies when making claims under statutes other than the IDEA (*Torrie v. Cwayna,* 1994), when challenging classroom procedures (*Hayes v. Unified School District No. 377,* 1989), or when seeking enforcement of administrative orders if state regulations provide for this through the administrative process (*Norris v. Board of Education of Greenwood Community School Corporation,* 1992).

Exhaustion Not Required

For the most part, courts agree that parents are not required to exhaust administrative remedies under a variety of circumstances (Clark, 2002). In the first of two cases on point, the Ninth Circuit agreed that parents were able to skip a due process hearing when their complaint was that they were denied access to that process (*Kerr Center Parents Association v. Charles,* 1990). In the second, the federal trial court in Arizona indicated that exhaustion would have been futile where a mother claimed that she was denied meaningful access to the IDEA's due process procedures (*Begay v. Hodel,* 1990).

Parties may not have to exhaust administrative remedies when complaints allege systemic failures. In such a case, the Second Circuit affirmed that a school board's alleged failure to prepare and implement IEPs, notify parents of meetings, provide parents with required progress reports, perform timely evaluations, provide adequate procedural safeguards, carry out their required responsibilities in a timely fashion, and offer appropriate training for staff members were systemic failures that could not be remedied through the administrative hearing process (*J.S. ex rel. N.S. v. Attica Central Schools,* 2004).

Challenges to school board policies that could violate the IDEA may not be subject to the administrative process. As such, the Ninth Circuit was convinced that a claim that the school day for specified special education students was shorter than for children in regular education was not subject to the exhaustion requirement because it had nothing to do with individual IEPs (*Christopher S. ex rel. Rita S. v. Stanislaus County Office of Education,* 2004).

Courts have considered exhaustion to be futile when hearing officers lacked authority to grant the requested relief. The Second Circuit decided that a father's complaint about the method by which hearing officers were selected was not subject to exhaustion since a sole hearing officer lacked the authority to alter the procedure (*Heldman v. Sobol*, 1992). Federal trial courts in New York also found that exhaustion was not required when the requested relief was that a child be placed in a school that was not on the state's list of approved placements because the hearing officer could not order a student to attend classes in an unapproved facility (*Straube v. Florida Union Free School District*, 1992), or in challenging an adjudication of officials of the state education department who rejected a parental request but declined to make an exception to general procedures (*Vander Malle v. Ambach*, 1987).

The previous section discussed cases wherein courts subjected class action suits to the exhaustion of remedies requirement. Yet, since not all courts agree, exhaustion may not be necessary in class action suits where the claims of plaintiffs are systemic in nature and hearing officers would not have the authority to grant the requested relief. For example, the Second Circuit affirmed that exhaustion was not required when a hearing officer could not order a systemwide change to correct the alleged wrongs (*J.G. v. Board of Education of Rochester City School District*, 1987). Exhaustion may be unnecessary in emergency situations if it would cause severe or irreparable harm to students. However, the Third Circuit held that since mere allegations of irreparable harm are insufficient to excuse exhaustion, a plaintiff must present actual evidence to support such a claim (*Komninos v. Upper Saddle River Board of Education*, 1994).

When litigation involves issues that are purely legal rather than factual, the Third Circuit was of the opinion that exhaustion may not be required (*Lester H. v. Gilhool*, 1990). Similarly, the Second Circuit determined that exhaustion may not be necessary if a state persistently fails to render expeditious decisions regarding a student's educational placement (*Frutiger v. Hamilton Central School District*, 1991).

Finally, courts have refused to apply the exhaustion requirement when students do not need special education. To this end, courts agree that parents do not have to exhaust administrative remedies in cases under Section 504 if their children are not receiving services under the IDEA, even if they are disabled (*Doe v. Belleville Public School District No. 118*, 1987; *Robertson v. Granite City Community Unit School District No. 9*, 1988).

Rights of Parties to a Hearing

Parties involved in due process hearings have the right to be accompanied and advised by counsel with special knowledge concerning the education of students with disabilities (20 U.S.C. § 1415(h)(1)). As such, the Supreme Court of Delaware held that the IDEA does not authorize nonattorneys to represent parents at hearings (*In re Arons*, 2000). Consequently, the court affirmed an order forbidding nonattorneys with special knowledge and training with respect to the problems of students with disabilities from representing parents at due process hearings.

The parties at hearings may present evidence, compel the attendance of witnesses, and cross-examine witnesses during these quasi-judicial proceedings (20 U.S.C. § 1415(h)(1)(2)). The parties can prohibit the introduction of evidence that is not disclosed at least five business days prior to hearings (34 C.F.R. § 300.512(a)(3)). At the same time, the parties have the right to obtain written or, at the option of the parents, electronic verbatim records of hearings, as well as findings of fact and decisions (20 U.S.C. §§ 1415(h)(3)-(4)).

In a procedural matter, the federal trial court in New Jersey observed that an indigent parent who could not afford to pay for it was entitled to receive a written transcript of a hearing at public expense so that she could challenge its results (*Militello v. Board of Education of the City of Union City*, 1992). The court contended that a copy of the transcript of the lengthy and complex hearing was an essential tool for the mother's effective and efficient review of its outcome. In a slightly different case, the First Circuit affirmed that educational officials could provide either a written transcript or an electronic record of the administrative hearings to indigent parents (*Edward B. v. Paul*, 1987).

Pursuant to the IDEA, hearing officers must render final orders within forty-five days of requests for hearings (34 C.F.R. § 300.515(a)). Even so, hearing officers can grant requests from the parties for extensions or continuances (34 C.F.R. § 300.515(c)). The results of hearings are final unless they are appealed (20 U.S.C. § 1415(i)(1)(A)).

In states with two-tiered due process hearing systems, officials must ensure that final appeals, based on the record, are reached within thirty days of requests for review (34 C.F.R. § 300.515(b)). At least one court decreed that the IDEA's finality requirement precludes a hearing officer from taking any action that interferes with rendering a final adjudicative order. The federal trial court in Delaware asserted that a hearing panel may not refer a case to some other body for review (*Slack v. State of Delaware Department of Public Instruction*, 1993). A hearing panel commented that a student was entitled to a residential placement but did not order the child to be moved to such a setting. Instead, the panel thought that a mechanism should have been established to evaluate options. The court concluded that referring the case for additional review did not comport with the IDEA's finality requirements, thereby undermining the concern for prompt resolution of placement disputes.

Once administrative review is complete, aggrieved parties may file suit in federal or state courts (20 U.S.C. § 1415(i)(2)(A)). Aggrieved parties are generally considered to be the losing parties or the ones who did not obtain the relief sought. While prevailing parties are ordinarily not viewed as aggrieved, the federal trial court in Delaware permitted parents who won on the legal issues but did not obtain the relief they sought to be treated as the aggrieved party so that they could seek judicial review (*Slack v. State of Delaware Department of Public Instruction*, 1993).

JUDICIAL REVIEW

As mentioned earlier, under the IDEA, either party can appeal the results of due process hearings to federal or state courts once they have exhausted administrative remedies. As important as this issue is, the IDEA is silent about whether cases are to be submitted to juries. Insofar as due process hearings generate their own record, the courts generally do not conduct trials *de novo*. In other words, courts ordinarily do not repeat investigations as if none had occurred administratively. Rather, the courts examine the records of hearings and hear new or additional testimony when necessary. Due to the importance Congress placed on the administrative process, the IDEA requires courts to give due weight to the results of due process hearings and overturn adjudications only when they are convinced that they were clearly erroneous.

Pro Se Parents

As a preliminary matter, while parents have the right to have attorneys represent them at trial, and parents who are lawyers can represent themselves, questions have arisen over whether parents who are not attorneys could represent their children in judicial proceedings under the IDEA. Consistent with many other IDEA issues, the courts were split on the question of whether parents who are not attorneys could act as *pro se* plaintiffs (literally, plaintiffs acting "on behalf of the self") in disputes over the education of their children who are in special education placements. Opinions on this issue ranged from letting non-attorney parents represent their interests and those of their children in all circumstances, to doing so in some situations, to prohibiting them from acting at all.

On one end of the spectrum the First Circuit held that parents can be aggrieved parties within the meaning of the IDEA and could sue a school board on behalf of the child regardless of whether the rights at issue were substantive or procedural (*Maroni v. Pemi-Baker Regional School District*, 2003). Similarly, a federal trial court in California agreed that parents had their own rights under the IDEA and could act pro se (*D.K. ex rel. Kumetz-Coleman v. Huntington Beach Union High School District*, 2006). In a midway position, the Third (*Collinsgru v. Palmyra Board of Education*, 1998) and Eleventh (*Devine v. Indian River County School Board*, 1997) Circuits found that Congress expressly permitted parents to represent their children in administrative proceedings pursuant to the IDEA but did not specifically permit parents to represent their children in court. Conversely, the Second (*Wenger v. Canastota Central School District*, 1998, 1999; *Tindall v. Poultney High School District*, 2005), Third (*Carpenter v. Pennell School District Elementary Unit*, 2003a, 2003b; *Montclair Board of Education v. M.W.D.*, 2006), Sixth (*Cavanaugh ex rel. Cavanaugh v. Cardinal Local School District*, 2005), and Seventh (*Navin v. Park Ridge School District*, 2001, 2002a, 2002b) Circuits and federal trial courts in New York (*Fauconier v. Committee on Special Education*, 2003) and Oregon (*C.O. v. Portland Public Schools*, 2005) agreed that parents cannot appear on behalf of their children in IDEA judicial actions.

The U.S. Supreme Court resolved the split among the Circuits in *Winkelman v. Parma City School District* (2007) when it decided that non-attorney parents of students with disabilities have substantive rights in their own names, independent of the rights of their children, to initiate litigation over whether their children are receiving a free appropriate public education. The dispute in *Winkelman* began when the parents of a student with disabilities brought suit pro se in a federal trial court to challenge a school board's IEP. After failing to gain relief they appealed to the Sixth Circuit, also proceeding pro se. The Sixth Circuit dismissed the appeal finding that the legislative purpose of the IDEA did not support the parents' right to proceed pro se (*Winkelman v. Parma City School District* (*Winkelman*), 2005). In reversing the Sixth Circuit's decision the high Court observed that the IDEA includes provisions governing four areas of relevance to the parents' claims: procedures to be followed when developing an IEP; criteria regulating the sufficiency of the education provided to a child; means for review that are to be made available when parents object to an IEP or to other aspects of the IDEA proceedings; and the requirement that school boards reimburse parents for certain expenses when it has failed to provide a FAPE. Noting that parents enjoy enforceable rights during administrative hearings, Justice Kennedy, writing for the majority, commented that it would have been inconsistent with the statutory scheme to bar them from continuing to assert those rights in federal court. In essence the Court ruled that the IDEA does not bar parents from seeking to vindicate the rights accorded them once the time comes for a civil action. Further, the Court interpreted the IDEA's references to parents' rights to mean that rights are conveyed to parents as well as to children. Through its text and structure, the Court stated, the IDEA creates for parents an independent stake in the procedures and costs implicated by the IDEA's process as well as in the substantive decisions to be made.

In a dissenting opinion Justice Scalia opined that parents have the right to proceed pro se when they seek reimbursement for private school expenses or to redress violations of their own procedural rights under the IDEA, but not when they seek a judicial declaration that their child's education is substantially inadequate. Scalia viewed the IDEA as granting parents two types of rights: reimbursement for private school expenditures when the school district has not made a free appropriate public education available, and procedural protections during the IEP development process. Inasmuch as those rights are accorded to parents themselves, Scalia suggested that they may proceed pro se in an action to vindicate them. On the other hand, he surmised that the right to a FAPE belongs to the child who receives the education and, although parents have an interest in seeing that the child receives a proper education, there is a difference between an interest and a statutory right.

The full effect of the *Winkelman* decision on school boards is, at this writing, unclear. To date only a small percentage of parents have filed suit pro se in IDEA cases. However, this ruling could encourage additional pro se actions. On the other hand, Congress could effectively abrogate the Supreme Court's ruling, as it has in the past, by amending the IDEA to prohibit pro se lawsuits.

Standing

In order to file suit, parties must have **standing**, or a legitimate interest, in the issues litigated. Put another way, parties must be able to show that they were faced with threatened injuries or deprivation of rights. As most of the cases in this book reveal, the vast majority of cases litigated on behalf of students with disabilities are filed by their parents; moreover, surrogate parents can file suit to protect the rights of these children (34 C.F.R. § 300.30(a)(5)). For example, the Second Circuit ruled that the father of a student with disabilities had standing to sue over the methods by which hearing officers were selected (*Heldman v. Sobol*, 1992). The court added that since the father had an enforceable right to an impartial hearing on behalf of his son, he had standing to challenge how hearing officers are selected.

Parents can lose their standing if they are no longer the legal guardians of their children. In such a case, the Fifth Circuit affirmed that under state law, a child's managing conservator, not her father, had the authority to file suit on her behalf (*Susan R.M. v. Northeast Independent School District*, 1987). In another dispute, where a divorce decree gave a mother the sole custody of her daughter, a federal trial court in Pennsylvania maintained that the father did not have standing to sue (*Carpenter v. Pennell School District Elementary Unit*, 2002, 2003a, 2003b).

In a case seeking reimbursement for the partial depletion of health insurance benefits that were used to procure special education services, the Fourth Circuit affirmed that a student had standing (*Shook v. Gaston County Board of Education*, 1989). The court noted that since using her insurance benefits to pay for special education diminished the student's resources because the policy capped her available benefits, she had a legitimate interest in the outcome of the litigation. In two separate actions, a federal trial court in Pennsylvania explained that an insurance company lacked standing under the IDEA when attempting to compel a board to provide services it had been paying for under health insurance policies (*Allstate Insurance Co. v. Bethlehem Area School District*, 1987; *Gehman v. Prudential Property and Casualty Insurance Company*, 1989). The court dismissed the cases on the basis that only aggrieved parents or school boards had access to the IDEA's due process mechanism.

The IDEA permits school officials to ask for hearings if parents refuse to consent to evaluations (34 C.F.R. § 300.300(a)(3)). Unfortunately, the courts do not agree on whether states can be aggrieved parties that challenge the results of due process hearings. Along these lines, the Ninth Circuit declared that a board could file such a suit (*Clovis Unified School District v. California Office of Administrative Hearings*, 1990). Similarly, the Seventh Circuit ascertained that a nonprofit corporation that operated a licensed child-care facility had standing to advocate for the rights of students with disabilities placed in its custody (*Family & Children's Center v. School City of Mishawaka*, 1994). The court observed that the corporation had standing because the denial of the students' IDEA rights would have deprived it of money to which it otherwise would have been entitled. According to the court, the corporation was an aggrieved party in light of the outcome of a due process hearing.

On the other hand, the Eleventh Circuit wrote that a school board lacked standing to seek to compel the state educational agency to provide special education services (*Andrews v. Ledbetter*, 1989). The court found that the IDEA was designed to resolve disputes about IEPs and that nothing in it permits local boards to sue states to compel them to fulfill their statutory duties. In like fashion, federal trial courts in New York (*Board of Education of the Seneca Falls Central School District v. Board of Education of the Liverpool Central School District*, 1990) and Indiana (*Metropolitan School District v. Buskirk*, 1997) agreed that school boards lacked standing to sue each other in disputes under the IDEA.

Burden of Proof

While the Supreme Court resolved who bears the burden of proof in challenging IEPs in due process hearings in *Schaffer*, the IDEA and its regulations remain silent on who bears the burden of proof in judicial disputes. As such, this is a question left for judicial discretion (Osborne, 2001). Insofar as the courts are unable to agree on who bears the burden of proof in judicial proceedings, two perspectives have emerged.

The First (*Doe v. Brookline School Committee*, 1983), Fourth (*Barnett v. Fairfax County School Board*, 1991), Fifth (*Christopher M. v. Corpus Christi Independent School District*, 1991), Sixth (*Dong v. Board of Education of the Rochester Community Schools*, 1999), Seventh (*Board of Education of Community Consolidated School District v. Illinois State Board of Education*, 1991), Tenth (*Johnson v. Independent School District No. 4*, 1990), and Eleventh Circuits (*Devine v. Indian River*, 2001) agree that the parties challenging IEPs or results of due process hearings bear the burden of proof. These courts are generally of the same mind that although the outcome of due process hearings is entitled to a degree of deference, the parties seeking to set aside administrative orders must demonstrate that the final results were inappropriate. In addition, the courts reasoned that since the IDEA creates a presumption in favor of then current placements, the parties attacking their terms must prove that they were inappropriate.

Conversely, the Third Circuit (*Oberti v. Board of Education of the Borough of Clementon School District*, 1993) and a federal trial court in Virginia (*Board of Education v. Michael M.*, 2000) placed the burden of proof on school boards. These courts agreed that since boards bear the ultimate responsibility for providing special education, they should have to prove that proposed IEPs are appropriate. The courts recognized the advantage school officials have over parents in IDEA proceedings. This approach has gained strength in suits in which compliance with the IDEA's least restrictive environment provision was at issue (*Oberti v. Board of Education of the Borough of Clementon School District*, 1993; *Mavis v. Sobol*, 1994).

Due to the fact that litigation may take more than a year, IEPs that are being questioned may have expired by the time courts act. In the meantime, the parties may have initiated challenges to more recently developed IEPs. In cases such as this, courts ordinarily treat the losing parties in disputes over original IEPs as bearing the burden of producing evidence of changed circumstances that rendered initial IEPs inappropriate (*Town of Burlington v. Department of Education, Commonwealth of Massachusetts*, 1984, 1985). When this happens, there is a presumption in favor of the placements that were ordered as a result of the first, disputed IEPs unless parties can prove that the circumstances have changed.

Given the Supreme Court's ruling in *Schaffer,* which placed the burden of proof in due process hearings on the party challenging IEPs, courts in the future may very well keep the burden of proof on that party throughout the proceedings. In a recent case, a federal trial court in Pennsylvania, following the Third Circuit precedent established in *Oberti v. Board of Education of the Borough of Clementon School District* (1993), wrote that the burden of proof remains on the same party throughout a case (*Leighty ex rel. Leighty v. Lauren School District*, 2006).

Judicial Deference

In line with the Supreme Court's position that judges should not substitute their views for those of school officials (*Board of Education of the Hendrick Hudson Central School District v. Rowley,* 1982), most jurists defer to educators on matters dealing with appropriate instructional methodologies as long as school officials followed procedural requirements. The Fourth Circuit thus reiterated the widely accepted notion that neither it nor a trial court should have disturbed an IEP simply because judges disagreed with its contents since the judiciary owes deference to educators as long as IEPs meet the IDEA's basic requirements (*Tice v. Botetourt County School Board,* 1990). Due to its having found that school officials failed to follow proper procedures in developing the IEP, the court refused to grant deference to the hearing officer's order.

The Supreme Court (*Board of Education of the Hendrick Hudson Central School District v. Rowley,* 1982) and other federal courts (*Roncker v. Walter,* 1983; *Briggs v. Board of Education of Connecticut,* 1989; *Kerkham v. Superintendent, District of Columbia Schools,* 1991) agree that the IDEA's mandate requiring courts to review the records of due process hearings implies that their results must be given due weight. Still, it is unclear how much weight is due these results. In *Rowley* the Court added that questions of methodology are for resolution by the states, clarifying that the judiciary should defer to hearing officers on questions of the content of IEPs and instructional methodology.

The First Circuit declared that a trial court must reach its own independent judgment based on the records of due process hearings as supplemented at trials (*Town of Burlington v. Department of Education, Commonwealth of Massachusetts,* 1984, 1985). The court specified that while the amount of weight to be afforded the result of hearings is left to the discretion of trial courts, judges must consider the records carefully and endeavor to respond to administrative resolutions of all material issues. In another dispute, the First Circuit affirmed that a trial court did not err in failing to overlook or misconstrue evidence where its judgment was based on a supportable finding that an IEP was reasonably calculated to address a student's needs (*Lenn v. Portland School Committee,* 1993).

In a related matter, federal trial courts in California (*Bertolucci v. San Carlos Elementary School District*, 1989) and New Jersey (*Woods v. New Jersey Department of Education*, 1993) rejected the notion that judges have broad power to overturn the orders of hearing officers. These courts shared the view that the IDEA's mandate for judicial review is not an open invitation for judges to substitute their views of sound educational policy for those of school officials. The Fourth Circuit also affirmed that a court is bound by an administrative record and additional evidence as produced at trial, but must act independently (*Burke County Board of Education v. Denton*, 1990). Conversely, the Fifth Circuit affirmed that courts need not defer to the results of hearings when their own reviews reveal that officers erroneously assessed the facts or misapplied the law (*Teague Independent School District v. Todd D.*, 1993).

The District of Columbia Circuit acknowledged that courts overturning the results of due process hearings must explain their grounds for doing so (*Kerkham v. McKenzie*, 1988). In addition, a trial court in the same jurisdiction pointed out that judges may reverse the orders of hearing officers only when they believe that school officials proved that the officers erred (*Block v. District of Columbia*, 1990). Previously, the federal trial court in Massachusetts noted that while a hearing officer's order must be accorded some deference, it is not entitled to great deference on matters of law (*Puffer v. Raynolds*, 1988).

In a two-tiered due process hearing scheme, courts defer to final orders (*Karl v. Board of Education of the Genesco Central School District*, 1984; *Thomas v. Cincinnati Board of Education*, 1990). If review procedures are flawed, courts defer to initial adjudications (*Puffer v. Raynolds*, 1988). In such a case, the Fourth Circuit reasoned that a hearing officer's judgment should not have been granted any weight since he discredited a witness he had not seen or heard testify while a local hearing officer relied on the credibility of the same witness (*Doyle v. Arlington County School Board*, 1991). **On remand**, a trial court considered the fact that all of the parents' witnesses had a record of testifying against the school board in evaluating the record of the due process hearing (*Doyle v. Arlington County School Board*, 1992). The Fourth Circuit again affirmed, but it did so without a written opinion (*Doyle v. Arlington County School Board*, 1994).

Admission of Additional Evidence

The IDEA permits courts to hear additional evidence at the request of a party (20 U.S.C. § 1415(i)(2)(C)(ii)). Even so, courts can limit the amounts and kinds of extra evidence that they are willing to admit, especially if such evidence has not been introduced prior to judicial review. In the first of two cases, the Eleventh Circuit affirmed that a trial court was within its discretion in refusing to receive and consider evidence that a school board wished to offer in addition to the record of a due process hearing (*Walker County School District v. Bennett*, 2000). In the second, the Sixth Circuit decided that a trial court erred in relying on additional evidence to address issues beyond those presented at a due process hearing over the appropriateness of a student's IEP (*Metropolitan Board of Public Education v. Guest*, 1999).

The First Circuit affirmed that a party seeking to admit additional evidence must justify its request (*Roland M. v. Concord School Committee*, 1990). A trial court refused to hear the testimony of witnesses for parents who could have testified at a due process hearing but whose testimony was deliberately withheld by their attorney. The panel determined that the trial court did not abuse its discretion in refusing to allow the witnesses to testify. In addition, a federal trial court in Illinois refused to admit evaluation materials that school officials had not previously submitted to the hearing officer (*Board of Education of the Paxton-Buckley-Loda Unit School District No. 10 v. Jeff S.*, 2002). Noting that withholding this information from the hearing officer severely undercut the role of the administrative hearing, the court also pointed out that such action deprived the court of the hearing officer's expertise on the matter.

On the other hand, the Sixth Circuit expressed the view that a lower court was justified in admitting additional evaluation materials (*Metropolitan Board of Public Education of the Metropolitan Government of Nashville and Davidson County v. Bellamy*, 2004). The court recognized that the parents had neither the opportunity nor the resources to procure additional evaluations before the due process hearing took place. In another interesting case, a federal trial court in Pennsylvania allowed parents to admit the testimony of witnesses who were available but did not testify at the due process hearing. The court ascertained that the admission of this testimony was justified because the burden of proof shifted from the school board to the parents during the time period between the due process hearing and the trial as a result of the Supreme Court's decision in *Schaffer*. With the burden of proof shifted to the parents, the court thought that it was reasonable for them to have changed their decision to introduce this testimony (*Antione M. v. Chester Upland School District*, 2006).

A party wishing to present additional evidence must make its intention to do so clearly known. In such an instance, the Seventh Circuit judged that if neither party makes its intention to submit additional evidence known, a court is entitled to assume that they wish to have the case resolved on the basis of the administrative record (*Hunger v. Leininger*, 1994). Further, the Sixth Circuit affirmed that it is appropriate for a trial court to consider evidence that a hearing officer failed to review (*Metropolitan Government of Nashville and Davidson County v. Cook*, 1990). The court stressed that the admission of additional evidence did not undercut the administrative process. Similarly, the Fifth Circuit agreed that a trial court gave due weight to the result of a due process hearing but was free to take additional evidence into consideration (*Teague Independent School District v. Todd D.*, 1993).

Due to delays that often occur between the time when placements are finalized and judicial review is initiated, additional evidence may be available about how students progressed in the disputed settings. It is not clear whether courts should admit evidence that develops after officials make disputed placements. The Ninth Circuit held that a trial court has the discretion to admit additional evidence concerning relevant events occurring after an administrative hearing (*Ojai Unified School District v. Jackson*, 1993). A federal trial court in Wisconsin also admitted evidence concerning progress a student had made in a home-based program during the time between the hearing and court review (*Konkel v. Elmbrook School District*, 2004). On the other hand, the Third Circuit affirmed that IEPs and placements should be reviewed from the perspective of the information that was available when the initial action was taken (*Fuhrmann v. East Hanover Board of Education*, 1993). While the court conceded that events that occur after a placement is made may be relevant, it concluded that they cannot be substituted for the threshold determination of whether an IEP was reasonably calculated to confer an appropriate education.

Mootness

Courts will not accept cases unless they present live controversies, meaning that the parties have real interests in their outcomes. Courts have thus rejected cases as **moot** where they could not grant effective relief due to a student's graduation (*Honig v. Doe*, 1988; *Thomas R.W. v. Massachusetts Department of Education*, 1997) or where relief would have served no purpose because a student moved (*Smith v. Special School District No. 1*, 1999). However, if the controversies that initiated disputes are no longer alive but are capable of repetition yet evading review, courts may still hear the cases. In such a dispute, the Supreme Court ruled that judges may adjudicate ongoing controversies and have jurisdiction if there is a reasonable likelihood that a party will again suffer the deprivation of the rights that initiated the suit (*Honig v. Doe*, 1988).

The Fifth Circuit declared a case moot after a school board agreed to provide a student with services (*Lee v. Biloxi School District*, 1992). In like fashion, the federal trial court in New Hampshire indicated that a case was moot where a school year ended and there was no reasonable expectation that the controversy would have recurred (*Greene v. Harrisville School District*, 1990). Additionally, federal trial courts in Indiana (*Merrifield v. Lake Central School Corporation*, 1991) and Texas (*McDowell v. Fort Bend Independent School District*, 1990) rejected claims as moot where students were no longer eligible to receive services because they had reached the maximum eligibility age under state law.

Once students are removed from disputed settings and receive new placements, placement issues are moot (*Robbins v. Maine School Administrative District No. 56*, 1992). At the same time, cases are moot if the parties no longer retain an interest in their outcome (*Stellato v. Board of Education of the Ellenville Central School District*, 1994).

In its only special education case involving mootness, the Supreme Court reasoned that a dispute was not moot for a twenty-year-old student who was still eligible to receive services under the IDEA where there could have been a reasonable expectation that he would have again been subjected to the deprivation of rights complained about in the litigation (*Honig v. Doe*, 1988). Other courts refused to treat cases as moot where issues were capable of repetition, such as when a school year ended (*Jenkins v. Squillacote*, 1991), when the basic complaint still existed (*Straube v. Florida Union Free School District*, 1992), when the IEP on which litigation was premised was superseded by a new IEP (*DeVries v. Spillane*,

1988), and when parents enrolled their children in private schools (*Daniel R.R. v. State Board of Education*, 1989; *Heldman v. Sobol*, 1992). The Circuit Court for the District of Columbia went so far as to assert that a case was not moot when parents approved an IEP because the board's past failures to adhere to the IDEA enhanced the probability that future violations would have occurred (*Abney ex rel. Kantor v. District of Columbia*, 1988).

Exchange of Information

Attorneys for the parties in IDEA proceedings generally exchange information prior to trials. Principles of fairness dictate that one side cannot withhold information that is crucial to one party's case because, just as in due process hearings, the goal is to have all possible evidence available to help measure the appropriateness of IEPs rather than prevail in disputes just for the sake of winning. For example, the federal trial court for the District of Columbia held that the school board had to provide parents with information about private schools, the qualifications of their teachers, and the disabilities of the students attending them since these matters were not privileged (*Fagan v. District of Columbia*, 1991). Further, the court acknowledged that the board was not required to provide information about due process hearings and suits challenging other placements since the parents' attorney could obtain this material through normal legal research.

Res Judicata

Based on the principle of **res judicata**, courts cannot hear cases or render judgments on matters that they have already resolved. *Res judicata* stands for the proposition that a final judgment by a court of competent jurisdiction is conclusive and acts as an absolute bar to a subsequent action involving the same claim. By way of illustration, the Eleventh Circuit, in a case that was before it for the second time, affirmed that under *res judicata*, a trial court's order prior to the first appeal precluded additional consideration of the issues (*Jenkins v. State of Florida*, 1991).

Settlement Agreements

During the course of disputes, parents and school officials often negotiate settlement agreements that effectively end controversies. The parties sometimes reach settlement agreements as a result of resolution sessions or mediation before due process hearings start or during litigation. When the parties agree on settlements during litigation, hearing officers or courts may either approve or reject them if they deem their terms to be contrary to public policy or existing law. In a representative case of this nature, the Eleventh Circuit decided that a trial court could vitiate a settlement agreement only if it violates public policy (*In re Smith*, 1991). Where the panel believed that a settlement agreement was not void as against public policy due to its high cost, the court issued an order to enforce its provisions to provide housing for a student with disabilities.

In a case from New Jersey, the federal trial court found that the existence of a settlement agreement that parents and school officials reached during a due process hearing did not bar it from hearing the case (*Woods v. New Jersey Department of Education,* 1992). The court decided that despite the settlement agreement, school officials still had the duty to provide the student with a FAPE. In another case, the same court asserted that a settlement agreement reached through mediation formed a contract between the parties but did not allow the board to avoid its responsibilities under the IDEA (*D.R. v. East Brunswick Board of Education,* 1993). The court emphasized that there was a presumption that the services agreed to by the parties when they entered into the agreement met the student's special education needs. Additionally, the court decreed that the parents had the right to question the terms of the agreement if there was a change in circumstances.

STATUTES OF LIMITATIONS

Earlier versions of the IDEA did not contain a statute of limitations for either requesting due process hearings or filing suits after exhausting administrative remedies (Osborne, 1996, 2004; Zirkel & Maher, 2003). Consequently, in amending the IDEA in 2004 Congress included specific statutes of limitations to govern the time lines for seeking such actions.

The IDEA and its regulations now require parties to request impartial due process hearings within two years of the date they knew or should have known about the actions that form the bases of their complaints (20 U.S.C. § 1415(f)(3)(C); 34 C.F.R. § 300.511(e)). If states have explicit time limitations for requesting hearings, these limitations apply. Limitations periods may be set aside if school boards misrepresented that they resolved the problems forming the bases of complaints or if officials withheld information that they should have provided to parents (20 U.S.C. § 1415(f)(3)(D); 34 C.F.R. § 300.511(f)). After final administrative decisions are rendered, parties have ninety days to file judicial appeals (20 U.S.C. § 1415(g)(2)(B); 34 C.F.R. § 300.516(b)). Again, if state laws provide otherwise, they prevail.

Beginning and Waiving Limitations Periods

Limitations periods generally begin when cases are resolved. In two separate disputes, the federal trial court in New Hampshire clarified that the statute of limitations begins to run on the day decisions are released, not the day the aggrieved parties receive copies of them in the mail (*I.D. v. Westmoreland School District,* 1991; *G.D. v. Westmoreland School District,* 1992). On the other hand, the Seventh Circuit affirmed that where a prevailing parent sought to recover attorneys' fees, the statute of limitations did not begin until after the expiration of the time when the school board could file an appeal of the hearing officer's adjudication (*McCartney C. v. Herrin Community Unit School District No. 4,* 1994). The court remarked that the parent could neither have recovered attorneys' fees until administrative and judicial proceedings were finished nor have known that the board would not have appealed the administrative order until after the time period to do so expired. In cases that do not necessarily involve appeals of due process hearings, courts agree that the clock begins to run on the day that students reach the age of majority (*Shook v. Gaston County Board of Education*, 1989), their eligibility for services ends (*Hall v. Knott County Board of Education*, 1991), or they graduate (*Richards v. Fairfax County School Board*, 1992).

Difficulties sometimes arise when parents are not fully aware of their procedural rights under the IDEA. According to a federal trial court in Illinois, a case filed after the statute of limitations expired was not untimely where parents were unaware of it and were not apprised of the deadline for challenging the results of a due process hearing (*Board of Education of the City of Chicago v. Wolinsky*, 1993). The court interpreted the IDEA as requiring state officials to inform parents of the full range of available procedural avenues. In addition, the federal trial court in New Hampshire declared that a case that was filed after the statute of limitations expired was not time-barred since the hearing officer failed to inform the parents of how much time they had to file an appeal (*Hebert v. Manchester, New Hampshire, School District*, 1993).

The First Circuit held that a suit that was filed after the statute of limitations expired was not barred where the parental delay was not unreasonable because in the interim they attempted to resolve their differences with the school board (*Murphy v. Timberlane Regional School District*, 1992). On remand, the federal trial court in New Hampshire found (*Murphy v. Timberlane Regional School District*, 1993), and the First Circuit affirmed (*Murphy v. Timberlane Regional School District*, 1994), that the case was not barred by the doctrine of laches, which applies when a party fails to assert a right, along with a lapse of time and other circumstances that put the other party at a disadvantage. The court conceded that school officials failed to show that witnesses were unavailable or had failed memories. In a conceptually related dispute, the Eleventh Circuit was of the opinion that since school officials never raised the issue of a suit's being time-barred, they waived the right to use the statute of limitations as a defense (*J.S.K. v. Hendry County School Board*, 1991).

Limitations periods may be tolled, or suspended, for good reason. For example, the federal trial court in Connecticut tolled the limitations period because a parent requested clarification of a hearing officer's order (*R.M. ex rel J.M. v. Vernon Board of Education*, 2002). In like fashion, the trial court in the District of Columbia tolled the limitations period where a parent requested reconsideration of a hearing officer's adjudication (*R.S. v. District of Columbia*, 2003). In another suit from the District of Columbia, the same court tolled the statute of limitations because school officials failed to inform the parents of the limitations period (*Abraham v. District of Columbia*, 2004).

CASES UNDER OTHER STATUTES

The IDEA is the primary federal statute protecting the rights of students with disabilities. Even so, parents can seek protection for the educational rights of their children with disabilities under other federal statutes and, in particular, under state laws that may provide greater protection than the IDEA (*Geis v. Board of Education*, 1985). In fact, the IDEA specifies that none of its provisions can be interpreted as restricting, or limiting, the rights, procedures, and remedies available under the Constitution, Title V of the Rehabilitation Act of 1973, or other federal statutes protecting the rights of students with disabilities (20 U.S.C. § 1415(1)). The IDEA adds that before parties can file suits under one of these other laws, they must exhaust all other available administrative remedies (20 U.S.C. § 1415(i)(A); *Quackenbush v. Johnson City School District*, 1983).

Most cases seeking relief under statutes other than the IDEA are filed pursuant to Section 1983 of the Civil Rights Act of 1871 (Section 1983) (42 U.S.C. § 1983), an expansive law used to enforce rights secured by federal law or the Constitution. A variety of courts have agreed that Section 1983 may be used to enforce the results of a due process hearing (*Robinson v. Pinderhughes*, 1987; *Reid v. Board of Education, Lincolnshire-Prairie View School District 103*, 1990; *Grace B. v. Lexington School Committee*, 1991) or to remedy a deprivation of due process or other rights secured by the IDEA (*Digre v. Roseville Schools Independent School District No. 623*, 1988; *Hiller v. Board of Education of the Brunswick Central School District*, 1988; *Mrs. W. v. Tirozzi*, 1989). Yet, courts have made it clear that cases filed under Section 1983 must be predicated on more than reallegations of claims presented under the IDEA (*Barnett v. Fairfax County School Board*, 1991), that Section 1983 cases are not viable when adequate remedies exist under other laws (*Fee v. Herndon*, 1990), and that Section 1983 cannot be used to expand the rights of students under the IDEA (*Crocker v. Tennessee Secondary School Athletic Association*, 1992). Recently, the First Circuit pointed out that parents cannot use Section 1983 to escape the strictures on damages under the IDEA, which preclude both punitive and compensatory awards where the claim was premised on a right created by the statute. The court reasoned that parents should not be allowed to circumvent the IDEA by pleading their case under Section 1983 (*Diaz-Fonseca v. Commonwealth of Puerto Rico*, 2006).

Pursuant to Section 1983, school officials acting under the color of state law, meaning that they proceeded as if they had the official authority to act as they did, may be liable for actions that have the effect of depriving students (or their parents) of rights secured by federal law. In such a case, a federal trial court in Indiana posited that an attorney hired to represent a school board in a special education case could be sued under Section 1983 (*Bray v. Hobart City School Corporation*, 1993). The student's parents successfully claimed that the advice the attorney gave the board led officials to deprive their son of his IDEA rights.

Section 504 of the Rehabilitation Act of 1973 (Section 504) prohibits discrimination against individuals with disabilities in programs receiving federal assistance (29 U.S.C. § 794). As might have been expected, parties frequently file suit alleging discrimination under Section 504 and the deprivation of rights under the IDEA. However, if disputes can be settled under the IDEA's provisions, courts will not turn to Section 504 for relief. A case from Pennsylvania is illustrative (*Gaudiello v. Delaware County Intermediate Unit*, 1992). The parents of a student with physical disabilities requested a due process hearing after school officials refused to permit him to have his service dog accompany him to class unless he moved to a less restrictive placement. After a hearing officer remarked that the student could have been educated in the less restrictive environment, his parents filed suit under Section 504 rather than challenge the hearing officer's order. In denying the parents' claim, a federal trial court treated the IDEA as the exclusive avenue through which they could bring an equal protection claim on behalf of their child's right to a FAPE. If relief is not available under the IDEA, a case may proceed under Section 504 (*University Interscholastic League v. Buchannan*, 1993).

The bottom line is that if school officials comply with the IDEA, courts are generally satisfied that they will have met the dictates of Section 504 (*Cordrey v. Euckert*, 1990; *Doe v. Alabama State Department of Education*, 1990; *Barnett v. Fairfax County School Board*, 1991). Additionally, as reflected by a judgment of the federal trial court in Maine, a party cannot rely on Section 504 to expand the rights available under the IDEA (*Carey v. Maine School Administrative District 17*, 1990).

CASE NO. 13—BURDEN OF PROOF AT DUE PROCESS HEARINGS

SCHAFFER *ex rel.* SCHAFFER

v.

WEAST

Supreme Court of the United States, 2005

546 U.S. 49

JUSTICE O'CONNOR delivered the opinion of the Court.

The Individuals with Disabilities Education Act (IDEA or Act) is a Spending Clause statute that seeks to ensure that "all children with disabilities have available to them a free appropriate public education." Under IDEA, school districts must create an "individualized education program" (IEP) for each disabled child. If parents believe their child's IEP is inappropriate, they may request an "impartial due process hearing." The Act is silent, however, as to which party bears the burden of persuasion at such a hearing. We hold that the burden lies, as it typically does, on the party seeking relief.

I

A

Congress first passed IDEA as part of the Education of the Handicapped Act in 1970 and amended it substantially in the Education for All Handicapped Children Act of 1975. . . . {Unless otherwise noted, the Court applied . . . the pre-2004 version of the statute because this is the version that was in effect during the proceedings below}

. . .

Parents and guardians play a significant role in the IEP process. They must be informed about and consent to evaluations of their child under the Act. Parents are included as members of "IEP teams." They have the right to examine any records relating to their child, and to obtain an "independent educational evaluation of the[ir] child." They must be given written prior notice of any changes in an IEP, and be notified in writing of the procedural safeguards available to them under the Act. If parents believe that an IEP is not appropriate, they may seek an administrative "impartial due process hearing." School districts may also seek such hearings, as Congress clarified in the 2004 amendments. They may do so, for example, if they wish to change an existing IEP but the parents do not consent, or if parents refuse to allow their child to be evaluated. As a practical matter, it appears that most hearing requests come from parents rather than schools.

Although state authorities have limited discretion to determine who conducts the hearings, and responsibility generally for establishing fair hearing procedures, Congress has chosen to legislate the central components of due process hearings. It has imposed minimal pleading standards, requiring parties to file complaints setting forth "a description of the nature of the problem" and "a proposed resolution of the problem to the extent known and available at the time." At the hearing, all parties may be accompanied by counsel, and may "present evidence and confront, cross-examine, and compel the attendance of witnesses." After the hearing, any aggrieved party may bring a civil action in state or federal court. Prevailing parents may also recover attorney's fees. Congress has never explicitly stated, however, which party should bear the burden of proof at IDEA hearings.

B

This case concerns the educational services that were due, under IDEA, to petitioner Brian Schaffer. Brian suffers from learning disabilities and speech-language impairments. From prekindergarten through seventh grade he attended a private school and struggled academically. In 1997, school officials informed Brian's mother that he needed a school that could better accommodate his needs. Brian's parents contacted respondent Montgomery County Public Schools System (MCPS) seeking a placement for him for the following school year.

MCPS evaluated Brian and convened an IEP team. The committee generated an initial IEP offering Brian a place in either of two MCPS middle schools. Brian's parents were not satisfied with the arrangement, believing that Brian needed smaller classes and more intensive services. The Schaffers thus enrolled Brian in another private school, and initiated a due process hearing challenging the IEP and seeking compensation for the cost of Brian's subsequent private education.

In Maryland, IEP hearings are conducted by administrative law judges (ALJs). After a 3-day hearing, the ALJ deemed the evidence close, held that the parents bore the burden of persuasion, and ruled in favor of the school district. The parents brought a civil action challenging the result. The United States District Court for the District of Maryland reversed and remanded, after concluding that the burden of persuasion is on the school district. Around the same time, MCPS offered Brian a placement in a high school with a special learning center. Brian's parents accepted, and Brian was educated in that program until he graduated from high school. The suit remained alive, however, because the parents sought compensation for the private school tuition and related expenses.

Respondents appealed. . . . While the appeal was pending, the ALJ reconsidered the case, deemed the evidence truly in "equipoise," and ruled in favor of the parents. The Fourth Circuit vacated and remanded the appeal so that it could consider the burden of proof issue along with the merits on a later appeal. The District Court reaffirmed its ruling that the school district has the burden of proof. On appeal, a divided panel of the Fourth Circuit reversed. Judge Michael, writing for the majority, concluded that petitioners offered no persuasive reason to "depart from the normal rule of allocating the burden to the party seeking relief." We granted *certiorari*, to resolve the following question: At an administrative hearing assessing the appropriateness of an IEP, which party bears the burden of persuasion?

II

A

The term "burden of proof" is one of the "slipperiest member[s] of the family of legal terms." Part of the confusion surrounding the term arises from the fact that historically, the concept encompassed two distinct burdens: the "burden of persuasion," *i.e.*, which party loses if the evidence is closely balanced, and the "burden of production," *i.e.*, which party bears the obligation to come forward with the evidence at different points in the proceeding. We note at the outset that this case concerns only the burden of persuasion, as the parties agree, and when we speak of burden of proof in this opinion, it is this to which we refer.

When we are determining the burden of proof under a statutory cause of action, the touchstone of our inquiry is, of course, the statute. The plain text of IDEA is silent on the allocation of the burden of persuasion. We therefore begin with the ordinary default rule that plaintiffs bear the risk of failing to prove their claims.

Thus, we have usually assumed without comment that plaintiffs bear the burden of persuasion regarding the essential aspects of their claims. For example, Title VII of the Civil Rights Act of 1964, does not directly state that plaintiffs bear the "ultimate" burden of persuasion, but we have so concluded. In numerous other areas, we have presumed or held that the default rule applies. . . .

The ordinary default rule, of course, admits of exceptions. For example, the burden of persuasion as to certain elements of a plaintiff's claim may be shifted to defendants, when such elements can fairly be characterized as affirmative defenses or exemptions. Under some circumstances this Court has even placed the burden of persuasion over an entire claim on the defendant. But while the normal default rule does not solve all cases, it certainly solves most of them. Decisions that place the *entire* burden of persuasion on the opposing party at the *outset* of a proceeding—as petitioners urge us to do here—are extremely rare. Absent some reason to believe that Congress intended otherwise, therefore, we will conclude that the burden of persuasion lies where it usually falls, upon the party seeking relief.

B

Petitioners contend first that a close reading of IDEA's text compels a conclusion in their favor. They urge that we should interpret the statutory words "due process" in light of their constitutional meaning, and apply the balancing test established by *Mathews v. Eldridge*. Even assuming that the Act incorporates constitutional due process doctrine, *Eldridge* is no help to petitioners, because "[o]utside the criminal law area, where special concerns attend, the locus of the burden of persuasion is normally not an issue of federal constitutional moment."

Petitioners next contend that we should take instruction from the lower court opinions of *Mills v. Board of Education* and *Pennsylvania Association for Retarded Children v. Commonwealth* (hereinafter *PARC*). IDEA's drafters were admittedly guided "to a significant extent" by these two landmark cases. As the court below noted, however, the fact that Congress "took a number of the procedural safeguards from *PARC* and *Mills* and wrote them directly into the Act" does not allow us to "conclude that Congress intended to adopt the ideas that it failed to write into the text of the statute."

Petitioners also urge that putting the burden of persuasion on school districts will further IDEA's purposes because it will help ensure that children receive a free appropriate public education. In truth, however, very few cases will be in evidentiary equipoise. Assigning the burden of persuasion to school districts might encourage schools to put more resources into preparing IEPs and presenting their evidence. But IDEA is silent about whether marginal dollars should be allocated to litigation and administrative expenditures or to educational services. Moreover, there is reason to believe that a great deal is already spent on the administration of the Act. Litigating a due process complaint is an expensive affair, costing schools approximately $8,000-to-$12,000 per hearing. Congress has also repeatedly amended the Act in order to reduce its administrative and litigation-related costs. For example, in 1997 Congress mandated that States offer mediation for IDEA disputes. In 2004, Congress added a mandatory "resolution session" prior to any due process hearing. It also made new findings that "[p]arents and schools should be given expanded opportunities to resolve their disagreements in positive and constructive ways," and that "[t]eachers, schools, local educational agencies, and States should be relieved of irrelevant and unnecessary paperwork burdens that do not lead to improved educational outcomes."

Petitioners in effect ask this Court to assume that every IEP is invalid until the school district demonstrates that it is not. The Act does not support this conclusion. IDEA relies heavily upon the expertise of school districts to meet its goals. It also includes a so-called "stay-put" provision, which requires a child to remain in his or her "then current educational placement" during the pendency of an IDEA hearing. Congress could have required that a child be given the educational placement that a parent requested during a dispute, but it did no such thing. Congress appears to have presumed instead that, if the Act's procedural requirements are respected, parents will prevail when they have legitimate grievances.

Petitioners' most plausible argument is that "[t]he ordinary rule, based on considerations of fairness, does not place the burden upon a litigant of establishing facts peculiarly within the knowledge of his adversary." But this "rule is far from being universal, and has many qualifications upon its application." School districts have a "natural advantage" in information and expertise, but Congress addressed this when it obliged schools to safeguard the procedural rights of parents and to share information with them. As noted above, parents have the right to review all records that the school possesses in relation to their child. They also have the right to an "independent educational evaluation of the[ir] child." The regulations clarify this entitlement by providing that a "parent has the right to an independent educational evaluation at public expense if the parent disagrees with an evaluation obtained by the public agency." IDEA thus ensures parents access to an expert who can evaluate all the materials that the school must make available, and who can give an independent opinion. They are not left to challenge the government without a realistic opportunity to access the necessary evidence, or without an expert with the firepower to match the opposition.

Additionally, in 2004, Congress added provisions requiring school districts to answer the subject matter of a complaint in writing, and to provide parents with the reasoning behind the disputed action, details about the other options considered and rejected by the IEP team, and a description of all evaluations, reports, and other factors that the school used in coming to its decision. Prior to a hearing, the parties must disclose evaluations and recommendations that they intend to rely upon. IDEA hearings are deliberately informal and intended to give ALJs the flexibility that they need to ensure that each side can fairly present its evidence. IDEA, in fact, requires state authorities to organize hearings in a way that guarantees parents and children the procedural protections of the Act. Finally, and perhaps most importantly, parents may recover attorney's fees if they prevail. These protections ensure that the school bears no unique informational advantage.

III

Finally, respondents and several States urge us to decide that States may, if they wish, override the default rule and put the burden always on the school district. Several States have laws or regulations purporting to do so, at least under some circumstances.... Because no such law or regulation exists in Maryland, we need not decide this issue today. Justice BREYER contends that the allocation of the burden ought to be left *entirely* up to the States. But neither party made this argument before this Court or the courts below. We therefore decline to address it.

We hold no more than we must to resolve the case at hand: The burden of proof in an administrative hearing challenging an IEP is properly placed upon the party seeking relief. In this case, that party is Brian, as represented by his parents. But the rule applies with equal effect to school districts: If they seek to challenge an IEP, they will in turn bear the burden of persuasion before an ALJ. The judgment of the United States Court of Appeals for the Fourth Circuit is, therefore, affirmed.

It is so ordered.

THE CHIEF JUSTICE took no part in the consideration or decision of this case.

Notes

1. Do you agree with this decision?

2. Is it appropriate for individual states to set their own burdens of proof? Can this lead to inconsistent results between states, making the rights of children with disabilities depend on where their parents live?

3. Chief Justice Roberts did not participate in this decision. Customarily the Justices do not give a reason for recusing themselves but most likely Chief Justice Roberts abstained because he was formerly associated with a law firm representing one of the parties in this case.

WINKELMAN ex rel. WINKELMAN
v. PARMA CITY SCHOOL DISTRICT

Supreme Court of the United States, 2007

127 S. Ct. 1994

Justice KENNEDY delivered the opinion of the Court.

Some four years ago, Mr. and Mrs. Winkelman, parents of five children, became involved in lengthy administrative and legal proceedings. They had sought review related to concerns they had over whether their youngest child, 6-year-old Jacob, would progress well at Pleasant Valley Elementary School, which is part of the Parma City School District in Parma, Ohio.

Jacob has autism spectrum disorder and is covered by the Individuals with Disabilities Education Act (Act or IDEA), . . . His parents worked with the school district to develop an individualized education program (IEP), as required by the Act. All concede that Jacob's parents had the statutory right to contribute to this process and, when agreement could not be reached, to participate in administrative proceedings including what the Act refers to as an "impartial due process hearing."

The disagreement at the center of the current dispute concerns the procedures to be followed when parents and their child, dissatisfied with the outcome of the due process hearing, seek further review in a United States District Court. The question is whether parents, either on their own behalf or as representatives of the child, may proceed in court unrepresented by counsel though they are not trained or licensed as attorneys. Resolution of this issue requires us to examine and explain the provisions of IDEA to determine if it accords to parents rights of their own that can be vindicated in court proceedings, or alternatively, whether the Act allows them, in their status as parents, to represent their child in court proceedings.

I

. . .

The school district proposed an IEP for the 2003–2004 school year that would have placed Jacob at a public elementary school. Regarding this IEP as deficient under IDEA, Jacob's nonlawyer parents availed themselves of the administrative review provided by IDEA. They filed a complaint alleging respondent had failed to provide Jacob with a free appropriate public education; they appealed the hearing officer's rejection of the claims in this complaint to a state-level review officer; and after losing that appeal they filed, on their own behalf and on behalf of Jacob, a complaint in the United States District Court for the Northern District of Ohio. . . . [T]hey challenged the administrative decision, alleging, among other matters: that Jacob had not been provided with a free appropriate public education; that his IEP was inadequate; and that the school district had failed to follow procedures mandated by IDEA. Pending the resolution of these challenges, the Winkelmans had enrolled Jacob in a private school at their own expense. They had also obtained counsel to assist them with certain aspects of the proceedings, although they filed their federal complaint, and later their appeal, without the aid of an attorney. The Winkelmans' complaint sought reversal of the administrative decision, reimbursement for private-school expenditures and attorney's fees already incurred, and, it appears, **declaratory relief**.

The District Court granted respondent's motion for judgment on the pleadings, finding it had provided Jacob with a free appropriate public education. Petitioners, proceeding without counsel, filed an appeal with the Court of Appeals for the Sixth Circuit. Relying on its recent decision in *Cavanaugh v. Cardinal Local School Dist.*, the Court of Appeals entered an order dismissing the Winkelmans' appeal unless they obtained counsel to represent Jacob. In *Cavanaugh* the Court of Appeals had rejected the proposition that IDEA allows nonlawyer parents raising IDEA claims to proceed *pro se* in federal court. The court ruled that the right to a free appropriate public education "belongs to the child alone," not to both the parents and the child. It followed, the court held, that "any right on which the [parents] could proceed on their own behalf would be derivative" of the child's right, so that parents bringing IDEA claims were not appearing on their own behalf. As for the parents' alternative argument, the court held, nonlawyer parents cannot litigate IDEA claims on behalf of their child because IDEA does not abrogate the common-law rule prohibiting nonlawyer parents from representing minor children. As the court in *Cavanaugh* acknowledged, its decision brought the Sixth Circuit in direct conflict with the First Circuit, which had concluded, under a theory of "statutory joint rights," that the Act accords to parents the right to assert IDEA claims on their own behalf. See *Maroni v. Pemi-Baker Regional School Dist.*

Petitioners sought review in this Court. In light of the disagreement among the Courts of Appeals as to whether a nonlawyer parent of a child with a disability may prosecute IDEA actions *pro se* in federal court, we granted certiorari.

II

Our resolution of this case turns upon the significance of IDEA's interlocking statutory provisions. Petitioners' primary theory is that the Act makes parents real parties in interest to IDEA actions, not "mer[e] guardians of their children's rights." If correct, this allows Mr. and Mrs. Winkelman back into court, for there is no question that a party may represent his or her own interests in federal court without the aid of counsel. Petitioners cannot cite a specific provision in IDEA mandating in direct and explicit terms that parents have the status of real parties in interest. They instead base their argument on a comprehensive reading of IDEA. Taken as a whole, they contend, the Act leads to the necessary conclusion that parents have independent, enforceable rights. Respondent, accusing petitioners of "knit[ting] together various provisions pulled from the crevices of the statute" to support these claims, reads the text of IDEA to mean that any redressable rights under the Act belong only to children.

We agree that the text of IDEA resolves the question presented. We recognize, in addition, that a proper interpretation of the Act requires a consideration of the entire statutory scheme. Turning to the current version of IDEA, which the parties agree governs this case, we begin with an overview of the relevant statutory provisions.

A

The goals of IDEA include "ensur[ing] that all children with disabilities have available to them a free appropriate public education" and "ensur[ing] that the rights of children with disabilities and parents of such children are protected." To this end, the Act includes provisions governing four areas of particular relevance to the Winkelmans' claim: procedures to be followed when developing a child's IEP; criteria governing the sufficiency of an education provided to a child; mechanisms for review that must be made available when there are objections to the IEP or to other aspects of IDEA proceedings; and the requirement in certain circumstances that States reimburse parents for various expenses. . . .

IDEA requires school districts to develop an IEP for each child with a disability, with parents playing "a significant role" in this process. . . . Parents serve as members of the team that develops the IEP. . . . IDEA accords parents additional protections that apply throughout the IEP process. . . . The statute also sets up general procedural safeguards that protect the informed involvement of parents in the development of an education for their child. . . .

. . .

When a party objects to the adequacy of the education provided, the construction of the IEP, or some related matter, IDEA provides procedural recourse: It requires that a State provide "[a]n opportunity for any party to present a complaint . . . with respect to any matter relating to the identification, evaluation, or educational placement of the child, or the provision of a free appropriate public education to such child." By presenting a complaint a party is able to pursue a process of review that, as relevant, begins with a preliminary meeting "where the parents of the child discuss their complaint" and the local educational agency "is provided the opportunity to [reach a resolution]." If the agency "has not resolved the complaint to the satisfaction of the parents within 30 days," the parents may request an "impartial due process hearing," which must be conducted either by the local educational agency or by the state educational agency, and where a hearing officer will resolve issues raised in the complaint.

. . .

. . . Once the state educational agency has reached its decision, an aggrieved party may commence suit in federal court: "Any party aggrieved by the findings and decision made [by the hearing officer] shall have the right to bring a civil action with respect to the complaint."

IDEA, finally, provides for at least two means of cost recovery that inform our analysis. First, in certain circumstances it allows a court or hearing officer to require a state agency "to reimburse the parents [of a child with a disability] for the cost of [private school] enrollment if the court or hearing officer finds that the agency had not made a free appropriate public education available to the child." Second, it sets forth rules governing when and to what extent a court may award attorney's fees. Included in this section is a provision allowing an award "to a prevailing party who is the parent of a child with a disability."

B

Petitioners construe these various provisions to accord parents independent, enforceable rights under IDEA. We agree. The parents enjoy enforceable rights at the administrative stage, and it would be inconsistent with the statutory scheme to bar them from continuing to assert these rights in federal court.

The statute sets forth procedures for resolving disputes in a manner that, in the Act's express terms, contemplates parents will be the parties bringing the administrative complaints. . . . Claims raised in these complaints are then resolved at impartial due process hearings, where, again, the statute makes clear that parents will be participating as parties. . . . The statute then grants "[a]ny party aggrieved by the findings and decision made [by the hearing officer] . . . the right to bring a civil action with respect to the complaint."

Nothing in these interlocking provisions excludes a parent who has exercised his or her own rights from statutory protection the moment the administrative proceedings end. Put another way, the Act does not *sub silentio* or by implication bar parents from seeking to vindicate the rights accorded to them once the time comes to file a civil action. Through its provisions for expansive review and extensive parental involvement, the statute leads to just the opposite result.

Respondent, resisting this line of analysis, asks us to read these provisions as contemplating parental involvement only to the extent parents represent their child's interests. In respondent's view IDEA accords parents nothing more than "collateral tools related to the child's underlying substantive rights—not freestanding or independently enforceable rights."

This interpretation, though, is foreclosed by provisions of the statute. IDEA defines one of its purposes as seeking "to ensure that the rights of children with disabilities and parents of such children are protected." The word "rights" in the quoted language refers to the rights of parents as well as the rights of the child; otherwise the grammatical structure would make no sense.

Further provisions confirm this view. IDEA mandates that educational agencies establish procedures "to ensure that children with disabilities and their parents are guaranteed procedural safeguards with respect to the provision of a free appropriate public education." It presumes parents have rights of their own when it defines how States might provide for the transfer of the "rights accorded to parents" by IDEA, and it prohibits the raising of certain challenges "[n]otwithstanding any other individual right of action that a parent or student may maintain under [the relevant provisions of IDEA]," To adopt respondent's reading of the statute would require an interpretation of these statutory provisions (and others) far too strained to be correct.

Defending its countertextual reading of the statute, respondent cites a decision by a Court of Appeals concluding that the Act's "references to parents are best understood as accommodations to the fact of the child's incapacity." This, according to respondent, requires us to interpret all references to parents' rights as referring in implicit terms to the child's rights—which, under this view, are the only enforceable rights accorded by IDEA. Even if we were inclined to ignore the plain text of the statute in considering this theory, we disagree that the sole purpose driving IDEA's involvement of parents is to facilitate vindication of a child's rights. It is not a novel proposition to say that parents have a recognized legal interest in the education and upbringing of their child. . . . There is no necessary bar or obstacle in the law, then, to finding an intention by Congress to grant parents a stake in the entitlements created by IDEA. Without question a parent of a child with a disability has a particular and personal interest in fulfilling "our national policy of ensuring equality of opportunity, full participation, independent living, and economic self-sufficiency for individuals with disabilities."

We therefore find no reason to read into the plain language of the statute an implicit rejection of the notion that Congress would accord parents independent, enforceable rights concerning the education of their children. We instead interpret the statute's references to parents' rights to mean what they say: that IDEA includes provisions conveying rights to parents as well as to children.

A variation on respondent's argument has persuaded some Courts of Appeals. The argument is that while a parent can be a "party aggrieved" for aspects of the hearing officer's findings and decision, he or she cannot be a "party aggrieved" with respect to all IDEA-based challenges. Under this view the causes of action available to a parent might relate, for example, to various procedural mandates, and reimbursement demands. The argument supporting this conclusion proceeds as follows: Because a "party aggrieved" is, by definition, entitled to a remedy, and parents are, under IDEA, only entitled to certain procedures and reimbursements as remedies, a parent cannot be a "party aggrieved" with regard to any claim not implicating these limited matters.

This argument is contradicted by the statutory provisions we have recited. True, there are provisions in IDEA stating parents are entitled to certain procedural protections and reimbursements; but the statute prevents us from placing too much weight on the implications to be drawn when other entitlements are accorded in less clear language. We find little support for the inference that parents are excluded by implication whenever a child is mentioned, and vice versa. . . . Without more, then, the language in IDEA confirming that parents enjoy particular procedural and reimbursement-related rights does not resolve whether they are also entitled to enforce IDEA's other mandates, including the one most fundamental to the Act: the provision of a free appropriate public education to a child with a disability.

We consider the statutory structure. The IEP proceedings entitle parents to participate not only in the implementation of IDEA's procedures but also in the substantive formulation of their child's educational program. Among other things, IDEA requires the IEP Team, which includes the parents as members, to take into account any "concerns" parents have "for enhancing the education of their child" when it formulates the IEP. The IEP, in turn, sets the boundaries of the central entitlement provided by IDEA: It defines a "'free appropriate public education'" for that parent's child.

The statute also empowers parents to bring challenges based on a broad range of issues. The parent may seek a hearing on "any matter relating to the identification, evaluation, or educational placement of the child, or the provision of a free appropriate public education to such child." To resolve these challenges a hearing officer must make a decision based on whether the child "received a free appropriate public education." When this hearing has been conducted by a local educational agency rather than a state educational agency, "any party aggrieved by the findings and decision rendered in such a hearing may appeal such findings and decision" to the state educational agency. Judicial review follows, authorized by a broadly worded provision phrased in the same terms used to describe the prior stage of review: "[a]ny party aggrieved" may bring "a civil action."

These provisions confirm that IDEA, through its text and structure, creates in parents an independent stake not only in the procedures and costs implicated by this process but also in the substantive decisions to be made. We therefore conclude that IDEA does not differentiate, through isolated references to various procedures and remedies, between the rights accorded to children and the rights accorded to parents. As a consequence, a parent may be a "party aggrieved" for purposes of [IDEA] with regard to "any matter" implicating these rights. The status of parents as parties is not limited to matters that relate to procedure and cost recovery. To find otherwise would be inconsistent with the collaborative framework and expansive system of review established by the Act. . . .

Our conclusion is confirmed by noting the incongruous results that would follow were we to accept the proposition that parents' IDEA rights are limited to certain nonsubstantive matters. The statute's procedural and reimbursement-related rights are intertwined with the substantive adequacy of the education provided to a child, and it is difficult to disentangle the provisions in order to conclude that some rights adhere to both parent and child while others do not. Were we nevertheless to recognize a distinction of this sort it would impose upon parties a confusing and onerous legal regime, one worsened by the absence of any express guidance in IDEA concerning how a court might in practice differentiate between these matters. It is, in addition, out of accord with the statute's design to interpret the Act to require that parents prove the substantive inadequacy of their child's education as a predicate for obtaining, for example, reimbursement under [IDEA], yet to prevent them from obtaining a judgment mandating that the school district provide their child with an educational program demonstrated to be an appropriate one. The adequacy of the educational program is, after all, the central issue in the litigation. The provisions of IDEA do not set forth these distinctions, and we decline to infer them.

The bifurcated regime suggested by the courts that have employed it, moreover, leaves some parents without a remedy. The statute requires, in express terms, that States provide a child with a free appropriate public education "at public expense," including specially designed instruction "at no cost to parents." Parents may seek to enforce this mandate through the federal courts, we conclude, because among the rights they enjoy is the right to a free appropriate public education for their child. Under the countervailing view, which would make a parent's ability to enforce IDEA dependant [sic] on certain procedural and reimbursement-related rights, a parent whose disabled child has not received a free appropriate public education would have recourse in the federal courts only under two circumstances: when the parent happens to have some claim related to the procedures employed; and when he or she is able to incur, and has in fact incurred, expenses creating a right to reimbursement. Otherwise the adequacy of the child's education would not be regarded as relevant to any cause of action the parent might bring; and, as a result, only the child could vindicate the right accorded by IDEA to a free appropriate public education.

The potential for injustice in this result is apparent. What is more, we find nothing in the statute to indicate that when Congress required States to provide adequate instruction to a child "at no cost to parents," it intended that only some parents would be able to enforce that mandate. The statute instead takes pains to "ensure that the rights of children with disabilities and parents of such children are protected." ...

We conclude IDEA grants parents independent, enforceable rights. These rights, which are not limited to certain procedural and reimbursement-related matters, encompass the entitlement to a free appropriate public education for the parents' child.

C

Respondent contends, though, that even under the reasoning we have now explained petitioners cannot prevail without overcoming a further difficulty. Citing our opinion in *Arlington Central School Dist. Bd. of Ed. v. Murphy,* respondent argues that statutes passed pursuant to the Spending Clause, such as IDEA, must provide "'clear notice'" before they can burden a State with some new condition, obligation, or liability. Respondent contends that because IDEA is, at best, ambiguous as to whether it accords parents independent rights, it has failed to provide clear notice of this condition to the States.

Respondent's reliance on *Arlington* is misplaced. In *Arlington* we addressed whether IDEA required States to reimburse experts' fees to prevailing parties in IDEA actions.

"[W]hen Congress attaches conditions to a State's acceptance of federal funds," we explained, "the conditions must be set out 'unambiguously.'" The question to be answered in *Arlington,* therefore, was whether IDEA "furnishes clear notice regarding the liability at issue." We found it did not.

The instant case presents a different issue, one that does not invoke the same rule. Our determination that IDEA grants to parents independent, enforceable rights does not impose any substantive condition or obligation on States they would not otherwise be required by law to observe. The basic measure of monetary recovery, moreover, is not expanded by recognizing that some rights repose in both the parent and the child. . . .

Respondent argues our ruling will, as a practical matter, increase costs borne by the States as they are forced to defend against suits unconstrained by attorneys trained in the law and the rules of ethics. Effects such as these do not suffice to invoke the concerns under the Spending Clause. . . .

III

The Court of Appeals erred when it dismissed the Winkelmans' appeal for lack of counsel. Parents enjoy rights under IDEA; and they are, as a result, entitled to prosecute IDEA claims on their own behalf. The decision by Congress to grant parents these rights was consistent with the purpose of IDEA and fully in accord with our social and legal traditions. It is beyond dispute that the relationship between a parent and child is sufficient to support a legally cognizable interest in the education of one's child; and, what is more, Congress has found that "the education of children with disabilities can be made more effective by . . . strengthening the role and responsibility of parents and ensuring that families of such children have meaningful opportunities to participate in the education of their children at school and at home."

In light of our holding we need not reach petitioners' alternative argument, which concerns whether IDEA entitles parents to litigate their child's claims *pro se.*

The judgment of the Court of Appeals is reversed, and the case is remanded for further proceedings consistent with this opinion.

It is so ordered.

Justice SCALIA, with whom Justice THOMAS joins, concurring in the judgment in part and dissenting in part.

I would hold that parents have the right to proceed *pro se* under the Individuals with Disabilities Education Act (IDEA), when they seek reimbursement for private school expenses or redress for violations of their own procedural rights, but not when they seek a judicial determination that their child's free appropriate public education (or FAPE) is substantively inadequate.

Whether parents may bring suits under the IDEA without a lawyer depends upon the interaction between the IDEA and the general *pro se* provision in the Judiciary Act of 1789. The latter . . . provides that "[i]n all courts of the United States *the parties* may plead and conduct their own cases personally or by counsel." The IDEA's right-to-sue provision, provides that "[a]ny *party aggrieved* by the findings and decision [of a hearing officer] shall have the right to bring a civil action with respect to the [administrative] complaint." Thus, when parents are "parties aggrieved" under the IDEA, they are "parties" within the meaning of [the Judiciary Act], entitled to sue on their own behalf.

As both parties agree, "party aggrieved" means "[a] party entitled to a remedy; espy., a party whose personal, pecuniary, or property rights have been adversely affected by another person's actions or by a court's decree or judgment." This case thus turns on the rights that the IDEA accords to parents, and the concomitant remedies made available to them. Only with respect to such rights and remedies are parents properly viewed as "parties aggrieved," capable of filing their own cases in federal court.

A review of the statutory text makes clear that, as relevant here, the IDEA grants parents only two types of rights. First, under certain circumstances "a court or a hearing officer may require the [school district] to reimburse *the parents*" for private school expenditures "if the court or hearing officer finds that the [school district] had not made a free appropriate public education available to the child." Second, parents are accorded a variety of procedural protections, both during the development of their child's individualized education program (IEP). It is clear that parents may object to procedural violations at the administrative due process hearing, and that a hearing officer may provide relief to parents for certain procedural infractions. Because the rights to reimbursement and to the various procedural protections are accorded to parents themselves, they are "parties aggrieved" when those rights are infringed, and may accordingly proceed *pro se* when seeking to vindicate them.

The Court goes further, however, concluding that parents may proceed *pro se* not only when they seek reimbursement or assert procedural violations, but also when they challenge the substantive adequacy of their child's FAPE—so that parents may act without a lawyer *in every IDEA case*. In my view, this sweeps far more broadly than the text allows. Out of this sprawling statute the Court cannot identify even *a single* provision stating that parents have the substantive right to a FAPE. The reason for this is readily understandable: The right to a free appropriate public education obviously inheres in the child, for it is he who receives the education. As the IDEA instructs, participating States must provide a "free appropriate public education . . . to all children with disabilities. . . ." The statute is replete with references to the fact that a FAPE belongs to the child. . . . The parents of a disabled child no doubt have an *interest* in seeing their child receive a proper education. But there is a difference between an *interest* and a statutory *right*. The text of the IDEA makes clear that parents have no *right* to the education itself.

The Court concedes, as it must, that while the IDEA gives parents the right to reimbursement and procedural protection in explicit terms, it does not do so for the supposed right to the education itself. The obvious inference to be drawn from the statute's clear and explicit conferral of discrete types of rights upon parents and children, respectively, is that it does not by accident confer the parent-designated rights upon children, or the children-designated rights upon parents. The Court believes, however, that "the statute prevents us from placing too much weight on [this] implicatio[n]." That conclusion is in error. Nothing in "the statute," undermines the obvious "implication" of Congress's scheme. What the Court relies upon for its conclusion that parents have a substantive right to a FAPE is not the "statutory structure," but rather the myriad *procedural* guarantees accorded to parents in the administrative process. But allowing parents, by means of these guarantees, to help shape the contours of their child's education is simply not the same as giving *them* the right to that education. Nor can the Court sensibly rely on the provisions governing due process hearings and administrative appeals, the various provisions that refer to the "parent's complaint," or the fact that the right-to-sue provision, refers to the administrative complaint, which in turn allows parents to challenge "any matter" relating to the provision of a FAPE. These provisions prove nothing except what all parties concede: that parents *may* represent their child *pro se* at the administrative level. ... Parents thus have the power, at the administrative stage, to litigate *all* of the various rights under the statute since at that stage they are acting not only on their *own* behalf, but on behalf of *their child* as well. This tells us nothing whatever about *whose* rights they are. The Court's spraying statutory sections about like buckshot cannot create a substantive parental right to education where none exists.

Harkening back to its earlier discussion of the IDEA's "text and structure" (by which it means the statute's procedural protections), the Court announces the startling proposition that, in fact, the "IDEA does not differentiate ... between the rights accorded to children and the rights accorded to parents." If that were so, the Court could have spared us its painful effort to craft a distinctive parental right out of scattered procedural provisions. But of course it is not so. The IDEA quite clearly differentiates between the rights accorded to parents and their children. As even petitioners' *amici* agree, "Congress specifically indicated that parents have rights under the Act that are separate from and independent of their children's rights." Does the Court seriously contend that a child has a right to reimbursement, when the statute most definitively provides that if "*the parents* of a child with a disability" enroll that child in private school, "a court ... may require the [school district] to reimburse *the parents* for the cost of that enrollment"? Does the Court believe that a child has a procedural right under [IDEA], which gives *parents* the power to excuse an IEP team member from attending an IEP meeting? The IDEA does not remotely envision communal "family" rights.

The Court believes that because parents must prove the substantive inadequacy of a FAPE before obtaining reimbursement, and because the suitability of a FAPE may also be at issue when procedural violations are alleged, it is "out of accord with the statute's design" to "prevent [parents] from obtaining a judgment mandating that the school district provide their child" with a FAPE. That is a total non sequitur. That Congress has required parents to demonstrate the inadequacy of their child's FAPE in order to vindicate their own rights says nothing about whether parents possess an underlying right to education. The Court insists that the right to a FAPE is the right "most fundamental to the Act." Undoubtedly so, but that sheds no light upon whom the right belongs to, and hence upon who can sue in their own right. Congress has used the phrase "party aggrieved," and it is this Court's job to apply that language, not to run from it.

The Court further believes that a distinction between parental and child rights will prove difficult to administer. I fail to see why that is so. Before today, the majority of Federal Courts of Appeals to have considered the issue have allowed parents to sue *pro se* with respect to some claims, but not with respect to the denial of a FAPE. . . . The Court points to no evidence suggesting that this majority rule has caused any confusion in practice. Nor do I see how it could, since the statute makes clear and easily administrable distinctions between parents' and children's legal entitlements.

Finally, the Court charges that the approach taken by the majority of Courts of Appeals would perpetuate an "injustice," since parents who do not seek reimbursement or allege procedural violations would be "without a remedy." That, of course, is not true. They will have the same remedy as all parents who sue to vindicate their children's rights: the power to bring suit, represented by counsel. But even indulging the Court's perception that it is unfair to allow some but not all IDEA parents to proceed *pro se,* that complaint is properly addressed to Congress, which structured the rights as it has, and limited suit to "party aggrieved." And there are good reasons for it to have done so. *Pro se* cases impose unique burdens on lower courts—and on defendants, in this case the schools and school districts that must hire their own lawyers. Since *pro se* complaints are prosecuted essentially for free, without screening by knowledgeable attorneys, they are much more likely to be unmeritorious. And for courts to figure them out without the assistance of plaintiff's counsel is much more difficult and time-consuming. In both categories of *pro se* parental suit permitted under a proper interpretation of the statute, one or the other of these burdens is reduced. Actions seeking reimbursement are less likely to be frivolous, since not many parents will be willing to lay out the money for private education without some solid reason to believe the FAPE was inadequate. And actions alleging procedural violations can ordinarily be disposed of without the intensive record-review that characterizes suits challenging the suitability of a FAPE.

* * *

Petitioners sought reimbursement, alleged procedural violations, and requested a declaration that their child's FAPE was substantively inadequate. I agree with the Court that they may proceed *pro se* with respect to the first two claims, but I disagree that they may do so with respect to the third.

Notes

1. In something of a surprise, the Court decided this case by a margin of seven to two. Most commentators thought that the Court would have ruled in favor of the board.

2. In his dissent, Justice Scalia expressed his concern that allowing parents who are not attorneys to initiate litigation can be costly to school systems. What additional costs could a school district incur by the ruling?

3. The Court failed to address what should take place if the interests of parents differ from those of their children. For example, if students in secondary schools disagree with their parents as to the content of their IEPs, it is possible that students and their parents, as well as their school boards, might all resort to litigation, creating the anomalous situation of having three different lawyers present. Further, if a noncustodial parent disagrees with the custodial parent and the student, then a fourth lawyer could be added to the mix.

4. Two related arguments against allowing parents to proceed on behalf of their children in IDEA cases is that their children, the real beneficiaries of the IDEA, should be represented by competent counsel and that their entitlements should not be compromised by the failure of their parents to obtain competent counsel. Conversely, others might argue that a child's entitlement would be compromised even further if parents were unable to file suit due to their inability to obtain counsel. Which side do you think has the better argument?

REFERENCES

Abney ex rel. Kantor v. District of Columbia, 849 F.2d 1491 (D.C. Cir. 1988).

Abraham v. District of Columbia, 338 F. Supp.2d 113 (D.D.C. 2004).

Alamo Heights Independent School District v. State Board of Education, 790 F.2d 1153 (5th Cir. 1986).

Allstate Insurance Co. v. Bethlehem Area School District, 678 F. Supp. 1132 (E.D. Pa. 1987).

Andrews v. Ledbetter, 880 F.2d 1287 (11th Cir. 1989).

Antkowiak v. Ambach, 838 F.2d 635 (2d Cir. 1988).

Antione M. v. Chester Upland School District, 420 F. Supp.2d 396 (E.D. Pa. 2006).

Arons, In re, 796 A.2d 867 (Del. 2000).

Association for Community Living in Colorado v. Romer, 992 F.2d 1040 (10th Cir. 1993).

Association for Retarded Citizens of Alabama v. Teague, 830 F.2d 158 (11th Cir. 1987).

Barnett v. Fairfax County School Board, 927 F.2d 146 (4th Cir. 1991), *cert. denied,* 502 U.S. 859 (1991).

Begay v. Hodel, 730 F. Supp. 1001 (D. Ariz. 1990).

Bertolucci v. San Carlos Elementary School District, 721 F. Supp. 1150 (N.D. Cal. 1989).

Beth B. v. Van Clay, 282 F.3d 493 (7th Cir. 2002).

Blackmon v. Springfield R-XII School District, 198 F.3d 648 (8th Cir. 1999).

Block v. District of Columbia, 748 F. Supp. 891 (D.D.C. 1990).

Board of Education of Community Consolidated School District v. Illinois State Board of Education, 938 F.2d 712 (7th Cir. 1991).

Board of Education of Strongville City School District v. Theado, 566 N.E.2d 667 (Ohio 1991).

Board of Education of the Baldwin Union Free School District v. Commissioner of Education, 610 N.Y.S.2d 426 (N.Y. Sup. Ct. 1994).

Board of Education of the City of Chicago v. Wolinsky, 842 F. Supp. 1080 (N.D. Ill. 1993).

Board of Education of the Hendrick Hudson Central School District v. Rowley, 458 U.S. 176 (1982).

Board of Education of the Paxton-Buckley-Loda Unit School District No. 10 v. Jeff S., 184 F. Supp.2d 790 (C.D. Ill. 2002).

Board of Education of the Seneca Falls Central School District v. Board of Education of the Liverpool Central School District, 728 F. Supp. 910 (W.D.N.Y. 1990).

Board of Education v. Michael M., 95 F. Supp.2d 600 (S.D. W. Va. 2000).

Bray v. Hobart City School Corporation, 818 F. Supp. 1226 (N.D. Ind. 1993).

Briggs v. Board of Education of Connecticut, 882 F.2d 688 (2d Cir. 1989).

Burke County Board of Education v. Denton, 895 F.2d 973 (4th Cir. 1990).

Burr v. Ambach, 863 F.3d 1071 (2d Cir. 1988), *vacated sub nom. Sobol v. Burr,* 492 U.S. 902 (1989a), *affirmed,* 888 F.2d 258 (2d Cir. 1989b), *cert. denied,* 494 U.S. 1005 (1990).

Canton Board of Education v. N.B. and R.B., 343 F. Supp.2d 123 (D. Conn. 2004).

Carey v. Maine School Administrative District 17, 754 F. Supp. 906 (D. Me. 1990).

Carlisle Area School v. Scott P., 62 F.3d 520 (3d Cir. 1995).

Carpenter v. Pennell School District Elementary Unit, 2002 WL 1832854 (E.D. Pa.2002), *affirmed sub nom. Carpenter v. Children for Youth Services,* 64 Fed.Appex. 850 (3d Cir. 2003a) (table), *cert. denied,* 540 U.S. 819 (2003b).

Cavanaugh ex rel. Cavanaugh v. Cardinal Local School District, 409 F.3d 753 (6th Cir. 2005).

Christopher M. v. Corpus Christi Independent School District, 933 F.2d 1285 (5th Cir. 1991).

Christopher S. ex rel. Rita S. v. Stanislaus County Office of Education, 384 F.3d 1205 (9th Cir. 2004).

Christopher W. v. Portsmouth School Committee, 877 F.2d 1089 (1st Cir. 1989).

Civil Rights Act of 1871, Section 1983, 42 U.S.C. § 1983.

Clark, S. G. (2002). Administrative remedy under IDEA: Must it be exhausting? *Education Law Reporter, 163,* 1–15.

Clovis Unified School District v. California Office of Administrative Hearings, 903 F.2d 635 (9th Cir. 1990).

C.O. v. Portland Public Schools, 406 F. Supp.2d 1157 (D. Or. 2005).

Cocores v. Portsmouth, New Hampshire School District, 779 F. Supp. 203 (D.N.H. 1991).

Collinsgru v. Palmyra Board of Education, 161 F.3d 225 (3d Cir. 1998).

Cordrey v. Euckert, 917 F.2d 1460 (6th Cir. 1990).

Cothern v. Mallory, 565 F. Supp. 701 (W.D. M0.1983).

Cox v. Jenkins, 878 F.2d 414 (D.C. Cir. 1989).

Crocker v. Tennessee Secondary Schools Athletic Association, 873 F.2d 933 (6th Cir. 1989), 980 F.2d 382 (6th Cir. 1992).

Daniel R.R. v. State Board of Education, 874 F.2d 1036 (5th Cir. 1989).

D.C. ex rel. S.K. v. Hamamoto, 97 Fed. Appx. 736 (9th Cir. 2004).

D.K. ex rel. Kumetz-Coleman v. Huntington Beach Union High School District, 428 F. Supp.2d 1088 (C.D. Cal. 2006).

Devine v. Indian River County School Board, 121 F.3d 576 (11th Cir. 1997).

Devine v. Indian River, 249 F.3d 1289 (11th Cir. 2001).

DeVries v. Spillane, 853 F.2d 264 (4th Cir. 1988).

Diaz-Fonseca v. Commonwealth of Puerto Rico, 451 F.3d 13 (1st Cir. 2006).

Digre v. Roseville School Independent School District No. 623, 841 F.2d 245 (11th Cir. 1988).

Doe v. Alabama State Department of Education, 915 F.2d 651 (11th Cir. 1990).

Doe v. Arizona Department of Education, 111 F.3d 678 (9th Cir. 1997).

Doe v. Belleville Public School District No. 118, 672 F. Supp. 342 (S.D. Ill. 1987).

Doe v. Board of Education of Tullahoma City Schools, 9 F.3d 455 (6th Cir. 1993).

Doe v. Brookline School Committee, 722 F.2d 910 (1st Cir. 1983).

Doe v. Smith, 879 F.2d 1340 (6th Cir. 1989).

Dong v. Board of Education of the Rochester Community Schools, 197 F.3d 793 (6th Cir. 1999).

Doyle v. Arlington County School Board, 953 F.2d 100 (4th Cir. 1991), *on remand,* 806 F. Supp. 1253 (E.D. Va. 1992), *affirmed,* 39 F.3d 1176 (4th Cir. 1994) (mem.).

D.R. v. East Brunswick Board of Education, 838 F. Supp. 184 (D.N.J. 1993).

Edward B. v. Paul, 814 F.2d 52 (1st Cir. 1987).

Evans v. Evans, 818 F. Supp. 1215 (N.D. Ind. 1993).

Fagan v. District of Columbia, 136 F.R.D. 5 (D.D.C. 1991).

Family & Children's Center v. School City of Mishawaka, 13 F.3d 1052 (7th Cir. 1994).

Fauconier v. Committee on Special Education, 2003 WL 21345549 (S.D.N.Y. 2003).

Fee v. Herndon, 900 F.2d 804 (5th Cir. 1990).

Frutiger v. Hamilton Central School District, 928 F.2d 68 (2d Cir. 1991).

Fuhrmann v. East Hanover Board of Education, 993 F.2d 1031 (3d Cir. 1993).

Gardener v. School Board of Caddo Parish, 958 F.2d 108 (5th Cir. 1992).

Garro v. State of Connecticut, 23 F.3d 734 (2d Cir. 1994).

Gaudiello v. Delaware County Intermediate Unit, 796 F. Supp. 849 (E.D. Pa. 1992).

G.D. v. Westmoreland School District, 783 F. Supp. 1532 (D.N.H. 1992).

Gehman v. Prudential Property and Casualty Insurance Company, 702 F. Supp. 1192 (E.D. Pa. 1989).

Geis v. Board of Education, 774 F.2d 575 (3d Cir. 1985).

Grace B. v. Lexington School Committee, 762 F. Supp. 416 (D. Mass. 1991).

Greene v. Harrisville School District, 771 F. Supp. 1 (D.N.H. 1990).

Grim v. Rhinebeck Central School District, 346 F.3d 377 (2d Cir. 2003).

Grymes v. Madden, 672 F.2d 321 (3d Cir. 1982).

Hacienda La Puente Unified School District of Los Angeles v. Honig, 976 F.2d 487 (9th Cir. 1992).

Hall v. Knott County Board of Education, 941 F.2d 402 (6th Cir. 1991).

Hayes v. Unified School District No. 377, 877 F.2d 809 (10th Cir. 1989).

Hebert v. Manchester, New Hampshire, School District, 833 F. Supp. 80 (D.N.H. 1993).

Heldman v. Sobol, 962 F.2d 148 (2d Cir. 1992).

Hiller v. Board of Education of the Brunswick Central School District, 674 F. Supp. 73 (N.D.N.Y. 1987), 687 F. Supp. 735 (N.D.N.Y. 1988).

Hoeft v. Tucson Unified School District, 967 F.2d 1298 (9th Cir. 1992).

Holmes v. Sobol, 690 F. Supp. 154 (W.D.N.Y. 1988).

Honig v. Doe, 484 U.S. 305 (1988).

Hunger v. Leininger, 15 F.3d 664 (7th Cir. 1994), *cert. denied*, 513 U.S. 839 (1994).

I.D. v. Westmoreland School District, 788 F. Supp. 632 (D.N.H. 1991).

Independent School District No. 623 v. Digre, 893 F.2d 987 (8th Cir. 1990).

Individuals with Disabilities Education Act of 2004, 20 U.S.C. §§ 1400–1482 (2005).

Jackson v. Fort Stanton Hospital and Training School, 757 F. Supp. 1243 (D.N.M. 1990).

Jenkins v. Squillacote, 935 F.2d 303 (D.C. Cir. 1991).

Jenkins v. State of Florida, 931 F.2d 1469 (11th Cir. 1991).

J.G. v. Board of Education of the Rochester City School District, 830 F.2d 444 (2d Cir. 1987).

Johnson v. Independent School District No. 4, 921 F.2d 1022 (10th Cir. 1990).

Johnson v. Lancaster-Lebanon Intermediate Unit No. 13, Lancaster City School District, 757 F. Supp. 606 (E.D. Pa. 1991).

J.S. ex rel. N.S. v. Attica Central Schools, 386 F.3d 107 (2d Cir. 2004).

J.S.K. v. Hendry County School Board, 941 F.2d 1563 (11th Cir. 1991).

Karl v. Board of Education of the Genesco Central School District, 736 F.2d 873 (2d Cir. 1984).

Kerkham v. McKenzie, 862 F.2d 884 (D.C. Cir. 1988).

Kerkham v. Superintendent, District of Columbia Schools, 931 F.2d 84 (D.C. Cir. 1991).

Kerr Center Parents Association v. Charles, 897 F.2d 1463 (9th Cir. 1990).

Komninos v. Upper Saddle River Board of Education, 13 F.3d 775 (3d Cir. 1994).

Konkel v. Elmbrook School District, 348 F. Supp.2d 1018 (E.D. Wis. 2004).

Kuszewski v. Chippewa Valley Schools, 117 F. Supp. 646 (E.D. Mich. 2000).

L.B. and J.B. ex rel. K.B. v. Nebo School District, 379 F.3d 966 (10th Cir. 2004).

L.E. ex rel. E.S. v. Ramsey Board of Education, 435 F.3d 384 (3d Cir. 2006).

Lee v. Biloxi School District, 963 F.2d 837 (5th Cir. 1992).

Leighty ex rel. Leighty v. Lauren School District, 457 F. Supp.2d 546 (W.D. Pa. 2006).

Lenn v. Portland School Community, 998 F.2d 1083 (1st Cir. 1993).

Lester H. v. Gilhool, 916 F.2d 865 (3d Cir. 1990).

Louis M. v. Ambach, 714 F. Supp. 1276 (N.D.N.Y. 1989).

Maroni v. Pemi-Baker Regional School District, 346 F.3d 247 (1st Cir. 2003).

Mavis v. Sobol, 839 F. Supp. 968 (N.D.N.Y. 1994).

McCartney C. v. Herrin Community Unit School District No. 4, 21 F.3d 173 (7th Cir. 1994).

McDowell v. Fort Bend Independent School District, 737 F. Supp. 386 (S.D. Tex. 1990).

McKenzie v. Smith, 771 F.2d 1527 (D.C. Cir. 1985).

Merrifield v. Lake Central School Corporation, 770 F. Supp. 468 (N.D. Ind. 1991).

Metropolitan Board of Public Education of the Metropolitan Government of Nashville and Davidson County v. Bellamy, 116 Fed. Appx. 570 (6th Cir. 2004).

Metropolitan Board of Public Education v. Guest, 193 F.3d 457 (6th Cir. 1999).

Metropolitan Government of Nashville and Davidson County v. Cook, 915 F.2d 232 (6th Cir. 1990).

Metropolitan School District v. Buskirk, 950 F. Supp. 899 (S.D. Ind. 1997).

Militello v. Board of Education of the City of Union City, 803 F. Supp. 974 (D.N.J. 1992).

Montclair Board of Education v. M.W.D., 182 Fed. Appx. 136 (3d Cir. 2006).

Mrs. W. v. Tirozzi, 706 F. Supp. 164 (D. Conn. 1989).

Murphy v. Timberlane Regional School District, 973 F.2d 13 (1st Cir. 1992), *on remand*, 819 F. Supp. 1127 (D.N.H.1993), *affirmed*, 22 F.3d 1186 (1st Cir. 1994), *cert. denied*, 513 U.S. 987 (1994).

Muth v. Central Bucks School District, 839 F.2d 113 (3d Cir. 1988), *affirmed on other grounds sub nom. Dellmuth v. Muth*, 491 U.S. 223 (1989).

Navin v. Park Ridge School District, 270 F.3d 1147 (7th Cir. 2001), *on remand*, 2002 WL 774300 (N.D. Ill. 2002a), *affirmed*, 49 Fed. Appx. 69 (7th Cir. 200b).

N.B. v. Alachua County School Board, 84 F.3d 1376 (11th Cir. 1996).

Norris v. Board of Education of Greenwood Community School Corporation, 797 F. Supp. 1452 (S.D. Ind. 1992).

Oberti v. Board of Education of the Borough of Clementon School District, 995 F.2d 1204 (3d Cir. 1993).

Ojai Unified School District v. Jackson, 4 F.3d 1467 (9th Cir. 1993), *cert. denied*, 513 U.S. 825 (1994).

Osborne, A. G. (1996). Statutes of limitations for filing a lawsuit under the Individuals With Disabilities Education Act. *Education Law Reporter, 106*, 959–970.

Osborne, A. G. (2001). Proving that you have provided a FAPE under IDEA. *Education Law Reporter, 151*, 367–372.

Osborne, A. G. (2004). Statutes of limitations for filing a lawsuit under the IDEA: A state by state analysis. *Education Law Reporter, 191*, 545–556.

Osborne, A. G., & Russo, C. J. (2005). The burden of proof in special education hearings: *Schaffer v. Weast. Education Law Reporter, 200*, 1–12.

Padilla v. School District No. 1, 233 F.3d 1268 (10th Cir. 2000).

Polera v. Board of Education of the Newburgh Enlarged City School District, 288 F.3d 478 (2d Cir. 2002).

Puffer v. Raynolds, 761 F. Supp. 838 (D. Mass. 1988).

Quackenbush v. Johnson City School District, 716 F.2d 141 (2d Cir. 1983).

Rehabilitation Act of 1973, Section 504, 29 U.S.C. §§ 792, 794 (1998).

Reid v. Board of Education, Lincolnshire-Prairie View School District 103, 765 F. Supp. 965 (N.D. Ill. 1990).

Richards v. Fairfax County School Board, 798 F. Supp. 338 (E.D. Va. 1992).

Riley v. Ambach, 668 F.2d 635 (2d Cir. 1981).

R.M. ex rel J.M. v. Vernon Board of Education, 208 F. Supp.2d 216 (D. Conn. 2002).

Robbins v. Maine School Administrative District No. 56, 807 F. Supp. 11 (D. Me. 1992).

Robertson v. Granite City Community Unit School District No. 9, 684 F. Supp. 1002 (S.D. Ill. 1988).

Robinson v. Pinderhughes, 810 F.2d 1270 (4th Cir. 1987).

Roland M. v. Concord School Community, 910 F.2d 983 (1st Cir. 1990), *cert. denied*, 499 U.S. 912 (1991).

Roncker v. Walter, 700 F.2d 1058 (6th Cir. 1983).

R.S. v. District of Columbia, 292 F. Supp.2d 23 (D.D.C. 2003).

Russo, C. J., & Osborne, A. G. (2006). The Supreme Court clarifies the burden of proof in special education due process hearings: *Schaffer ex rel. Schaffer v. Weast. Education Law Reporter, 208*, 705–717.

Sanders v. Santa Fe Pub. Schools, 383 F.Supp.2d 1305 (D.N.M. 2004).

Schaffer v. Weast, 546 U.S. 49 (2005).

Seattle School District No. 1 v. B.S., 82 F.3d 1493 (9th Cir. 1996).

Section 504, Rehabilitation Act of 1973, 29 U.S.C. § 792.

Section 1983, Civil Rights Act of 1871, 42 U.S.C. § 1983.

Shook v. Gaston County Board of Education, 882 F.2d 119 (4th Cir. 1989).

Slack v. State of Delaware Department of Public Instruction, 826 F. Supp. 115 (D. Del. 1993).

Smith, In re, 926 F.2d 1027 (11th Cir. 1991).

Smith v. Special School District No. 1, 184 F.3d 764 (8th Cir. 1999).

Spencer v. District of Columbia, 416 F. Supp.2d 5 (D.D.C. 2006).

Stellato v. Board of Education of the Ellenville Central School District, 842 F. Supp. 1512 (N.D.N.Y. 1994).

Straube v. Florida Union Free School District, 801 F. Supp. 1164 (S.D.N.Y. 1992).

Susan R.M. v. Northeast Independent School District, 818 F.2d 455 (5th Cir. 1987).

Teague Independent School District v. Todd D., 999 F.2d 127 (5th Cir. 1993).

Thomas R.W. v. Massachusetts Department of Education, 130 F.3d 477 (1st Cir. 1997).

Thomas v. Cincinnati Board of Education, 918 F.2d 618 (6th Cir. 1990).

Tice v. Botetourt County School Board, 908 F.2d 1200 (4th Cir. 1990).

Tindall v. Poultney High School District, 414 F.3d 281 (2d Cir. 2005).

Torrie v. Cwayna, 841 F. Supp. 1434 (W.D. Mich. 1994).

Town of Burlington v. Department of Education, Commonwealth of Massachusetts, 736 F.2d 773 (1st Cir. 1984), *affirmed on other grounds sub nom. Burlington School Committee v. Department of Education of the Commonwealth of Massachusetts,* 471 U.S. 359 (1985).

T.S. v. Ridgefield Board of Education, 10 F.3d 87 (2d Cir. 1993).

University Interscholastic League v. Buchannan, 848 S.W.2d 298 (Tex. App. 1993).

Vander Malle v. Ambach, 667 F. Supp. 1015 (S.D.N.Y. 1987).

Walker County School District v. Bennett, 203 F. 3d 1293 (11th Cir. 2000).

Weast v. Schaffer, 377 F.3d 449 (4th Cir. 2004), *affirmed sub nom. Schaffer v. Weast,* 546 U.S. 49 (2005).

Wenger v. Canastota Central School District, 146 F.3d 123 (2d Cir. 1998), *cert. denied,* 526 U.S. 1025 (1999).

Wenkart, R. D. (2004). The burden of proof in IDEA due process hearings. *Education Law Reporter, 187,* 817–823.

West Platte R-II School District v. Wilson ex rel. L.W., 439 F.3d 783 (8th Cir. 2006).

Winkelman v. Parma City School District, 150 Fed. Appx. 406 (6th Cir. 2005), 127 S. Ct. 1994 (2007).

Woods v. New Jersey Department of Education, 796 F. Supp. 767 (D.N.J. 1992); 823 F. Supp. 254 (D.N.J. 1993).

Zirkel, P. A., & Maher, P. J. (2003). The statute of limitations under the Individuals with Disabilities Education Act. *Education Law Reporter, 175,* 1–5.

8

Remedies for Failure to Provide a Free Appropriate Public Education

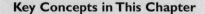

Key Concepts in This Chapter

❖ Damages

❖ Tuition Reimbursement

❖ Compensatory Educational Services

❖ Attorney Fees

If school officials fail to provide students with disabilities with the free appropriate public education (FAPE) called for in the Individuals with Disabilities Education Act (IDEA), the courts can grant appropriate relief based on the preponderance of evidence standard (20 U.S.C. § 1415(i)(2); 34 C.F.R. § 300.516(c)(3)).

Courts typically award such relief as reimbursement for tuition and other costs that parents incur when they unilaterally place their children in the schools of their choice. Courts can also grant parents who cannot afford to pay prospectively for placing their children in private schools awards of compensatory educational services. Further, courts can grant prevailing parents reimbursement for their legal expenses. While courts are generally reluctant to award **punitive damages** against school boards, recent litigation indicates that this attitude may be changing.

A great deal of litigation has focused on remedies in special education, including key cases that made their way to the United States Supreme Court. Many of the remedies that exist to compensate for the failure of school officials to provide a FAPE are based on case law. As such, in amending the IDEA, Congress provided additional guidance about the types of remedies that are available to students and parents, along with establishing the circumstances under which they may be granted. In fact, some legislative changes occurred in response to judicial interpretations of the IDEA. This chapter provides information on the remedies available to parents and students, including those based on provisions in the IDEA and those that emerged from case law.

This chapter begins with an overview of the most common remedies fashioned by the courts: tuition reimbursement and compensatory educational services. The next sections review attorney fees before discussing the evolving law of damages.

TUITION REIMBURSEMENT

When administrative or judicial proceedings involving placement disputes are pending pursuant to the IDEA, students must remain in their then current educational placements unless their parents and school officials or states agree otherwise (20 U.S.C. § 1415(j); 34 C.F.R. § 300.318(a)). Parents who are concerned that the current placements of their children are inappropriate may not wish to have the children remain in those placements for the length of time it takes to reach final settlements. In these situations, parents frequently remove their children from their current placements and enroll them in private facilities. Parents who prevail in their placement challenges can, under appropriate circumstances, be reimbursed for the costs of tuition and other expenses associated with unilateral private placements. While case law provided parents with this relief, the IDEA and its regulations now explicitly authorize tuition reimbursement (20 U.S.C. § 1412(a)(10)(C)(ii); 34 C.F.R. § 300.148).

The Supreme Court and Parental Reimbursement

The United States Supreme Court rendered two important judgments regarding tuition reimbursement for parents who unilaterally placed their children in private schools. In *Burlington School Committee v. Department of Education,*

Commonwealth of Massachusetts (*Burlington*) (1985) the Court affirmed that the IDEA allowed reimbursement as long as the parents' chosen placement was determined to be the appropriate placement for their child. The Court declared that when Congress empowered the judiciary to grant appropriate relief, it intended to include retroactive relief as an available remedy. The Court reasoned that reimbursement merely requires school boards to pay the expenses that they would have incurred all along if officials had initially developed proper individualized education programs (IEPs). If reimbursement were not available, the Court explained that the rights of students to a FAPE and parental rights to participate fully in developing appropriate IEPs pursuant to the IDEA's procedural safeguards would have been less than complete. The Court maintained that parental violations of the IDEA's status quo provision do not constitute waiver of the right to request tuition reimbursements. However, the Court cautioned parents who make unilateral placements that they do so at their own financial risk since they will not be reimbursed if school officials can show that they proposed, and had the capacity to implement, appropriate IEPs.

Eight years later, in *Florence County School District Four v. Carter* (*Carter*) (1993), the Supreme Court unanimously affirmed that parentally chosen placements need not be in state-approved facilities in order for them to obtain tuition reimbursements. In *Carter*, parents who were dissatisfied with the IEP that school officials developed for their daughter placed her in a private school that was not on the state's list of approved facilities. Eventually, a trial court found that insofar as the school board's proposed IEP was inadequate, it had to reimburse the parents for the cost of the private school placement. The Fourth Circuit affirmed, noting that the private school provided an educational program that met the Supreme Court's standard of appropriateness as enunciated in *Board of Education of the Hendrick Hudson Central School District v. Rowley* (*Rowley*) (1982), even though it was not state approved and did not fully comply with the IDEA. The Fourth Circuit asserted that when the board defaulted on its obligations under the IDEA, reimbursement for the parental placement at a facility that was not approved by the state was not forbidden as long as the educational program met the *Rowley* standard. The Supreme Court agreed, emphasizing that the IDEA is designed to ensure that all students with disabilities receive an education that is both appropriate and free. The Court pointed out that barring reimbursement under the circumstances in *Carter* would have defeated the IDEA's statutory purposes.

Reimbursement Ordered Under *Burlington* and *Carter*

Parents can be denied tuition reimbursement awards if courts find that school officials offered, and had the capacity to implement, appropriate IEPs (20 U.S.C. § 1412(a)(10)(C)(i); 34 C.F.R. § 300.148(a)). Once courts agree that proposed IEPs are appropriate, they do not need to examine the appropriateness of parentally chosen placements. Even so, courts often award tuition reimbursement when parents can demonstrate that their school boards failed to offer appropriate IEPs and that the facilities they selected provided their children with appropriate educational programs.

Parentally Chosen Placements Must Be Appropriate, Not Perfect

According to *Burlington,* parents can be reimbursed for private school costs when their chosen placements are appropriate and those of school board officials are inappropriate. Recognizing that parents are not experts when it comes to making educational placements, courts do not expect them to make the exact required placements. Rather, as long as hearing officers or courts are satisfied that parentally chosen placements are more appropriate than those proposed by school boards, the judiciary generally awards reimbursement, even when the settings are not identical to those that are finally judged to be appropriate. The courts grant parents such latitude because they are aware that when parents make unilateral placements, they may not have as many options available to them as do school boards. Consequently, parents may not necessarily make the exact appropriate placement decisions made by school officials. Not surprisingly, courts ruled that reimbursement is still an available remedy (*Garland Independent School District v. Wilks,* 1987).

On the other hand, parents are not entitled to full reimbursement if courts discern that their chosen placements exceed what was required and were more costly than necessary (*Alamo Heights Independent School District v. State Board of Education,* 1986). The amount of advice and counsel that school officials provide to parents who seek to make unilateral placements may influence the extent of reimbursement awards. The Eleventh Circuit agreed that a residential placement was required for an autistic child but was troubled by the fact that the parents had chosen one in Tokyo, Japan (*Drew P. v. Clarke County School District,* 1987, 1989). The court affirmed that while the parents were entitled to some reimbursement, it did not think that a placement so far from home was necessary. Other courts denied full reimbursement to parents who chose residential placements when private day schools could have provided an appropriate education (*Board of Education of Oak Park & River Forest High School District No. 200 v. Illinois State Board of Education,* 1988; *Lascari v. Board of Education of the Ramapo Indian Hills Regional High School District,* 1989). Under these circumstances, courts generally award reimbursement for educational expenses at schools but not for room and board.

Parents are not entitled to tuition reimbursement for unilaterally obtained placements if they are not appropriate, even when school boards fail to offer appropriate IEPs. For example, in Connecticut the federal trial court held that a school board's IEP was not appropriate because school personnel committed several procedural errors. The court denied the parental request for reimbursement because their chosen placement was inappropriate since the school was not staffed by professionals who could deliver the special education services the student needed (*P.J. v. State of Connecticut State Board of Education,* 1992). Similarly, the Second Circuit posited that reimbursement was unwarranted where a hearing officer determined that a board's proposed placement was inappropriate but that the parents' chosen placement was also unacceptable (*M.S. ex rel. S.S. v. Board of Education of the City School District of the City of Yonkers,* 2000).

Courts can award parents reimbursement under *Carter* if their chosen facilities can deliver appropriate services, regardless of whether they or their staffs are certificated. The Ninth Circuit awarded reimbursement to the parents of an autistic student who unilaterally enrolled him in a private clinic that was not certified to provide special education services (*Union School District v. Smith,* 1994). The court affirmed that although school officials failed to offer a FAPE, the student received educational benefit from his placement at the private clinic. Likewise, the federal trial court in Maryland declared that parents were entitled to be reimbursed for tuition expenses at a private school that was not approved to provide special education services because evidence indicated that the student received a FAPE while there (*Gerstmyer v. Howard County Public Schools,* 1994). The Second Circuit affirmed that parents who enrolled their child in a program that was not staffed by certified individuals were entitled to reimbursement because the program still offered an appropriate education (*Still v. DeBuono,* 1996). The court concluded that the promise of the IDEA would have been defeated if reimbursement were barred when the parentally chosen providers were not certified and the reason the service was not provided by the state was that there was a shortage of qualified providers.

The Third Circuit affirmed a monetary award to compensate a mother for the time she spent providing services to her preschool-age daughter. After the mother unsuccessfully requested the addition of Lovaas therapy to her daughter's program, she received training to provide it herself and offered the services to her child. In finding that the child's program was inadequate, the court remanded to the hearing officer to consider an appropriate remedy. The hearing officer awarded reimbursement to compensate the parent for the time she spent providing therapy to her child. Subsequently, the federal trial court and the Third Circuit agreed with that award since the services that the mother provided were appropriate and the county's denial of those services constituted a violation of the IDEA (*Bucks County Department of Mental Health/Mental Retardation v. Commonwealth of Pennsylvania,* 2004).

School Boards Must Be Given the Opportunity to Act

In *Burlington,* the Supreme Court ruled that parents who violated the status quo provision did not waive their right to tuition reimbursement. Yet, in post-*Burlington* cases, courts agreed that parents waived their right to reimbursement when they made unilateral placements before giving school board officials opportunities to address their concerns. To this end, parents must notify school officials that they are dissatisfied with the IEPs of their children and afford educators the opportunity to take appropriate corrective action. This case law is now incorporated into the IDEA and its regulations (20 U.S.C. § 1412(a)(10)(C)(iii); 34 C.F.R. § 300.148(d)).

Pursuant to the IDEA and its regulations, reimbursement costs may be reduced or denied in four situations. First, costs can be reduced or denied if at the most recent IEP team meetings that parents attended prior to removal of their children from public schools, they did not inform the teams that they were rejecting the proposed placements of their children; notice must include a statement of parental concerns and their intent to enroll their children in private schools at public expense (20 U.S.C. § 1412(a)(10)(C)(iii)(I)(aa); 34 C.F.R. § 300.148 (d)(1)(i)).

Second, costs can be reduced or denied if at least ten business days (including any holidays that occur on business days) prior to the removal of children from public schools parents do not provide school officials with written notice of their intent to do so (20 U.S.C. § 1412(a)(10)(C)(iii)(I); 34 C.F.R. § 300.148(d)(1)(ii)). Third, if, prior to parental removal of their children from public schools educational officials informed parents of their intent to evaluate the students (along with statements of the purposes of the evaluations that were appropriate and reasonable) but the parents did not make them available (20 U.S.C. § 1412(a)(10)(C)(iii)(II); 34 C.F.R. § 300.148(d)(2)). Fourth, costs can be reduced or denied if courts find that parents acted unreasonably (20 U.S.C. § 1412(a)(10)(C)(iii)(III); 34 C.F.R. § 300.148(d)(3)).

A dispute from the Eighth Circuit, although litigated before these provisions were incorporated into the IDEA, provides an illustration of how parents can be denied reimbursement awards. The court affirmed that parents were not entitled to reimbursement because they unilaterally changed their daughter's placement rather than afford officials a chance to change her educational program (*Evans v. District No. 17 of Douglas County*, 1988). The court decided that insofar as there was no indication that the educators would have refused to change the student's program, they were entitled to have the opportunity to modify the child's IEP and placement. The court maintained that parents must put school officials on notice that they disagree with the educational programs of their children and must be given the opportunity to modify placements voluntarily before parents can take unilateral actions. Ten years later, the same court denied reimbursement to parents who removed their child from school after one day in the eighth grade, without any discussion of accommodations to meet his needs (*Schoenfield v. Parkway School District*, 1998).

Courts frequently deny reimbursement awards when parents take unilateral actions before giving school officials opportunities to intervene. Generally, courts reason that equity prevents reimbursement awards from accruing prior to the time school officials could evaluate students and make placement recommendations (*Ash v. Lake Oswego School District*, 1991, 1992; *Tucker v. Calloway County Board of Education*, 1998; *Johnson v. Metro Davidson County School System*, 2000; *L.K. ex rel. J.H. v. Board of Education for Transylvania County*, 2000). Parents may also forfeit their right to tuition reimbursement by failing to cooperate with school officials in the evaluation process (*Patricia P. v. Board of Education of Oak Park and River Forest High School District No. 200*, 2000). As stated above, the IDEA requires parents to provide school officials with written notification of their intent to enroll their child in private schools at public expense if they hope to obtain reimbursement awards. Parents who fail either to challenge the IEPs of their children or to provide school officials with the written notice required by the IDEA prior to making unilateral placements are not entitled to reimbursements (*Yancy v. New Baltimore City Board of School Commissioners*, 1998; *Nein v. Greater Clark County School Corporation*, 2000; *Greenland School District v. Amy N.*, 2004; *Ms. M. ex rel. K.M. v. Portland School Committee*, 2004).

Controversy has developed over new language in the IDEA that limits the obligation of school boards to reimburse parents. According to this language:

> If the parents of a child with a disability, who previously received special education and related services under the authority of a public agency, enroll the child in a private elementary school or secondary school without the consent of or referral by the public agency, a court or a hearing officer may require the agency to reimburse the parents for the cost of that enrollment if the court or hearing officer finds that the agency had not made a free appropriate public education available to the child in a timely manner prior to that enrollment. (20 U.S.C. § 1412(a)(10)(C)(ii))

The question has arisen as to whether that clause means that school boards are not required to reimburse the parents of students who have been unilaterally enrolled in private schools if the children never attended the public schools. Insofar as the Second Circuit affirmed that the IDEA does not preclude reimbursement in such a situation (*Frank G. v. Board of Education of Hyde Park,* 2006; *Board of Education of the City School District of the City of New York v. Tom F* (*Tom F.*), 2006, 2007), the Supreme Court agreed to hear the appeal in the latter case.

Amazingly, only ten days after hearing oral arguments, and just as this book was headed to press, the Supreme Court issued a one line opinion that "The judgment is affirmed by an equally divided Court (*Tom F.,* 2007 WL 2935030 (2007))." The Court added without further explanation that that "Justice Kennedy took no part in the decision of this case (*Tom F.,* 2007 WL 2935030 (2007))."

Insofar as *Tom F.* is a plurality, it remains binding precedent only in New York, Connecticut, and Vermont, the three states that comprise the Second Circuit. As such, the issue remains unsettled throughout the rest of the United States. Unfortunately, since the Court chose not to clarify the meaning of the provisions at issue, it leaves the door open to further litigation, and increased costs to school systems, as parents will undoubtedly make unilateral placements of their children in non-public schools and seek judicial reimbursement.

Parents Entitled to Reimbursement
If School Boards Commit Procedural Errors

The fact that school officials devised appropriate educational programs for students is insufficient to preclude reimbursement awards. IEP teams must spell out appropriate placements in properly executed IEPs. Procedural errors are sufficient grounds for awarding reimbursement for unilateral placements because, under *Rowley,* an educational placement is inappropriate if it is not contained in a properly executed IEP. For example, the Third Circuit held that reimbursement is warranted when a school board proposes an appropriate program but the IEP is defective on procedural grounds (*Muth v. Central Bucks School District,* 1988). Here school officials proposed a placement that was later deemed appropriate, but they failed to write an IEP for that proposal. In like fashion, the Fourth Circuit affirmed a reimbursement award in positing that school board officials failed to provide a FAPE for a child (*Board of Education of the County of Cabell v. Dienelt*, 1988). The trial court had decided that the board's program was inappropriate due to procedural defects since officials failed to conduct annual reviews and involve the parents in the IEP process.

If parents are unhappy with the education of their children, as noted, they must give school officials chances to evaluate students and propose appropriate placements. Boards may also be liable for tuition reimbursement if officials do not properly evaluate children. In one case, the Fourth Circuit affirmed that parents were justified in making a unilateral placement when school board officials failed to propose an appropriate placement due to an improper evaluation of the child (*Hudson v. Wilson*, 1987). The court maintained that the parents did not waive their right to reimbursement when they removed their child from the public schools before board personnel could conduct further assessments and propose a final IEP.

The IDEA requires parents to provide school officials with notice of their intent to place their children in private facilities in order to qualify for reimbursement. Even so, courts may excuse parental failure to notify officials if educators did not comply with proper procedures. For instance, the federal trial court in Maryland found that parents could not be denied reimbursement in failing to notify school board officials of their intent where educators failed to provide the parents with the notice of procedural requirements called for by state law and the IDEA (*Mayo v. Baltimore City Public Schools*, 1999).

As reflected by a case from Ohio, improperly written IEPs can serve as the basis for reimbursement awards. The Sixth Circuit, noting that flaws in an IEP were not harmless technical errors, awarded reimbursement to a parent who rejected an IEP that neither provided an objective means to measure progress nor adequately explained the services the student would have received (*Cleveland Heights–University Heights City School District v. Boss*, 1998). In addition, the Second Circuit approved a reimbursement award to parents who enrolled their child in a private school after school officials proposed a Section 504 accommodation plan instead of an IEP (*Muller v. Committee on Special Education of the East Islip Union Free School District*, 1998). The trial court decreed that the student qualified for special education as emotionally disturbed. Moreover, the Sixth Circuit awarded parents reimbursement in concluding that officials denied a child a FAPE because they predetermined his placement (*Deal ex rel. Deal v. Hamilton County Department of Education*, 2004). Previously, the Fourth Circuit was of the opinion that procedural errors must actually interfere with the provision of a FAPE before parents are entitled to reimbursement awards. When parents sought summer services and officials failed to consider their request properly, the court treated this as a harmless error since the evidence revealed that the student was not entitled to summer services (*DiBuo v. Board of Education of Worcester County*, 2002).

Parental Delays or Failure to Cooperate May Affect Reimbursement Awards

In New York, a federal trial court thought that nothing prohibited parents from being reimbursed even if they cause delays in the hearing process (*Eugene B.*

v. Great Neck Union Free School District, 1986). The court decided that the parents could still be reimbursed because their choice of a private school was the appropriate placement. In response to a request for reimbursement, school officials responded that since the parents caused several delays in the proceedings, they should not have been compensated for the periods of each of the delays. The court disagreed, stating that the board was responsible for the private school tuition for the entire time period regardless of whether there were delays in the proceedings.

On the other hand, the parents can be denied reimbursement if they delay unreasonably in requesting hearings. The Third Circuit was of the view that parents waived their right to reimbursement if they did not initiate review proceedings within a reasonable period of time (*Bernardsville Board of Education v. J.H.*, 1994). When the parents waited two years before filing their claim, the court observed that such a delay, absent mitigating factors, was unreasonable. Echoing this rationale in another case, the same court subsequently remarked that parents who enrolled their children, gifted students with learning disabilities, in a private school, but waited sixteen months before requesting tuition reimbursement, were not entitled to recover the costs for the time period prior to their request for a hearing (*Warren G. v. Cumberland County School District*, 1999). State statutes of limitations may impose additional restrictions on the time frames within which parents may file reimbursement claims.

Parents can lose awards or have them reduced if they frustrate attempts by school officials to develop IEPs. A federal trial court in California contended that a parent's failure to cooperate fully with attempts by school officials to design an educational program justified the reduction of a reimbursement award (*Glendale Unified School District v. Almasi*, 2000). In Wisconsin, where a parent refused a recommended evaluation but later placed the child in a residential facility, the school board refused to pay the tuition at the facility because it had not made the placement. The trial court agreed that since the board could not have been faulted for failing to act in the face of parental resistance, the parent was not entitled to reimbursement (*Suzawith v. Green Bay Area School District*, 2000).

Reimbursements for Related Services

Along with tuition, courts consistently award reimbursement for the costs of related services. The criteria for reimbursement of related services are the same as for tuition expenses: Parents must demonstrate that the services were required for their children to receive an appropriate education. In most cases, related services are provided at private schools in conjunction with special education services. However, courts award reimbursement for the costs of privately obtained related services when school boards fail to provide needed services in conjunction with public special education placements.

Parents have received reimbursement awards for the costs of psychotherapy or counseling services (*Max M. v. Thompson*, 1983, 1984, *sub nom. Max M. v. Illinois State Board of Education*, 1986; *Gary A. v. New Trier High School District No. 203*, 1986; *Doe v. Anrig*, 1987; *Vander Malle v. Ambach*, 1987; *Tice v. Botetourt*

County School District, 1990; *Babb v. Knox County School System*, 1992; *Straube v. Florida Union Free School District*, 1992). In many of these cases, the therapeutic services were provided to students who were placed in private schools or psychiatric facilities due to emotional difficulties. In others, parents obtained the counseling services privately to supplement the services that their children received in public schools. Regardless of the setting where students receive special education services, parents seeking reimbursement awards must show that their children would not benefit from special education without psychotherapy or counseling.

School officials must provide needed transportation because children cannot benefit from special education services if they cannot get to class. Officials must even provide students who attend private schools at public expense with appropriate transportation. Frequently, tuition reimbursement awards include compensation for other necessary costs such as transportation. Even when tuition reimbursement is not an issue, courts may make such awards to parents when school officials fail to provide appropriate transportation. For example, the First Circuit awarded the father of a child with physical disabilities who drove his son to school himself reimbursement since school personnel failed to make appropriate arrangements (*Hurry v. Jones*, 1984). In another case, a trial court in New York reimbursed a care provider for costs associated with transporting a student to an educational facility for children with physical disabilities (*Taylor v. Board of Education of Copake-Taconic Hills Central School District*, 1986). The award in this case included reimbursement for hiring a babysitter to watch other children while the caretaker transported the child to the center. A trial court in South Dakota awarded reimbursement for transportation for a student who moved into the district with an IEP calling for door-to-door transportation (*Malehorn v. Hill City School District*, 1997). After officials in the new district determined that the student did not require special transportation, her mother appealed. While a hearing officer upheld the action of school officials, the court explained that the board was required to honor the terms of the previous IEP until such time as it could be reviewed.

Parents have recovered reimbursement awards for other related services, such as occupational therapy (*Rapid City School District v. Vahle*, 1990) and speech therapy (*Johnson v. Lancaster-Lebanon Intermediate Unit 13, Lancaster City School District*, 1991). The Ninth Circuit went so far as to affirm a reimbursement award for the cost of lodging for a student and his mother that was required because the facility he attended was not within daily commuting distance of the family's residence (*Union School District v. Smith*, 1994).

Hearing Officers and Reimbursement Awards

Although the courts granted all of the reimbursement awards cited in this section, parents do not necessarily have to seek judicial review in order to obtain reimbursements. Hearing officers have the authority to grant reimbursement awards along with other forms of appropriate equitable relief. In one such case, a trial court in North Carolina ruled that reimbursement was included within the IDEA's provision that a hearing may be conducted on any matter relating to a FAPE (*S-1 v. Spangler*, 1986, 1987, 1993, 1994). In addition, the court pointed out that Congress did not intend to give courts any greater powers of equity than those given to a hearing officer. The IDEA currently grants hearing officers the authority to grant reimbursement awards (20 U.S.C. § 1412(a)(10)(C)(ii); 34 C.F.R. § 300.148(b)).

COMPENSATORY EDUCATIONAL SERVICES

Courts grant awards of compensatory educational services when school officials fail to provide children with a FAPE and their parents lack the financial means to obtain alternate services or for whatever reason have chosen not to obtain services privately. Students are thus forced to remain in inappropriate programs while administrative hearings are pending. As a result, children can lose several years of appropriate educational services during the often lengthy appeals process. Generally, students are entitled to compensatory services during time periods when they would otherwise have been ineligible for services. In most cases involving the remedy of compensatory services, courts apply the *Burlington* rationale to evaluate whether services are warranted (Zirkel & Hennessy, 2001).

Awards of Compensatory Services

The courts acknowledge that they have had the authority to award compensatory services since Congress empowered them to fashion appropriate remedies to cure deprivations of rights secured by the IDEA. Courts agree that compensatory services, like reimbursement, merely compensate students for the inappropriate education they received while placement issues were in dispute or school board officials failed to act properly.

The theory behind compensatory educational services awards is that appropriate remedies are not limited to those parents who can afford to provide their children with alternate educational placements while litigation is pending (*White v. State of California*, 1987; *Lester H. v. Gilhool*, 1990; *Todd D. v. Andrews*, 1991; *Manchester School District v. Christopher B.*, 1992; *Murphy v. Timberlane Regional School District*, 1992, 1993, 1994a). Generally, compensatory services must be provided for periods equal to the time students were denied services (*Valerie J. v. Derry Cooperative School* District, 1991; *Manchester School District v. Christopher B.*, 1992; *Big Beaver Falls Area School District v. Jackson*, 1993). In addition, plaintiffs can recover compensatory awards even after students pass the ceiling age for eligibility under the IDEA (*Pihl v. Massachusetts Department of Education*, 1993; *State of West Virginia ex rel. Justice v. Board of Education of the County of Monongalia*, 2000).

A case from the Eleventh Circuit illustrates the similarity between awards of tuition reimbursement and compensatory services. That court affirmed that an award of compensatory educational services was similar to one for tuition reimbursement insofar as it was necessary to preserve the student's right to a FAPE (*Jefferson County Board of Education v. Breen*, 1988). The court wrote that without compensatory services awards, the rights of students under the IDEA would depend on the ability of their parents to obtain services privately while due process hearings progressed. Along the same line, the Eighth Circuit found that compensatory educational services were available to the parent of a student with disabilities who could not afford to provide appropriate educational services himself during the lengthy court battle (*Miener v. Missouri*, 1986). In granting the award, the court added that Congress did not intend for the entitlements of children to a FAPE to rest on the ability of their parents to pay for the costs of placements up front. Yet another court agreed that if compensatory services were not available, the parents would have gained a Pyrrhic victory because their child's right to a FAPE would have been illusory (*Cremeans v. Fairland Local School District Board of Education*, 1993).

Students may receive compensatory services even after they earn valid high school diplomas. The federal trial court in Massachusetts awarded compensatory educational services to a student who earned a high school diploma after discovering that the school officials failed to follow proper procedures (*Puffer v. Raynolds*, 1988). The court reasoned that the fact that the student earned a diploma was not an indication that she had not required special education services but rather was evidence that she succeeded despite the shortcomings of her educational program. The court ordered the school board to provide services equal in scope to what it should have provided prior to the student's graduation. A federal trial court in New York also thought that a student who graduated was entitled to compensatory educational services while attending college, but not in the form of tuition (*Straube v. Florida Union Free School District*, 1992). Further, the federal trial court in New Hampshire ordered a board to provide compensatory services to a student for the time when he was denied educational services (*Valerie J. v. Derry Cooperative School District*, 1991).

Compensatory services awards accrue from the point that school officials know, or should have known, that IEPs were inadequate (*M.C. ex rel. J.C. v. Central Regional School District*, 1996; *Ridgewood Board of Education v. N.E.*, 1999). Generally, compensatory services are provided for a period of time equal to the length of the deprivation.

Hearing officers can grant awards of compensatory educational services. As with the power to confer tuition reimbursement, courts recognized that hearing officers may fashion appropriate relief, which sometimes requires an award of compensatory services (*Cocores v. Portsmouth, NH School District*, 1991; *Big Beaver Falls Area School District v. Jackson*, 1993).

Denials of Compensatory Services

Awards of compensatory services, as with tuition reimbursement, are available only when parents can demonstrate that their children were denied the

FAPE mandated by the IDEA (*Timms v. Metropolitan School District,* 1982, 1983; *Martin v. School Board of Prince George County,* 1986; *Garro v. State of Connecticut,* 1994). Nevertheless, a federal trial court in Tennessee denied an award of compensatory education in positing that the homebound program that a student received was inappropriate, but the school board and the parents were unaware of the existence of an appropriate program (*Brown v. Wilson County School District,* 1990). Insofar as school officials had not taken any actions that resulted in the denial of a FAPE, the court maintained that the board was not required to provide compensatory services.

The Third Circuit pointed out that compensatory services are warranted only when parents can demonstrate that their children underwent prolonged or gross deprivations of the right to a FAPE (*Carlisle Area School District v. Scott P.,* 1995). Absent such evidence, the court denied an award of compensatory services where an administrative appeals panel ordered officials to include additional services in the student's IEP. The Eighth Circuit also affirmed that a student was not entitled to compensatory services absent a showing of egregious circumstances or culpable conduct on the part of school officials (*Yankton School District v. Schramm,* 1995, 1996).

In a case from New York, the Second Circuit affirmed that the parents of a student who was seriously injured in an automobile accident failed to demonstrate that he regressed as a result of the school board's failure to provide special education services in a timely fashion. As such, the courts decided that the student was not entitled to compensatory services (*Wenger v. Canastota Central School District,* 1997, 1999). Likewise, a school board's timely action to correct deficiencies in a student's IEP led the federal trial court in New Jersey to deny compensatory services (*D.B. v. Ocean Township Board of Education,* 1997). Failure to take advantage of offered services may be a ground for denial of awards of compensatory services. In such a case, the Ninth Circuit uncovered evidence that school officials offered parents extra tutoring and summer school for their child, but they rejected the proposal (*Parents of Student W. v. Puyallup School District No. 3,* 1994). As such, the court affirmed the denial of the parents' request for compensatory services. Two years later, the federal trial court in Minnesota denied compensatory speech therapy services where parents withdrew their son from his educational program and rejected the services offered by school officials (*Moubry v. Independent School District No. 696,* 1996).

ATTORNEY FEES AND COSTS

The IDEA contains one of the most comprehensive mechanisms that Congress ever created for dispute resolution. Litigation is expensive, and many parents, after succeeding in their disputes with school boards, believe that they should be reimbursed for their costs in securing the rights of their children. Many parents sense that they achieve nugatory victories if they prevail in showing that school officials failed to provide the FAPE their children were entitled to receive under the IDEA but are left with large legal bills. Initially, most courts viewed awards of attorney fees as awards for damages (see, e.g., *Diamond v. McKenzie*, 1985).

In *Smith v. Robinson* (1984) the Supreme Court interpreted the IDEA as not permitting parents to recover their legal expenses. Unhappy with this outcome, Congress amended the IDEA in 1986 by adding the Handicapped Children's Protection Act (HCPA) (20 U.S.C. § 1415(I)(3)) to its provisions. The HCPA permits courts to provide awards of reasonable attorney fees to parents who prevail against school boards in any actions or proceedings brought pursuant to the IDEA. Awards are based on the prevailing rates in the communities in which cases arose. Courts have the authority to judge what is a reasonable amount of time spent preparing and arguing cases in terms of the issues litigated. Awards may be limited if school boards made settlement offers more than ten days before the proceedings began that were equal to or more favorable than the final relief that parents obtained. In addition, fee awards may be reduced if courts find that parents unreasonably protracted disputes, the hourly rates of attorneys were excessive, or the time spent and legal services furnished were excessive in light of the issues litigated. While attorney fees may be awarded for representation at administrative and judicial hearings, they are unavailable for representation at IEP meetings unless such sessions are convened in response to administrative or judicial orders (20 U.S.C. § 1415(i)(3)(D)(ii); 34 C.F.R. § 300.517(c)(2)(ii)).

Hearing officers cannot grant awards of attorney fees because this authority is reserved for the courts (*Mathern v. Campbell County Children's Center*, 1987). However, parents do not necessarily have to go to court to recover their legal expenses. Agreements may be worked out with school boards for payment of the parents' legal expenses. If parents are required to file court action to recover attorney fees and they succeed, they may recover their costs in filing fee petitions as well (*Angela L. v. Pasadena Independent School District*, 1990). Parents do not need to exhaust administrative remedies prior to filing fee petitions since hearing officers cannot award attorney fees (*J.G. v. Board of Education of the Rochester City School District*, 1986, 1987; *Esther C. v. Ambach*, 1988; *Sidney K. v. Ambach*, 1988).

If Parents Prevail

One of the most often litigated issues under the IDEA's attorney fees provision deals with whether parents were prevailing parties. While on its face the issue seems straightforward, unfortunately, it is not. Most special education disputes involve multiple issues, and parents may have had only partial success. Courts generally define prevailing parents as those who succeeded on most of the issues litigated. Even so, in some cases where parents have not prevailed on all issues, the courts have granted partial awards.

Full Awards

For the most part, courts grant full awards when parents prevail on the major issues in the litigation, even if they did not succeed on some minor points. In most instances, the work performed litigating the minor issues is inseparable from that litigating the major issue, is insignificant compared to that required by the major issue, and/or is performed in conjunction with the work completed for the major issue (*Turton v. Crisp County School District*, 1988; *Angela L. v. Pasadena Independent School District*, 1990; *Phelan v. Bell*, 1993). Courts generally conclude that the parents are the prevailing party when they acquire the primary relief sought in the principal issues in their suit (*Barbara R. v. Tirozzi*, 1987; *Kristi W. v. Graham Independent School District*, 1987; *Neisz v. Portland Public School District*, 1988; *Mitten v. Muscogee County District*, 1989).

Parents may receive full reimbursement of their legal expenses even when they do not prevail on all issues. Generally, courts grant full awards if the time spent litigating the various issues cannot be easily apportioned on an issue-by-issue basis. In an illustrative case, the Sixth Circuit awarded attorney fees to parents who did not receive the residential placement they requested but succeeded in obtaining additional services (*Krichinsky v. Knox County Schools*, 1992). In other cases, courts agreed that parents were entitled to full fee awards because the matters before the administrative hearings were intertwined and could not have been viewed as a series of separate claims, and the parents received most of what they requested (*Moore v. Crestwood Local School District*, 1992; *Noyes v. Grossmont Union High School District*, 2004).

Partial Awards

Parents can receive partial awards of attorney fees even if they do not prevail on the most significant question in the litigation but do succeed on some of the issues. At the same time, parents may receive partial awards when they prevail on some of their claims and the issues litigated are distinct enough so that the work done on each claim can be separated from the work done on all others (*Max M. v. Illinois State Board of Education*, 1988; *Burr v. Sobol*, 1990; *Koswenda v. Flossmoor School District No. 161*, 2002). Requested fee awards may be reduced for various other reasons. If a court thinks that a requested hourly rate or the number of hours billed was excessive (*Mr. D. v. Glocester School Committee*, 1989; *Hall v. Detroit Public Schools*, 1993; *Troy School District v. Boutsikaris*, 2003) or finds fault with the time sheets submitted by attorneys (*In re Conklin*, 1991; *Smith v. District of Columbia*, 2004), the court can make adjustments in requested fee awards. In one case, a federal trial court in Indiana reduced a requested fee amount in determining that the parents' counsel unnecessarily protracted the proceedings (*Howey v. Tippecanoe School Corporation*, 1990). Another court ruled that an attorney who was unfamiliar with special education laws could not bill for the time and research spent in learning the statutes (*King v. Floyd County Board of Education*, 1998).

Courts do not always reduce awards by evaluating the number of hours spent litigating each issue and reducing them by the amount of fees charged for unsuccessfully litigating certain issues. Sometimes, awards are adjusted in proportion to the parents' overall success and failure in the litigation. As such, when the federal trial court in New Jersey had difficulty apportioning legal costs issue by issue, it simply reduced the requested fee award by fifty percent because the parents had not achieved their primary objectives, even though they were successful on several other significant issues (*Field v. Haddonfield Board of Education*, 1991).

If Parents Do Not Prevail

Parents cannot recover their legal expenses when school boards are the prevailing parties. It should go without saying that parents who do not succeed on any of their claims do not achieve prevailing party status (*Wheeler v. Towanda Area School District*, 1991). As discussed in the previous section, parents may receive limited reimbursement awards if they prevail on at least some of their claims. Parents cannot be awarded attorney fees if their legal relationships with their boards are unaltered following litigation, even if they received minor victories (*Salley v. St. Tammany Parish School Board*, 1995; *Board of Education of Downers Grove Grade School District No. 58 v. Steven L.*, 1996; *Metropolitan School District of Lawrence Township v. M.S.*, 2004). Parents also are not the prevailing party if the changes that occur are not a direct result of the litigation but are caused by other factors.

As noted, courts sometimes grant parents partial reimbursement of their legal expenses if they obtain some but not all of the relief that they sought. If the relief obtained is insignificant, courts may not grant even partial awards. As reflected by a case from the Seventh Circuit, parents were not entitled to an award of attorney fees, even though they obtained an order that conferred some benefits on their daughter since they did not succeed on most of their claims (*Hunger v. Leininger*, 1994). Additionally, a federal trial court in Wisconsin denied a fee request writing that the relief the parents obtained was minimal in light of their overall objectives (*Linda T. ex rel. William A. v. Rice Lake Area School District*, 2004).

Courts may deny fee awards if they deem that parents unnecessarily protracted proceedings (*Fischer v. Rochester Community Schools*, 1991) or the problems they complained of could have been resolved without resort to administrative or judicial review (*Combs v. School Board of Rockingham County*, 1994). Parents may not receive fee awards if they request administrative hearings before the school boards have had full opportunities to develop appropriate IEPs (*Johnson v. Bismarck Public School District*, 1991; *Patricia E. v. Board of Education of Community High School District No. 155*, 1995; *Payne v. Board of Education, Cleveland City Schools*, 1996; *W.L.G. v. Houston County Board of Education*, 1997).

Catalyst Theory

In the past, courts awarded attorney fees based on the catalyst theory, even if an administrative hearing or judicial action never took place (see, e.g., *Doucet v. Chilton County Board of Education*, 1999; *Daniel S. v. Scranton School District*, 2000). Under the catalyst theory, courts can award fees if suits, or even threats of litigation, bring about change in a defendant's behavior, causing a termination in proceedings. However, recent litigation appears to have struck down the catalyst theory (Wenkart, 2002).

In a nonschool case, *Buckhannon Board & Care Home v. West Virginia Department of Health and Human Resources* (*Buckhannon*) (2001), the Supreme Court rejected the catalyst theory on the basis that a prevailing party must prevail before the courts in judgments on the merits or through consent decrees (Osborne, 2003). Subsequently, circuit courts denied fee requests by relying on the rationale in *Buckhannon*, explaining that the high Court's analysis governed claims filed pursuant to the IDEA (*J.C. v. Regional School District No. 10*, 2002; *John T. by Paul T. and Joan T. v. Delaware County Intermediate Unit*, 2003; *T.D. v. LaGrange School District No. 102*, 2003; *Doe v. Boston Public Schools*, 2004; Osborne, 2005).

Fees for Administrative Hearings

The IDEA permits parents to recover attorney fees if they prevail in "any action or proceeding" brought under its procedural safeguards (20 U.S.C. § 1415(i)(3)(B); 34 C.F.R. § 300.517(a)). The meaning of the phrase "any action or proceeding" has been in dispute. Many school boards have claimed that it refers only to court actions and that attorney fees are not recoverable for work performed at the administrative hearing level. After some controversy, it is well settled that attorney fees are available for representation at administrative hearings even if disputes are settled without judicial action. In addition, it is well settled that parents can file suits solely for the purpose of recovering legal expenses (Osborne & DiMattia, 1991).

The District of Columbia Circuit resolved the leading, and most controversial, case on the topic in 1990 (*Moore v. District of Columbia*, 1990). Initially, a divided three-judge panel decreed that congressional language in the HCPA provided for awards of attorney fees only where the losing parties in administrative actions appealed to the courts and prevailed in judicial actions (*Moore v. District of Columbia*, 1989). According to the court, fees could not be awarded to parents who prevailed at the administrative level and brought judicial action only to obtain attorney fees. While this opinion was contrary to the majority of cases from the other circuits, the court granted a rehearing en banc (Osborne & DiMattia, 1991). On further review, the court vacated its earlier judgment, declaring that attorney fees were available for administrative proceedings. This time the court concluded that Congress, using the phrase "any action or proceeding," meant to authorize fees for parents who prevailed in civil actions or administrative proceedings. The court added that the legislative history of the HCPA supported its interpretation. Subsequently, courts unanimously agreed that parents who prevailed at the administrative level could recover their legal expenses (Osborne & DiMattia, 1991).

Settlement Offers

School boards can lessen their liability by attempting to reach settlements with parents before beginning administrative hearings. One section of the HCPA provides that fees are unavailable for legal representation that occurs after school boards make written settlement offers if the final relief that parents obtain is not more favorable than the settlement offers. School boards must make settlement offers at least ten days before the scheduled start of due process hearings (20 U.S.C. § 1415(i)(3)(D)(i); 34 C.F.R. § 300.517(c)(2)(i)).

In order to avoid paying fee awards, settlement offers from school boards must be deemed to be equal to or better than the final relief that parents obtained. Settlement offers need not be identical to final administrative orders in order to stop the time clocks of attorneys from ticking. Parents are not entitled to awards of attorney fees when the final relief they obtain is substantially similar to (*Hyden v. Board of Education of Wilson County*, 1989) or less favorable than (*Mr. L. and Mrs. L. v. Woonsocket Education Department*, 1992) the offers made by school boards. On the other hand, parents can be reimbursed for their legal costs when they win more favorable terms than their boards offer (*Capistrano Unified School District v. Wartenberg*, 1995; *Virginia McC. v. Corrigan-Camden Independent School District*, 1995). Courts may be called on to consider whether settlement offers were, in fact, more favorable than the final results obtained through administrative proceedings. In such a case, a federal trial court in Ohio rejected a board's claim of a more favorable settlement offer because the offer did not include specific details (*Gross ex rel. Gross v. Perrysburg Exempted Village School District*, 2004).

Courts recognized that parents are entitled to collect attorney fees for legal work that was completed up to the time of settlement offers, even when hearings are canceled because parents accepted the offers (*E.P. v. Union County Regional High School District No. 1*, 1989; *Shelly C. v. Venus Independent School District*, 1989; *Barlow-Gresham Union High School District No. 2 v. Mitchell*, 1991). Yet, in the wake of *Buckhannon*, lower courts have denied fees when the parties reached settlement agreements before completing administrative hearings (*Brandon K. v. New Lenox School District*, 2001; *J.S. v. Ramapo Central School District*, 2001; *Jose Luis R. v. Joliet Township H.S. District 204*, 2002; *P.O. ex rel. L.T. and T.O. v. Greenwich Board of Education*, 2002; *Algeria v. District of Columbia*, 2004; *Smith v. District of Columbia*, 2004; *Smith ex rel. Smith v. Fitchburg Public Schools*, 2005). Still, attorney fees may be awarded for settlement agreements if hearing officers or courts sanction the agreements. Courts agreed that incorporating settlement agreements into orders or reading them into records gives them the judicial imprimatur called for by *Buckhannon* (*D.M. ex rel. G.M. and C.M. v. Board of Education, Center Moriches Union Free School District*, 2003; *Abraham v. District of Columbia*, 2004).

The issue of settlement offers is not completely resolved. At least one court maintained that parents who gained the relief they sought through mediation or a settlement agreement are entitled to attorney fees in spite of *Buckhannon*. In this dispute, a federal trial court in California reasoned that applying *Buckhannon* to settlement agreements under the IDEA would contravene the act's preference for early settlements (*Noyes v. Grossmont Union High School District*, 2004).

Fees to Attorneys From Public Agencies

Many parents use attorneys from public advocacy agencies in special education litigation. These agencies provide low-cost or free legal services via sliding scale fee arrangements. Courts agree that when parents who are represented by public agency attorneys prevail in special education actions, the attorneys are entitled to be reimbursed at the prevailing rate in their communities even if the fees are higher than the one that the agencies would have charged the parents (*Eggers v. Bullitt County School District*, 1988; *Mitten v. Muscogee County School District*, 1989; *Yankton School District v. Schramm*, 1996).

Fees to Lay Advocates and Pro Se Parents

Parents often, especially in the early stages of disputes, rely on the aid of lay advocates to advise and represent them in meetings with school boards. Although the services of lay advocates may be beneficial in resolving disputes, because they are not attorneys, advocates cannot be reimbursed for legal representation (*Arons v. New Jersey State Board of Education*, 1988). If advocates work in conjunction with attorneys, it is possible that they may be reimbursed for their services as part of the attorneys' costs (*Heldman v. Sobol*, 1994). Even so, representation solely by lay advocates is not reimbursable (*Connors v. Mills*, 1998).

Most courts agree that parents who represent themselves may not be compensated under the IDEA even if they are members of the bar (*Rappaport v. Vance*, 1993; *Heldman v. Sobol*, 1994; *Miller v. West Lafayette Community School Corporation*, 1996; *Doe v. Board of Education of Baltimore County*, 1998; *Erickson v. Board of Education of Baltimore County*, 1998; *Woodside v. School District of Philadelphia Board of Education*, 2001). On the other hand, a federal trial court in Georgia decreed that nothing in the language of the IDEA prohibits an award of fees to an attorney-parent (*Matthew V. v. DeKalb County School System*, 2003).

Fees for Expert Witnesses

The IDEA permits parents to recover other costs of bringing special education suits along with attorney fees (Osborne, 2005). However, for years the courts did not agree on whether parents could recover the costs of expert witness fees. A variety of federal courts found that parents may include the costs of expert witnesses in their requests for attorney fee awards, reasoning that these expenses are often a necessary part of administrative hearings (*Chang v. Board of Education of Glen Ridge Township*, 1988; *Turton v. Crisp County School District*, 1988; *Aronow v. District of Columbia*, 1992; *P.L. by Mr. and Mrs. L. v. Norwalk Board of Education*, 1999; *Mr. J. v. Board of Education*, 2000; *Pazik v. Gateway Regional School District*, 2001; *Brillon v. Klein Independent School District*, 2003; *Murphy v. Arlington Central School District Board of Education*, 2005). A trial court in Georgia even held that parents were entitled to be reimbursed for the services of an expert who did not testify but who did contribute to the development of the case (*Turton v. Crisp County School District*, 1988). On the other hand, the federal trial court in New Jersey refused to reimburse parents for the full costs of an expert witness because it was of the opinion that even though the expert witness was helpful, the expert's presence was not necessary (*E.M. v. Millville Board of Education*, 1994).

Other courts have denied requests for reimbursement of expert witnesses. Recently, the District of Columbia Circuit denied expert witness fees, reasoning that the IDEA does not enable a prevailing party to shift expert witness fees (*Goldring v. District of Columbia*, 2005). On at least two occasions the Eighth Circuit denied expert witness fees in deciding that nothing in the plain language of the IDEA suggests that the courts are authorized to award fees for expert witnesses (*Neosho R-V School District v. Clark*, 2003; *Missouri Department of Elementary and Secondary Education v. Springfield R-12 School District*, 2004). Similarly, the Seventh Circuit declined to award expert witness fees absent specific authorization within the statute (*T.D. v. LaGrange School District No. 102*, 2003). Previously, a federal trial court in North Carolina denied a request for reimbursement of expert witness fees on the basis that the IDEA does not provide for an award of expert witness fees (*Eirschele v. Craven County Board of Education*, 1998).

As is typically the case, the Supreme Court intervened to resolve the difference between the Circuits and to ensure a more uniform interpretation of the IDEA. In *Arlington Central School District v. Murphy* (2006), the Supreme Court, reversing the Second Circuit's earlier order to the contrary, interpreted the IDEA as not permitting parents to be reimbursed for the services of expert witnesses or consultants who assisted them in their disputes with school boards (Osborne & Russo, 2006). Although recognizing that this created the anomalous situation whereby parents who prevailed in their disputes with their school boards could recover attorney fees but not expenses to cover the costs associated with expert witnesses or consultants who helped them to win their cases, the Court concluded that since Congress was aware of this fact but refused to modify the IDEA accordingly, it saw no reason to rewrite the statute.

Fees for Representation in Complaint Resolution Procedures

The IDEA's regulations require states to adopt procedures to resolve complaints filed by organizations or individuals over alleged violations of the IDEA (34 C.F.R. §§ 300.151–300.153). Whether fees are available for representation in filing complaints through the IDEA's complaint resolution procedures is unsettled. The Ninth Circuit and the federal trial court in Vermont agreed that fees may be awarded for representation in the filing of complaints under a state's or the IDEA's complaint resolution procedures (*Upper Valley Association of Handicapped Citizens v. Blue Mountain Union School District No. 21*, 1997; *Lucht v. Molalla River School District*, 1999). Conversely, the federal trial court in Minnesota denied a fee award for an attorney who filed a complaint on behalf of a student with disabilities (*Megan C. v. Independent School District No. 625*, 1999). The court ascertained that the filing of a complaint was not an action or proceeding for purposes of recovering attorney fees under the IDEA. Similarly noting that the IDEA does not authorize a complaint resolution procedure, the Second Circuit affirmed that fees are not reimbursable for representation at complaint resolution proceedings (*Vultaggio v. Board of Education, Smithtown Central School District*, 2003).

Fees for Representation at IEP Meetings

The IDEA specifically prohibits reimbursements of attorney fees for attendance at IEP meetings unless such sessions were convened as a result of administrative or judicial actions (20 U.S.C. § 1415(i)(3)(D)(ii); 34 C.F.R. § 300.517(c)(2)(ii)). Courts consistently denied fees for representation at IEP meetings (*E.C. ex rel. R.C. v. Board of Education of South Brunswick Township*, 2001). On the other hand, at least one court allowed reimbursement for the time an attorney spent scheduling an IEP meeting when that effort was the direct result of a court order (*Watkins v. Vance*, 2004).

Awards to School Boards

The IDEA allowed for recovery of legal expenses by prevailing parents, but did not originally grant school boards the right to seek reimbursement for their legal expenses if they prevailed in litigation. Using their general powers of equity, courts have sometimes, albeit reluctantly, awarded attorney fees to boards in determining that parental claims were frivolous or unnecessarily prolonged the litigation. The First Circuit, for example, concluded that a board was entitled to reimbursement of legal expenses under Appellate Rule 38 in finding that the parents' suit was "completely devoid of merit and plagued by unnecessary delay" (*Caroline T. v. Hudson School District*, 1990, p. 757). The court commented that the parents engaged in tactics throughout the proceedings that led to undue delays and also failed to cooperate in negotiations to settle the dispute. In another case, a federal trial court in New York denied a prevailing board's request for attorney fees based on the claim that the parents brought the action in bad faith (*Hiller v. Board of Education of the Brunswick Central School District*, 1990). The court was convinced that since both parties proceeded in good faith, they should bear their own costs.

In a major change, the 2004 amendments included a provision that permits school boards to seek reimbursement of their legal expenses when parents file complaints that are later found to be frivolous, unreasonable, or without foundation or when the litigation was continued after it clearly became frivolous, unreasonable, or without foundation (20 U.S.C. § 1415(i)(3)(B)(i)(II); 34 C.F.R. § 300.517(a)(ii)). Moreover, boards may obtain awards when parents' suits are filed for improper purposes, cause unnecessary delays, or needlessly increase the cost of litigation (20 U.S.C. § 1415(i)(3)(B)(i)(III); 34 C.F.R. § 300.517(a)(iii)). Under this section, awards are to be levied against the parents' attorneys, not the parents themselves. In light of past judicial reluctance to award attorney fees to boards under their general powers of equity, even under circumstances similar to those described within the statute, it remains to be seen whether boards will use this provision to recover some of the costs of litigation.

By the same token, school boards may not continue litigation that is clearly frivolous, unreasonable, or without foundation or engage in any tactics that unnecessarily prolong litigation or otherwise abuse the process. Under the Federal Rules of Civil Procedure, a federal trial court in California sanctioned a board and its attorney for raising frivolous objections, making misstatements, and mischaracterizing facts (*Moser v. Bret Harte Union High School District,* 2005).

DAMAGES

The term *damages,* by its broad definition, refers to monetary relief that is awarded to compensate aggrieved parties for their losses (Zirkel & Osborne, 1987). The term as used in this chapter is defined in a narrower context. Here the term *damages* refers to monetary awards given to persons who were injured by the actions of another for punitive purposes (Garner, 1999). For the purposes of this chapter, compensatory awards, such as reimbursement for tuition and other out-of-pocket expenses, are not considered to be damages awards. In the context of special education cases, courts treated punitive damages as a separate entity from compensation for lost services.

Failure to Provide a FAPE

In general, courts have historically agreed that damages are unavailable under the IDEA unless school boards flagrantly failed to comply with the act's procedural requirements (Osborne & Russo, 2001). The Seventh Circuit, in a case where the parents actually sought tuition reimbursement, insisted that monetary awards were not available under the IDEA unless exceptional circumstances existed (*Anderson v. Thompson,* 1981). One of those exceptional circumstances occurs when school boards act in bad faith by failing to comply with the IDEA's procedural provisions in an egregious manner. Although this case involved an award of tuition reimbursement, other courts either cited the Seventh Circuit's judgment or used analogous reasoning to declare that damages are not available under the IDEA (*Marvin H. v. Austin Independent School District,* 1983; *Powell v. DeFore,* 1983; *Gary A. v. New Trier High School District No. 203,* 1986; *Barnett v. Fairfax County School Board,* 1991).

The Supreme Court specifically struck down the Seventh Circuit's treatment of reimbursement as a damages award in *Burlington School Committee v. Department of Education, Commonwealth of Massachusetts* (1985). Even so, the legal principle that courts can award damages only when school boards act in bad faith has survived (*Charlie F. v. Board of Education of Skokie School District 68,* 1996). The Fifth Circuit asserted that a damages award is inconsistent with the IDEA's goals and that appropriate relief does not include punitive damages when school boards act in good faith (*Marvin H. v. Austin Independent School District,* 1983). Similarly, the Fourth Circuit affirmed that damages are unavailable unless it can be shown that boards acted in bad faith or committed intentional acts of discrimination (*Barnett v. Fairfax County School Board,* 1991). A trial court in New York decreed that while damages are allowed for bad faith or egregious failures to comply with the IDEA, they are unwarranted when officials make good-faith efforts to provide appropriate placements but commit misjudgments (*Gerasimou v. Ambach,* 1986). On the other hand, a federal trial court in Michigan indicated that when a court finds that school board placements are inappropriate, they are limited to fashioning appropriate placements (*Sanders v. Marquette Public Schools*, 1983). The court held that damages were unavailable even if parents could show that school officials acted in bad faith or grossly misused their professional discretion. Another federal trial court in Michigan was of the opinion that the recovery of monetary, nonrestitutional damages was not allowed under the IDEA (*Wayne County Regional Education Service Agency v. Pappas*, 1999).

The Fourth Circuit ruled that awards of compensatory and punitive damages are inconsistent with the IDEA's structure (*Sellers v. School Board of the City of Manassas*, 1998). Reasoning that a claim that a student was denied a FAPE was indistinguishable from one of educational malpractice, the court emphasized that such damages were simply inconsistent with the IDEA's scheme. The Tenth Circuit subsequently agreed with this rationale, adding that the IDEA may not provide the basis for a Section 1983 claim (*Padilla v. School District No. 1 in the City and County of Denver*, 2000).

In like fashion, the Second Circuit maintained that a damages award would not only have been inconsistent with the IDEA's goals but would have undercut its carefully structured procedure for administrative remedies (*Polera v. Board of Education of the Newburgh Enlarged City School District*, 2002). Echoing this sentiment, the First Circuit reasoned that the IDEA's primary purpose is to ensure a FAPE, not provide a mechanism for compensating personal injury (*Nieves-Marquez v. Commonwealth of Puerto Rico*, 2003).

Torts

The purpose of tort remedies is to compensate individuals for injuries that resulted from the unreasonable conduct of others. **Torts** are civil wrongs, other than breaches of **contract**, committed against someone's person or property. Torts may result from either intentional or unintentional acts. In order to receive damages awards, litigants must prove negligence on the part of persons who allegedly committed the torts. Awards may be granted to compensate injured parties for their actual losses as well as for punitive purposes (Russo, 2006). In the realm of special education, since the nature of the disabilities of students may increase their likelihood of injury, school officials may have to adopt a heightened standard of care (Mawdsley, 2001).

In Louisiana, a state court indicated that school boards are not liable for injuries that students in inclusive settings sustained as long as their placements were reasonable (*Brooks v. St. Tammany Parish School Board*, 1987). Another state court, in California, thought that tort damages were unavailable under the IDEA for a claim that a student was denied a FAPE (*White v. State of California*, 1987). The court decided that the appropriate remedy for a denial of services would have been an award of compensatory educational services. Also, a state court in Michigan observed that damages for negligence were not recoverable under the IDEA for a board's failure to evaluate a student properly (*Johnson v.*

Clark, 1987). The court was not convinced that Congress intended for the IDEA to serve as a vehicle for a private cause of action for damages.

The Sixth Circuit affirmed that the IDEA does not create a right to recover damages for loss of earning power attributed to the failure to provide a FAPE (*Hall v. Knott County Board of Education*, 1991). The student sued to recover lost wages allegedly resulting from an insufficient education. The same court later remarked that a student could not receive damages for an emotional injury he allegedly suffered when he was wrongfully barred from participating in sports (*Crocker v. Tennessee Secondary School Athletic Association*, 1992).

Section 1983

Section 1983 of the Civil Rights Act of 1871 (42 U.S.C. § 1983), a very brief but expansively interpreted federal statute, permits courts to grant punitive damages. The courts can grant these damages to punish individuals who, "acting under the color of state law," meaning that they behave as if they had the authority to do so, deprive others of rights, privileges, and immunities secured by the Constitution and laws of the United States. In recent years, courts have agreed that Section 1983 may be used as a back door to gain an award of damages for violations of the IDEA (Osborne & Russo, 2001; Mawdsley, 2002; Osborne, 2002; Wenkart, 2004).

In an often-cited case from New Jersey, the mother of a child who was eventually placed in a special education setting sought damages on the basis that school officials persistently refused to evaluate her son and provide him with necessary special education services (*W.B. v. Matula* (*Matula*), 1995). A trial court denied the motion for damages, but, on further review, the Third Circuit reversed in favor of the mother. In interpreting the enactment of the HCPA as meaning that violations of the IDEA can be redressed in private causes of action under Section 1983 and Section 504, the court declared that Congress "expressly contemplated that the courts would fashion remedies not specifically enumerated in IDEA" (*W.B. v. Matula*, 1995, pp. 494–495). Even so, the panel cautioned

> that in fashioning a remedy for an IDEA violation, a district court may wish to order educational services, such as compensatory education beyond a child's age of eligibility, or reimbursement for providing at private expense what should have been offered by the school, rather than **compensatory damages** for generalized pain and suffering. (*W.B. v. Matula*, 1995, p. 495)

Nonetheless, the panel "did not preclude the awarding of monetary damages" (p. 495) and left it up to the trial court to fashion appropriate relief. More recently, however, the Third Circuit has apparently abrogated its *Matula* decision. In *A.W. v. Jersey City Public Schools* (2007), the court revisited the issue and this time ruled that because the IDEA includes a comprehensive judicial remedy, Section 1983 cannot be used to redress violations of the IDEA.

Actions under Section 1983 seeking damages for violations of the IDEA's procedural protections may be particularly viable. For example, the federal trial court in Minnesota held that there is an enforceable Section 1983 interest implicit in the IDEA's procedural protections such that a case could be brought under Section 1983 to enforce the procedural rights contained in the IDEA (*Brantley v. Independent School District No. 625, St. Paul Public Schools,* 1996). Trial courts in other states have conceded that damages may be available under Section 1983 for violations of the IDEA (*Emma C. v. Eastin,* 1997; *Cappillino v. Hyde Park Central School District,* 1999; *B.H. v. Southington Board of Education,* 2003).

On the other hand, the Eighth Circuit noted that since parents cannot recover damages under the IDEA, they cannot do so under Section 1983 for IDEA violations (*Bradley v. Arkansas Department of Education,* 2002). Likewise, a federal trial court in California was of the view that parents cannot bypass the procedural and remedial scheme of the IDEA by repackaging their claim as one under Section 1983 so that a jury may grant their requests for damages (*Alex G. ex rel. Stephen G. v. Board of Trustees of Davis Joint Unified School District,* 2004). With the Third Circuit's reversal of its *Matula* decision, it now appears that the majority view is that Section 1983 cannot be used to recover damages for IDEA violations.

CASE NO. 15—UNILATERAL PARENTAL PLACEMENTS IN NON-STATE-APPROVED FACILITIES

FLORENCE COUNTY SCHOOL DISTRICT FOUR

v.

CARTER

United States Supreme Court, 1993

510 U.S. 7

Justice O'CONNOR delivered the opinion of the Court.

The Individuals with Disabilities Education Act (IDEA or Act), requires States to provide disabled children with a "free appropriate public education." . . . This case presents the question whether a court may order reimbursement for parents who unilaterally withdraw their child from a public school that provides an inappropriate education under IDEA and put the child in a private school that provides an education that is otherwise proper under IDEA, but does not meet all the requirements of § 1401(a)(18). We hold that the court may order such reimbursement, and therefore affirm the judgment of the Court of Appeals.

I

Respondent Shannon Carter was classified as learning disabled in 1985, while a ninth grade student in a school operated by petitioner Florence County School District Four. School officials met with Shannon's parents to formulate an individualized education program (IEP) for Shannon, as required under IDEA. The IEP provided that Shannon would stay in regular classes except for three periods of individualized instruction per week, and established specific goals in reading and mathematics of four months' progress for the entire school year. Shannon's parents were dissatisfied, and requested a hearing to challenge the appropriateness of the IEP. Both the local educational officer and the state educational agency hearing officer rejected Shannon's parents' claim and concluded that the IEP was adequate. In the meantime, Shannon's parents had placed her in Trident Academy, a private school specializing in educating children with disabilities. Shannon began at Trident in September 1985 and graduated in the spring of 1988.

Shannon's parents filed this suit in July 1986, claiming that the school district had breached its duty under IDEA to provide Shannon with a "free appropriate public education," § 1401(a)(18), and seeking reimbursement for tuition and other costs incurred at Trident. After a bench trial, the District Court ruled in the parents' favor. . . . The District Court concluded that Shannon's education was "appropriate" under IDEA, and that Shannon's parents were entitled to reimbursement of tuition and other costs.

The Court of Appeals for the Fourth Circuit affirmed. The court agreed that the IEP proposed by the school district was inappropriate under IDEA. . . . Accordingly, "when a public school system has defaulted on its obligations under the Act, a private school placement is 'proper under the Act' if the education provided by the private school is 'reasonably calculated to enable the child to receive educational benefits.'"

The court below recognized that its holding conflicted with *Tucker v. Bay Shore Union Free School Dist.*, in which the Court of Appeals for the Second Circuit held that parental placement in a private school cannot be proper under the Act unless the private school in question meets the standards of the state education agency. We granted certiorari to resolve this conflict among the Courts of Appeals.

II

In *School Comm. of Burlington v. Department of Ed. of Mass.*, we held that IDEA's grant of equitable authority empowers a court "to order school authorities to reimburse parents for their expenditures on private special education for a child if the court ultimately determines that such placement, rather than a proposed IEP, is proper under the Act." Congress intended that IDEA's promise of a "free appropriate public education" for disabled children would normally be met by an IEP's provision for education in the regular public schools or in private schools chosen jointly by school officials and parents. In cases where cooperation fails, however, "parents who disagree with the proposed IEP are faced with a choice: go along with the IEP to the detriment of their child if it turns out to be inappropriate or pay for what they consider to be the appropriate placement." For parents willing and able to make the latter choice, "it would be an empty victory to have a court tell them several years later that they were right but that these expenditures could not in a proper case be reimbursed by the school officials." Because such a result would be contrary to IDEA's guarantee of a "free appropriate public education," we held that "Congress meant to include retroactive reimbursement to parents as an available remedy in a proper case."

As this case comes to us, two issues are settled: (1) the school district's proposed IEP was inappropriate under IDEA, and (2) although Trident did not meet the § 1401(a)(18) requirements, it provided an education otherwise proper under IDEA. This case presents the narrow question whether Shannon's parents are barred from reimbursement because the private school in which Shannon enrolled did not meet the § 1401(a)(18) definition of a "free appropriate public education." We hold that they are not, because § 1401(a)(18)'s requirements cannot be read as applying to parental placements.

Section 1401(a)(18)(A) requires that the education be "provided at public expense, under public supervision and direction." Similarly, § 1401(a)(18)(D) requires schools to provide an IEP, which must be designed by "a representative of the local educational agency," and must be "establish[ed]," "revise[d]," and "review[ed]" by the agency, § 1414(a)(5). These requirements do not make sense in the context of a parental placement. In this case, as in all *Burlington* reimbursement cases, the parents' rejection of the school district's proposed IEP is the very reason for the parents' decision to put their child in a private school. In such cases, where the private placement has necessarily been made over the school district's objection, the private school education will not be under "public supervision and direction." Accordingly, to read the § 1401(a)(18) requirements as applying to parental placements would effectively eliminate the right of unilateral withdrawal recognized in *Burlington*. Moreover, IDEA was intended to ensure that children with disabilities receive an education that is both appropriate and free. To read the provisions of § 1401(a)(18) to bar reimbursement in the circumstances of this case would defeat this statutory purpose.

Nor do we believe that reimbursement is necessarily barred by a private school's failure to meet state education standards. Trident's deficiencies, according to the school district, were that it employed at least two faculty members who were not state-certified and that it did not develop IEP's. As we have noted, however, the § 1401(a)(18) requirements—including the requirement that the school meet the standards of the state educational agency do not apply to private parental placements. Indeed, the school district's emphasis on state standards is somewhat ironic. As the Court of Appeals noted, "it hardly seems consistent with the Act's goals to forbid parents from educating their child at a school that provides an appropriate education simply because that school lacks the stamp of approval of the same public school system that failed to meet the child's needs in the first place." Accordingly, we disagree with the Second Circuit's theory that "a parent may not obtain reimbursement for a unilateral placement if that placement was in a school that was not on [the State's] approved list of private" schools. Parents' failure to select a program known to be approved by the State in favor of an unapproved option is not itself a bar to reimbursement.

Furthermore, although the absence of an approved list of private schools is not essential to our holding, we note that parents in the position of Shannon's have no way of knowing at the time they select a private school whether the school meets state standards. South Carolina keeps no publicly available list of approved private schools, but instead approves private school placements on a case-by-case basis. In fact, although public school officials had previously placed three children with disabilities at Trident . . . Trident had not received blanket approval from the State. South Carolina's case-by-case approval system meant that Shannon's parents needed the cooperation of state officials before they could know whether Trident was state-approved. As we recognized in *Burlington,* such cooperation is unlikely in cases where the school officials disagree with the need for the private placement.

III

The school district also claims that allowing reimbursement for parents such as Shannon's puts an unreasonable burden on financially strapped local educational authorities. The school district argues that requiring parents to choose a state approved private school if they want reimbursement is the only meaningful way to allow States to control costs; otherwise States will have to reimburse dissatisfied parents for any private school that provides an education that is proper under the Act, no matter how expensive it may be.

There is no doubt that Congress has imposed a significant financial burden on States and school districts that participate in IDEA. Yet public educational authorities who want to avoid reimbursing parents for the private education of a disabled child can do one of two things: give the child a free appropriate public education in a public setting, or place the child in an appropriate private setting of the State's choice. This is IDEA's mandate, and school officials who conform to it need not worry about reimbursement claims.

Moreover, parents who, like Shannon's, "unilaterally change their child's placement during the pendency of review proceedings, without the consent of state or local school officials, do so at their own financial risk." They are entitled to reimbursement only if a federal court concludes both that the public placement violated IDEA and that the private school placement was proper under the Act.

Finally, we note that once a court holds that the public placement violated IDEA, it is authorized to "grant such relief as the court determines is appropriate." Under this provision, "equitable considerations are relevant in fashioning relief," and the court enjoys "broad discretion" in so doing. Courts fashioning discretionary equitable relief under IDEA must consider all relevant factors, including the appropriate and reasonable level of reimbursement that should be required. Total reimbursement will not be appropriate if the court determines that the cost of the private education was unreasonable.

Accordingly, we affirm the judgment of the Court of Appeals.

So ordered.

Notes

1. Is this outcome in the best interest of students with disabilities?

2. How far can, or should, courts go in extending this rationale? For example, what if parents wished to send their children to religiously affiliated charter schools? What if parents sought reimbursement for costs associated with homeschooling?

ARLINGTON CENTRAL SCHOOL DISTRICT BOARD OF EDUCATION

v.

MURPHY

United States Supreme Court, 2006

_U.S._, 126 S. Ct. 2455

Justice ALITO delivered the opinion of the Court.

The Individuals with Disabilities Education Act (IDEA or Act) provides that a court "may award reasonable attorneys' fees as part of the costs" to parents who prevail in an action brought under the Act. We granted certiorari to decide whether this fee-shifting provision authorizes prevailing parents to recover fees for services rendered by experts in IDEA actions. We hold that it does not.

I

Respondents Pearl and Theodore Murphy filed an action under the IDEA on behalf of their son, Joseph Murphy, seeking to require petitioner Arlington Central School District Board of Education to pay for their son's private school tuition for specified school years. Respondents prevailed in the District Court and the Court of Appeals for the Second Circuit affirmed.

As prevailing parents, respondents then sought $29,350 in fees for the services of an educational consultant, Marilyn Arons, who assisted respondents throughout the IDEA proceedings. The District Court granted respondents' request in part. It held that only the value of Arons' time spent between the hearing request and the ruling in respondents' favor could properly be considered charges incurred in an "action or proceeding brought" under the Act. This reduced the maximum recovery to $8,650. The District Court also held that Arons, a nonlawyer, could be compensated only for time spent on expert consulting services, not for time spent on legal representation, but it concluded that all the relevant time could be characterized as falling within the compensable category, and thus allowed compensation for the full $8,650.

The Court of Appeals for the Second Circuit affirmed. Acknowledging that other Circuits had taken the opposite view, the Court of Appeals for the Second Circuit held that "Congress intended to and did authorize the reimbursement of expert fees in IDEA actions." . . .

We granted certiorari to resolve the conflict among the Circuits with respect to whether Congress authorized the compensation of expert fees to prevailing parents in IDEA actions. We now reverse.

II

Our resolution of the question presented in this case is guided by the fact that Congress enacted the IDEA pursuant to the Spending Clause. Like its statutory predecessor, the IDEA provides federal funds to assist state and local agencies in educating children with disabilities "and conditions such funding upon a State's compliance with extensive goals and procedures."

Congress has broad power to set the terms on which it disburses federal money to the States, but when Congress attaches conditions to a State's acceptance of federal funds, the conditions must be set out "unambiguously." . . . States cannot knowingly accept conditions of which they are "unaware" or which they are "unable to ascertain." Thus, in the present case, we must view the IDEA from the perspective of a state official who is engaged in the process of deciding whether the State should accept IDEA funds and the obligations that go with those funds. We must ask whether such a state official would clearly understand that one of the obligations of the Act is the obligation to compensate prevailing parents for expert fees. In other words, we must ask whether the IDEA furnishes clear notice regarding the liability at issue in this case.

III

A

In considering whether the IDEA provides clear notice, we begin with the text. We have "stated time and again that courts must presume that a legislature says in a statute what it means and means in a statute what it says there." When the statutory "language is plain, the sole function of the courts—at least where the disposition required by the text is not absurd—is to enforce it according to its terms."

The governing provision of the IDEA, 20 U.S.C. § 1415(i)(3)(B), provides that "[i]n any action or proceeding brought under this section, the court, in its discretion, may award reasonable attorneys' fees as part of the costs" to the parents of "a child with a disability" who is the "prevailing party." While this provision provides for an award of "reasonable attorneys' fees," this provision does not even hint that acceptance of IDEA funds makes a State responsible for reimbursing prevailing parents for services rendered by experts.

Respondents contend that we should interpret the term "costs" in accordance with its meaning in ordinary usage and that § 1415(i)(3)(B) should therefore be read to "authorize reimbursement of all costs parents incur in IDEA proceedings, including expert costs." This argument has multiple flaws. For one thing, as the Court of Appeals in this case acknowledged, "'costs' is a term of art that generally does not include expert fees." The use of this term of art, rather than a term such as "expenses," strongly suggests that § 1415(i)(3)(B) was not meant to be an open-ended provision that makes participating States liable for all expenses incurred by prevailing parents in connection with an IDEA case—for example, travel and lodging expenses or lost wages due to time taken off from work. Moreover, contrary to respondents' suggestion, § 1415(i)(3)(B) does not say that a court may award "costs" to prevailing parents; rather, it says that a court may award reasonable attorney's fees "as part of the costs" to prevailing parents. This language simply adds reasonable attorney's fees incurred by prevailing parents to the list of costs that prevailing parents are otherwise entitled to recover. This list of otherwise recoverable costs is obviously the list set out in 28 U.S.C. § 1920, the general statute governing the taxation of costs in federal court, and the recovery of witness fees under § 1920 is strictly limited by § 1821, which authorizes travel reimbursement and a $40 per diem. Thus, the text of 20 U.S.C. § 1415(i)(3)(B) does not authorize an award of any additional expert fees, and it certainly fails to provide the clear notice that is required under the Spending Clause.

Other provisions of the IDEA point strongly in the same direction. While authorizing the award of reasonable attorney's fees, the Act contains detailed provisions that are designed to ensure that such awards are indeed reasonable. The absence of any comparable provisions relating to expert fees strongly suggests that recovery of expert fees is not authorized. Moreover, the lack of any reference to expert fees in § 1415(d)(2) gives rise to a similar inference. This provision, which generally requires that parents receive "a full explanation of the procedural safeguards" available under § 1415 and refers expressly to "attorneys' fees," makes no mention of expert fees.

B

Respondents contend that their interpretation of § 1415(i)(3)(B) is supported by a provision of the Handicapped Children's Protection Act of 1986 that required the General Accounting Office (GAO) to collect certain data, § 4(b)(3), (hereinafter GAO study provision), but this provision is of little significance for present purposes. The GAO study provision directed the Comptroller General, acting through the GAO, to compile data on, among other things: "(A) the specific amount of attorneys' fees, costs, and expenses awarded to the prevailing party" in IDEA cases for a particular period of time, and (B) "the number of hours spent by personnel, including attorneys and consultants, involved in the action or proceeding, and expenses incurred by the parents and the State educational agency and local educational agency."

Subparagraph (A) would provide some support for respondents' position if it directed the GAO to compile data on awards to prevailing parties of the expense of hiring consultants, but that is not what subparagraph (A) says. Subparagraph (A) makes no mention of consultants or experts or their fees.

Subparagraph (B) similarly does not help respondents. Subparagraph (B), which directs the GAO to study "the number of hours spent [in IDEA cases] by personnel, including . . . consultants," says nothing about the award of fees to such consultants. Just because Congress directed the GAO to compile statistics on the hours spent by consultants in IDEA cases, it does not follow that Congress meant for States to compensate prevailing parties for the fees billed by these consultants. Respondents maintain that "Congress' direction to the GAO would be inexplicable if Congress did not anticipate that the expenses for 'consultants' would be recoverable," but this is incorrect. There are many reasons why Congress might have wanted the GAO to gather data on expenses that were not to be taxed as costs. Knowing the costs incurred by IDEA litigants might be useful in considering future procedural amendments (which might affect these costs) or a future amendment regarding fee shifting. And, in fact, it is apparent that the GAO study provision covered expenses that could not be taxed as costs. For example, the GAO was instructed to compile statistics on the hours spent by all attorneys involved in an IDEA action or proceeding, even though the Act did not provide for the recovery of attorney's fees by a prevailing state or local educational agency. Similarly, the GAO was directed to compile data on "expenses incurred by the parents," not just those parents who prevail and are thus eligible to recover taxed costs.

In sum, the terms of the IDEA overwhelmingly support the conclusion that prevailing parents may not recover the costs of experts or consultants. Certainly the terms of the IDEA fail to provide the clear notice that would be needed to attach such a condition to a State's receipt of IDEA funds.

IV

Thus far, we have considered only the text of the IDEA, but perhaps the strongest support for our interpretation of the IDEA is supplied by our decisions and reasoning in *Crawford Fitting* and *Casey*. In light of those decisions, we do not see how it can be said that the IDEA gives a State unambiguous notice regarding liability for expert fees.

In *Crawford Fitting*, the Court rejected an argument very similar to respondents' argument that the term "costs" in § 1415(i)(3)(B) should be construed as an open-ended reference to prevailing parents' expenses. It was argued in *Crawford Fitting* that Federal Rule of Civil Procedure 54(d), which provides for the award of "costs" to a prevailing party, authorizes the award of costs not listed in 28 U.S.C. § 1821. The Court held, however, that Rule 54(d) does not give a district judge "discretion to tax whatever costs may seem appropriate;" rather, the term "costs" in Rule 54(d) is defined by the list set out in § 1920. Because the recovery of witness fees is strictly limited by § 1821, the Court observed, a broader interpretation of Rule 54(d) would mean that the Rule implicitly effected a partial repeal of those provisions. But, the Court warned, "[w]e will not lightly infer that Congress has repealed §§ 1920 and 1821, either through Rule 54(d) or any other provision not referring explicitly to witness fees."

The reasoning of *Crawford Fitting* strongly supports the conclusion that the term "costs" in 20 U.S.C. § 1415(i)(3)(B), like the same term in Rule 54(d), is defined by the categories of expenses enumerated in 28 U.S.C. § 1920. This conclusion is buttressed by the principle, recognized in *Crawford Fitting*, that no statute will be construed as authorizing the taxation of witness fees as costs unless the statute "refer[s] explicitly to witness fees."

Our decision in *Casey* confirms even more dramatically that the IDEA does not authorize an award of expert fees. In *Casey*, as noted above, we interpreted a fee-shifting provision, 42 U.S.C. § 1988, the relevant wording of which was virtually identical to the wording of 20 U.S.C. § 1415(i)(3)(B). We held that § 1988 did not empower a district court to award expert fees to a prevailing party. To decide in favor of respondents here, we would have to interpret the virtually identical language in 20 U.S.C. § 1415 as having exactly the opposite meaning. Indeed, we would have to go further and hold that the relevant language in the IDEA *unambiguously means* exactly the opposite of what the nearly identical language in 42 U.S.C. § 1988 was held to mean in *Casey*.

The Court of Appeals, as noted above, was heavily influenced by a *Casey* footnote, but the court misunderstood the footnote's meaning. The text accompanying the footnote argued, based on an analysis of several fee-shifting statutes, that the term "attorney's fees" does not include expert fees. In the footnote, we commented on petitioners' invocation of the Conference Committee Report relating to 20 U.S.C. § 1415(i)(3)(B), which stated: "'The conferees intend[ed] that the term "attorneys' fees as part of the costs" include reasonable expenses and fees of expert witnesses and the reasonable costs of any test or evaluation which is found to be necessary for the preparation of the . . . case.'" This statement, the footnote commented, was "an apparent effort to *depart* from ordinary meaning and to define a term of art." The footnote did not state that the Conference Committee Report set out the correct interpretation of § 1415(i)(3)(B), much less that the Report was sufficient, despite the language of the statute, to provide the clear notice required under the Spending Clause. The thrust of the footnote was simply that the term "attorneys' fees," standing alone, is generally not understood as encompassing expert fees. Thus, *Crawford Fitting* and *Casey* strongly reinforce the conclusion that the IDEA does not unambiguously authorize prevailing parents to recover expert fees.

V

Respondents make several arguments that are not based on the text of the IDEA, but these arguments do not show that the IDEA provides clear notice regarding the award of expert fees. Respondents argue that their interpretation of the IDEA furthers the Act's overarching goal of "ensur[ing] that all children with disabilities have available to them a free appropriate public education," 20 U.S.C. § 1400(d)(1)(A) as well as the goal of "safeguard[ing] the rights of parents to challenge school decisions that adversely affect their child." These goals, however, are too general to provide much support for respondents' reading of the terms of the IDEA. The IDEA obviously does not seek to promote these goals at the expense of all other considerations, including fiscal considerations. Because the IDEA is not intended in all instances to further the broad goals identified by the respondents at the expense of fiscal considerations, the goals cited by respondents do little to bolster their argument on the narrow question presented here.

Finally, respondents vigorously argue that Congress clearly intended for prevailing parents to be compensated for expert fees. They rely on the legislative history of § 1415 and in particular on the following statement in the Conference Committee Report, discussed above: "The conferees intend that the term 'attorneys' fees as part of the costs' include reasonable expenses and fees of expert witnesses and the reasonable costs of any test or evaluation which is found to be necessary for the preparation of the . . . case."

Whatever weight this legislative history would merit in another context, it is not sufficient here. Putting the legislative history aside, we see virtually no support for respondents' position. Under these circumstances, where everything other than the legislative history overwhelming suggests that expert fees may not be recovered, the legislative history is simply not enough. In a Spending Clause case, the key is not what a majority of the Members of both Houses intend but what the States are clearly told regarding the conditions that go along with the acceptance of those funds. Here, in the face of the unambiguous text of the IDEA and the reasoning in *Crawford Fitting* and *Casey,* we cannot say that the legislative history on which respondents rely is sufficient to provide the requisite fair notice.

* * *

We reverse the judgment of the Court of Appeals for the Second Circuit and remand the case for further proceedings consistent with this opinion.

It is so ordered.

Notes

1. This was the first education case in which Justice Alito authored the Court's majority opinion. The vote was six to three.

2. Even in conceding that the Court stayed close to the text in interpreting the IDEA, is it fair for parents to have to pay for experts and consultants who help them prevail in obtaining services for their children? Put another way, after the Supreme Court denied prevailing parents the opportunity to recover attorney fees, Congress amended the IDEA. Although it has refused to do so in recent years, should Congress amend the IDEA to permit parents to recover fees for expert witnesses and consultants who assisted in helping them win their cases?

3. In the lengthier of the two dissents, Justice Breyer, joined by Justices Stevens and Souter, disagreed with the Court on two primary points. First, he interpreted the GAO Report as permitting fee awards to prevailing parents. Second, he maintained that interpreting the IDEA as allowing prevailing parents to recover the disputed fees would have advanced its goals. Although he joined Justice Breyer's dissent, Justice Souter thought it necessary to pen a separate paragraph length dissent to emphasize his support for the disputed GAO report.

REFERENCES

Abraham v. District of Columbia, 338 F. Supp.2d 113 (D.D.C. 2004).

Alamo Heights Independent School District v. State Board of Education, 790 F.2d 1153 (5th Cir. 1986).

Alex G. ex rel. Stephen G. v. Board of Trustees of Davis Joint Unified School District, 332 F. Supp.2d 1315 (E.D. Cal. 2004).

Algeria v. District of Columbia, 391 F.3d 262 (D.C. Cir. 2004).

Anderson v. Thompson, 658 F.2d 1205 (7th Cir. 1981).

Angela L. v. Pasadena Independent School District, 918 F.2d 1188 (5th Cir. 1990).

Appellate Rule 38, Fed.R.App.P. 38.

Arlington Central School District Board of Education v. Murphy, 126 S. Ct. 2455 (2006), *reversing Murphy v. Arlington Central School District*, 402 F.3d 332 (2d Cir. 2005).

Aronow v. District of Columbia, 780 F. Supp. 46 (D.D.C. 1992), 791 F. Supp. 318 (D.D.C. 1992).

Arons v. New Jersey State Board of Education, 842 F.2d 58 (3d Cir. 1988).

Ash v. Lake Oswego School District, 766 F. Supp. 852 (D. Or. 1991), *affirmed*, 980 F.2d 585 (9th Cir. 1992).

A.W. v. Jersey City Public Schools, 486 F.3d 791 (3d Cir. 2007).

Babb v. Knox County School System, 965 F.2d 104 (6th Cir. 1992).

Barbara R. v. Tirozzi, 665 F. Supp. 141 (D. Conn. 1987).

Barlow-Gresham Union High School District No. 2 v. Mitchell, 940 F.2d 1280 (9th Cir. 1991).

Barnett v. Fairfax County School Board, 927 F.2d 146 (4th Cir. 1991).

Bernardsville Board of Education v. J.H., 42 F.3d 149 (3d Cir. 1994).

B.H. v. Southington Board of Education, 273 F. Supp.2d 194 (D. Conn. 2003).

Big Beaver Falls Area School District v. Jackson, 624 A.2d 806 (Pa. Commw. Ct. 1993).

Board of Education of Downers Grove Grade School District No. 58 v. Steven L., 89 F.3d 464 (7th Cir. 1996).

Board of Education of Oak Park & River Forest High School District No. 200 v. Illinois State Board of Education, 21 F. Supp.2d 862 (N.D. Ill. 1988), *vacated and remanded on other grounds sub nom. Board of Education of Oak Park & River Forest High School District No. 200 v. Kelly E.*, 207 F.3d 931 (7th Cir. 2000).

Board of Education of the City School District of the City of New York v. Tom F., 193 Fed. Appx. 26 (2d Cir. 2006), *affirmed by an equally divided court*, 2007 WL 2935030 (2007).

Board of Education of the County of Cabell v. Dienelt, 843 F.2d 813 (4th Cir. 1988).

Board of Education of the Hendrick Hudson Central School District v. Rowley, 458 U.S. 176 (1982).

Bradley v. Arkansas Department of Education, 301 F.3d 952 (8th Cir. 2002).

Brandon K. v. New Lenox School District, 2001 WL 1491499 (N.D. Ill. 2001).

Brantley v. Independent School District No. 625, St. Paul Public Schools, 936 F. Supp. 649 (D. Minn. 1996).

Brillon v. Klein Independent School District, 274 F. Supp.2d 864 (S.D. Tex. 2003).

Brooks v. St. Tammany Parish School Board, 510 S0.2d 51 (La. App. Ct. 1987).

Brown v. Wilson County School District, 747 F. Supp. 436 (M.D. Tenn. 1990).

Buckhannon Board & Care Home v. West Virginia Department of Health and Human Resources, 532 U.S. 598 (2001).

Bucks County Department of Mental Health/Mental Retardation v. Commonwealth of Pennsylvania, 379 F.3d 61 (3d Cir. 2004).

Burlington School Committee v. Department of Education, Commonwealth of Massachusetts, 471 U.S. 359 (1985).

Burr v. Sobol, 748 F. Supp. 97 (S.D.N.Y. 1990).

Capistrano Unified School District v. Wartenberg, 59 F.3d 884 (9th Cir. 1995).

Cappillino v. Hyde Park Central School District, 40 F. Supp.2d 513 (S.D.N.Y. 1999).

Carlisle Area School District v. Scott P., 62 F.3d 520 (3d Cir. 1995).

Caroline T. v. Hudson School District, 915 F.2d 752 (1st Cir. 1990).

Chang v. Board of Education of Glen Ridge Township, 685 F. Supp. 96 (D.N.J. 1988).

Charlie F. v. Board of Education of Skokie School District 68, 98 F.3d 989 (7th Cir. 1996).

Civil Rights Act of 1871, Section 1983, 42 U.S.C. § 1983.

Cleveland Heights–University Heights City School District v. Boss, 144 F.3d 391 (6th Cir. 1998).

Cocores v. Portsmouth, NH School District, 779 F. Supp. 203 (D.N.H. 1991).

Combs v. School Board of Rockingham County, 15 F.3d 357 (4th Cir. 1994).

Conklin, In re, 946 F.2d 306 (4th Cir. 1991).

Connors v. Mills, 34 F. Supp.2d 795 (N.D.N.Y. 1998).

Cremeans v. Fairland Local School District Board of Education, 633 N.E.2d 570 (Ohio App. Ct. 1993).

Crocker v. Tennessee Secondary School Athletic Association, 980 F.2d 382 (6th Cir. 1992).

Daniel S. v. Scranton School District, 230 F.3d 90 (3d Cir. 2000).

D.B. v. Ocean Township Board of Education, 985 F. Supp. 457 (D.N.J. 1997).

Deal ex rel. Deal v. Hamilton County Department of Education, 392 F.3d 840 (6th Cir. 2004).

Diamond v. McKenzie, 602 F. Supp. 632 (D.D.C. 1985).

DiBuo v. Board of Education of Worcester County, 309 F.3d 184 (4th Cir. 2002).

D.M. ex rel. G.M. and C.M. v. Board of Education, Center Moriches Union Free School District, 296 F. Supp.2d 400 (E.D.N.Y. 2003).

Doe v. Anrig, 651 F. Supp. 424 (D. Mass. 1987).

Doe v. Board of Education of Baltimore County, 165 F.3d 260 (4th Cir. 1998).

Doe v. Boston Public Schools, 358 F.3d 20 (1st Cir. 2004).

Doucet v. Chilton County Board of Education, 65 F. Supp.2d 1249 (M.D. Ala. 1999).

Drew P. v. Clarke County School District, 676 F. Supp. 1559 (M.D. Ga. 1987), *affirmed*, 877 F.2d 927 (11th Cir. 1989).

E.C. ex rel. R.C. v. Board of Education of South Brunswick Township, 792 A.2d 583 (N.J. Sup. Ct. 2001).

Eggers v. Bullitt County School District, 854 F.2d 892 (6th Cir. 1988).

Eirschele v. Craven County Board of Education, 7 F. Supp.2d 655 (E.D.N.C. 1998).

E.M. v. Millville Board of Education, 849 F. Supp. 312 (D.N.J. 1994).

Emma C. v. Eastin, 985 F. Supp. 940 (N.D. Cal. 1997).

E.P. v. Union County Regional High School District No. 1, 741 F. Supp. 1144 (D.N.J. 1989).

Erickson v. Board of Education of Baltimore County, 162 F.3d 289 (4th Cir. 1998).

Esther C. v. Ambach, 535 N.Y.S.2d 462 (N.Y. App. Div. 1988).

Eugene B. v. Great Neck Union Free School District, 635 F. Supp. 753 (E.D.N.Y. 1986).

Evans v. District No. 17 of Douglas County, 841 F.2d 824 (8th Cir. 1988).

Field v. Haddonfield Board of Education, 769 F. Supp. 1313 (D.N.J. 1991).

Fischer v. Rochester Community Schools, 780 F. Supp. 1142 (E.D. Mich. 1991).

Florence County School District Four v. Carter, 510 U.S. 7 (1993).

Frank G. v. Board of Education of Hyde Park, 459 F.3d 356 (2d Cir. 2006).

Garland Independent School District v. Wilks, 657 F. Supp. 1163 (N.D. Tex. 1987).

Garner, B. A. (Ed.). (1999). *Black's law dictionary* (7th ed.). St. Paul, MN: West.

Garro v. State of Connecticut, 23 F.3d 734 (2d Cir. 1994).

Gary A. v. New Trier High School District No. 203, 796 F.2d 940 (7th Cir. 1986).

Gerasimou v. Ambach, 636 F. Supp. 1504 (E.D.N.Y. 1986).

Gerstmyer v. Howard County Public Schools, 850 F. Supp. 361 (D. Md. 1994).

Glendale Unified School District v. Almasi, 122 F. Supp.2d 1093 (C.D. Cal. 2000).

Goldring v. District of Columbia, 416 F.3d 70 (D.C. Cir. 2005).

Greenland School District v. Amy N., 358 F.3d 150 (1st Cir. 2004).

Gross ex rel. Gross v. Perrysburg Exempted Village School District, 306 F. Supp.2d 726 (N.D. Ohio 2004).

Hall v. Detroit Public Schools, 823 F. Supp. 1377 (E.D. Mich. 1993).

Hall v. Knott County Board of Education, 941 F.2d 402 (6th Cir. 1991).

Heldman v. Sobol, 846 F.3d 285 (S.D.N.Y. 1994).

Hiller v. Board of Education of the Brunswick Central School District, 743 F. Supp. 958 (N.D.N.Y. 1990).

Howey v. Tippecanoe School Corporation, 734 F. Supp. 1485, (N.D. Ind. 1990).

Hudson v. Wilson, 828 F.2d 1059 (4th Cir. 1987).

Hunger v. Leininger, 15 F.3d 664 (7th Cir. 1994).

Hurry v. Jones, 734 F.2d 879 (1st Cir. 1984).

Hyden v. Board of Education of Wilson County, 714 F. Supp. 290 (M.D. Tenn. 1989).

Individuals with Disabilities Education Act, 20 U.S.C. §§ 1400–1482 (2005).

J.C. v. Regional School District No. 10, 278 F.3d 119 (2d Cir. 2002).

Jefferson County Board of Education v. Breen, 853 F.2d 853 (11th Cir. 1988).

J.G. v. Board of Education of the Rochester City School District, 648 F. Supp. 1452 (W.D.N.Y. 1986), *affirmed*, 830 F.2d 444 (2d Cir. 1987).

John T. by Paul T. and Joan T. v. Delaware County Intermediate Unit, 318 F.3d 545 (3d Cir. 2003).

Johnson v. Bismarck Public School District, 949 F.2d 1000 (8th Cir. 1991).

Johnson v. Clark, 418 N.W.2d 466 (Mich. Ct. App. 1987).

Johnson v. Lancaster-Lebanon Intermediate Unit 13, Lancaster City School District, 757 F. Supp. 606 (E.D. Pa. 1991).

Johnson v. Metro Davidson County School System, 108 F. Supp.2d 906 (M.D. Tenn. 2000).

Jose Luis R. v. Joliet Township H.S. District 204, 2002 WL 54544 (N.D. Ill. 2002).

J.S. v. Ramapo Central School District, 165 F. Supp.2d 570 (S.D.N.Y. 2001).

King v. Floyd County Board of Education, 5 F. Supp.2d 504 (E.D. Ky. 1998).

Koswenda v. Flossmoor School District No. 161, 227 F. Supp.2d 979 (N.D. Ill. 2002).

Krichinsky v. Knox County Schools, 963 F.2d 847 (6th Cir. 1992).

Kristi W. v. Graham Independent School District, 663 F. Supp. 86 (N.D. Tex. 1987).

Lascari v. Board of Education of the Ramapo Indian Hills Regional High School District, 560 A.2d 1180 (N.J. 1989).

Lester H. v. Gilhool, 916 F.2d 865 (3d Cir. 1990).

Linda T. ex rel. William A. v. Rice Lake Area School District, 337 F. Supp.2d 1135 (W.D. Wis. 2004).

L.K. ex rel. J.H. v. Board of Education for Transylvania County, 113 F. Supp.2d 856 (W.D.N.C. 2000).

Lucht v. Molalla River School District, 225 F.3d 1023 (9th Cir. 1999).

Malehorn v. Hill City School District, 987 F. Supp. 772 (D.S.D. 1997).

Manchester School District v. Christopher B., 807 F. Supp. 860 (D.N.H. 1992).

Martin v. School Board of Prince George County, 348 S.E.2d 857 (Va. Ct. App. 1986).

Marvin H. v. Austin Independent School District, 714 F.2d 1348 (5th Cir. 1983).

Mathern v. Campbell County Children's Center, 674 F. Supp. 816 (D. Wyo. 1987).

Matthew V. v. DeKalb County School System, 244 F. Supp.2d 1331 (N.D. Ga. 2003).

Mawdsley, R. D. (2001). Standard of care and students with disabilities. *Education Law Reporter, 148*, 553–571.

Mawdsley, R. D. (2002). A section 1983 cause of action under the IDEA? Measuring the effect of *Gonzaga University v. Doe. Education Law Reporter, 170*, 425–438.

Mayo v. Baltimore City Public Schools, 40 F. Supp.2d 331 (D. Md. 1999).

Max M. v. Illinois State Board of Education, 684 F. Supp. 514 (N.D. Ill. 1988), *affirmed*, 859 F.2d 1297 (7th Cir. 1988).

Max M. v. Thompson, 566 F. Supp. 1330 (N.D. Ill. 1983), 592 F. Supp. 1437 (N.D. Ill. 1984), *sub nom. Max M. v. Illinois State Board of Education*, 629 F. Supp. 1504 (N.D. Ill. 1986).

M.C. ex rel. J.C. v. Central Reg. School District, 81 F.3d 389 (3d Cir. 1996).

Megan C. v. Independent School District No. 625, 57 F. Supp.2d 776 (D. Minn. 1999).

Metropolitan School District of Lawrence Township v. M.S., 818 N.E.2d 978 (Ind. Ct. App. 2004).

Miener v. Missouri, 800 F.2d 749 (8th Cir. 1986).

Miller v. West Lafayette Community School Corporation, 665 N.E.2d 905 (Ind. 1996).

Missouri Department of Elementary and Secondary Education v. Springfield R-12 School District, 358 F.3d 992 (8th Cir. 2004).

Mitten v. Muscogee County District, 877 F.2d 932 (11th Cir. 1989).

Moore v. Crestwood Local School District, 804 F. Supp. 960 (N.D. Ohio 1992).

Moore v. District of Columbia, 886 F.2d 335 (D.C. Cir. 1989); 907 F.2d 165 (D.C. Cir. 1990).

Moser v. Bret Harte Union High School District, 366 F. Supp.2d 944 (E.D. Cal. 2005).

Moubry v. Independent School District No. 696, 951 F. Supp. 867 (D. Minn. 1996).

Mr. D. v. Glocester School Community, 711 F. Supp. 66 (D.R.I. 1989).

Mr. J. v. Board of Education, 98 F. Supp.2d 226 (D. Conn. 2000).

Mr. L. and Mrs. L. v. Woonsocket Education Department, 793 F. Supp. 41 (D.R.I. 1992).

M.S. ex rel. S.S. v. Board of Education of the City School District of the City of Yonkers, 231 F.3d 96 (2d Cir. 2000).

Ms. M. ex rel. K.M. v. Portland School Committee, 360 F.3d 267 (1st Cir. 2004).

Muller v. Committee on Special Education of the East Islip Union Free School District, 145 F.3d 95 (2d Cir. 1998).

Murphy v. Arlington Central School District Board of Education, 402 F.3d 332 (2d Cir. 2005).

Murphy v. Timberlane Regional School District, 973 F.2d 13 (1st Cir. 1992), *on remand*, 819 Supp. 1127 (D.N.H. 1993), *affirmed*, 22 F.3d 1186 (1st Cir. 1994a), *contempt finding*, 855 F. Supp. 498 (D.N.H. 1994b).

Muth v. Central Bucks School District, 839 F.2d 113 (3d Cir. 1988), *reversed and remanded on other grounds sub nom. Dellmuth v. Muth*, 491 U.S. 223 (1989).

Nein v. Greater Clark County School Corporation, 95 F. Supp.2d 961 (S.D. Ind. 2000).

Neisz v. Portland Public School District, 684 F. Supp. 1530 (D. Or. 1988).

Neosho R-V School District v. Clark, 315 F.3d 1022 (8th Cir. 2003).

Nieves-Marquez v. Commonwealth of Puerto Rico, 353 F.3d 108 (1st Cir. 2003).

Noyes v. Grossmont Union High School District, 331 F. Supp.2d 1233 (S.D. Cal. 2004).

Osborne, A. G. (2002). Can Section 1983 be used to redress violations of the IDEA? *Education Law Reporter, 161*, 21–32.

Osborne, A. G. (2003). Attorneys' fees under the IDEA after *Buckhannon:* Is the catalyst theory still viable? *Education Law Reporter, 175*, 397–407.

Osborne, A. G. (2005). Update on attorneys' fees under the IDEA. *Education Law Reporter, 193*, 1–12.

Osborne, A. G., & DiMattia, P. (1991). Attorney fees are available for administrative proceedings under the EHA. *Education Law Reporter, 66*, 909–920.

Osborne, A. G., & Russo, C. J. (2001). Are damages an available remedy when a school district fails to provide an appropriate education under IDEA? *Education Law Reporter, 152*, 1–14.

Osborne, A. G., & Russo, C. J. (2006). The Supreme Court rejects parental reimbursement for expert witness fees under the IDEA: *Arlington Central School District Board of Education v. Murphy. Education Law Reporter, 213*, 333–348.

Padilla v. School District No. 1 in the City and County of Denver, 233 F.3d 1268 (10th Cir. 2000).

Parents of Student W. v. Puyallup School District No. 3, 31 F.3d 1489 (9th Cir. 1994).

Patricia E. v. Board of Education of Community High School District No. 155, 894 F. Supp. 1161 (N.D. Ill. 1995).

Patricia P. v. Board of Education of Oak Park and River Forest High School District No. 200, 203 F.3d 462 (7th Cir. 2000).

Payne v. Board of Education, Cleveland City Schools, 88 F.3d 392 (6th Cir. 1996).

Pazik v. Gateway Regional School District, 130 F. Supp.2d 217 (D. Mass. 2001).

Phelan v. Bell, 8 F.3d 369 (6th Cir. 1993).

Pihl v. Massachusetts Department of Education, 9 F.3d 184 (1st Cir. 1993).

P.J. v. State of Connecticut State Board of Education, 788 F. Supp. 673 (D. Conn. 1992).

P.L. by Mr. and Mrs. L. v. Norwalk Board of Education, 64 F. Supp.2d 61 (D. Conn. 1999).

P.O. ex rel. L.T. and T.O. v. Greenwich Board of Education, 210 F. Supp.2d 76 (D. Conn. 2002).

Polera v. Board of Education of the Newburgh Enlarged City School District, 288 F.3d 478 (2nd Cir. 2002).

Powell v. DeFore, 699 F.2d 1078 (11th Cir. 1983).

Puffer v. Raynolds, 761 F. Supp. 838 (D. Mass. 1988).

Rapid City School District v. Vahle, 922 F.2d 476 (8th Cir. 1990).

Rappaport v. Vance, 812 F. Supp. 609 (D. Md. 1993).

Ridgewood Board of Education v. N.E., 172 F.3d 238 (3d Cir. 1999).

Rehabilitation Act, Section 504, 29 U.S.C. § 794.

Russo, C. J. (2006). Negligence. In C. J. Russo (Ed.), *Key legal issues for schools: The ultimate resource for school business officials* (pp. 83–97). Lanham, MD: Rowman & Littlefield Education.

S-1 v. Spangler, 650 F. Supp. 1427 (M.D.N.C. 1986), *vacated and remanded due to mootness*, 832 F.2d 294 (4th Cir. 1987), *on remand* (unpublished opinion), *affirmed sub nom. S-1 v. State Board of Education*, 6 F.3d 160 (4th Cir. 1993), *rehearing en banc, reversed*, 21 F.3d 49 (4th Cir. 1994).

Salley v. St. Tammany Parish School Board, 57 F.3d 458 (5th Cir. 1995).

Sanders v. Marquette Public Schools, 561 F. Supp. 1361 (W.D. Mich. 1983).

Schoenfield v. Parkway School District, 138 F.3d 379 (8th Cir. 1998).

Sellers v. School Board of the City of Manassas, 141 F.3d 524 (4th Cir. 1998).

Shelly C. v. Venus Independent School District, 878 F.2d 862 (5th Cir. 1989).

Sidney K. v. Ambach, 535 N.Y.S.2d 468 (N.Y. App. Div. 1988).

Smith ex rel Smith v. Fitchburg Public Schools, 401 F.3d 16 (1st Cir. 2005).

Smith v. District of Columbia, 117 Fed. Appx. (D.C. Cir. 2004).

Smith v. Robinson, 468 U.S. 992 (1984).

State of West Virginia ex rel. Justice v. Board of Education of the County of Monongalia, 539 S.E.2d 777 (W.Va. 2000).

Still v. DeBuono, 101 F.3d 888 (2d Cir. 1996).

Straube v. Florida Union Free School District, 778 F. Supp. 774 (S.D.N.Y. 1991), 801 F. Supp. 1164 (S.D.N.Y. 1992).

Suzawith v. Green Bay Area School District, 132 F. Supp.2d 718 (D. Wis. 2000).

Taylor v. Board of Education of Copake-Taconic Hills Central School District, 649 F. Supp. 1253 (N.D.N.Y. 1986).

T.D. v. LaGrange School District No. 102, 349 F.3d 469 (7th Cir. 2003).

Tice v. Botetourt County School District, 908 F.2d 1200 (4th Cir. 1990).

Timms v. Metropolitan School District, EHLR 554:361 (S.D. Ind. 1982), *affirmed,* 718 F.2d 212 (7th Cir. 1983), *amended,* 722 F.2d 1310 (7th Cir. 1983).

Todd D. v. Andrews, 933 F.2d 1576 (11th Cir. 1991).

Troy School District v. Boutsikaris, 250 F. Supp.2d 720 (E.D. Mich. 2003).

Tucker v. Calloway County Board of Education, 136 F.3d 495 (6th Cir. 1998).

Turton v. Crisp County School District, 688 F. Supp. 1535 (M.D. Ga. 1988).

Union School District v. Smith, 15 F.3d 1519 (9th Cir. 1994).

Upper Valley Association of Handicapped Citizens v. Blue Mountain Union School District No. 21, 973 F. Supp. 429 (D. Vt. 1997).

Valerie J. v. Derry Cooperative School District, 771 F. Supp. 483 (D.N.H. 1991).

Vander Malle v. Ambach, 667 F. Supp. 1015 (S.D.N.Y. 1987).

Virginia McC. v. Corrigan-Camden Independent School District, 909 F. Supp. 1023 (E.D. Tex. 1995).

Vultaggio v. Board of Education, Smithtown Central School District, 343 F.3d 598 (2nd Cir. 2003).

Warren G. v. Cumberland County School District, 190 F.3d 80 (3d Cir. 1999).

Watkins v. Vance, 328 F. Supp.2d 27, (D.D.C. 2004).

Wayne County Regional Education Service Agency v. Pappas, 56 F. Supp.2d 807 (E.D. Mich. 1999).

W.B. v. Matula, 67 F.3d 484 (3d Cir. 1995).

Wenger v. Canastota Central School District, 979 F. Supp. 147 (N.D.N.Y. 1997), *affirmed,* 181 F.3d 84, 136 Ed.Law Rep. 226 (2d Cir. 1999) (mem.).

Wenkart, R. D. (2002). Attorneys' fees under the IDEA and the demise of the catalyst theory. *Education Law Reporter, 165,* 439–445.

Wenkart, R. D. (2004). The award of section 1983 damages under the IDEA. *Education Law Reporter, 183,* 313–335.

Wheeler v. Towanda Area School District, 950 F.2d 128 (3d Cir. 1991).

White v. State of California, 240 Cal. Rptr. 732 (Cal. Ct. App. 1987).

W.L.G. v. Houston County Board of Education, 975 F. Supp. 1317 (M.D. Ala. 1997).

Woodside v. School District of Philadelphia Board of Education, 248 F.3d 129 (3d Cir. 2001).

Yancy v. New Baltimore City Board of School Commissioners, 24 F. Supp.2d 512 (D. Md. 1998).

Yankton School District v. Schramm, 900 F. Supp. 1182 (D.S.D. 1995), *affirmed,* 93 F.3d 1369 (8th Cir. 1996).

Zirkel, P. A., & Hennessy, M. K. (2001). Compensatory educational services in special education cases: An update. *Education Law Reporter, 150,* 311–332.

Zirkel, P. A., & Osborne, A. G. (1987). Are damages available in special education suits? *Education Law Reporter, 42,* 497–508.

Emerging Issues

❖

Each year, a large number of suits are filed under the Individuals with Disabilities Education Act (IDEA) over basic issues associated with educating students with disabilities. Even so, a variety of important issues that educators need to be aware of have not been subject to much litigation. The fact that there has not been much litigation on these important issues does not mean that there will not be any in the future. In fact, due to the significance of these issues and their importance to both school boards and parents, many are emerging as hot topics.

This chapter reflects on seldom-litigated issues that did not fit neatly into any of the previous chapters. The chapter reviews issues associated with child find, state testing programs, state responsibility to ensure compliance, responsibility of insurance carriers, disbursement of federal funds, policy letters issued by the Department of Education, programs for infants and toddlers under Part C of the IDEA, and report cards and transcripts for students with disabilities.

CHILD FIND

The IDEA requires states and local school boards to locate, identify, and evaluate all children with disabilities who need special education and related services (20 U.S.C. § 1412(a)(3)). This directive includes children who are homeless, wards of the state, and in private schools. In light of the various educational settings of children, school boards must employ child find procedures to locate parentally placed private school students with disabilities that are similar to the ones that they use for children in public schools (20 U.S.C. § 1412(a)(10)(III)). The child find provision further instructs school personnel to develop and implement practical methods for determining which students are currently receiving services.

Failure to evaluate in a timely manner students who demonstrate signs of having disabilities could violate the child find provision. For example, the federal trial court in Hawaii held that the state's Department of Education violated the child find provisions because officials had, or should have had, reason to suspect that a high school student had a disability (*Department of Education, State of Hawaii v. Cari Rae S.*, 2001). In examining the record, the court discovered that officials had reason to suspect that the student had a disability and should have evaluated her sooner. Similarly, a federal trial court in Pennsylvania found fault with school officials who were aware of a student's systematic academic and behavioral decline but instead of evaluating him chose to monitor his progress (*Hicks ex rel. Hicks v. Purchase Line School District*, 2003).

A case from the District of Columbia illustrates the principle that school officials have an affirmative duty to act when parents express concerns about their children. The mother of a second grader asked a school counselor for help because she was concerned that her son was having difficulty learning. Later that same year, the mother met with the child's teacher and the school's principal to discuss her son's academic, behavior, and attention problems. In spite of the mother's expressed concern, her son was neither evaluated nor identified as a student with disabilities until he was retained in the fourth grade. A hearing officer, whose order was confirmed by the federal trial court, noted that since school officials failed to provide the child with an appropriate education by not identifying him earlier, he was entitled to compensatory educational services (*Reid v. District of Columbia*, 2004, 2005).

The IDEA's child find requirements have special significance in light of the statute's disciplinary provisions. The IDEA requires school authorities to provide the IDEA's procedural protections to disciplinary situations in which students have not been identified as disabled but school personnel should have known that they had disabilities (20 U.S.C.A. § 1415(k)(5); 34 C.F.R. § 300.534). Given this requirement, it is incumbent on school board officials to be diligent in identifying all students who may have disabilities. This topic is discussed in greater detail in Chapter 6.

STATE TESTING PROGRAMS

The No Child Left Behind Act (NCLB) has mandated greater accountability in the nation's classrooms. In response to the NCLB's calls for greater accountability, all states have developed and are administering tests in major subject areas at several grade levels (20 U.S.C. § 6311). At the same time, the IDEA requires states to include students with disabilities in any general state or school district assessment programs (20 U.S.C. § 1412(a)(16)). Depending on the grade level, these tests may be used either as graduation requirements to assure that students receiving diplomas have specified knowledge bases or to identify children who, because they have not achieved competency in basic skills, may require remedial instruction.

State testing programs are not new. Many testing programs predate the NCLB and were once known as minimum competency tests or basic skills tests. Not surprisingly, states with testing programs in place had to revise them in order to meet the more stringent requirements of the NCLB. While some of the cases discussed under this heading predate the NCLB, the legal principles that emerged are still applicable.

It is well settled that states have the authority to establish graduation requirements and may expect students to pass competency tests before being able to receive standard high school diplomas. In an early case from Florida, the Eleventh Circuit ruled that when competency tests were used as graduation requirements, they had to be valid and reliable measures of what had been taught. Further, the court explained that students had to be given sufficient notice that they must pass such tests in order to receive standard diplomas. The court also made it clear that competency tests may not be racially, linguistically, or ethnically discriminatory (*Debra P. v. Turlington*, 1984).

Other early courts examining the issue upheld the requirement that students must pass tests to receive standard high school diplomas (*Anderson v. Banks*, 1981, 1982; *Board of Education of Northport-East Northport Union Free School District v. Ambach*, 1983; *Brookhart v. Illinois State Board of Education*, 1983). Further, most courts agreed that in order for these tests to have been valid diploma requirements, students had to have been given sufficient notice and their Individualized Education Programs (IEPs) should have included instruction in the areas to be tested. Of course in the NCLB era, all students have, or should have, received notice.

To enable students with disabilities to take state-administered tests may require some modifications. School personnel may be required to modify how tests are administered but cannot be required to alter the actual content of examinations. For example, students who are visually impaired should be given Braille versions of tests, while students with physical challenges may need assistance writing or filling in the circles on machine-scored answer sheets. Conversely, school officials are not required to develop and administer tests with fewer items or easier items for students with intellectual or cognitive impairments (*Brookhart v. Illinois Board of Education*, 1983; *Rene v. Reed*, 2001). In sum, school officials must make accommodations that allow students to take tests but are not obligated to modify the content of items.

At least one court indicated that the NCLB does not require school boards to base determinations as to whether students with disabilities have received a free appropriate public education (FAPE) on the results of state tests (*Leighty v. Laurel School District*, 2006). In addition, the court pointed out that the NCLB does not oblige educators to develop IEPs specifically to enhance a student's scores on state tests. Importantly, the court agreed that the NCLB's assessments could be used as one factor in the overall evaluation of whether students received a meaningful education. Thus it appears that the failure of students to pass state mandated tests does not mean that school boards did not provide them with a FAPE, but passing test scores may be one indicator that school boards have complied with the law.

STATE RESPONSIBILITY TO ENSURE COMPLIANCE

A careful reading of the IDEA reveals that its provisions often refer to states rather than local education agencies or school boards. This distinction emerges because IDEA funds are allocated to states for distribution to local school boards (20 U.S.C. § 1411(a)). Under these provisions, states are required to submit plans that assure that they have policies and procedures in place to ensure that they meet all of the IDEA's requirements (20 U.S.C. § 1412(a)). This also means that states have the primary responsibility under the IDEA to provide a FAPE and to ensure compliance with its dictates (*M.A. ex rel. E.S. v. State-Operated School District of Newark*, 2003).

The Fourth Circuit made it clear that state officials are ultimately responsible for making certain that all students within their jurisdictions receive a FAPE (*Gadsby v. Grasmick*, 1997). For that reason, the court wrote that the state could be liable if officials failed to comply with their duty to assure compliance with the IDEA's substantive requirements. Similarly, the Fifth Circuit emphasized that both a local school board and the state could be liable for the failure to provide a FAPE (*St. Tammany Parish School Board v. State of Louisiana*, 1998).

Along the same lines, a federal trial court in Illinois was of the opinion that the state failed to meet its responsibilities under the IDEA to ensure compliance with the statute's least restrictive environment (LRE) provision (*Corey H. v. Board of Education of the City of Chicago*, 1998). The court maintained that officials acting on behalf of the state failed to monitor and enforce compliance with the

LRE mandate. While the court added that the state was not required to micro-manage local school systems, its officials had the duty to correct situations where boards failed to comply with the IDEA's LRE mandate.

RESPONSIBILITY OF INSURANCE CARRIERS

A question that has not been widely litigated addresses the responsibility of insurance companies in providing assistance, most often in the form of related services, for students with disabilities. It is well settled that insurance companies are not relieved of their obligations to provide services to children with disabilities simply because the services may be available to students under the IDEA. To this end, insurance companies or other third-party payers may not use the IDEA to avoid their responsibilities to insured parties or clients.

On two separate occasions, a federal trial court in Pennsylvania dismissed claims by insurance companies that sought to have school boards assume responsibility for providing special education and related services to students who became disabled as a result of injuries sustained in automobile accidents (*Allstate Insurance Company v. Bethlehem Area School District*, 1987; *Gehman v. Prudential Property and Casualty Insurance Company*, 1989). In both cases the court dismissed the claims because the insurance companies did not have standing to sue inasmuch as only students and their parents may invoke the provisions of the IDEA. Yet, in dicta, one court wrote that the IDEA neither alters nor disturbs the relationship between parents and their insurers, nor shifts obligations from insurance companies to school boards.

The Second Circuit decided that a student who required the services of a nurse twenty-four hours a day was entitled to have them provided in school under the Medicaid program (*Detsel v. Sullivan*, 1990). The court was persuaded that since providing private-duty nursing services in a school setting was basically equivalent to making them available in the student's home, it was the responsibility of Medicaid. In a similar case involving Medicaid, the federal trial court in Connecticut struck down a state regulation that restricted the provision of home health services to those offered actually only in homes (*Skubel v. Sullivan*, 1996). In a class action suit, where officials denied the requests of students who needed round-the-clock nursing services for benefits at schools and on transportation vehicles, the court held that the state regulation implementing Medicaid impermissibly interpreted the law as preventing children from receiving needed services for which they were qualified.

As far-reaching as their duties may be, insurance companies are not required to provide or pay for services that are educational in nature. Companies are also not obligated to pay for services that are not within the terms of their policies. For instance, in New York, a state court noted that a school for children with dyslexia was an academic institution and not a hospital as defined by the parents' insurance policy (*Schonfeld v. Aetna Life Insurance and Annuity Company*, 1993). The court was convinced that where the school and the program it provided were not medically approved or recognized as a method for remediating dyslexia, an insurance company was not responsible for a student's tuition.

On the other hand, the IDEA's guarantee that special education services are to be provided at no cost to parents means that they cannot be forced to use their insurance policies to pay for benefits that their children should otherwise have received if using them imposes a cost on the parents. In one such situation, a federal trial court in Iowa ordered an insurance carrier to reimburse parents for the costs of an independent evaluation of their son (*Raymond S. v. Ramirez*, 1996). Insofar as the parents' policy included a lifetime cap that was reduced by the amount of the evaluation, the court explained that parents would have suffered a financial loss because using their insurance to pay for the evaluation would have decreased their available lifetime coverage under their policy. However, the court also directed the parents to reimburse the company for the costs of the evaluations that were not covered by their policy.

DISBURSEMENT OF FEDERAL FUNDS

The United States Department of Education (USDOE) disburses federal special education funds to local school boards through state education agencies (SEAs). SEAs may then delegate responsibility for disbursement to their chief school officers. In a case from Louisiana, when the state Board of Elementary and Secondary Education disagreed with the Superintendent of Education's disbursement of IDEA funds, officials notified the USDOE of their concerns. Following an audit, the USDOE agreed that funds were misapplied and ordered the SEA to refund $700,000. The SEA objected because its officials had not actually disbursed the funds but only passed them on to local school systems. Even so, the Fifth Circuit affirmed that since the SEA was the actual recipient of the funds, it was responsible for overseeing their expenditure (*Louisiana State Board of Elementary and Secondary Education v. United States Department of Education*, 1989).

Congress has never fully funded the IDEA (Ilg & Russo, 2004). Yet, the IDEA provides that federal funds are to be used to assist school boards in providing special education and related services to students with disabilities (20 U.S.C. § 1411(a)(1)). In an important limitation, IDEA funds may not be used to supplant state funds for special education (20 U.S.C. § 1412(a)(17)(C)). In such a dispute, the Ninth Circuit held that this provision requires states to maintain fiscal effort, even if officials must reallocate funds in doing so (*State of Washington v. U.S. Department of Education*, 1990). If costs decline, the court posited, funds must be used to provide new programs that school boards previously could not have afforded. According to the court, the only exceptions to the maintenance of expenditures requirement exist when there are decreases in enrollments or if there were unusual expenditures in the previous years.

In another issue with regard to funding, the Fourth Circuit was of the view that the IDEA requires hearings whenever the USDOE attempts to discontinue funding to SEAs based on perceived violations of the statute (*Virginia Department of Education v. Riley,* 1994). The USDOE withheld fifty million dollars in Virginia's IDEA funds because, in its opinion, the commonwealth's plan included a regulation that was incompatible with the IDEA. When officials in Virginia failed to change the regulation, the USDOE withheld federal funds pending a hearing. In ruling that notice and a hearing were required before the funds were actually withheld, the Fourth Circuit commented, "It seems only proper that a department which so emphasizes procedural fairness on the part of states would exercise that same fairness in its dealings with them" (p. 86).

POLICY LETTERS

As indicated in the first chapter of this book, special education is governed by statutes, regulations, and court decisions. In addition, from time to time the USDOE issues policy letters that clarify administrative regulations or provide interpretations of what federal law requires. Policy letters may be issued in response to questions raised by parents, state or local school board officials, or other interested parties. These letters are published in the *Federal Register* and are reproduced by several loose-leaf law reporting services. While courts often refer to these policy letters for guidance in interpreting the IDEA's requirements, questions arise as to the amount of authority that these advisories carry. For the most part, courts will consider an agency's interpretation of its own rules, but a policy letter does not carry the same weight as other traditional canons of statutory interpretation, such as a statute's legislative history.

The Seventh Circuit found that a policy letter issued by the USDOE concerning its interpretation of requirements for providing services to students with disabilities was an interpretive rule not subject to the Administrative Procedures Act's (APA) (2005) notice and comment requirements (*Metropolitan School District of Wayne Township v. Davila,* 1992). The APA outlines public notice procedures that must be followed if a federal agency promulgates a legislative rule. The court concluded that the letter was not a legislative rule but, rather, was advisory insofar as it simply stated what the USDOE thought that the IDEA required.

PROGRAMS FOR INFANTS AND TODDLERS

In 1986 Congress passed one of its more expansive amendments to the IDEA by creating a discretionary grant program to assist states in providing special education services to children with disabilities from birth through the age of two (Education of the Handicapped Amendments, 1986). The purpose of these grants, as contained in what is now known as Part C of the IDEA, is to provide financial assistance to states "to develop and implement a statewide, comprehensive, coordinated, multidisciplinary, interagency system that provides early intervention services for infants and toddlers with disabilities and their families" (20 U.S.C. § 1431(b)(1)).

States and local school boards must thus use the grants to provide direct services and support services to eligible children and their families. Children with high probability of experiencing substantial developmental delays without early intervention services are eligible under this part (20 U.S.C. § 1432(1)). Eligible infants and toddlers are those who are experiencing developmental delay in one or more of the following areas: physical development, cognitive development, communication development, social or emotional development, or adaptive development (20 U.S.C. § 1432(1)(4)(C)).

The infant and toddler legislation specifies that officials must develop written individualized family service plans (IFSPs) for all eligible children (20 U.S.C. § 1436). IFSPs are similar to IEPs except that they also address the needs of the families of children with disabilities. IFSPs should be developed after multidisciplinary assessments of the unique strengths and needs of infants or toddlers and an identification of services appropriate to meeting those needs. In addition, agency officials must conduct assessments of the resources, priorities, and concerns of the families in order to identify the supports and services that would be needed to enhance their abilities to meet the developmental needs of infants or toddlers with disabilities. For the most part, standards for judging the appropriateness of IFSPs are similar to those for IEPs (*Wagner v. Short*, 1999).

Insofar as the preschool amendment calls for interagency cooperation in the delivery of services to infants, toddlers, and their families, the IDEA maintains that all families must be assigned individuals who are responsible for coordinating services across agency lines (20 U.S.C. § 1436((d)(7)). Coordinators are to provide a single point of contact to help parents obtain the services and assistance they need and to provide an ongoing process to assist families in gaining access to early intervention services. The IDEA's infant and toddler provisions also contain procedural safeguards similar to those found in Part B for school-age students with disabilities and their parents (20 U.S.C. § 1439). Even though several agencies may be involved in providing services to infants or toddlers, SEAs are ultimately accountable for their delivery.

REPORT CARDS AND TRANSCRIPTS

Questions often arise over how students with disabilities who are educated predominantly in inclusive settings should be graded. At the same time, questions arise about whether report cards may indicate that students were in special education courses as part of their overall educational programs. Similar questions arise about notations on student transcripts. The USDOE recently issued a policy letter that answers these and other questions (*Letter to Hudler*, 2006). Pursuant to these guidelines:

1. Report cards may indicate that students are receiving special education and related services; however, report cards must also include meaningful explanations of the progress made by students, such as grades.

2. Educators may assign grades based on usual grade-level standards for special education students who participate in regular education classes. Grades for classes with different course content or classes using modified or alternate curricula should be based on standards to reflect progress or the level of achievement for their content.

3. Report cards for students who have IEPs may distinguish between special education programs and general education classes if the course content in the programs is different.

4. Educators may make notations on report cards to distinguish that students worked under modified curricula in general education.

5. Student transcripts may not indicate that children were enrolled in special education programs, received special education, or had disabilities. Even so, transcripts may note that students took classes with modified or alternate curricula.

6. Student transcripts may not mention that children received accommodations in general education classes.

The differences between what is allowed on report cards and on transcripts are due to the different purposes of each record. Report cards are generally provided to parents, who should already be aware of the information. On the other hand, transcripts might be provided to postsecondary admissions offices, prospective employers, or others who do not have a legal right to that information. Educators should keep these distinctions in mind when dealing with these important student records.

❖ **CASE NO. 17—STATE TESTING**

RENE

v.

REED

Court of Appeals of Indiana, 2001

751 N.E.2d 736

OPINION

MATTINGLY-MAY, Judge.

   Meghan Rene and certain other students with disabilities ("the Students") who were or are required to pass the Indiana graduation qualifying examination ("the GQE") brought a class action against Dr. Suellen Reed as Indiana Superintendent of Public Instruction ("the State"). They sought declaratory and injunctive relief, alleging the State violated their due process rights by imposing the GQE as a condition of high school graduation because the State had not previously required disabled students to meet the standards the State had implemented to prepare students for the GQE. Therefore, the Students say, it did not necessarily expose them to some of the material tested on the GQE. The Students also assert the State violated the Individuals with Disabilities Education Act (IDEA) because they were denied certain test-taking adaptations and modifications required for them pursuant to the IDEA. The trial court entered judgment for the State, and we affirm.

FACTS

   . . . The Complaint, filed by their parents on the Students' behalf, set forth claims under 42 U.S.C. § 1983 and the Individuals with Disabilities Education Act, . . . ("IDEA"). The Students, . . . claim that the Appellee/Defendant, Dr. Suellen Reed (Dr. Reed), in her official capacity as Indiana State Superintendent of Public Instruction, violated their due process rights under the United States Constitution and the Indiana Constitution by requiring them to take and pass the Graduation Qualifying Examination ("GQE") when they had previously been exempted from standardized testing and/or had not been taught the subject matter on the tests. The Students . . . claim that Dr. Reed violated their rights under the IDEA by requiring them to take the GQE without the testing accommodations and adaptations required by the Students' case conferences and individualized education programs.

   In Indiana, students participate in the Indiana Statewide Testing for Educational Progress (ISTEP) testing program in the third, sixth, eighth and tenth grades. . . . This test measures achievement in mathematics and language arts. . . . The GQE is a portion of the tenth grade ISTEP examination. Subject to two exceptions, all Indiana high school students who wish to receive a high school diploma must take and pass the GQE. . . . This includes students with disabilities. . . .

   . . . Prior to the change in the state statute requiring that students pass the GQE, case conference could indicate that a student with disabilities was excused from taking the GQE or other standardized testing, while still on the diploma track. . . . Prior to the GQE, students with disabilities on the diploma track received a high school diploma if they satisfied the requirements of their IEPs and the general state curriculum requirements, regardless of whether they took the standardized tests. Furthermore, prior to the GQE, there was not a requirement that in order to graduate, a student master the skills that are now tested by the GQE examination. The Students allege that as a result, many students with disabilities who were on a diploma track were not taught the information now tested on the GQE. Indeed, the State has acknowledged that there was no requirement that, prior to the GQE, students with disabilities be taught the skills which are now tested on the graduation examination.

[Meghan Rene] attends Ben Davis High School in Indianapolis, Indiana, and has received special education since the first grade. Prior to the GQE requirement, Meghan had always been excused from standardized testing. Meghan's IEP provided that she was in the diploma program and if she completed all her course work and complied with her IEP, she would receive a diploma. Meghan's IEP further provided that she be excused from standardized testing and also indicated that all tests were to be read to her. Meghan was first informed that she had to take the GQE in the fall of 1997. Meghan first took the exam in the fall of 1997 and the examination was not read to her. Also, Meghan's IEP provided that she be allowed to use a calculator during testing. This accommodation was also disallowed when she took the GQE. Meghan failed the exam, and as of February 1999, had yet to pass the GQE....

DUE PROCESS

. . .

A. Notice of the GQE Requirement

. . .

There was evidence in the case before us to support the trial court's determination that the students had adequate notice of the GQE requirement. The State notes the school districts had at least five years' notice of the GQE requirement, and the Students and their parents had at least three....

Debra P. [v. *Turlington*] and *Anderson v. Banks*, ... support the proposition that three years is sufficient notice. In *Anderson,* two years' notice of a requirement that graduating students would need to demonstrate performance at a ninth-grade level was adequate where, as here, the test could be retaken and remediation was provided. In *Debra P.,* one year of notice was found insufficient where the state had not submitted evidence that the test covered material required to be taught in the classroom. On remand, the injunction was lifted after the state provided such evidence.... We cannot say the trial court erred to the extent it determined the State provided adequate notice that the Students would be subject to the GQE requirement.

B. Exposure to the Curriculum

The Students assert non-disabled students had ten years to prepare for the GQE requirement while the disabled students, who do not learn at a normal rate, had only three.

. . .

The trial court found the Students had been exposed to the curriculum tested on the GQE, and we cannot characterize that finding as clearly erroneous. In its findings of fact, the court noted that state law requires remedial assistance be provided to all students who do not meet the academic standards required to pass the GQE, and stated "Given the multiple remediation opportunities mandated by state law for students who take but do not pass the GQE, the Court finds it implausible that the Plaintiff class was not exposed throughout their high school career to the subjects tested on the GQE." . . .

The Students correctly note there was evidence presented that in order to learn the material tested on the GQE, students must have the appropriate base knowledge from earlier courses and from building blocks that were in place in elementary school. They note that disabled students, by definition, learn at a slower pace than other students. But, they assert, there was evidence that even after the imposition of the GQE requirement, the curriculum for a significant number of disabled students had not been "realigned to the proficiencies tested on the examination."

. . .

INDIVIDUALS WITH DISABILITIES EDUCATION ACT

The trial court made no findings of fact with regard to the students in Class B, who alleged a violation of the IDEA in the form of the State's failure to honor certain modifications and accommodations in the test-taking process. As its only conclusion of law on that issue, the trial court stated the Students had failed to "cite supporting law for their position that the State's policies violate IDEA," . . . and therefore they had not established a *prima facie* case on that issue.

We note initially that the IDEA does not require specific results, but instead it mandates only that disabled students have access to specialized and individualized educational services. Therefore, denial of a diploma to handicapped children who cannot achieve the educational level necessary to pass a standardized graduation exam is not a denial of the "free appropriate public education" the IDEA requires. . . . Further, the imposition of such a standardized exam does not violate the IDEA where, as in the case before us, the exam is not the sole criterion for graduation. . . ." Congress' desire to provide specialized educational services . . . cannot be read as imposing any particular substantive educational standard upon the states." *Board of Educ. of Hendrick Hudson Central Sch. Dist. Westchester County v. Rowley.*

. . . The IEPs of the members of Class B state that the class members are on the diploma track but are to be excused from standardized testing or are to have certain accommodations during testing. While the definition of "free appropriate public education" mandated by the IDEA includes special education that meets the standards of the State educational agency, . . . *Rowley* notes that it "must also comport with the child's IEP. . . ."

Because the State is requiring all the members of Class B to take and pass the GQE without certain adaptations or accommodations, the Students assert the IDEA is violated. "[S]tate procedures which more stringently protect the rights of the handicapped and their parents are consistent with the [IDEA's predecessor statute] and thus enforceable." . . . However, "those [procedures] that merely add additional steps not contemplated in the scheme of the Act are not enforceable." . . . The State, the Students say, accordingly cannot choose to honor some, but not other, of the modifications and adaptations called for in the IEP and cannot require a disabled student to take the GQE if he or she is properly exempted by the case conference.

We cannot say the trial court erred to the extent it determined the State need not honor certain accommodations called for in the Students' IEPs where those accommodations would affect the validity of the test results. The court had evidence before it that the State does permit a number of accommodations typically called for in IEPs. However, the State does not permit accommodations for "cognitive disabilities" that can "significantly affect the meaning and interpretation of the test score." . . .

For example, the State permits accommodations such as oral or sign language responses to test questions, questions in Braille, special lighting or furniture, enlarged answer sheets, and individual or small group testing. By contrast, it prohibits accommodations in the form of reading to the student test questions that are meant to measure reading comprehension, allowing unlimited time to complete test sections, allowing the student to respond to questions in a language other than English, and using language in the directions or in certain test questions that is reduced in complexity.

Neither the Students nor the State have directed us to decisions that directly address whether the IDEA is violated by prohibiting on a standardized graduation exam accommodations for "cognitive disabilities" that are provided for in a student's IEP. However, a number of administrative decisions have addressed one such accommodation—that of providing the services of a reader for a reading comprehension test. In those decisions, Office of Civil Rights hearing officers have found that states could properly require students to take a reading comprehension test without providing the services of a reader. For example, in *Mobile County Bd. of Education*, the hearing officer decided the State could properly deny an accommodation in the form of a reader on the Alabama "exit exam."

The IEP represents "an educational plan developed specifically for the child [that] sets out the child's present educational performance, establishes annual and short-term objectives for improvements in that performance, and describes the specially designed instruction and services that will enable the child to meet those objectives." ... The GQE, by contrast, is an assessment of the outcome of that educational plan. We therefore decline to hold that an accommodation for cognitive disabilities provided for in a student's IEP must necessarily be observed during the GQE, or that the prohibition of such an accommodation during the GQE is necessarily inconsistent with the IEP. We cannot say the trial court erred when it determined the prohibition of certain accommodations did not violate the IDEA.

CONCLUSION

While the Students have an interest protected by due process in fair implementation of the GQE requirement, we cannot say the trial court erred when it found the Students were exposed during their schooling to the subjects tested on the GQE, that they had adequate notice of that graduation requirement, and that the remediation and additional opportunities to take the GQE were an adequate remedy if due process was violated. The trial court further did not err to the extent it found the State's refusal to allow certain test-taking accommodations did not violate the IDEA. Accordingly, we affirm.

Notes

1. It is well settled that before standardized tests can be implemented as diploma requirements, students must be given proper notice. More than one court held that three years is sufficient notice to students. The plaintiffs in *Rene* argued that three years was insufficient, particularly since they generally needed a longer time period to master material due to their special educational needs. Do you think that three years notice is sufficient for high school students with disabilities?

2. Accommodations that allow students to take tests in a different manner, such as large-print versions, are mandatory, but modifications that alter their content are not required. Would reading word problems on mathematics tests to students with learning disabilities alter their content? Would allowing students with learning disabilities extra time to complete multiple-choice tests alter their content?

CASE NO. 18—STATE RESPONSIBILITY TO ENSURE COMPLIANCE WITH THE IDEA

GADSBY

v.

GRASMICK

United States Court of Appeals, Fourth Circuit, 1997

109 F.3d 940

OPINION

HAMILTON, Circuit Judge:

Eric Gadsby and his parents, Carol and John Gadsby, appeal the district court's adverse judgment against them. In their complaint, the Gadsbys allege that the Maryland State Department of Education (MSDE) violated the Individuals with Disabilities Education Act (IDEA), . . . and should be held liable for the costs of Eric's private school placement for the 1993–94 school year. Because the district court incorrectly held that the Gadsbys had no potentially valid cause of action against MSDE, we vacate its judgment in favor of MSDE and remand for further proceedings consistent with this opinion.

I

Because this appeal involves both IDEA and various State statutory and administrative provisions, it is helpful to begin our discussion with an overview of the relevant code provisions before reviewing the particular facts of this dispute.

A

IDEA, known originally as the Education of the Handicapped Act, was enacted to ensure that all children with disabilities have access to a "free appropriate public education" to meet their unique needs. . . . To effectuate this goal, Congress established a three-tiered funding, administration, and implementation scheme, under which the state must submit a plan of compliance to the Secretary of Education which provides federal IDEA funds to the state. The state is then responsible for administering the funds on the state level, including the distribution of federal funds to local education agencies (LEAs) and the implementation of policies and procedures to ensure that each LEA expends the funds in a manner consistent with the purpose and substantive provisions of IDEA. . . . In order to qualify for IDEA funds, each LEA must apply to the state education agency (SEA) and provide certain assurances of compliance with IDEA. . . . The LEA then provides services directly to children with disabilities using the funds obtained from the SEA. . . .

A state wishing to receive funding under IDEA must have in effect a policy assuring all children with disabilities a free appropriate public education and establish specific procedures to ensure compliance with IDEA by both state and local education agencies. . . . Of particular import to this litigation is IDEA's directive to the states to establish policies and procedures for developing and implementing interagency agreements between the SEA and other state and local agencies to define the financial responsibility of each agency for the provision of a free appropriate public education to each child with a disability and to resolve interagency disputes. . . .

The LEA, on the other hand, must apply to the state for funds under IDEA. . . . In the event that an LEA has no program for a free appropriate public education in place or fails to maintain an existing program, [the IDEA] provides a stopgap measure, ensuring the provision of a free appropriate public education:

> Whenever . . . a[n] [LEA] . . . is unable or unwilling to establish and maintain programs of free appropriate public education which meet the requirements established in subsection (a) . . . the [SEA] shall use the payments which would have been available to such [LEA] to provide special education and related services directly to handicapped children residing in the area served by such [LEA]. . . .

Thus, IDEA delegates supervisory authority to the SEA, which is responsible for administering funds, setting up policies and procedures to ensure local compliance with IDEA, and filling in for the LEA by providing services directly to students in need where the LEA is either unable or unwilling to establish and maintain programs in compliance with IDEA. The LEA, on the other hand, is responsible for the direct provision of services under IDEA, including the development of an individualized education program (IEP) for each disabled student, the expenditure of IDEA funds to establish programs in compliance with IDEA, and the maintenance of records and the supply of information to the SEA as needed to enable the SEA to function effectively in its supervisory role under IDEA.

Although the SEA's role under IDEA is primarily supervisory, [the IDEA] places the ultimate responsibility for the provision of a free appropriate public education to each student on the SEA:

The State educational agency shall be responsible for assuring that the requirements of this subchapter are carried out and that all educational programs for handicapped children within the State, including all such programs administered by any other State or local agency, will be under the general supervision of the persons responsible for educational programs for handicapped children in the State educational agency and shall meet education standards of the State educational agency. This paragraph shall not be construed to limit the responsibility of agencies other than educational agencies in a State from providing or paying for some or all of the costs of a free appropriate public education to be provided handicapped children in the State. . . .

B

Eric Gadsby, a seventeen-year-old with learning disabilities, is a resident of the City of Baltimore. Although Eric attended a private day school through the eighth grade, in May 1993, Eric and his parents requested that the Baltimore City Public Schools (BCPS) evaluate Eric for special education services. By the beginning of the 1993–94 school year, however, BCPS had failed to develop an individualized education program (IEP) for Eric, as required by IDEA, . . . and the Gadsbys enrolled Eric in the Forman School, a private residential school in Connecticut.

BCPS developed its first IEP for Eric on October 13, 1993. Under the IEP proposed by BCPS, Eric would attend regular public school classes for twenty hours a week and receive ten hours of special education services a week.

In November 1993, the Gadsbys challenged the proposed IEP and requested a local due process hearing. . . . Prior to the hearing, the Gadsbys and BCPS agreed to settle their dispute. Under the terms of their settlement, BCPS agreed to pay the portion of Eric's tuition at the Forman School that the LEA is required to pay under Maryland's [education statutes], and the Gadsbys agreed not to proceed with the local due process hearing. . . . BCPS also agreed to apply to MSDE for "its approval and contribution for the remainder of the tuition." . . . Finally, BCPS agreed to "stay neutral" if there was a dispute between the Gadsbys and MSDE or either of the coordinating councils. At no time prior to the hearing request or during the course of settlement negotiations was MSDE made aware of the Gadsbys' situation.

On April 19, 1994, BCPS submitted Eric's application for State funding to MSDE. MSDE officials determined that the BCPS application contained serious deficiencies preventing its consideration. Therefore, on May 9, 1994, MSDE returned the application without decision, giving two specific reasons: (1) the State statute providing for reimbursement of private tuition by MSDE did not apply because a settlement had been reached between BCPS and the Gadsbys concerning the financial responsibility of each party for Eric's Forman School placement; and (2) prior approval by both the LCC and the SCC was required for all out-of-state residential placements, . . . MSDE specifically referred BCPS to a May 1992 directive from Nancy Grasmick, State Superintendent of Schools, in which Ms. Grasmick stated that MSDE would not accept applications for approval of placements in unapproved programs. Instead, according to MSDE's letter to BCPS, an LEA that enters into an agreement concerning the placement of a child in an unapproved program may have to bear the full cost of such a placement. In its letter to BCPS explaining its position, MSDE stated that either BCPS should submit its application for approval of Eric's out-of-state residential placement to the LCC, as required for approval of an out-of-state residential placement, . . .

MSDE did not send a copy of the May 9 letter to the Gadsbys or otherwise notify the Gadsbys of its refusal to consider BCPS's application on behalf of Eric. However, on May 23, 1994, counsel for BCPS sent a copy of the letter to the Gadsbys' counsel.

Following the return of its application from MSDE, BCPS submitted its application to the LCC. On June 17, 1994, the LCC held a meeting to consider the application. Although the Gadsbys had been informed of the meeting and invited to attend, they did not attend. The LCC rejected the application, finding that based on BCPS's description of Eric's needs, he did not need the level of care provided by a residential treatment center and, therefore, was not eligible for a residential placement.

On September 26, 1994, the Gadsbys filed an administrative appeal under IDEA, challenging MSDE's return of BCPS's tuition reimbursement application. . . . A three-member Maryland State Department of Education Hearing Review Board (Board) convened to consider the Gadsbys' appeal. . . .

On October 31, 1994, the parties submitted the following stipulated facts:

(1) Eric Gadsby was placed at the Forman School unilaterally by his parents in September 1993.

(2) After the Gadsbys requested that Eric be screened by BCPS in May 1993, BCPS committed serious procedural violations in its development of Eric's individualized education program (IEP), which deprived Eric of any public educational opportunities for the 1993–94 school year.

(3) Until BCPS submitted an application for State funding of Eric's 1993–94 Forman School placement in April 1994, the Maryland State Department of Education (MSDE) had never been informed of any issue concerning Eric's educational program, nor had MSDE been consulted as to the terms of the settlement agreement reached by BCPS and the Gadsbys in February 1994.

(4) BCPS failed to meet State statutory conditions for obtaining State funding of Eric's out-of-state residential placement in submitting the funding application to MSDE in April 1994.

(5) Eric received educational benefits at the Forman School during the 1993–94 school year.

(6) The Forman School is not approved for State special education funding and has not been found by MSDE to meet State and federal special education standards or otherwise provide an appropriate education to students with disabilities, as defined by federal and State special education statutes and regulations. . . .

The Board issued its decision on January 6, 1995. The first issue it considered was whether IDEA applied to the dispute. At the hearing, MSDE first argued that IDEA did not apply to the dispute because the dispute was between an LEA and an SEA regarding the SEA's decision to fund or not to fund a particular out-of-state placement. According to MSDE, IDEA does not require an SEA to reimburse an LEA for a private school placement, and, therefore, IDEA should not even apply. The Board concluded that IDEA applied to the dispute, however, because, ultimately, the dispute concerned the deprivation of a public educational opportunity for Eric and the funding of that education, matters clearly encompassed by IDEA.

Having determined that the provisions of IDEA applied to the dispute, the Board next considered whether MSDE had complied with the statutory notice requirements under IDEA when it returned BCPS's application concerning reimbursement for Eric's private school tuition. . . . The Gadsbys argued that MSDE had failed to comply with IDEA's notice requirement when it returned BCPS's application on behalf of Eric without providing any notice of its decision to the Gadsbys. The Board found that at the time that MSDE returned BCPS's application on behalf of Eric, it had sufficient information upon which to base its refusal to consider the application and to provide the Gadsbys with an explanation supporting its action. Because MSDE had failed to give the Gadsbys any notice of the denial, the Board concluded that MSDE had violated the notice provisions of IDEA. The Board found that MSDE's procedural violations effectively denied Eric a free appropriate public education under IDEA and, therefore, MSDE was responsible for its portion of Eric's private school placement. . . .

On March 29, 1995, the Gadsbys filed suit against Walter G. Amprey, Superintendent of BCPS; Nancy S. Grasmick, MSDE Superintendent; and MSDE in the United States District Court for the District of Maryland, seeking to enforce the Board's decision. On April 21, 1995, Amprey filed a motion to dismiss, asserting that BCPS had fulfilled its obligations under the settlement agreement and that it was not a party to the proceeding before the Board. On April 24, 1995, MSDE and Grasmick filed an answer and counterclaim, seeking to reverse the Board's decision and dismissal of the complaint.

On August 2, 1995, the district court entered its opinion and order granting Amprey's motion to dismiss and reversing and vacating the Board's decision. The district court stated that because there was no dispute as to any material fact regarding either the complaint or the counterclaim, it would resolve Amprey's motion to dismiss, as well as the merits of the dispute.

The district court first recognized that, under IDEA, BCPS was obligated to provide Eric with a free appropriate public education. The district court noted that under IDEA, if parents and the LEA disagree about the services a child needs, there is an elaborate set of administrative and judicial review procedures which exist under federal and State law. In this case, the district court noted that the Gadsbys and BCPS decided not to pursue this review process, but rather they resolved their dispute privately. The district court found that because the Gadsbys settled with BCPS, MSDE was never given the opportunity to evaluate whether Eric was entitled to a residential placement under IDEA. Therefore, MSDE's decision to return the application to BCPS did not relate to whether Eric was entitled to a residential placement under IDEA, but rather related only to whether BCPS could receive a State subsidy for the placement. According to the district court, MSDE's refusal to consider Eric's initial application was merely its insistence that BCPS, like other LEAs, follow statutorily required procedures when asking for State reimbursement for residential placements. The district court concluded the MSDE did not need to inform the Gadsbys of its decision. Therefore, the district court held that the Board was erroneous as a matter of law and that Eric and his parents had no valid cause of action against any defendant. The district court then granted defendant Amprey's motion to dismiss and vacated the Board's decision.

On August 14, 1995, the Gadsbys filed a motion to alter or amend the district court's order ... In their motion, the Gadsbys argued, *inter alia,* that the district court did not address their facial challenge to Maryland's process for approving residential placements for children with disabilities.

On February 6, 1996, the district court entered a second opinion and order denying the Gadsbys' motion to alter or amend its previous order. The district court stated that in their motion the Gadsbys merely reargued matters previously litigated. With regard to the Gadsbys' facial challenge to Maryland's procedural mechanism for approving residential placements, the district court stated that while not explicitly addressed in its previous order, this argument was implicitly rejected. The district court noted that it found in its previous order that MSDE's decision related only to whether BCPS could receive a subsidy from MSDE, not to whether Eric was entitled to a residential placement under IDEA, and concluded, therefore, that IDEA's procedural requirements did not apply to MSDE's refusal to consider Eric's application. According to the district court, it follows from this conclusion that IDEA does not apply to Maryland's procedure for evaluating LEA applications for discretionary State subsidies. Because it had implicitly rejected the Gadsbys' facial challenge to Maryland's process for approving residential placements in its previous order, the district court denied their motion to alter its previous order on this basis.

Also on February 6, 1996, the district court entered its judgment against the Gadsbys, reversing and vacating the Board's decision and dismissing all of the Gadsbys' claims with prejudice. The Gadsbys noted a timely appeal.

II

On appeal, the Gadsbys argue that they are entitled to reimbursement for the remainder of Eric's Forman School tuition from MSDE because: (1) the State of Maryland failed to provide Eric a free appropriate public education as required by IDEA; and (2) MSDE violated IDEA's notice provisions when it denied reimbursement for Eric's Forman School tuition without notice to the Gadsbys, thereby violating Eric's right to a free appropriate public education. After setting forth the appropriate standard of review, we address each argument in turn.

A

The district court in this case granted defendant Walter G. Amprey's motion to dismiss, . . . and rendered judgment in favor of all defendants based on the parties' stipulated facts. At the time that it entered its opinion and order dismissing the Gadsbys' claims against all defendants, only defendant Amprey had filed a motion to dismiss. All parties had briefed the merits of their respective positions, however, and, as stated above, the district court relied on the facts as stipulated for the Board hearing in resolving the dispute. . . .

B

As set forth above, IDEA requires states to provide a free appropriate public education to all of its children with disabilities. . . . There is no dispute in this case that the LEA failed to develop an IEP for Eric Gadsby prior to the beginning of the 1993–94 school year, thus violating IDEA. . . . The dispute, rather, revolves around the remedy for the violation. . . .

. . . [T]he remedy ordered by the Board in this case—reimbursement of Eric's private school tuition—is an appropriate remedy under IDEA where the LEA fails to develop an appropriate IEP by the beginning of the school year. The Gadsbys assert, however, not only that they are entitled to reimbursement for the costs of Eric's Forman School tuition, but also that MSDE must pay the portion of the reimbursement funds that the LEA did not pay pursuant to their settlement. The Gadsbys assert, first, that MSDE is ultimately responsible under IDEA for the provision of a free appropriate public education to all students with disabilities in the State of Maryland. Second, the Gadsbys assert that under State law MSDE is required to contribute a portion of the reimbursement costs. . . . MSDE responds, however, that its duty to contribute to the reimbursement of a student's private school tuition depends on the LEA's compliance with State law. MSDE argues that because the application for reimbursement came from the LEA and the LEA failed to comply with MSDE requirements, it had no obligation to grant the LEA's application for reimbursement on Eric's behalf. . . . According to MSDE, because the LEA violated IDEA in this case, the parents must assert their claim for reimbursement against the LEA, not the SEA. Thus, MSDE argues that where the parents have settled with the LEA, they cannot turn to the SEA for the remainder of the tuition.

The first issue in this case, then, is whether the Gadsbys may assert a cause of action against MSDE for reimbursement of the cost of Eric's tuition at the Forman School based on BCPS's failure to develop an appropriate IEP for Eric, where: (1) BCPS's application on behalf of Eric failed to comply with State law requirements for the approval of an out-of-state private placement; and (2) the Gadsbys have already settled with the LEA, *i.e.*, BCPS, for a portion of these costs and released BCPS from any further liability. In resolving this issue, our first task is to determine whether an SEA may ever be held liable for the failure to provide a free appropriate public education to a child with a disability within its jurisdiction. If we determine that an SEA may be held liable, our next task is to determine the impact of Maryland's laws and regulations on an MSDE's potential liability-that is, whether MSDE may avoid liability for reimbursement costs otherwise appropriate under *Burlington* and *Carter* by arguing that BCPS failed to comply with Maryland's laws and regulations established to comply with IDEA. Finally, as between the LEA and the SEA, we must decide under what circumstances an SEA may be held liable for the reimbursement costs of a child's private school tuition, where the parents or guardians of the child are entitled to reimbursement . . .

2

The first question we must address to resolve the issue of MSDE's liability for the failure to develop an IEP for Eric is whether an SEA may ever be held liable where there is a failure to provide a free appropriate public education to a particular child within its jurisdiction. . . .

3

In answering the first question, whether an SEA may be held responsible for the failure to provide a particular child with a free appropriate public education, "[w]e begin, as we must, by examining the statutory language." . . . This language suggests that, ultimately, it is the SEA's responsibility to ensure that each child within its jurisdiction is provided a free appropriate public education. Therefore, it seems clear that an SEA may be held responsible if it fails to comply with its duty to assure that IDEA's substantive requirements are implemented.

This conclusion is further supported by [the IDEA], which provides that where an LEA is either unable or unwilling to establish and maintain programs for the provision of a free appropriate public education, "the [SEA] shall use the payments which would have been available to such [LEA] to provide special education and related services directly to handicapped children residing in the area served by such [LEA]." . . . Under this provision, once an LEA is either unable or unwilling to establish and maintain programs in compliance with IDEA, the SEA is responsible for directly providing the services to disabled children in the area. . . . It follows, therefore, that the SEA in such a case could be held liable if it fails to provide those services.

Our conclusion that an SEA may be held liable under IDEA where the state fails to provide a free appropriate public education to a child with a disability is buttressed by the legislative history of [the IDEA]. This legislative history indicates that [the state responsibility clause] was included in the statute to "assure a single line of responsibility with regard to the education of handicapped children." . . . Therefore, we hold that the SEA is ultimately responsible for the provision of a free appropriate public education to all of its students and may be held liable for the state's failure to assure compliance with IDEA.

    . . .

5

Finally, we address the question of when an SEA, as opposed to an LEA, may be held liable for the reimbursement costs of a child's private school tuition, where the parents or guardians of the child are entitled to reimbursement. . . . The Gadsbys assert that an SEA may under any circumstance be held liable where a disabled child is not provided with a free appropriate public education and the parents unilaterally place the child in a private program. MSDE argues, however, that because the LEA has the duty to develop an IEP for each child, only the LEA is liable for reimbursement costs where it fails to fulfill that duty.

Because the remedy of reimbursement for private school tuition is an equitable remedy imposed at the discretion of the district court and held to be appropriate by the Supreme Court . . . there is no statutory language specifically authorizing such a remedy, much less designating what governmental entity must pay the costs of reimbursement and when. Therefore, we "must examine the statute as a whole, giving due weight to design, structure, and purpose as well as to aggregate language." . . .

There is nothing in either the language or the structure of IDEA that limits the district court's authority to award reimbursement costs against the SEA, the LEA, or both in any particular case. By contrast, both the language and the structure of IDEA suggest that either or both entities may be held liable for the failure to provide a free appropriate public education, as the district court deems appropriate after considering all relevant factors. . . .

One relevant factor to be considered by the district court in fashioning relief is the relative responsibility of each agency for the ultimate failure to provide a child with a free appropriate public education. It may well be the case that in some instances it would be unfair to hold the SEA liable for reimbursement costs of private school tuition, where the LEA was primarily responsible for the failure. On the other hand, there may be cases in which it would be unfair to hold the LEA liable for costs, where, for example, there was no appropriate facility within the LEA's jurisdiction for the child and the SEA failed to provide an alternative. . . .

We disagree, then, both with MSDE, which asserts that an SEA can never be held liable for an LEA's failure to develop an IEP, and with the Gadsbys, who assert that an SEA should always be held liable for an LEA's failure to provide a free appropriate public education, regardless of the particular circumstances of the case. Instead, we hold, . . . that district courts have broad discretion in granting appropriate relief under IDEA. This relief may include an award of reimbursement of private school tuition against the SEA, the LEA, or both. This relief may only be awarded, however, after the district court considers all relevant factors in fashioning appropriate equitable relief.

6

Applying these principles to the facts of this case, we hold that the district court erred when it held that MSDE could not be held liable in this case because its decision to return BCPS's application on behalf of Eric implicated only State law, not IDEA. As established above, an SEA may be held liable for the reimbursement of a child's private school tuition under IDEA, even if state law requirements regarding the approval of the private placement are not met. In addition, an SEA may be held liable for reimbursement costs, even where the LEA fails to develop an appropriate IEP for the child.

Because the district court erred in holding that MSDE could not be held liable under IDEA, we must remand the case for the district court to determine what, if any, relief is appropriate. In so doing, the district court should consider all relevant factors, including the relative responsibility of each agency involved in the failure to provide Eric with a free appropriate public education and, if the court determines that the award of reimbursement costs of Eric's Forman School tuition is appropriate, the reasonable level of reimbursement that should be awarded. We note that the district court is free to hold MSDE, BCPS, or both agencies liable as it deems appropriate after considering all relevant factors.

. . .

III

For the reasons set forth above, we vacate the district court's judgment in favor of MSDE and remand the matter to the district court for further proceedings consistent with this opinion.

VACATED AND REMANDED FOR FURTHER PROCEEDINGS.

Notes

1. The Fourth Circuit ruled that the state of Maryland was responsible for paying a portion of the reimbursement award that the parents received in making a unilateral private placement. Would a state be responsible for providing special education services in the first place if a local school board defaulted on its obligation?

2. Is a state educational agency responsible for monitoring local school boards to make sure they are in compliance with all of the IDEA's myriad requirements? What if state officials fail in their duty? Should they be sanctioned?

REFERENCES

Administrative Procedures Act, 5 U.S.C. § 553 (2005).

Allstate Insurance Company v. Bethlehem Area School District, 678 F. Supp. 1132 (E.D. Pa. 1987).

Anderson v. Banks, 520 F. Supp. 472 (S.D. Ga. 1981), *modified,* 540 F. Supp. 761 (S.D. Ga. 1982).

Board of Education of Northport-East Northport Union Free School District v. Ambach, 469 N.Y.S.2d 699 (N.Y. 1983).

Brookhart v. Illinois State Board of Education, 697 F.2d 179 (7th Cir. 1983).

Corey H. v. Board of Education of the City of Chicago, 995 F. Supp. 900 (N.D. Ill. 1998).

Debra P. v. Turlington, 730 F.2d 1405 (11th Cir. 1984).

Department of Education, State of Hawaii v. Cari Rae S., 158 F. Supp. 1190 (D. Haw. 2001).

Detsel v. Sullivan, 895 F.2d 58 (2d Cir. 1990).

Education of the Handicapped Amendments, P.L. 99–457 (1986).

Gadsby v. Grasmick, 109 F.3d 940 (4th Cir. 1997).

Gehman v. Prudential Property and Casualty Insurance Company, 702 F. Supp. 1192 (E.D. Pa. 1989).

Hicks ex rel. Hicks v. Purchase Line School District, 251 F. Supp.2d 1250 (W.D. Pa. 2003).

Ilg, T. J., & Russo C. J. (2004). Funding and special education and the IDEA: Promises, promises. In K. DeMoss & K. Wong (Eds.), *Money, politics, and law: Intersections and conflicts in the provision of educational opportunity.* Annual yearbook of the American Education Finance Association (pp. 101–113). New York: Eye on Education.

Individuals with Disabilities Education Act, 20 U.S.C. §§ 1400–1482 (2005).

Leighty v. Laurel School District, 457 F. Supp.2d 546 (W.D. Pa. 2006).

Letter to Hudler, United States Department of Education, Office for Civil Rights, 2006.

Louisiana State Board of Elementary and Secondary Education v. United States Department of Education, 881 F.2d 204 (5th Cir. 1989).

M.A. ex rel. E.S. v. State-Operated School District of Newark, 344 F.3d 335 (3d Cir. 2003).

Metropolitan School District of Wayne Township v. Davila, 969 F.2d 485 (7th Cir. 1992).

No Child Left Behind Act, 20 U.S.C. §§ 6301–7941 (2002).

Raymond S. v. Ramirez, 918 F. Supp. 1280 (N.D. Iowa 1996).

Reid v. District of Columbia, 310 F. Supp.2d 137 (D.D.C. 2004), *reversed on other grounds,* 401 F.3d 516 (D.C. Cir. 2005).

Rene v. Reed, 751 N.E.2d 736 (Ind. Ct. App. 2001).

Schonfeld v. Aetna Life Insurance and Annuity Company, 593 N.Y.S.2d 250 (N.Y. App. Div. 1993).

Skubel v. Sullivan, 925 F. Supp. 930 (D. Conn. 1996).

St. Tammany Parish School Board v. State of Louisiana, 142 F.3d 776 (5th Cir. 1998).

State of Washington v. U.S. Department of Education, 905 F.2d 274 (9th Cir. 1990).

Virginia Department of Education v. Riley, 23 F.3d 80 (4th Cir. 1994), *reversed on other grounds en banc,* 106 F.3d 559 (4th Cir. 1997).

Wagner v. Short, 63 F. Supp.2d 672 (D. Md. 1999).

10

Antidiscrimination Statutes

❖

Key Concepts in This Chapter
❖ Interaction of Various Laws
❖ Discrimination Claims
❖ Otherwise Qualified
❖ Reasonable Accommodations

As noted earlier, in addition to the Individuals with Disabilities Education Act (IDEA) (2005), the rights of students with disabilities are protected under two other significant pieces of legislation. The first law, Section 504 of the Rehabilitation Act of 1973 (Section 504) (2005), which traces its origins back to 1918, a time when the American government sought to provide rehabilitation services for military veterans of World War I, was the first federal civil rights statute protecting the rights of the disabled. According to Section 504, which is codified as part of federal labor law rather than education law, "[n]o otherwise qualified individual with a disability . . . shall, solely by reason of her or his disability, be excluded from participation in, be denied the benefits of, or be subjected to discrimination under any program or activity receiving Federal financial assistance" (29 U.S.C. § 794). Section 504 effectively prohibits recipients of federal financial assistance, public and nonpublic, from discriminating against individuals with disabilities in the provision of services or employment.

The second statute, the Americans with Disabilities Act (ADA), was enacted in 1990 "to provide a comprehensive national mandate for the elimination of discrimination against individuals with disabilities" (42 U.S.C. § 12101(b)(2)). Congress expanded the scope of Section 504's coverage by passing the ADA to provide protection to individuals with disabilities throughout society (*Vande Zande v. State of Wisconsin Department of Administration*, 1994). While the ADA effectively extends the protections of Section 504 to the private sector, it has not had a major effect on the delivery of a free appropriate public education (FAPE) under the IDEA. Instead, the ADA's greatest impact has been on the employment of individuals with disabilities. Moreover, while the ADA, like Section 504, prohibits discrimination against individuals on the basis of their disabilities, it does not require the delivery of a FAPE (Wenkart, 1993). The IDEA still remains the major statute that guarantees a student's right to receive a free appropriate public education. In light of the broad range of protections that Section 504 and the ADA provide, this chapter examines the key provisions of these statutes.

ELIGIBILITY

It is important to keep in mind that while Section 504 covers not only children but also employees, parents, and others who visit schools, like the ADA, it does so without any age restrictions. Even so, this book focuses on the rights of students. Section 504 defines an individual with a disability as one "who (i) has a physical or mental impairment which substantially limits one or more of such person's major life activities, (ii) has a record of such an impairment, or (iii) is regarded as having such an impairment (29 U.S.C.A. § 706(7)(B))." The regulations define physical or mental impairments as including

(A) any physiological disorder or condition, cosmetic disfigurement, or anatomical loss affecting one or more of the following body systems: neurological; musculoskeletal; special sense organs; respiratory, including speech organs; cardiovascular; reproductive, digestive, genito-urinary; hemic and lymphatic; skin; and endocrine; or

(B) any mental or psychological disorder, such as mental retardation, organic brain syndrome, emotional or mental illness, and specific learning disorders. (45 C.F.R. § 84.3(j)(2)(i), 34 C.F.R. § 104.3(j)(2)(i))

A note accompanying this list indicates that it merely provides examples of the types of impairments that are covered; it is not meant to be exhaustive.

In order to have records of impairment, individuals must have histories of, or been identified as having, mental or physical impairments that substantially limit one or more major life activities. As defined in one of Section 504's regulations, individuals who are regarded as having impairments are those who have

(A) a physical or mental impairment that does not substantially limit major life activities but that is treated by a recipient as constituting such a limitation; (B) a physical or mental impairment that substantially limits major life activities only as a result of the attitudes of others toward such impairment; or (C) none of the impairments . . . but is treated by a recipient as having such an impairment. (34 C.F.R. § 104.3(j)(2)(iv))

"'Major life activities' means functions such as caring for one's self, performing manual tasks, walking, seeing, hearing, speaking, breathing, learning, and working" (34 C.F.R. § 104.3(j)(2)(ii)). Once students are identified as having disabilities, the next step is to evaluate whether they are "otherwise qualified." In order to be "otherwise qualified," students must be "(i) of an age during which nonhandicapped persons are provided such services, (ii) of any age during which it is mandatory under state law to provide such services to handicapped persons, or (iii) [a student] to whom a state is required to provide a free appropriate public education [under the IDEA] (34 C.F.R. § 104.3(l)(2))." Students who are "otherwise qualified," meaning that they are eligible to participate in programs or activities despite the existence of impairments, must be permitted to take part in programs or activities as long as it is possible to do so by means of "reasonable accommodations" (34 C.F.R. § 104.39).

Once identified, qualified students are entitled to an appropriate public education, regardless of the nature or severity of their impairments. In order to guarantee eligible children an appropriate education, Section 504's regulations include due process requirements for evaluation and placement similar to those under the IDEA (34 C.F.R. § 104.36). In making modifications for students, as discussed in greater detail later in this chapter, educators must provide aid, benefits, and/or services that are comparable to those available to children who do not have impairments.

Students with severe disabilities may sometimes require special education classes or other services that are not offered in the general education environment. Whenever students must be removed from regular classes to receive programming, the services have to be provided in facilities that are comparable to those provided for the education of peers who do not have impairments. For example, a federal trial court in Pennsylvania found that the commonwealth's Secretary of Education violated Section 504 by failing to ensure that the educational facilities for students with disabilities were comparable to those of peers who did not have disabilities (*Hendricks v. Gilhool*, 1989). The court emphasized that the facilities did not have to be precisely equivalent but observed that in this instance they were substantially unequal. The court ruled that officials violated Section 504 when they relocated special education classes to lesser facilities to accommodate classes for students without disabilities.

In addition to Section 504, the ADA provides a comprehensive federal mandate to eliminate discrimination against people with disabilities and to provide "clear, strong, consistent and enforceable standards" (42 U.S.C.A. § 12101(b)(2)) to this end. The ADA's broad definition of a disability is comparable with the one in Section 504: "(a) a physical or mental impairment that substantially limits one or more of the major life activities; (b) a record of such an impairment; or (c) being regarded as having such an impairment" (§ 12102(2)). Further, as under Section 504, "major life activities" includes "caring for one's self, performing manual tasks, walking, seeing, hearing, speaking, breathing, learning, and working" (34 C.F.R. § 36.104) . The ADA, like Section 504, does not require individuals to have certificates from doctors or psychologists in order to be covered by it, but school officials can ask for proof (Kaesberg & Murray, 1994).

According to the Supreme Court, persons are otherwise qualified for purposes of Section 504 if they are capable of meeting all of a program's requirements in spite of their disabilities (*School Board of Nassau County, Florida v. Arline*, 1987; *Southeastern Community College v. Davis*, 1979). If persons are otherwise qualified, recipients of federal funds are expected to make reasonable accommodations to allow them to participate in programs or activities unless doing so would create undue hardships on the programs (34 C.F.R. § 104.12(a)). As with Section 504, under the ADA otherwise qualified individuals with disabilities must be provided with reasonable accommodations so that they may participate in programs provided by public entities (42 U.S.C. § 12111(9)). Public entities include state and local governments, agencies, and other instrumentalities of a government (42 U.S.C. § 12131(1)). Insofar as schools are public entities under the ADA, they are prohibited from discriminating against individuals with disabilities in much the same way as under Section 504 (42 U.S.C. § 12132). While the ADA includes extensive requirements to provide access to public transportation for the disabled, public school transportation is specifically exempted from these provisions (42 U.S.C. § 12141).

Section 504 offers a degree of protection against discrimination to students who have disabilities but are not eligible to receive services under the IDEA. Under the IDEA students must fall into one of the categories of disabilities outlined within the statute, and must require special education services as a result of that disability, to receive services (20 U.S.C. § 1401(a)(1)(A)). However, the protections of Section 504 reach a much wider population.

One of the best examples of the broader reach of Section 504 involves students with infectious diseases. Under the IDEA, students with infectious diseases are entitled to special education services only if their academic performance is adversely affected by their illnesses (34 C.F.R. § 300.8). Yet, pursuant to Section 504, students with infectious diseases such as HIV/AIDS cannot be discriminated against or excluded from schools unless there is a high risk of transmission of their diseases (*Doe v. Belleville Public School District*, 1987; *Doe v. Dolton Elementary School District*, 1988; *Martinez v. School Board of Hillsborough County*, 1988, 1989; *New York State Association for Retarded Children v. Carey*, 1979; *Ray v. School District of DeSoto County*, 1987; *Thomas v. Atascadero Unified School District*, 1987). A case from a federal trial court in Illinois is illustrative (*Doe v.*

Dolton Elementary School District, 1988). When officials excluded a student from attending regular classes and all extracurricular activities after he was diagnosed as having AIDS, the court decided that he was entitled to the protection of Section 504 because he was regarded as having a physical impairment that substantially interfered with his life activities. The court added that because there was no significant risk that the student would have transmitted AIDS in the classroom setting, the school officials who sought to exclude him violated his rights under Section 504.

The majority of public school students with disabilities are covered by the IDEA, Section 504, and the ADA. For this reason, plaintiffs frequently file suits alleging violations of all three statutes. Generally, courts agree that compliance with the IDEA regarding the provision of a FAPE establishes compliance with Section 504 and the ADA (*Barnett v. Fairfax County School Board,* 1989, 1991; *Cordrey v. Euckert,* 1990; *Doe v. Alabama State Department of Education,* 1990). Still, the IDEA's requirements for a FAPE are more stringent than those under Section 504 (*Colin K. v. Schmidt,* 1983; *Darlene L. v. Illinois Board of Education,* 1983).

When considering differences between the IDEA and Section 504, the federal trial court in Massachusetts went so far as to explain that school officials did not violate the latter when they offered special education services to a student with learning disabilities in a manner that was not procedurally correct (*Puffer v. Raynolds,* 1988). The court reasoned that since the officials offered the services, he was neither discriminated against nor denied the services. Further, the court pointed out that the procedural errors had to be addressed via the IDEA's due process mechanism. Similarly, the Fourth Circuit was of the opinion that a school board did not violate Section 504 by refusing to provide special education services in a student's neighborhood school when the needed services were available in a centralized location (*Barnett v. Fairfax County School Board,* 1991). The court maintained that officials had not discriminated against the student because he was not denied services.

When school systems provide services to students under Section 504 or the ADA, they must be appropriate. In one such case, a federal trial court in New Hampshire posited that a student who alleged that he had not been provided with educational services that adequately addressed his learning disability presented a claim under Section 504 (*I.D. v. Westmoreland School District,* 1992).

Some students who do not qualify for special education services under the IDEA may be eligible for accommodation plans under Section 504 that are discussed later in this chapter. Even so, the different statutes have distinct purposes so that the services that students are entitled to receive may vary under each. A case from the District of Columbia is illustrative. The federal trial court upheld the school board's finding that a student with attention deficit hyperactivity disorder (ADHD) was not eligible for services under IDEA because his educational performance was not adversely affected by his ADHD (*Lyons v. Smith,* 1993). On the other hand, the court was convinced that a hearing officer could have ordered the board to provide special education services to the student, who was designated as otherwise qualified under Section 504 in appropriate circumstances.

The court did emphasize that Section 504 does not require affirmative efforts to overcome the student's disability but simply is designed to prevent discrimination on the basis of the disability. Consequently, in some situations, boards may need to provide special education services to students with disabilities in order to eliminate discrimination.

Concerns also arise as to whether students with disabilities who are incarcerated are entitled to receive special education services (*Green v. Johnson*, 1982). In such a situation, a federal trial court in Illinois indicated that Section 504 is applicable to correctional facilities (*Donnell C. v. Illinois State Board of Education*, 1993). Insofar as correctional facilities receive federal funds to provide educational services to inmates, the court said that they fall within the scope of Section 504.

The major thrust of the ADA has been to extend the protections of Section 504 to the private sector while clarifying other issues by codifying judicial interpretations of the latter. Due to the similarities between the two statutes, compliance with Section 504 generally translates to compliance with the ADA (*Vande Zande v. State of Wisconsin Department of Administration*, 1994). While most suits are filed on the basis of both Section 504 and the ADA, students generally receive no greater relief under the ADA than under Section 504. Of course, in rare situations where the ADA has adopted stricter standards, school boards are required to meet those greater requirements. As such, when school officials make diligent good faith efforts to comply with Section 504, they should not run into difficulty with the ADA (Miles, Russo, & Gordon, 1991).

DISCRIMINATION PROHIBITED

Unlike the IDEA, which requires school officials to identify, assess, and serve students with disabilities, Section 504 and the ADA are antidiscrimination statutes to the extent that they prohibit school officials and others from offering unequal opportunities to qualified individuals. In a case illustrating this principle, the federal trial court in Arizona emphasized that a student did not need to prove that an act of discrimination was intentional in order to present an actionable claim under Section 504 (*Begay v. Hodel*, 1990). According to the court, the failure of school officials to correct a situation that resulted in a denial of access suggested an impermissible disparate impact sufficient to present such a claim under Section 504. When officials failed to correct architectural barriers in the student's high school which, in turn, forced her to attend a school several miles away, causing her to have to commute over poor roads, thereby aggravating her condition, and forcing her to withdraw from school, the court concluded that they violated her rights.

The Second Circuit noted that Section 504 does not require that all students with disabilities receive identical benefits (*P.C. v. McLaughlin*, 1990). Recognizing that courts must allow for professional judgment, the court indicated that a student would have to show that more suitable arrangements were available but were not offered in order to substantiate a discrimination claim under Section 504.

School officials cannot discriminate against students with disabilities on the basis of the means by which they address their impairments. In a case from California, a federal trial court was of the view that as long as the means by which a student addressed her circumstances were reasonable, school officials could not discriminate against her on the basis of how she chose to address her condition (*Sullivan v. Vallejo City Unified School District*, 1990).

As reflected in any number of cases discussed in previous chapters, courts declined to intervene in situations where parents disagreed with the methodologies used in specific placements as long as school officials could demonstrate that their selected approaches were appropriate. In a case from Nebraska, the federal trial court agreed that the ADA does not provide parents with any additional clout regarding the choice of methodology (*Petersen v. Hastings Public Schools*, 1993). The court asserted that since the methodology selected by school officials to instruct students with hearing impairments was no less effective than the one preferred by their parents, it met the requirements of the ADA.

In a noneducation dispute with implications for schools, a federal trial court in Pennsylvania held that although a public entity was not prohibited from providing benefits, services, or advantages to individuals with disabilities or to a particular class of individuals with disabilities beyond those required by the ADA, it could not discriminate in the provision of affirmative services (*Easley v. Snider*, 1993). The court wrote that providing services to persons with physical disabilities while not providing the same to individuals with physical and mental disabilities constituted discrimination since there was no rational reason for excluding those physically disabled individuals who also had mental disabilities from the benefits of the program.

In yet another noneducation case of significance, a federal trial court in Florida acknowledged that the elimination of all recreation programs for individuals with disabilities violated the ADA where similar programs were still offered to those who did not have disabilities (*Concerned Parents to Save Dreher Park Center v. City of West Palm Beach*, 1994). City officials eliminated the programs due to fiscal constraints, but the court wrote that any benefits provided to persons who did not have disabilities had to have been made available on an equal basis to those with disabilities. Therefore, the court thought that since city officials chose to provide recreation services to people who were not disabled, the ADA required them to offer equal opportunities for persons with disabilities.

OTHERWISE QUALIFIED STUDENTS WITH DISABILITIES

In *Southeastern Community College v. Davis* (1979), its first case interpreting the provisions of Section 504, the Supreme Court ruled that in order to be considered otherwise qualified, students with disabilities must be able to participate in programs or activities in spite of their impairments as long as they can do so with reasonable accommodations. Although *Davis* was set in the context of higher education, its implications for elementary and secondary schools are the same: Students must meet all of the usual qualifications for participation. The student who filed suit unsuccessfully challenged her being denied admission to a nursing program because she was hearing impaired and relied on lipreading to understand speech. In upholding the actions of officials who denied the student's application due to safety considerations, the Court reasoned that Section 504 did not require educational institutions to disregard the disabilities of applicants or to make substantial modifications in their programs to allow participation. The Court emphasized that legitimate physical qualifications could be essential to participation in programs.

A federal trial court in Kentucky applied the principles from *Davis* in declaring that a blind student who had multiple disabilities in addition to a visual impairment and was denied admission to the state's school for the blind was not otherwise qualified. The court asserted that since the student did not meet the school's admission criteria that applicants demonstrate the ability for academic and vocational learning, self-care, and independent functioning, he was not entitled to attend (*Eva N. v. Brock*, 1990). While the court agreed that school officials did not have to admit the student, the IDEA still obligated them to provide the student with a FAPE. The Supreme Court of Ohio later upheld the denial of a blind student's application to attend medical school on the ground that the accommodations that she sought were not reasonable because they would have required fundamental alterations to the essential nature of the program and/or since they imposed undue financial or administrative burdens on the school (*Ohio Civil Rights Commission v. Case Western Reserve University*, 1996). Conversely, a federal trial court in Tennessee decreed that a student who suffered from an autoimmune disease was otherwise qualified to attend a private school because she had the necessary academic qualifications (*Thomas v. Davidson Academy*, 1994).

In the area of sports participation, the Seventh Circuit affirmed that when a coach refused to select a student for his high school's basketball team, this did not violate his rights under Section 504 (*Doe v. Eagle-Union Community School Corporation*, 2001a). The court recognized that even though the student had a Section 504 alternative learning plan, he was not selected for the team because the coach did not believe that he was otherwise qualified insofar as he lacked the requisite skill level. The Supreme Court refused to hear a further appeal in the case (*Doe v. Eagle-Union Community School Corporation*, 2001b).

Parents who have disabilities also may exert rights under Section 504 in order to obtain services that allow them to better participate in the educational programs of their children. In such a case, the Second Circuit affirmed that part of a judgment which ordered a school board to provide hearing-impaired parents with the services of a sign-language interpreter so that they could participate in school-related functions (*Rothschild v. Grottenthaler*, 1990). The court was convinced that as parents of students attending the school, they were otherwise qualified to participate in parent-oriented activities but would have been unable to do so without accommodations.

REASONABLE ACCOMMODATIONS

Section 504 and the ADA do not require school boards to disregard completely the disabilities of those who wish to participate in their programs and activities. Boards must allow participation when doing so would require them to make only reasonable accommodations. Officials are not required to make substantial modifications or fundamental alterations to programs and activities (*Southeastern Community College v. Davis* (*Davis*), 1979). The requirement to provide reasonable accommodations to allow individuals with disabilities to participate does not carry with it the duty that boards must lower their standards. Reasonable accommodations do require adaptations to allow access but do not require officials to eliminate essential prerequisites to participation.

Once identified, qualified students are entitled to an appropriate public education, regardless of the nature or severity of their impairments. To guarantee that an appropriate education is made available, Section 504's regulations include due process requirements for evaluation and placement similar to those under the IDEA (34 C.F.R. § 104.36). In making accommodations for students, educators must provide aid, benefits, and/or services that are comparable to those available to children who do not have impairments. Accordingly, qualified students must receive comparable materials, teacher quality, length of school term, and daily hours of instruction. Moreover, programs for qualified children should not be separate from those available to students who are not impaired, unless such segregation is necessary for these children to be successful. While school officials are not prohibited from offering separate programs for students with impairments, these children cannot be required to attend such classes unless they cannot be served adequately in other settings (34 C.F.R. § 104.4(b)(3)). If such programs are offered separately, facilities must, of course, be comparable (34 C.F.R. § 104.34(c)).

Reasonable accommodations may involve minor adjustments, such as providing a hearing interpreter for a student (*Barnes v. Converse College*, 1977), permitting a child to be accompanied by a service dog (*Sullivan v. Vallejo City Unified School District*, 1990), modifying a behavior policy to accommodate a student with an autoimmune disease who was disruptive (*Thomas v. Davidson Academy*, 1994), and/or using nonverbal signals to make a student aware of inappropriate sensory stimulation and giving the student preferred seating in the school lunchroom to minimize environmental influences that might have disrupted the student's ability to concentrate on the task at hand (*Molly L. ex rel. B.L. v. Lower Merion School District*, 2002). At the same time, school officials do not have to grant all requests for accommodation. For example, in addition to the cases discussed below under the defenses to Section 504, a federal trial court in Missouri ruled that school officials did not have to establish a "scent-free" environment for a child with severe asthma because she was not otherwise qualified to participate in its educational program (*Hunt v. St. Peter School*, 1997). The court added that the school's voluntary "scent-free" policy met Section 504's "minor adjustment" standard. Additionally, a federal trial court in Pennsylvania rejected claims that school officials violated the Section 504 rights of a student who was classified as other health impaired in refusing to provide him with video teleconferencing equipment so that he could participate in classroom activities when he was absent (*Eric H. ex rel. John H. v. Methacton School District*, 2003). In agreeing with the board's determination that the presence of the equipment in the classroom was disruptive to students in the class, the court noted that officials did not violate Section 504 because the student was not denied benefits that would have been provided to children who were not disabled.

On the other hand, where a student in New York was unable to attend school due to a chronic illness, the Second Circuit ruled that the refusals of educational officials to provide her with reasonable accommodations, such as not requiring her to climb stairs if she felt too sick and allowing her to lie down on a couch if she needed to rest, presented actionable claims under both Section 504 and the ADA (*Weixel v. Board of Education of the City of New York*, 2002). Further, when school officials forced a student with asthma to perform physical exercise as a punishment, thereby triggering an attack of his illness, a federal trial court in Tennessee, in rejecting the school board's request for summary judgment, concluded that educators violated his rights under the ADA (*Moss v. Shelby County*, 2005). The court held that school officials should have modified their standard punishment to accommodate the student's asthma.

Academic modifications might include permitting children more time to complete examinations or assignments, using peer tutors, distributing outlines in advance, employing specialized curricular materials, and/or permitting students to use laptop computers to record answers on examinations. In modifying facilities, school officials do not have to make every classroom and/or area of buildings accessible; it may be enough to bring services to children, such as offering keyboards for musical instruction in accessible classrooms rather than revamping entire music rooms for students who wish to take piano classes.

In a related concern, Section 504's only regulation directly addressing private schools stipulates that officials in such schools may not exclude students on the basis of their conditions if they can, with minor adjustments, be provided with an appropriate education (34 C.F.R. § 104.39(a)). This regulation also states that private schools "may not charge more for the provision of an appropriate education to handicapped persons than to nonhandicapped persons except to the extent that any additional charge is justified by a substantial increase in cost to the recipient (34 C.F.R. § 104.39(b))." As such, private schools may be able to charge additional costs to parents of children with impairments.

In a case from Texas that made its way to the Supreme Court, the justices interpreted the delivery of basic school health services to a student with physical impairments that would have allowed her to be present in a classroom as a reasonable accommodation (*Tatro v. State of Texas*, 1980, 1981, 1983, 1984). Insofar as the student needed to be catheterized approximately every four hours, a service that a school nurse, health aide, or other trained layperson were all capable of carrying out, courts agreed that when school officials refused to provide such a service, they violated her Section 504 rights.

In recent years, parents have filed suit under the IDEA seeking programs in fully inclusive settings for their children with severe disabilities. In ordering inclusive placements for many of these students, courts also are turning to Section 504 for guidance. In one case, the federal trial court in New Jersey commented that excluding a student from the regular education classroom without first investigating and providing reasonable accommodations violated Section 504 (*Oberti v. Board of Education of the Borough of Clementon School District*, 1992, 1993). The court explained that a segregated special education placement may be the program of choice only when it is necessary for the child to receive educational benefit.

Returning to sports and extracurricular activities, disputes often arise over whether school boards and athletic associations can be required to waive nonessential eligibility requirements. On the one hand, at least two courts directed athletic associations to waive age limitation requirements to allow students who repeated grades due to their learning disabilities to participate in sports (*Hoot v. Milan Area Schools*, 1994; *University Interscholastic League v. Buchanan*, 1993). The courts agreed that where the association allowed waivers of other rules, a waiver of the rule prohibiting students over the age of nineteen from participating in sports was a reasonable accommodation. Further, the Sixth Circuit affirmed that in preventing a transfer student from participating in sports when he changed schools solely due to his need to receive special education services, officials violated his rights under Section 504 (*Crocker v. Tennessee Secondary School Athletic Association*, 1990). In an admittedly different factual context, the Sixth Circuit subsequently decided that a high school athletic association's eight-semester eligibility rule did not violate either Section 504 or the ADA and that a student's claim that it violated his rights was without merit (*McPherson v. Michigan High School Athletic Association*, 1997). Previously, the Eighth Circuit held that since a student who challenged an athletic association's age restrictions was not otherwise qualified under either the ADA or Section 504 because he exceeded the age limit, he was not entitled to relief (*Pottgen v. Missouri State High School Activities Association*, 1994).

In a non-age-related case involving sports, a federal trial court in Illinois rejected the claims of a student athlete who was suspended from his football and lacrosse teams for disciplinary infractions (*Long v. Board of Education, District 128*, 2001). The court posited that waiving the athletic code of conduct would have been an unreasonable accommodation under Section 504 and the ADA because it would have sent the message to others that student athletes could thwart the enforcement of team rules by threatening legal actions, thereby making it difficult for school officials to maintain effective control over their athletic programs.

Most jurisdictions have instituted requirements that students pass comprehensive state-administered tests in order to graduate with standard high school diplomas. This requirement has become more prevalent following the passage of the No Child Left Behind Act. Under Section 504 and the ADA, school boards may be required to modify test-taking situations to allow students with disabilities to complete their examinations. Even so, school officials are not required to alter the content of the tests themselves (*Brookhart v. Illinois State Board of Education*, 1983). While altering the content of tests to accommodate the inability of individuals to learn amounts to a substantial modification, modifying the manner in which examinations are administered to accommodate student disabilities is probably reasonable. In other words, allowing a visually impaired student to take a Braille version of a test is a reasonable accommodation, but changing the content of an examination to make it easier would likely not be required.

A significant number of disputes over testing accommodations that were litigated in the context of postsecondary institutions apply to situations in elementary and secondary schools. These cases help to illustrate the point that accommodations in how tests are administered are required, but alterations to their contents are not. In one such case, a federal trial court in New York ordered additional accommodations for a visually impaired law school graduate who was sitting for the bar examination. Although the Board of Bar Examiners granted some but not all of the graduate's requested accommodations, since her physician testified that they were necessary, the court ordered that they be made on the ground that the purpose of the ADA was to guarantee that those with disabilities not be disadvantaged but put on an equal footing with others (*D'Amico v. New York State Board of Law Examiners*, 1993). Conversely, another case from New York involving a law school graduate reveals that applicants are not entitled to accommodations just because they may have failed an examination in the past without accommodations (*Pazer v. New York State Board of Law Examiners*, 1994). The court was convinced that requested accommodations were not necessary for a student who claimed to have a learning disability, since the testimony of an acknowledged expert on dyslexia proved to be credible and persuasive in establishing that he did not have such a condition.

As discussed below under defenses, accommodations that are unduly costly, create an excessive monitoring burden, or expose other individuals to excessive risk are not required. In an illustrative case, the Eighth Circuit decided that inoculating staff members against the hepatitis B virus so that a carrier of that disease could attend a learning center program went beyond the requirements of Section 504 (*Kohl v. Woodhaven Learning Center*, 1989). Similarly, a federal trial court in Kentucky ruled that a school for the blind could not be required to hire additional staff or modify the mission of the institution to accept a student who did not meet the minimum qualifications for admission to the school (*Eva N. v. Brock*, 1990).

Admission Evaluations

Insofar as some public schools may require students with disabilities to take admission examinations and/or be interviewed prior to being accepted and/or placed, in order to evaluate whether applicants are otherwise qualified, provisions in Section 504 address this situation. The regulations cover four areas: pre-placement evaluation, evaluation, placement, and reevaluation (34 C.F.R. § 104.35).

As to pre-placement evaluations, the regulations require school officials to evaluate all children who, due to their conditions, need or are believed to need special education or related services. These evaluations are to be completed before officials take any action with respect to the initial placements of children in regular or special education, as well as prior to making any later significant changes in placement.

Section 504's evaluation provisions require school officials to follow procedures similar to those under the IDEA. These provisions require officials to validate tests and other evaluation materials for the specific purposes for which they are used and to ensure that they are administered by trained personnel in conformance with the instructions provided by their producers. These materials must also be tailored to assess specific areas of educational need and cannot be designed to provide a single general intelligence quotient. Further, these materials must be selected and administered in a way that best ensures that when tests are administered to students with impaired sensory, manual, or speaking skills, the results accurately reflect their aptitude or achievement level or whatever other factors the tests purport to measure, rather than reflecting their impaired sensory, manual, or speaking skills, except where those skills are the factors that the tests purport to measure.

When school officials apply placement procedures to students under Section 504, their interpretations of data must consider information from a variety of sources, including aptitude and achievement tests, teacher recommendations, physical condition, social and cultural background, and adaptive behaviors that have been documented and carefully considered. In addition, not only must any such decisions be made by groups of persons, including knowledgeable individuals, but all children must be periodically reevaluated in a manner consistent with the dictates of the IDEA.

Under Section 504, schools relying on examinations or interviews may be required to provide reasonable accommodations to applicants with impairments. While school officials are not required to alter the content of examinations or interviews, they may have to make accommodations in how tests are administered or interviews are conducted. Put another way, school officials would not be required to make examinations easier so that students who simply lacked the requisite knowledge could pass, but they would have to alter the conditions under which examinations are administered or interviews are conducted so that students with impairments who have the requisite knowledge and skills to pass or express themselves fully could do so despite their condition.

The accommodations that educators provide for examinations may be as simple as providing quiet rooms without distractions, essentially private rooms away from others for students who suffer from attention deficit hyperactivity disorder, or procuring the services of a reader or Braille versions of examinations for applicants who are blind. Moreover, students with physical disabilities may require special seating arrangements, such as scribes to record answers to questions, and/or to be permitted to use computers to record answers on examinations. In like fashion, whether as part of examinations or admission interviews, students who are hearing impaired might be entitled to the services of sign-language interpreters to communicate directions that are normally given orally. At the same time, school officials may be required to provide students with learning disabilities with extra time to complete examinations or may have to make computers available to children who are more comfortable with them than with traditional paper-and-pencil tests.

Prior to receiving accommodations, students must prove that they have such conditions as learning disabilities (*Argen v. New York State Board of Law Examiners,* 1994) and that the extra time to take examinations is necessary due to their impairments. The purpose of providing the extra time is to allow students who might have difficulty processing information sufficient opportunity to show that they are capable of answering the questions.

In a major difference from the IDEA, which requires school officials to identify, assess, and serve students with disabilities, under Section 504, students and/or their parents, are responsible for making school officials aware of the fact that they need testing or interviewing accommodations. To this end, administrators should require proof that students have impairments in need of accommodation in order to demonstrate knowledge and skills on examinations. Students, through their parents, should also suggest which accommodations would be most appropriate. In considering whether students are entitled to accommodations, school officials must make individualized inquiries. School officials may be liable for violating Section 504 if they refuse to make testing accommodations or make modifications only for students with specified impairments.

Section 504 Service Plans

As noted, students who qualify under the Section 504 definition are entitled to reasonable accommodations so that they may access school programs. Making accommodations may involve alterations to physical plants, such as building wheelchair ramps or removing architectural barriers, so that students may physically enter and get around school buildings. School officials must also allow students to bring service dogs into classrooms (*Sullivan v. Vallejo City Unified School District*, 1990), but the officials are not required to provide accommodations that go beyond what would be considered reasonable. Accommodations that are excessively expensive, that expose the school's staff to excessive risk, or that require substantial modifications to the missions or purposes of programs are not required.

Neither Section 504 nor its regulations mandate the creation of written agreements with regard to student accommodations or specify the content of such documents. Even so, school officials in many districts meet with parents to formalize the accommodations and services that they will provide to eligible students. These written agreements are euphemistically referred to as

Section 504 service plans. In practical terms, school officials should be sure to include the following components in each written Section 504 service plan:

Demographic data: student's name, date of birth, school identification number, grade, school, teacher, parents' names, address, telephone numbers, and the like

Team members: a listing of all team members who contributed to the development of the service plan, and their respective roles

Impairment: a detailed description of the student's impairment and its severity, along with an explanation of how it impedes the child's educational progress

Accommodations and services: a detailed description of the accommodations and services to be offered under the plan, including the frequency and location of services, where they will be provided, and by whom they will be provided

In addition, officials should attach the evaluative reports or assessments that helped to determine the nature of a student's impairments and the need for accommodations and services.

DEFENSES

Even if children appear to be "otherwise qualified," school officials can rely on one of three defenses to avoid being charged with noncompliance with Section 504. This represents a major difference between Section 504 and the IDEA, since no such defenses are applicable under the latter. Another major difference between the laws is that the federal government provides public schools with direct federal financial assistance to help fund programs under the IDEA, but offers no financial incentives to aid institutions, public or nonpublic, as they seek to comply with the dictates of Section 504. Interestingly, these defenses emerged largely as a result of two Supreme Court cases not involving students in elementary and secondary schools.

In *Southeastern Community College v. Davis* (1979), the Court held that officials at a community college did not violate the rights of an unsuccessful applicant to a nursing program. The Court explained that since officials denied the applicant entry on the basis that her hearing impairment would have made it unsafe for her to participate, she was not otherwise qualified to do so. On the other hand, in the Court's first case on Section 504 in a school setting, *School Board of Nassau County, Florida v. Arline (Arline)* (1987), it affirmed that educational officials violated a teacher's rights by discharging her due to recurrences of tuberculosis. In determining that the teacher was otherwise qualified for the job, the Court created a four-part test for use in cases involving contagious diseases. The elements that the Court relied on in ordering the teacher's reinstatement were the nature of the risk, its duration, its severity, and the probability that the disease would be transmitted and cause varying degrees of harm. On remand, a federal trial court in Florida agreed that since the teacher was otherwise qualified, she was entitled to return to her job (*Arline v. School Board of Nassau County*, 1988).

The first defense under Section 504 is that officials can be excused from making accommodations that result in "a fundamental alteration in the nature of [a] program" (*Southeastern Community College v. Davis*, 1979, p. 410). The second defense permits school officials to avoid compliance if modifications impose an "undue financial burden" (*Davis*, p. 412) on an institution or entity as a whole. The third defense is that an otherwise qualified student with a disability can be excluded from a program if the student's presence creates a substantial risk of injury to himself, herself, or others (*School Board of Nassau County, Florida v. Arline*, 1987). As such, a student with a severe visual impairment could be excluded from using a scalpel in a biology laboratory. However, in order to comply with Section 504, school officials would probably have to offer a reasonable accommodation such as providing a computer-assisted program to achieve an instructional goal similar to the one that would have been achieved in a laboratory class.

Finally, Section 504, which is enforced by the Office of Civil Rights, requires each recipient of federal financial aid to file an assurance of compliance; provide notice to students and their parents that their programs are nondiscriminatory; engage in remedial actions where violations are proven; take voluntary steps to overcome the effects of conditions that resulted in limiting the participation of students with disabilities in their programs; conduct a self-evaluation; designate a staff member, typically at the central-office level, as compliance coordinator; and adopt grievance procedures (34 C.F.R. § 104.5).

Effect of Mitigating Measures

In 1999 the Supreme Court addressed a trio of cases that, when taken together, indicate that officials must consider mitigating, or corrective, measures when evaluating whether individuals have disabilities under the ADA. Although these cases were resolved in noneducation employment contexts, they have implications for evaluating whether students are disabled. Further, even though these disputes involved only the ADA, due to the similarity of the statutes they also have implications for the interpretation of Section 504.

In *Sutton v. United Airlines* (*Sutton*) (1999), the Supreme Court ruled that if individuals are taking measures to correct for, or mitigate, impairments, the effects of those measures must be taken into account when considering whether they are substantially limited in major life activities. In essence, the Court distinguished between individuals currently being substantially limited, as opposed to being potentially or hypothetically substantially limited, when attempting to demonstrate the existence of disabilities. In other words, the Court reasoned that individuals whose physical or mental impairments are corrected through medication or other measures do not have impairments that presently limit major life activities. Accordingly, such persons would neither meet the ADA's definition of individuals with disabilities nor be entitled to accommodations.

The Supreme Court resolved the second case, *Murphy v. United Parcel Service* (1999), by referencing its previous order in *Sutton,* noting that determination of whether impairments substantially limit one or more major life activities is made in light of the mitigating measures that individuals employ. In the final case, *Albertsons, Inc. v. Kirkingburg* (1999), the Court added that it makes no difference whether corrective measures are undertaken with artificial aids, such as medication or devices, or measures taken with the body's own systems, such as an individual adapting to having monocular vision.

In all three of these cases the Supreme Court emphasized that findings of whether persons are disabled under the ADA must be individualized inquiries. In a later case, *Toyota Motor Manufacturing v. Williams* (2002), the Court pointed out that impairments must prevent or severely restrict individuals from performing activities that are of central importance to most people's daily lives. The Court explained that the impact of impairments must be permanent or long term in order to be considered.

Under these cases, elementary or secondary students who have impairments that can be easily corrected would not qualify as individuals with disabilities under either the ADA or Section 504. For example, as in *Sutton,* a student with poor vision that can be fully corrected with lenses would not have a disability. However, it is important to note that many corrective devices improve functioning for individuals but may not fully mitigate the effects of their impairments. Accordingly, school officials must conduct individualized assessments in considering whether impairments, even when partially corrected, limit major life activities. In elementary or secondary school settings, the inquiry as to whether students have disabilities needs to consider, among other things, whether their impairments affect the major life activity of learning.

One question that has not been answered is whether persons who choose not to use available mitigating measures or devices would qualify as individuals with disabilities under the ADA and Section 504. For example, even though many students are prescribed medication for attention deficit hyperactivity disorder, for various reasons many parents choose not to have their children take the psychothropic medications that are usually prescribed. In such situations, where student impairments can be fully mitigated through use of medications, it is unclear whether students would qualify as disabled under the statutes if their parents were unwilling to administer the medications. Interestingly, the IDEA prohibits states and school systems from requiring children to take medications as a condition of attending school, being evaluated, or receiving services (20 U.S.C. § 1412(a)(25)). Even so, it is unclear whether courts will interpret the ADA and Section 504 as not allowing school personnel to consider whether students could take measures to mitigate impairments in making such evaluations.

❖

CASE NO. 19—THE MEANING OF "OTHERWISE QUALIFIED"

SOUTHEASTERN COMMUNITY COLLEGE

v.

DAVIS

Supreme Court of the United States, 1979

442 U.S. 397

Justice POWELL delivered the opinion of the Court.

This case presents a matter of first impression for this Court: Whether § 504 of the Rehabilitation Act of 1973, which prohibits discrimination against an "otherwise qualified handicapped individual" in federally funded programs "solely by reason of his handicap," forbids professional schools from imposing physical qualifications for admission to their clinical training programs.

I

Respondent, who suffers from a serious hearing disability, seeks to be trained as a registered nurse. During the 1973–1974 academic year she was enrolled in the College Parallel program of Southeastern Community College, a state institution that receives federal funds. Respondent hoped to progress to Southeastern's Associate Degree Nursing program, completion of which would make her eligible for state certification as a registered nurse. In the course of her application to the nursing program, she was interviewed by a member of the nursing faculty. It became apparent that respondent had difficulty understanding questions asked, and on inquiry she acknowledged a history of hearing problems and dependence on a hearing aid. She was advised to consult an audiologist.

On the basis of an examination at Duke University Medical Center, respondent was diagnosed as having a "bilateral, sensori-neural hearing loss." A change in her hearing aid was recommended, as a result of which it was expected that she would be able to detect sounds "almost as well as a person would who has normal hearing." But this improvement would not mean that she could discriminate among sounds sufficiently to understand normal spoken speech. Her lipreading skills would remain necessary for effective communication: "While wearing the hearing aid, she is well aware of gross sounds occurring in the listening environment. However, she can only be responsible for speech spoken to her, when the talker gets her attention and allows her to look directly at the talker."

Southeastern next consulted Mary McRee, Executive Director of the North Carolina Board of Nursing. On the basis of the audiologist's report, McRee recommended that respondent not be admitted to the nursing program. In McRee's view, respondent's hearing disability made it unsafe for her to practice as a nurse. In addition, it would be impossible for respondent to participate safely in the normal clinical training program, and those modifications that would be necessary to enable safe participation would prevent her from realizing the benefits of the program: "To adjust patient learning experiences in keeping with [respondent's] hearing limitations could, in fact, be the same as denying her full learning to meet the objectives of your nursing programs."

After respondent was notified that she was not qualified for nursing study because of her hearing disability, she requested reconsideration of the decision. The entire nursing staff of Southeastern was assembled, and McRee again was consulted. McRee repeated her conclusion that on the basis of the available evidence, respondent "has hearing limitations which could interfere with her safely caring for patients." Upon further deliberation, the staff voted to deny respondent admission.

Respondent then filed suit in the United States District Court for the Eastern District of North Carolina, alleging both a violation of § 504 of the Rehabilitation Act of 1973 and a denial of equal protection and due process. After a bench trial, the District Court entered judgment in favor of Southeastern . . .

. . . the District Court concluded that respondent was not an "otherwise qualified handicapped individual" protected against discrimination by § 504. . . .

On appeal, the Court of Appeals for the Fourth Circuit reversed. It did not dispute the District Court's findings of fact, but held that the court had misconstrued § 504. . . . the appellate court believed that § 504 required Southeastern to "reconsider plaintiff's application for admission to the nursing program without regard to her hearing ability." It concluded that the District Court had erred in taking respondent's handicap into account in determining whether she was "otherwise qualified" for the program, rather than confining its inquiry to her "academic and technical qualifications." . . .

Because of the importance of this issue to the many institutions covered by § 504, we granted certiorari. We now reverse.

II

As previously noted, this is the first case in which this Court has been called upon to interpret § 504. It is elementary that "[t]he starting point in every case involving construction of a statute is the language itself." Section 504 by its terms does not compel educational institutions to disregard the disabilities of handicapped individuals or to make substantial modifications in their programs to allow disabled persons to participate. Instead, it requires only that an "otherwise qualified handicapped individual" not be excluded from participation in a federally funded program "solely by reason of his handicap," indicating only that mere possession of a handicap is not a permissible ground for assuming an inability to function in a particular context.

The court below, however, believed that the "otherwise qualified" persons protected by § 504 include those who would be able to meet the requirements of a particular program in every respect except as to limitations imposed by their handicap. Taken literally, this holding would prevent an institution from taking into account any limitation resulting from the handicap, however disabling. It assumes, in effect, that a person need not meet legitimate physical requirements in order to be "otherwise qualified." We think the understanding of the District Court is closer to the plain meaning of the statutory language. An otherwise qualified person is one who is able to meet all of a program's requirements in spite of his handicap.

The regulations promulgated by the Department of HEW to interpret § 504 reinforce, rather than contradict, this conclusion. According to these regulations, a "[q]ualified handicapped person" is, "[w]ith respect to postsecondary and vocational education services, a handicapped person who meets the academic and technical standards requisite to admission or participation in the [school's] education program or activity. . . ."

A... note emphasizes that legitimate physical qualifications may be essential to participation in particular programs. We think it clear, therefore, that HEW interprets the "other" qualifications which a handicapped person may be required to meet as including necessary physical qualifications.

III

The remaining question is whether the physical qualifications Southeastern demanded of respondent might not be necessary for participation in its nursing program. It is not open to dispute that, as Southeastern's Associate Degree Nursing program currently is constituted, the ability to understand speech without reliance on lipreading is necessary for patient safety during the clinical phase of the program. As the District Court found, this ability also is indispensable for many of the functions that a registered nurse performs.

Respondent contends nevertheless that § 504, properly interpreted, compels Southeastern to undertake affirmative action that would dispense with the need for effective oral communication. First, it is suggested that respondent can be given individual supervision by faculty members whenever she attends patients directly. Moreover, certain required courses might be dispensed with altogether for respondent. It is not necessary, she argues, that Southeastern train her to undertake all the tasks a registered nurse is licensed to perform. Rather, it is sufficient to make § 504 applicable if respondent might be able to perform satisfactorily some of the duties of a registered nurse or to hold some of the positions available to a registered nurse.

Respondent finds support for this argument in portions of the HEW regulations discussed above. In particular, a provision applicable to postsecondary educational programs requires covered institutions to make "modifications" in their programs to accommodate handicapped persons, and to provide "auxiliary aids" such as sign-language interpreters. Respondent argues that this regulation imposes an obligation to ensure full participation in covered programs by handicapped individuals and, in particular, requires Southeastern to make the kind of adjustments that would be necessary to permit her safe participation in the nursing program.

We note first that on the present record it appears unlikely respondent could benefit from any affirmative action that the regulation reasonably could be interpreted as requiring. [A federal regulation], for example, explicitly excludes "devices or services of a personal nature" from the kinds of auxiliary aids a school must provide a handicapped individual. Yet the only evidence in the record indicates that nothing less than close, individual attention by a nursing instructor would be sufficient to ensure patient safety if respondent took part in the clinical phase of the nursing program. Furthermore, it also is reasonably clear that [the regulation] does not encompass the kind of curricular changes that would be necessary to accommodate respondent in the nursing program. In light of respondent's inability to function in clinical courses without close supervision, Southeastern, with prudence, could allow her to take only academic classes. Whatever benefits respondent might realize from such a course of study, she would not receive even a rough equivalent of the training a nursing program normally gives. Such a fundamental alteration in the nature of a program is far more than the "modification" the regulation requires.

Moreover, an interpretation of the regulations that required the extensive modifications necessary to include respondent in the nursing program would raise grave doubts about their validity. If these regulations were to require substantial adjustments in existing programs beyond those necessary to eliminate discrimination against otherwise qualified individuals, they would do more than clarify the meaning of § 504. Instead, they would constitute an unauthorized extension of the obligations imposed by that statute.

The language and structure of the Rehabilitation Act of 1973 reflect a recognition by Congress of the distinction between the evenhanded treatment of qualified handicapped persons and affirmative efforts to overcome the disabilities caused by handicaps. Section 501(b), governing the employment of handicapped individuals by the Federal Government, requires each federal agency to submit "an affirmative action program plan for the hiring, placement, and advancement of handicapped individuals. . . ." These plans "shall include a description of the extent to which and methods whereby the special needs of handicapped employees are being met." Similarly, § 503(a), governing hiring by federal contractors, requires employers to "take affirmative action to employ and advance in employment qualified handicapped individuals. . . ."

Under § 501(c) of the Act, by contrast, state agencies such as Southeastern are only "encourage[d] . . . to adopt and implement such policies and procedures." Section 504 does not refer at all to affirmative action, and except as it applies to federal employers it does not provide for implementation by administrative action. A comparison of these provisions demonstrates that Congress understood accommodation of the needs of handicapped individuals may require affirmative action and knew how to provide for it in those instances where it wished to do so.

Although an agency's interpretation of the statute under which it operates is entitled to some deference, "this deference is constrained by our obligation to honor the clear meaning of a statute, as revealed by its language, purpose, and history." Here, neither the language, purpose, nor history of § 504 reveals an intent to impose an affirmative-action obligation on all recipients of federal funds. Accordingly, we hold that even if HEW has attempted to create such an obligation itself, it lacks the authority to do so.

IV

We do not suggest that the line between a lawful refusal to extend affirmative action and illegal discrimination against handicapped persons always will be clear. It is possible to envision situations where an insistence on continuing past requirements and practices might arbitrarily deprive genuinely qualified handicapped persons of the opportunity to participate in a covered program. Technological advances can be expected to enhance opportunities to rehabilitate the handicapped or otherwise to qualify them for some useful employment. Such advances also may enable attainment of these goals without imposing undue financial and administrative burdens upon a State. Thus, situations may arise where a refusal to modify an existing program might become unreasonable and discriminatory. Identification of those instances where a refusal to accommodate the needs of a disabled person amounts to discrimination against the handicapped continues to be an important responsibility of HEW.

In this case, however, it is clear that Southeastern's unwillingness to make major adjustments in its nursing program does not constitute such discrimination. The uncontroverted testimony of several members of Southeastern's staff and faculty established that the purpose of its program was to train persons who could serve the nursing profession in all customary ways. This type of purpose, far from reflecting any animus against handicapped individuals is shared by many if not most of the institutions that train persons to render professional service. It is undisputed that respondent could not participate in Southeastern's nursing program unless the standards were substantially lowered. Section 504 imposes no requirement upon an educational institution to lower or to effect substantial modifications of standards to accommodate a handicapped person.

Respondent's argument misses the point. Southeastern's program, structured to train persons who will be able to perform all normal roles of a registered nurse, represents a legitimate academic policy, and is accepted by the State. In effect, it seeks to ensure that no graduate will pose a danger to the public in any professional role in which he or she might be cast. Even if the licensing requirements of North Carolina or some other State are less demanding, nothing in the Act requires an educational institution to lower its standards.

One may admire respondent's desire and determination to overcome her handicap, and there well may be various other types of service for which she can qualify. In this case, however, we hold that there was no violation of § 504 when Southeastern concluded that respondent did not qualify for admission to its program. Nothing in the language or history of § 504 reflects an intention to limit the freedom of an educational institution to require reasonable physical qualifications for admission to a clinical training program. Nor has there been any showing in this case that any action short of a substantial change in Southeastern's program would render unreasonable the qualifications it imposed.

V

Accordingly, we reverse the judgment of the court below, and remand for proceedings consistent with this opinion.

So ordered.

Notes

1. One could argue that if parents were fully aware of the parameters of Section 504, then schools would have to operate differently. Would this be good?

2. Note that all students who are covered by Section 504 are not necessarily protected by the IDEA's more specific eligibility requirements.

3. What are the implications of *Davis* on participation in sports or other extracurricular activities? What if their conditions place student athletes, such as those who may be visually impaired, at greater risks of injury? What does it mean to these students? Other participants?

CASE NO. 20—DEFENSES UNDER SECTION 504

SCHOOL BOARD OF NASSAU COUNTY, FLORIDA

v.

ARLINE

Supreme Court of the United States, 1987

480 U.S. 273

Justice BRENNAN delivered the opinion of the Court.

Section 504 of the Rehabilitation Act of 1973 prohibits a federally funded state program from discriminating against a handicapped individual solely by reason of his or her handicap. This case presents the questions whether a person afflicted with tuberculosis, a contagious disease, may be considered a "handicapped individual" within the meaning of § 504 of the Act, and, if so, whether such an individual is "otherwise qualified" to teach elementary school.

I

From 1966 until 1979, respondent Gene Arline taught elementary school in Nassau County, Florida. She was discharged in 1979 after suffering a third relapse of tuberculosis within two years. After she was denied relief in state administrative proceedings, she brought suit in federal court, alleging that the school board's decision to dismiss her because of her tuberculosis violated § 504 of the Act.

... Arline was hospitalized for tuberculosis in 1957. For the next 20 years, Arline's disease was in remission. Then, in 1977, a culture revealed that tuberculosis was again active in her system; cultures taken in March 1978 and in November 1978 were also positive.

The superintendent of schools for Nassau County, Craig Marsh, then testified as to the school board's response to Arline's medical reports. After both her second relapse, in the spring of 1978, and her third relapse in November 1978, the school board suspended Arline with pay for the remainder of the school year. At the end of the 1978–1979 school year, the school board held a hearing, after which it discharged Arline, "not because she had done anything wrong," but because of the "continued reoccurence [sic] of tuberculosis." In her trial memorandum, Arline argued that it was "not disputed that the [school board dismissed her] solely on the basis of her illness. Since the illness in this case qualifies the Plaintiff as a 'handicapped person' it is clear that she was dismissed solely as a result of her handicap in violation of Section 504." The District Court held, however, that although there was "[n]o question that she suffers a handicap," Arline was nevertheless not "a handicapped person under the terms of that statute." The court found it "difficult ... to conceive that Congress intended contagious diseases to be included within the definition of a handicapped person." The court then went on to state that, "even assuming" that a person with a contagious disease could be deemed a handicapped person, Arline was not "qualified" to teach elementary school.

The Court of Appeals reversed, holding that "persons with contagious diseases are within the coverage of section 504," and that Arline's condition "falls ... neatly within the statutory and regulatory framework" of the Act. The court remanded the case "for further findings as to whether the risks of infection precluded Mrs. Arline from being 'otherwise qualified' for her job and, if so, whether it was possible to make some reasonable accommodation for her in that teaching position" or in some other position. We granted certiorari and now affirm.

II

In enacting and amending the Act, Congress enlisted all programs receiving federal funds in an effort "to share with handicapped Americans the opportunities for an education, transportation, housing, health care, and jobs that other Americans take for granted." To that end, Congress not only increased federal support for vocational rehabilitation, but also addressed the broader problem of discrimination against the handicapped by including § 504, an antidiscrimination provision patterned after Title VI of the Civil Rights Act of 1964. Section 504 of the Rehabilitation Act reads in pertinent part:

> No otherwise qualified handicapped individual in the United States, as defined in section 706(7) of this title, shall, solely by reason of his handicap, be excluded from participation in, be denied the benefits of, or be subjected to discrimination under any program or activity receiving Federal financial assistance. . . . 29 U.S.C. § 794.

In 1974 Congress expanded the definition of "handicapped individual" for use in § 504 to read as follows:

> [A]ny person who (i) has a physical or mental impairment which substantially limits one or more of such person's major life activities, (ii) has a record of such an impairment, or (iii) is regarded as having such an impairment." 29 U.S.C. § 706(7)(B).

The amended definition reflected Congress' concern with protecting the handicapped against discrimination stemming not only from simple prejudice, but also from "archaic attitudes and laws" and from "the fact that the American people are simply unfamiliar with and insensitive to the difficulties confront[ing] individuals with handicaps." To combat the effects of erroneous but nevertheless prevalent perceptions about the handicapped, Congress expanded the definition of "handicapped individual" so as to preclude discrimination against "[a] person who has a record of, or is regarded as having, an impairment [but who] may at present have no actual incapacity at all."

In determining whether a particular individual is handicapped as defined by the Act, the regulations promulgated by the Department of Health and Human Services are of significant assistance. As we have previously recognized, these regulations were drafted with the oversight and approval of Congress; they provide "an important source of guidance on the meaning of § 504." The regulations are particularly significant here because they define two critical terms used in the statutory definition of handicapped individual. "Physical impairment" is defined as follows:

> [A]ny physiological disorder or condition, cosmetic disfigurement, or anatomical loss affecting one or more of the following body systems: neurological; musculoskeletal; special sense organs; respiratory, including speech organs; cardiovascular; reproductive, digestive, genito-urinary; hemic and lymphatic; skin; and endocrine.

In addition, the regulations define "major life activities" as "functions such as caring for one's self, performing manual tasks, walking, seeing, hearing, speaking, breathing, learning, and working."

III

Within this statutory and regulatory framework, then, we must consider whether Arline can be considered a handicapped individual. According to . . . testimony . . . Arline suffered tuberculosis "in an acute form in such a degree that it affected her respiratory system," and was hospitalized for this condition. Arline thus had a physical impairment as that term is defined by the regulations, since she had a "physiological disorder or condition . . . affecting [her] . . . respiratory [system]." This impairment was serious enough to require hospitalization, a fact more than sufficient to establish that one or more of her major life activities were substantially limited by her impairment. Thus, Arline's hospitalization for tuberculosis in 1957 suffices to establish that she has a "record of . . . impairment" within the meaning of 29 U.S.C. § 706(7)(B)(ii), and is therefore a handicapped individual.

Petitioners concede that a contagious disease may constitute a handicapping condition to the extent that it leaves a person with "diminished physical or mental capabilities," Brief for Petitioners 15, and concede that Arline's hospitalization for tuberculosis in 1957 demonstrates that she has a record of a physical impairment. Petitioners maintain, however, that Arline's record of impairment is irrelevant in this case, since the school board dismissed Arline not because of her diminished physical capabilities, but because of the threat that her relapses of tuberculosis posed to the health of others.

We do not agree with petitioners that, in defining a handicapped individual under § 504, the contagious effects of a disease can be meaningfully distinguished from the disease's physical effects on a claimant in a case such as this. Arline's contagiousness and her physical impairment each resulted from the same underlying condition, tuberculosis. It would be unfair to allow an employer to seize upon the distinction between the effects of a disease on others and the effects of a disease on a patient and use that distinction to justify discriminatory treatment.

Nothing in the legislative history of § 504 suggests that Congress intended such a result. That history demonstrates that Congress was as concerned about the effect of an impairment on others as it was about its effect on the individual. . . .

Allowing discrimination based on the contagious effects of a physical impairment would be inconsistent with the basic purpose of § 504, which is to ensure that handicapped individuals are not denied jobs or other benefits because of the prejudiced attitudes or the ignorance of others. By amending the definition of "handicapped individual" to include not only those who are actually physically impaired, but also those who are regarded as impaired and who, as a result, are substantially limited in a major life activity, Congress acknowledged that society's accumulated myths and fears about disability and disease are as handicapping as are the physical limitations that flow from actual impairment. Few aspects of a handicap give rise to the same level of public fear and misapprehension as contagiousness. Even those who suffer or have recovered from such noninfectious diseases as epilepsy or cancer have faced discrimination based on the irrational fear that they might be contagious. The Act is carefully structured to replace such reflexive reactions to actual or perceived handicaps with actions based on reasoned and medically sound judgments: the definition of "handicapped individual" is broad, but only those individuals who are both handicapped and otherwise qualified are eligible for relief. The fact that some persons who have contagious diseases may pose a serious health threat to others under certain circumstances does not justify excluding from the coverage of the Act all persons with actual or perceived contagious diseases. Such exclusion would mean that those accused of being contagious would never have the opportunity to have their condition evaluated in light of medical evidence and a determination made as to whether they were "otherwise qualified." Rather, they would be vulnerable to discrimination on the basis of mythology—precisely the type of injury Congress sought to prevent. We conclude that the fact that a person with a record of a physical impairment is also contagious does not suffice to remove that person from coverage under § 504.

IV

The remaining question is whether Arline is otherwise qualified for the job of elementary schoolteacher. To answer this question in most cases, the district court will need to conduct an individualized inquiry and make appropriate findings of fact. Such an inquiry is essential if § 504 is to achieve its goal of protecting handicapped individuals from deprivations based on prejudice, stereotypes, or unfounded fear, while giving appropriate weight to such legitimate concerns of grantees as avoiding exposing others to significant health and safety risks. The basic factors to be considered in conducting this inquiry are well established. In the context of the employment of a person handicapped with a contagious disease, we agree with amicus American Medical Association that this inquiry should include . . . "[findings of] facts, based on reasonable medical judgments given the state of medical knowledge, about (a) the nature of the risk (how the disease is transmitted), (b) the duration of the risk (how long is the carrier infectious), (c) the severity of the risk (what is the potential harm to third parties) and (d) the probabilities the disease will be transmitted and will cause varying degrees of harm."

In making these findings, courts normally should defer to the reasonable medical judgments of public health officials. The next step in the "otherwise-qualified" inquiry is for the court to evaluate, in light of these medical findings, whether the employer could reasonably accommodate the employee under the established standards for that inquiry.

Because of the paucity of factual findings by the District Court, we, like the Court of Appeals, are unable at this stage of the proceedings to resolve whether Arline is "otherwise qualified" for her job. . . .

We hold that a person suffering from the contagious disease of tuberculosis can be a handicapped person within the meaning of § 504 of the Rehabilitation Act of 1973, and that respondent Arline is such a person. We remand the case to the District Court to determine whether Arline is otherwise qualified for her position. The judgment of the Court of Appeals is Affirmed.

Notes

1. Was this decision wise? Was it safe for the school community?

2. What are *Arline*'s implications for students with contagious diseases such as HIV/AIDS or hepatitis B? How would a school board's response be different for students with more contagious

diseases based on the increased risk of infection? Under what circumstances could students with contagious diseases be excluded from inclusive programs in public schools?

3. *Davis* and *Arline* demonstrate that in order to be otherwise qualified, individuals with disabilities must be able to meet all of a program's requirements in spite of their impairments. Even so, Section 504 and the ADA require officials to make reasonable accommodations so that individuals may, in fact, meet programmatic requirements. In addition to those discussed in the text, what are some other reasonable accommodations that are typically provided in school settings?

REFERENCES

Albertsons, Inc. v. Kirkingburg, 527 U.S. 555 (1999).

Americans with Disabilities Act, 42 U.S.C.A. §§ 12101 *et seq.* (2005).

Argen v. New York State Board of Law Examiners, 860 F. Supp. 84, (W.D.N.Y. 1994).

Arline v. School Board of Nassau County, 692 F. Supp. 1286 (M.D. Fla.1988).

Barnes v. Converse College, 436 F. Supp. 635 (D.S.C. 1977).

Barnett v. Fairfax County School Board, 721 F. Supp. 757 (E.D. Va. 1989), *affirmed*, 927 F.2d 146 (4th Cir. 1991).

Begay v. Hodel, 730 F. Supp. 1001 (D. Ariz. 1990).

Brookhart v. Illinois State Board of Education, 697 F.2d 179 (7th Cir. 1983).

Colin K. v. Schmidt, 715 F.2d 1 (1st Cir. 1983).

Concerned Parents to Save Dreher Park Center v. City of West Palm Beach, 846 F. Supp. 986 (S.D. Fla. 1994).

Cordrey v. Euckert, 917 F.2d 1460 (6th Cir. 1990).

Crocker v. Tennessee Secondary School Athletic Association, 735 F. Supp. (M.D. Tenn. 1990), *affirmed without published opinion sub nom. Metropolitan Government of Nashville and Davidson County v. Crocker*, 908 F.2d 973 (6th Cir. 1990).

D'Amico v. New York State Board of Law Examiners, 813 F. Supp. 217 (W.D.N.Y. 1993).

Darlene L. v. Illinois Board of Education, 568 F. Supp. 1340 (N.D. Ill. 1983).

Doe v. Alabama State Department of Education, 915 F.2d 651 (11th Cir. 1990).

Doe v. Belleville Public School District, 672 F. Supp. 342 (S.D. Ill. 1987).

Doe v. Dolton Elementary School District, 694 F. Supp. 440 (N.D. Ill. 1988).

Doe v. Eagle-Union Community School Corporation, 2 Fed Appx. 567 (7th Cir. 2001a), 534 U.S. 1042 (2001b).

Donnell C. v. Illinois State Board of Education, 829 F. Supp. 1016 (N.D. Ill. 1993).

Easley v. Snider, 841 F. Supp. 668 (E.D. Pa. 1993).

Eric H. ex rel. John H. v. Methacton School District, 265 F. Supp.2d 513 (E.D. Pa. 2003).

Eva N. v. Brock, 741 F. Supp. 626 (E.D. Ky. 1990).

Green v. Johnson, 513 F. Supp. 965 (D. Mass. 1982).

Hendricks v. Gilhool, 709 F. Supp. 1362 (E.D. Pa. 1989).

Hoot v. Milan Area Schools, 853 F. Supp. 243 (E.D. Mich. 1994).

Hunt v. St. Peter School, 963 F. Supp. 843 (W.D. Mo. 1997).

I.D. v. Westmoreland School District, 788 F. Supp. 634 (D.N.H. 1992).

Individuals with Disabilities Education Act, 20 U.S.C.A. §§ 1400–1482 (2005).

Kaesberg, M. A., & Murray, K. T. (1994). Americans with Disabilities Act. *Education Law Reporter, 90*, 11–20.

Kohl v. Woodhaven Learning Center, 865 F.2d 930 (8th Cir. 1989).

Long v. Board of Education, District 128, 167 F. Supp.2d 988 (N.D. Ill. 2001).

Lyons v. Smith, 829 F. Supp. 414 (D.D.C. 1993).

Martinez v. School Board of Hillsborough County, 861 F.2d 1502 (11th Cir. 1988), *on remand*, 711 F. Supp. 1066 (M.D. Fla. 1989).

McPherson v. Michigan High School Athletic Association, 119 F.3d 453 (6th Cir. 1997).

Miles, A. S., Russo, C. J., & Gordon, W. M. (1991). The reasonable accommodations provisions of the Americans with Disabilities Act. *Education Law Reporter, 69*, 1–8.

Molly L. ex rel. B.L. v. Lower Merion School District, 194 F. Supp.2d 422 (E.D. Pa. 2002).

Moss v. Shelby County, 401 F. Supp2d 850 (W.D. Tenn. 2005)

Murphy v. United Parcel Service, 527 U.S. 516 (1999).

New York State Association for Retarded Children v. Carey, 612 F.2d 644 (2d Cir. 1979).

No Child Left Behind Act, 20 U.S.C. §§ 6301–7941 (2002).

Oberti v. Board of Education of the Borough of Clementon School District, 801 F. Supp. 1393 (D.N.J. 1992), *affirmed*, 995 F.2d 1204 (3d Cir. 1993).

Ohio Civil Rights Commission v. Case Western Reserve University, 666 N.E.2d 1376 (Ohio 1996).

Pazer v. New York State Board of Law Examiners, 849 F. Supp. 284 (S.D.N.Y. 1994).

P.C. v. McLaughlin, 913 F.2d 1033 (2d Cir. 1990).

Petersen v. Hastings Public Schools, 831 F. Supp. 742 (D. Neb. 1993).

Pottgen v. Missouri State High School Activities Association, 40 F.3d 926 (8th Cir. 1994).

Puffer v. Raynolds, 761 F. Supp. 838 (D. Mass. 1988).

Ray v. School District of DeSoto County, 666 F. Supp. 1524 (M.D. Fla. 1987).

Rehabilitation Act, Section 504, 29 U.S.C.A. § 794 (2005).

Rothschild v. Grottenthaler, 907 F.2d 286 (2d Cir. 1990).

School Board of Nassau County, Florida v. Arline, 480 U.S. 273 (1987).

Southeastern Community College v. Davis, 442 U.S. 397 (1979).

Sullivan v. Vallejo City Unified School District, 731 F. Supp. 947 (E.D. Cal. 1990).

Sutton v. United Air Lines, 527 U.S. 471 (1999).

Tatro v. State of Texas, 625 F.2d 557 (5th Cir. 1980), *on remand* 516 F. Supp. 968 (N.D. Tex. 1981), *affirmed*, 703 F.2d 823 (5th Cir. 1983), *affirmed sub nom. Irving Independent School District v. Tatro*, 468 U.S. 883 (1984).

Thomas v. Atascadero Unified School District, 662 F. Supp. 376 (C.D. Cal. 1987)

Thomas v. Davidson Academy, 846 F. Supp. 611 (M.D. Tenn. 1994).

Toyota Motor Manufacturing v. Williams, 534 U.S. 184 (2002).

University Interscholastic League v. Buchanan, 848 S.W.2d 298 (Tex. App. Ct. 1993).

Vande Zande v. State of Wisconsin Department of Administration, 851 F. Supp. 353 (W.D. Wis. 1994).

Weixel v. Board of Educ. of the City of New York, 287 F.3d 138 (2d Cir. 2002).

Wenkart, R. D. (1993). The Americans with Disabilities Act and its impact on public education. *Education Law Reporter, 82*, 291–302.

Glossary

Administrative appeal: a quasi-judicial proceeding before an independent hearing officer or administrative law judge.

Administrative law judge (ALJ): an individual presiding at an administrative due process hearing who has the power to administer oaths, hear testimony, rule on questions of evidence, and make determinations of fact. The role of an administrative law judge in IDEA proceedings is identical to that of an independent hearing officer.

Affirm: to uphold the decision of a lower court in an appeal.

Annual review: a review of a student's progress in a special education program and an examination of his or her future special education needs held at least once each year. An annual review may repeat some of the original assessments for the purpose of assessing progress but generally is not as thorough as the original evaluation. The student's Individualized Education Program is revised and updated at the annual review conference.

Appeal: a resort to a higher court seeking review of a judicial action.

Appellate court: a court that can only hear appeals and so has appellate jurisdiction.

Case law: law that results from court opinions; this is also referred to as *common law* or *judge-made law.*

***Certiorari* (literally, "to be informed"):** a writ issued by an appeals court indicating that it will review a lower court's decision, abbreviated as *cert.*

C.F.R. (abbreviation for Code of Federal Regulations): the repository regulations promulgated by various federal agencies to implement laws passed by Congress.

Civil action: a dispute between two private parties or a private party and the state to enforce, redress, or protect private rights.

Civil right: a personal right guaranteed by the United States Constitution (or a state constitution) or a federal (or state) statute.

Class action: a suit brought on behalf of named plaintiffs as well as others who may be similarly situated.

Common law: the body of law that developed as a result of court decisions, customs, and precedents; it is also sometimes referred to a *case law* or *judge-made law*.

Compensatory damages: a judicial award intended to compensate a plaintiff for an actual loss.

Consent decree: an agreement between parties to a suit that is sanctioned by a court that essentially settles the dispute by mutual consent.

Contract: an agreement between two parties that creates a legal obligation to do or not to do something; a contract can be written or oral.

Damages: a judicial award to compensate an injured party; damages can be legal (or monetary), in the form of a payment by the party causing the injury, or equitable (see the definition of *equitable relief* below).

Declaratory relief: a judicial decree that clarifies a party's legal rights but that does not order consequential relief.

Defendant: the party against whom a suit is brought.

***De novo* (literally, "from new"):** a trial *de novo* refers to a situation where a court hears evidence and testimony that may have been previously heard by a lower court or administrative body.

***Dictum* or *dicta* (literally, "remark" or "remarks"):** a gratuitous statement (or statements) in a judicial opinion that, being beyond the facts and issues of a case, cannot be binding on future cases; this is also referred to as *obiter dictum* or *obiter dicta* (literally, "a remark or remarks by the way").

***En banc* (literally, "in the bench"):** a judicial session in which the entire membership of a court participates in a decision rather than a single judge or select panel of judges; a rehearing *en banc* may be granted if a select panel of judges has rendered a decision that is contrary to decisions rendered by similar courts.

Equitable relief: justice administered according to fairness; a form of relief that orders a party to do something or to refrain from doing something when monetary damages are inadequate to make an injured party whole.

***Et seq.* (abbreviated, and more commonly used form of *et sequentes*, literally, "and the following"):** this is generally used in a citation to indicate "and the sections that follow."

Evaluation team: a group of individuals who perform assessments on the student to determine whether the child has a disability and, if so, what special education and related services he or she will require. An evaluation team is composed of individuals such as the classroom teacher, a special education teacher, an administrator, a psychologist, the parents of the student (and in some cases the student), and other specialists. Different states have various names for the evaluation team, such as multidisciplinary team, committee on special education, pupil personnel services team, or pupil placement team.

Ex parte (**literally, "by or for one party"**): an action initiated at the request of one party and without notice to the other party.

Expulsion: a long-term exclusion from school, generally for disciplinary purposes; ordinarily, a disciplinary exclusion of more than ten days is considered an expulsion.

Ex relatione (**abbreviated as, and more commonly used as,** *ex rel.;* **literally, "upon relation or information"**): a term in a case title indicating that the legal proceedings were instituted by the state on behalf of an individual who had an interest in the matter.

Full inclusion: the practice of educating students with disabilities in a fully inclusive setting with children who do not have disabilities; this has also been referred to as *mainstreaming.*

Holding: the part of a court's decision that applies the law to the facts of the case.

Independent hearing officer: an impartial third-party decision-maker who conducts an administrative hearing and renders a decision on the merits of the dispute.

Injunction: an equitable remedy, or court order, forbidding a party to from taking a contemplated action, restraining a party from continuing an action, or requiring a party to take some action.

In loco parentis (**literally, "in the place of the parent"**): this deals with situations where school (or other public) officials act in the place of a child's parents.

In re (**literally, "in the matter of"**): indicating that there are no adversarial parties in a judicial proceeding, this refers to the fact that a court is considering only a *res* ("thing"), not a person.

Judgment: a decision of a court that has the authority to resolve a dispute.

Jurisdiction: the legal right by which a court exercises its authority; this also refers to the geographic area within which a court has the authority to rule.

Moot: when a real, or live, controversy no longer exists; a suit becomes moot if, for example, there is no longer any dispute because a student with a disability turns twenty-one.

On remand: this occurs when a higher court returns a case to a lower court with directions that it take further action.

Opinion: a court's written explanation of its judgment.

Per curiam (**literally, "for or by the court"**): an unsigned decision of the court as opposed to one signed by a specific judge.

P.L.: the abbreviation for Public Law; a Public Law is a statute passed by Congress. The IDEA was initially referred to as 94–142, the 142nd piece of legislation introduced during the 94th Congress.

Plaintiff: the party bringing a suit to court.

Precedent: a judicial opinion that is binding on lower courts in a given jurisdiction; this is also referred to as *binding precedent* to distinguish it from *persuasive precedent* (such as *dicta*), which is not binding.

Preponderance of the evidence: the level of proof required in a civil suit; evidence that has the greater weight or is more convincing. Conversely, a criminal case requires proof beyond a reasonable doubt.

Pro se **(literally, "for himself or herself"):** this refers to a person who represents himself or herself in court.

Prospective: looking toward the future; prospective relief provides a remedy in the future, typically by either ordering a party to do or to refrain from doing something.

Punitive damages: compensation awarded to a plaintiff that is over and above the actual loss suffered; these damages are designed to punish the defendant for wrongful action and to act as an incentive to prevent similar action in the future.

Reevaluation: a complete and thorough reassessment of the student. Generally, all of the original assessments will be repeated, but additional assessments must be completed if necessary; the IDEA requires educators to reevaluate each child with a disability at least every three years.

Remand: to return a case to a lower court, usually with specific instructions for further action.

Res judicata **(literally, "a thing decided"):** a rule that a final judgment of a court is conclusive and acts to prevent subsequent action on the same claim.

Reverse: to revoke a lower court's decision in an appeal.

Settlement agreement: an out-of-court agreement made by the parties to a lawsuit to settle the case by resolving the major issues that initiated the litigation.

Sovereign immunity: a legal prohibition against suing the government without its consent.

Special education: instruction specifically designed to meet the unique needs of a student with disabilities.

Standing: an individual's right to bring a suit to court; in order to have standing an individual must be directly affected by, and have a real interest in, the issues litigated.

Stare decisis **(literally, "let the decision stand"):** this refers to adherence to precedent.

State-level review officer (or panel): an impartial person (or panel of usually three or more persons) who reviews the decisions of an independent hearing officer from an administrative due process proceeding under the IDEA. The

IDEA provides that if administrative due process hearings are held at the local school district level, provisions must be made for an appeal at the state level.

Statute of limitations: specifies the period of time within which a suit must be filed.

Sub nomine **(abbreviated *sub nom.*; literally, "under the name"):** indicates that a case was on appeal under a different name than the one used at the lower court level.

Suspension: a short-term exclusion from school, usually for less than ten days, typically for disciplinary purposes.

Tort: a civil wrong other than breach of contract; the most common tort is negligence.

U.S.C. (abbreviation for United States Code): the official compilation of statutes enacted by Congress.

Vacate: to set aside a lower court's decision in an appeal.

DEPARTMENT OF SPECIAL EDUCATION WEB SITES, BY STATE

Alabama: http://www.alsde.edu/html/sections/section_detail.asp?section=65&footer=sections

Alaska: http://www.eed.state.ak.us/tls/sped/

Arizona: http://www.ade.state.az.us/ess/

Arkansas: http://arksped.k12.ar.us/

California: www.cde.ca.gov/sp/se/

Colorado: www.cde.state.co.us/cdesped/index.asp

Connecticut: www.state.ct.us/sde/deps/special/

Delaware: www.decec.org/index.php

District of Columbia: http://www.seo.dc.gov/seo/cwp/view,a,1222,q,561151.asp/

Florida: http://www.fldoe.org/ese/ese-home.asp

Georgia: http://public.doe.k12.ga.us/ci_exceptional.aspx

Hawaii: http://doe.k12.hi.us/specialeducation/

Idaho: http://www.sde.idaho.gov/SpecialEducation/default.asp

Illinois: www.isbe.state.il.us/spec-ed/

Indiana: http://www.doe.state.in.us/exceptional/speced/

Iowa: http://www.iowa.gov/educate/content/view/574/591/

Kansas: www.kansped.org/

Kentucky: www.education.ky.gov/KDE/Instructional+Resources/Student+and+Family+Support/Exceptional+Children/default.htm

Louisiana: http://www.louisianaschools.net/lde/ssd/2442.html

Maine: http://www.maine.gov/education/speced/

Maryland: http://www.marylandpublicschools.org/MSDE/divisions/earlyinterv/

Massachusetts: www.doe.mass.edu/sped/

Michigan: http://www.michigan.gov/mde/0,1607,7–140–6530_6598—,00.html

Minnesota: http://education.state.mn.us/MDE/Learning_Support/Special_Education/index.html

Mississippi: www.mde.k12.ms.us/special_education/

Missouri: http://www.dese.mo.gov/divspeced/

Montana: www.opi.state.mt.us/

Nebraska: www.nde.state.ne.us/SPED/sped.html

Nevada: http://www.doe.nv.gov/teachers/specialeducation.html

New Hampshire: www.ed.state.nh.us/education/doe/organization/instruction/bose.htm

New Jersey: www.state.nj.us/njded/specialed/

New Mexico: www.ped.state.nm.us/seo/index.htm

New York: www.vesid.nysed.gov/specialed/home.html

North Carolina: www.ncpublicschools.org/ec/

North Dakota: www.dpi.state.nd.us/speced/index.shtm

Ohio: www.ode.state.oh.us/exceptional_children/

Oklahoma: www.sde.state.ok.us/home/defaultie.html

Oregon: www.ode.state.or.us/search/results/?=40

Pennsylvania: www.pde.state.pa.us/special_edu/site/default.asp

Rhode Island: www.ridoe.net/Special_needs/Default.htm

South Carolina: http://ed.sc.gov/agency/offices/ec/

South Dakota: http://doe.sd.gov/oess/specialed/index.asp

Tennessee: www.state.tn.us/education/speced/

Texas: www.mde.k12.ms.us/special_education/

U.S. Virgin Islands: http://www.doe.vi/

Utah: www.usoe.k12.ut.us/sars/

Vermont: www.state.vt.us/educ/new/html/pgm_sped.html

Virginia: www.pen.k12.va.us/VDOE/sess/

Washington: www.k12.wa.us/SpecialEd/default.aspx

West Virginia: http://wvde.state.wv.us/ose/

Wisconsin: www.dpi.state.wi.us/dpi/dlsea/een/index.html

Wyoming: http://www.k12.wy.us/se.asp

Index

The Corwin Press logo—a raven striding across an open book—represents the union of courage and learning. Corwin Press is committed to improving education for all learners by publishing books and other professional development resources for those serving the field of PreK–12 education. By providing practical, hands-on materials, Corwin Press continues to carry out the promise of its motto: **"Helping Educators Do Their Work Better."**